Short
Selling

THE FRANK J. FABOZZI SERIES

Fixed Income Securities, Second Edition by Frank J. Fabozzi
Focus on Value: A Corporate and Investor Guide to Wealth Creation by James L.
Grant and James A. Abate
Handbook of Global Fixed Income Calculations by Dragomir Krgin
Managing a Corporate Bond Portfolio by Leland E. Crabbe and Frank J. Fabozzi
Real Options and Option-Embedded Securities by William T. Moore
Capital Budgeting: Theory and Practice by Pamela P. Peterson and Frank J. Fabozzi
The Exchange-Traded Funds Manual by Gary L. Gastineau
Professional Perspectives on Fixed Income Portfolio Management, Volume 3 edited
by Frank J. Fabozzi
Investing in Emerging Fixed Income Markets edited by Frank J. Fabozzi and
Efstathia Pilarinu
Handbook of Alternative Assets by Mark J. P. Anson
The Exchange-Traded Funds Manual by Gary L. Gastineau
The Global Money Markets by Frank J. Fabozzi, Steven V. Mann, and
Moorad Choudhry
The Handbook of Financial Instruments edited by Frank J. Fabozzi
Collateralized Debt Obligations: Structures and Analysis by Laurie S. Goodman
and Frank J. Fabozzi
Interest Rate, Term Structure, and Valuation Modeling edited by Frank J. Fabozzi
Investment Performance Measurement by Bruce J. Feibel
The Handbook of Equity Style Management edited by T. Daniel Coggin and
Frank J. Fabozzi
The Theory and Practice of Investment Management edited by Frank J. Fabozzi and
Harry M. Markowitz
Foundations of Economic Value Added: Second Edition by James L. Grant
Financial Management and Analysis: Second Edition by Frank J. Fabozzi and
Pamela P. Peterson
Measuring and Controlling Interest Rate and Credit Risk: Second Edition by
Frank J. Fabozzi, Steven V. Mann, and Moorad Choudhry
Professional Perspectives on Fixed Income Portfolio Management, Volume 4 edited
by Frank J. Fabozzi
The Handbook of European Fixed Income Securities edited by Frank J. Fabozzi
and Moorad Choudhry
The Handbook of European Structured Financial Products edited by Frank J.
Fabozzi and Moorad Choudhry
The Mathematics of Financial Modeling and Investment Management by Sergio M.
Focardi and Frank J. Fabozzi

Short
Selling

Strategies, Risks, and Rewards

FRANK J. FABOZZI

EDITOR

WILEY
John Wiley & Sons, Inc.

Contents

Foreword

Short selling is un-American. It is done by rogues, thieves, and especially pessimists, who are, of course, the worst of the lot. It is a terrible, terrible thing and must be stopped in our lifetime. We should halt it, restrict it, or at the very least revile those who make it their vocation.

The above sentiments are sadly not imaginary or rare. Rather, they genuinely reflect much of the investing public's view of short selling. In fact, attacks have included proposals to make short selling harder (the existing "uptick rule" already makes it hard), or to make it impossible by banning it outright (presumably along with pessimism itself, and perhaps the infield fly rule). These criticisms and draconian proposals all increase in volume and seriousness when the stock market goes through a tough time. At such times many claim short sellers are the cause of the market's decline. Finally, at the low point for stock prices, many members of Congress invariably reexamine whether shorting should be allowed, or more simply, consider just legislating that the Dow go up 50 points a day.

Of course, the media does not help. A rising stock market is a good thing for ratings and circulation. This country is, of course, biased toward rooting for stocks to go up, and people watch and read more about this stuff when it is fun (i.e., going up). Thus, short sellers, with their gloomy attitude, are not generally media friendly. In fact, even some pro-free enterprise media outlets sometimes throw away their *laissez faire* stance when it comes to short selling, particularly "in times of crisis" (defined as an overvalued market getting a bit less overvalued). Apparently, they have some confusion regarding the difference between supporting a free capital market versus supporting an expensive one.

Well, to sum up the theme of this foreword, opponents of short selling are not merely wrong. They are incredibly wrong, both factually and morally. Short sellers are among the heroes of capitalism and we owe them our thanks not our opprobrium. The opponents of short selling are either exceptionally economically challenged, or run to a natural tendency to ban anything they do not like. There's a word for the political system favored by people like that and it is not democracy (but does rhyme with Motalitarianism).

Extensive theory may be helpful, but it is not necessary, to understand why the ability to implement a pessimistic view (e.g., to sell short) improves market efficiency and thus makes the market safer for all participants. Without short selling, prices are in a sense uncapped. As valuations get excessive the only way to express a negative view is to go on a buying strike. It is analogous to a voter who disliked the incumbent, but found the only option was to stay home, as voting for the challenger was prohibited (again, we have seen systems like that in the world, but we are just not supposed to have one here). It seems quite intuitive that if we restrict the ability to express pessimistic views, prices will on net be biased towards the optimistic outlook. Of course the goal of efficient financial markets is to have prices reflect our collective best guess, somewhere between optimistic and pessimistic. It follows that overpriced stocks and stock markets, including incredibly destructive bubbles, are best fought by allowing all opinions to affect prices. For instance, the recent market/tech bubble would in all likelihood have been less egregious with fewer hurdles to short selling. To put it simply, widows and orphans are on net protected, not damaged by short sellers. Of course, for this all to be true, short sellers must, as most of them claim, be following rational strategies and not following the same wild momentum strategies as others just on the short side.

Luckily, short sellers as a group, at least according to the reported hedge-fund indices, do what they say they do. A simple study of their returns makes it clear they are net short stocks.[1] If this seems less than revelatory, consider that doing what you say you are going to do is not

---

[1] Using the short selling index from CSFB/Tremont and returns on the S&P 500, and value-growth stocks and small-large stocks (HML and SMB from Professor Ken French's website http://mba.tuck.dartmouth.edu/pages/faculty/ken.french/ respectively) run the following regression (all returns are either on long/short portfolios or excess over cash) monthly from 1994–2003:

CSFB Short return
= intercept + $\beta_1 \times$ S&P 500 + $\beta_2 \times$ [value-growth] + $\beta_3 \times$ [small-large]

Running this regression leads to t-statistics on the betas of −16.4 (S&P 500), +3.1 (value-growth), and −7.4 (small-large) with an adjusted R-squared of 76.7%. Next add one additional term to capture a potentially changing market beta through time. This is an "interaction" term representing this month's S&P 500 times the S&P 500's return over the prior year. If this comes in with a positive (negative) slope it means that short sellers ran a higher (lower) market beta after rolling years that the market went up. Its t-statistic is −2.65 (so short sellers get shorter after market rallies) with the statistical significance of the other factors unchanged (though the value-growth t-statistic falls to a still significant +2.09, perhaps as this dynamic beta captures part of the time pattern of value's return).

always a slam dunk in today's capital markets. More novel, shorts are biased to get shorter when the market has been strong, that is, in aggregate they fight a market trend.[2] They are biased to short smaller than average stocks and, perhaps most importantly, to short expensive stocks. In a world that often feels dominated by momentum investing and one-way market cheerleading, they are short. They get more short when the market goes up and less when it falls. And, when it comes to stock selection, they are most short the most expensive growth stocks. While individual short sellers might differ, in aggregate, they are not shorting distressed companies to drive them to doom with misleading Internet chat. Rather, in aggregate, short sellers are the Praetorian Guard of the financial markets. These activities logically, and in fact, lead to a more stable market where bubbles (both in aggregate and in relative value) are fought by the short sellers (though as 1999–2000 shows, not necessarily fought enough), and not, like done by much of the rest of the investing world, simply ridden until the eventual ugly denouement.

Why do they do it? Consider the hurdles short sellers face. Stocks, on average, rise over time. This is both an empirical fact and a theoretically mandated occurrence. The long-run equity risk premium is positive. Short sellers swim against this tide, taking their capital and betting against "stocks for the long run." Second, short sellers bet against the idea that markets are efficient. While some of the returns to short selling can be construed as just picking up a value premium which may be rational, clearly the shorts themselves believe they are taking the rational side in an irrational world. Also, the specific stocks they short, tend to be ones prevailing wisdom favors, nay adores, and in the early days of a short position they are often laughed at (with the last laugh often forgotten).

Furthermore, the risks of shorting may be greater than other investments. Some used to laugh at the common observation, "Don't short because you can lose an infinite amount of money." Then 1999 came along and proved the "fools" uttering this statement were not so wrong. Truth be told however, the infinite loss possibility argument is still a bit silly, as a diversified portfolio of shorts is definitely amenable to risk control. But, it would be disingenuous not to acknowledge that shorting involves some risk control challenges beyond those of traditional long-only management.

Finally, successfully utilizing short selling does not just involve picking stocks that will ultimately fall, but convincing your investors to stick with you when you are too early, and your portfolio of shorts moves from 2× to 4× overvalued. Short sellers, by definition, tend to lose when

---

[2] Probably meaning their feelings about valuations dominate any effect from getting "squeezed" which might lead to them moving to less short after strong markets.

most others are winning, and lose even more when this is happening in the context of an irrational bubble (as they get much shorter in the most overvalued names). In principle, this should be the most palatable time for a rough patch, as diversification is half the point of a short or market neutral investment. But, it just does not work out that way. When you lose and others are mostly winning, you have to defend yourself from the charge that you are foolish, that you have lost your edge, that what used to work does not work anymore because it is a "new world," or put more eloquently, "You stink, let us out of our lockup please."

So, why do they do it? Greed, in the best capitalistic sense, is of course part of it. They believe enough in their skill at identifying the overvalued, the frauds, and the scams, that over the long run they will be more than compensated for the many hurdles they face. But, while not completely fungible, many or most of the skills in successful short-ing work on the long-only side as well, with none of the hurdles above. So why do they choose short selling? Well, like many who excel in any field, you will find the short sellers choose short selling partly because they have no choice. When they see the public fooled into buying over-valued nonsense, when they see fraud perpetrated without retribution, and when they see hucksters lauded by a stock market dying to anoint the next emperor without clothes, they have no choice but to fight. They feel a personal affront at the overvalued going up day after day, and bubble-vision covering it in breathless admiration. They feel they must do something about it. Ultimately, the shorts are in it to make money, but if they can do that while being right when everyone else is wrong (and actually help right a wrong) more the better. People acting in their own interest, but also making the world better. Kind of how capitalism is supposed to work no?

That brings us to this book, which is something special. It is not a coincidence that this book wasn't published in late 2002/early 2003 when so many hastily scribed, rush-job books on shorting came out at the nadir of a bear market. These works were light on the content, and heavy on the "You too Can Get Rich by Shorting" sentiments, generally including a couple of "if you had only shorted *blank* at *blank* price you would have made blank by now." This book is different. The quality of the authors, a collection of learned and respected academics and practi-tioners, speaks to that, as does the coverage, scope, and seriousness of the topics. This is not about getting rich quickly. It is about how short-ing works, what short sellers actually do, how shorts uncover the over-valued and the true ponzi schemes, economically why short selling is important, the true impediments to shorting, and a host of other sober, vital, and often neglected topics. It is not just about the canonical short-only manager uncovering fraud and overvaluation as implicitly described above, it is also a detailed description of how shorting can be part of an overall optimal portfolio, and can be pursued in all different forms with all different types of managers (a systematic market-neutral manager, a generally long manager who uses shorts to reduce risk and hopefully add alpha, or a truly dedicated short manger).

This book not only pulls together much of the scattered literature on short selling, but also adds dramatically to our body of knowledge. It is not a "get rich quickly by shorting" book. But, reading this book might help you become a better investor, as I believe it has done for me. And, if there is a better way than this to get rich slowly, or at least to stay solvent by avoiding scams, it has yet to be discovered.

Clifford S. Asness
Managing and Founding Principal
AQR Capital Management, LLC

Preface

Short Selling: Strategies, Risks, and Rewards provides the most recent theory and empirical evidence on the practice of short selling. The chapters in this book, contributed by leading practitioners and academics, explain not just the complex mechanics of short selling and the associated risks, but also why some stocks can be expected to become overpriced, strategies for exploiting overpricing, and how short selling can improve portfolio performance and market efficiency. Each chapter contains information relevant to both institutional and individual investors who are currently using or may be contemplating using short selling as a part of their investment management strategy.

I wish to express my deep gratitude to the contributors of this book. A special thanks to Edward Miller who contributed three chapters covering the underlying theory on why markets become overpriced (theory of divergence of opinion) and the implications for investment management when there are restrictions on short selling.

This book could not have been completed without the assistance of Steven Jones and Glen Larsen. In addition to their contribution of three chapters to the book, they reviewed all chapters in the book, suggested the organization of the chapters, and identified several contributors.

Robert Krail of AQR Capital provided helpful comments on selected portions of the manuscript.

I am grateful to Clifford Asness for reading the page proofs and providing the foreword.

Frank J. Fabozzi

About the Editor

Frank J. Fabozzi, Ph.D., CFA, CPA is the Frederick Frank Adjunct Professor of Finance in the School of Management at Yale University. Prior to joining the Yale faculty, he was a Visiting Professor of Finance in the Sloan School of Management at MIT. Frank is a Fellow of the International Center for Finance at Yale University, the editor of the *Journal of Portfolio Management*, a member of Princeton University's Advisory Council for the Department of Operations Research and Financial Engineering, and a trustee of the BlackRock complex of closed-end funds and Guardian Life sponsored open-end mutual funds. He has authored several books in investment management and in 2002 was inducted into the Fixed Income Analysts Society's Hall of Fame. He earned a doctorate in economics from the City University of New York in 1972.

Contributing Authors

James A. Abate	GAM USA Inc.
Lee Atzil	Elm Ridge Capital
Arturo Bris	Yale School of Management
Jeff Cohen	Susquehanna Intl Group, LLLP
Frank J. Fabozzi	Yale School of Management
Gary L. Gastineau	ETF Consultants LLC
William N. Goetzmann	Yale School of Management
James L. Grant	JLG Research
Ron Gutfleish	Elm Ridge Capital
David Haushalter	Susquehanna Intl Group, LLLP
Bruce I. Jacobs	Jacobs Levy Equity Management
Steven L. Jones	Indiana University, Kelley School of Business — Indianapolis
Owen A. Lamont	Yale School of Management and NBER
Glen Larsen	Indiana University, Kelley School of Business — Indianapolis
Kenneth N. Levy	Jacobs Levy Equity Management
Edward M. Miller	University of New Orleans
Adam V. Reed	University of North Carolina at Chapel Hill
Ning Zhu	University of California, Davis

CHAPTER 1

Introduction

Frank J. Fabozzi, Ph.D., CFA
Fredrick Frank Adjunct Professor of Finance
School of Management
Yale University

Steven L. Jones, Ph.D.
Associate Professor of Finance
Indiana University, Kelley School of Business — Indianapolis

Glen Larsen, Ph.D., CFA
Professor of Finance
Indiana University, Kelley School of Business — Indianapolis

Selling a long position is the most obvious means of avoiding losses in what is perceived to be an overpriced asset. Short selling, on the other hand, offers a means not just to avoid losses but also to profit from knowledge of overpricing. Although the opportunity to short sell is not new, the surge in hedge funds, many of which used short selling to profit in the bear market, has focused renewed attention on the subject. In fact, many believe that the competition for alpha will force pension funds to relax the "no-short" constraint on their active managers.[1] But for many investors, short selling remains an obscure, even mysterious subject, seemingly more akin to art than investment science.

---

[1] See Bob Litterman, "The Active Risk Puzzle: Implications for the Asset Management Industry," *The Active Alpha Investing Series* (Goldman Sachs Asset Management, March 2004).

This book reflects the most recent theory and empirical evidence on the practice of short selling. The chapters that follow explain not just the complex mechanics of short selling, but also why we might expect some stocks to become overpriced, strategies for exploiting overpricing, including the use of derivatives, and how short selling can improve portfolio performance and market efficiency. Each chapter contains information relevant to both institutional and individual investors who are currently using or may be contemplating the use of short selling as a part of their investment management strategy. Special emphasis is placed on the risks associated with short selling. For example, short selling is generally viewed as more risky than long investing because prices can always go higher, which implies unlimited losses for a short position.

This book is divided into four sections. Section One covers the mechanics of short selling. The mechanics are relatively complex compared to a normal buy transaction. In Chapter 2, Jeff Cohen, David Haushalter, and Adam Reed explain how short selling, or shorting, a stock in the cash market involves selling a stock that you do not own. The shorted stock is borrowed through a broker and sold in the open market with the proceeds from the sale placed in escrow. Some institutional investors may earn "rebate" interest on these escrowed proceeds. Returning the borrowed shares satisfies the loan; hence, the short seller profits from a decline in price by "selling high and then buying low." In order to short sell, you must have a margin account and your broker must be able to locate the shares to loan you. The short seller faces the risk that the borrowed shares may be recalled by the lender early (recall risk), as well as the risk of being caught in a so-called "short squeeze," where price spikes due to price pressure from too many shorts attempting to cover (i.e., buy back the stock) at the same time.

There are alternatives to selling short in the cash market. An investor seeking to benefit from an anticipated decline in the price of a stock, broad-based stock market index, or narrow-based stock market index (e.g., a sector or industry) may be able to do so in the futures or options markets. Selling futures has several advantages to selling short in the cash market. Buying puts and selling calls are two ways to implement a short-selling strategy in the options market. There are trade-offs between buying puts, selling calls, and borrowing the stock in the cash market in order to sell short. The relative merits of using futures and options for short selling, along with a review of futures and options and their investment characteristics, are covered by Frank Fabozzi in Chapter 3.

In Chapter 4, Gary Gastineau describes how short selling exchange-traded funds (ETFs) can mitigate the risks associated with shorting individual stocks. For example, it is essentially impossible to suffer a short squeeze in ETF shares because the number of shares in an ETF can be increased on any given trading day. A second advantage is that the "uptick" rule does not apply to ETFs. On the NYSE exchange, this rule means that a short sale may only be done on an uptick or a zero-plus tick; that is, a price that is the same price as the last trade, but higher in price than the previous trade at a different price. On the NASDAQ, you cannot short on the bid side of the market when the current inside bid is lower than the previous inside bid (a downtick). A third advantage that Gastineau discusses relates to hedging with ETF shares instead of derivative contracts. Derivative contracts have limited lives. The most active contracts in any futures market are the near month and the next settlement after the near month. Equity index futures contracts will usually be rolled over about four times a year in longer-term risk management applications. While risk managers could take futures positions with more distant settlements, liquidity is usually concentrated in the nearest contracts. Consequently, risk managers typically use the near or next contract and roll the position forward as it approaches expiration. ETF shares allow for a hedge of indefinite length without "roll risk."

The five chapters in Section Two cover the theory and evidence on short selling. In Chapter 5, Edward Miller points out that restrictions on short selling mean that prices are often set by the most optimistic investors, with little limited trading opportunities for the less optimistic investors, other than to sell there holdings. The result is potential overpricing in some stocks. The opportunity to short sell such overpriced stocks is exploitable only when the overpricing is due to factors that are likely to be revealed in the relatively near future. Possible opportunities arise from optimistic errors such as extrapolating growth too far in the future, not allowing for new entry or market saturation, or just omitting low probability adverse events from expectations.

Miller builds on these points in Chapter 6 by arguing that a substantial divergence of investor opinion about a stock implies a negative expected return. This is because restrictions on short selling prevent unfavorable opinions from being fully reflected in stock prices. Therefore, with restricted short selling, divergence of opinion tends to raise prices, and profits can be improved by avoiding stocks with high divergence of opinion, especially those analysts disagree about. Miller further demonstrates that because risk correlates with divergence of opinion, the return to risk, both systematic and nonsystematic, is less than what investors would otherwise require. This leads Miller to suggest that typical investors should overweight the less risky stocks in their portfolio.

Owen Lamont provides evidence of overpricing by showing that stocks with high short sale constraints tend to experience particularly low returns in the future in Chapter 7. Lamont also reviews specific cases where extremely high short-sale constraints led to extremely high overpricing and thus extremely low subsequent returns. He concludes with a discussion suggesting that the "tech stock mania" of 1998–2000 was attributable to the reluctance of pessimists to go short.

Steven Jones and Glen Larsen illustrate, in Chapter 8, how short selling has the potential to improve upon the mean-variance return performance of portfolios. The opportunity to short sell effectively doubles the number of assets, and this clearly offers the potential to reduce portfolio variance since the covariances of the second set of stocks (potentially held short) have the opposite sign from the respective covariances in the first set of stocks (potentially held long). Jones and Larsen stress that while short selling offers the potential to improve realized portfolio efficiency, there is no guarantee of portfolio efficiency improvement without perfect foresight. That is, if one can be certain of the forecasted means and covariances, then short selling improves mean-variance efficiency as a simple matter of portfolio mathematics. A review of the current empirical research suggests that covariance forecasts are so fraught with error that realized portfolio efficiency might actually be improved by restricting or even prohibiting short positions. Jones and Larsen point out, however, that this empirical research focuses on risk reduction and ignores the potential for identifying overpriced stocks. They also emphasize that short positions must be actively managed due the risk of recall and the transitory nature of overpricing.

In Chapter 9, Jones and Larsen provide an overview and analysis of nearly all of the academic research, from the past 25 years, on the information content of short sales. In opposition to Miller's overpricing hypothesis, mentioned above, the rational-expectations-based literature argues that overpricing could persist only where high levels of short interest are unanticipated, prior to announcement. However, the empirical evidence on whether short interest can be used to predict future returns is quite mixed, with much of the debate turning on the timing of the interval over which to measure the accumulation of short interest or future returns. Jones and Larsen conclude that there is ample evidence of overpricing in stocks that are costly to short, but short sales and short interest, while potentially useful, provide no easily discernible signal.

The question remains as to whether there are any proven strategies for spotting short-sale candidates? Three techniques are discussed in Section Three. In Chapter 10, Ron Gutfleish and Lee Atzi discuss their strategy for "buying stress and shorting comfort." The strategy is intended to take advantage of the tendency of perpetual optimists, cheerleaders (including analysts and portfolio managers), and speculators to ignore signs that their expectations are not being confirmed. Gutfleish and Atzi look for evidence that a company is beginning to compromise its future in order to continue to produce the earnings or sales growth trajectory that their followers expect. Firms may be able to trade off future performance for current results for a number of quarters to keep Wall Street happy. Just a couple of the accounting gimmicks they watch for are: (1) a heavy reliance on nonrecurring events and (2) businesses with high operating leverage that run factories full out while accumulating excess inventory. The latter gimmick allows management to book lower unit costs and inflate gross margins, while writing off the inventory later as a nonrecurring charge.

In Chapter 11, James Abate and James Grant show that while short selling based on poor or deteriorating fundamentals is a time-tested strategy, it has all too often been implemented using accounting earnings and relative valuation indicators. They offer guidance on how to use *net present value* (NPV) and *economic value added* (EVA) as part of an active short selling strategy. The financial characteristics of firms that have created economic value as well as those that have destroyed it are analyzed. Abate and Grant conclude that EVA provides a robust framework, consistent with finance theory, for selecting both long and short candidates.

In Chapter 12, Bruce Jacobs and Kenneth Levy describe how a market-neutral portfolio is constructed from long and short positions so as to incur virtually no systematic or market risk. Long–short portfolios free investors from the nonnegativity constraint imposed on long-only portfolios and relax the restrictions imposed by benchmark portfolio weights. The result is increased flexibility in both the pursuit of return and in the control of risk. Jacobs and Levy also suggest that active portfolio managers can achieve improved performance with an integrated optimization that considers both the long and short positions simultaneously. To a large extent, however, the performance of a market-neutral portfolio is determined by the value-added through security analysis and selection.

The topic of short selling and market efficiency is covered in Section Four. The importance of short selling to the global equity market is investigated in Chapter 13 by Arturo Bris, William Goetzmann, and Ning Zhu. They collected information on short sales regulations and practices for about 80 markets around the world. Their survey of world markets suggests that, while as much as 93% of the world's equity market capitalization is potentially shortable, there are also particular regions of the world where it is difficult to take a short position. These include several countries in Southeast Asia and South America. In addition, Bris, Goetzmann, and Zhu find important periods when nonshortable securities are a major determinant of the global equity portfolio. While stocks in these markets might be slightly less prone to extreme price drops, they are also less efficiently priced. For a large sample of countries in which short sales are not allowed or not practiced in the local market, they find a migration of capital over the last decade towards the *American Depository Receipt* (ADR) or *Global Depository Receipt* (GDR) market. The trend appears to be that markets with regulations facilitating efficiency are winning the battle for international capital flows. This is to some extent because the issue of whether a security is easily shortable is an important one for many institutional investors and investment managers.

In Chapter 14, the final chapter of the book, Edward Miller notes that modern financial theory makes an important distinction between diversifiable and nondiversifiable (or systematic risk). He argues that divergence of opinion is correlated with both. This, in the presence of restrictions on short selling, has interesting implications for the security market efficiency and thus investment policy. The marginal investors in stocks with high divergence of opinion are more likely to be overly optimistic. The implication is that share prices will not reflect the valuations of informed investors because they are restricted in short selling the overvalued stocks. Just a few of the financial puzzles that Miller attributes to divergence of opinion in the presence of restrictions on short selling include: (1) Why bearing nonsystematic risk may be rewarded; (2) why the rewards to systematic risk (i.e., beta) are lower than standard finance theory predicts; (3) why closed-end funds usually trade at discount; and (4) why value additivity does not hold in mergers and divestitures.

The Mechanics of Short Selling

CHAPTER 2

Mechanics of the Equity Lending Market

Jeff Cohen
Securities Lending Manager
Susquehanna Intl Group, LLLP

David Haushalter, Ph.D.
Corporate Research and Educational Associate
Susquehanna Intl Group, LLLP

Adam V. Reed, Ph.D.
Assistant Professor of Finance
University of North Carolina at Chapel Hill

Short sellers sell stock they do not own. The equity lending market exists to match these short sellers with owners of the stock willing to lend their shares for a fee. The equity lending market's importance is emphasized by its size: securities loans in the United States are estimated to be worth $700 billion.[1]

Despite its obvious importance to the operation of financial markets, the equity lending market is arcane. The market is dominated by loans negotiated over the phone between borrowers and lenders. Although there have been significant improvements in recent years, there is no widely used electronic quote or trade network in the equity lending market.

---

[1] *Securities Lending Transactions: Market Development and Implications*, Technical Committee of the International Organization of Securities Commissions (July 1999).

In this chapter, we discuss the mechanics of equity loans, the participants and their roles, and how rebate rates (prices) are determined in the market.

THE LENDING PROCESS

An investor who wants to sell a stock short must first find a party willing to lend the shares.[2] Once a lender has been located and the shares are sold short, exchange procedures generally require that the short-seller deliver shares to the buyer on the third day after the transaction $(t + 3)$ and post an initial margin requirement at its brokerage firm. Under Regulation T, the initial margin requirement is 50%. Self-regulatory organizations (e.g., NYSE and NASD) require the short seller to maintain a margin of at least 30% of the market value of the short position as the market price fluctuates.

As described in Exhibit 2.1, the proceeds from the short sale are deposited with the lender of the stock. For U.S. stocks, the lender requires 102% of the value of the loan in collateral. The value of the loan is marked to market daily; an increase in the stock price will result in the lender requiring additional collateral for the loan, and a decrease in the stock price will result in the lender returning some of the collateral to the borrower. When the borrower returns the shares to the lender, the collateral will be returned.

While a stock is on loan, the lender invests the collateral and receives interest on this investment. Generally, the lender returns part of the interest to the borrower in the form of a negotiated *rebate rate*. Therefore, rather than fees, the primary cost to the borrower is the difference between the current market interest rate and the rebate rate the lender pays the borrower on the collateral. A lender's benefit from participating in this market is the ability to earn the spread between these rates. Although the earnings from this interest spread are often split between several parties participating in the lending process, the interest can add low risk return to a lender's portfolio.

---

[2] One exception to this rule is for market makers. For example, the NYSE requires affirmative determination (a locate) of borrowable or otherwise attainable shares for members who are not market makers, specialists or odd lot brokers in fulfilling their market-making responsibilities. Similar rules exist for the NASD and AMEX exchanges. See Richard Evans, Christopher Geczy, David Musto, and Adam Reed, "Failure *Is* an Option: Impediments to Short Selling and Options Prices," working paper, University of North Carolina, March 2003.

EXHIBIT 2.1   Equity Loan Structure

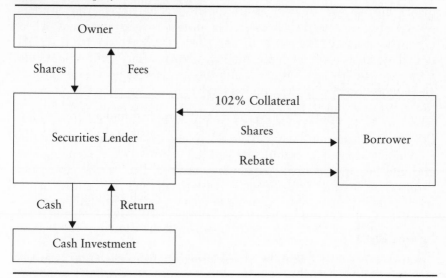

LENDERS

Traditionally, custodian banks that clear and hold positions for large institutional investors have been the largest equity lenders. With the beneficial owner's permission, custodian banks can act as lending agents for the beneficial owners by lending shares to borrowers. The custodian bank and the beneficial owners share in any revenue generated by securities lending with a prearranged fee sharing agreement. A typical arrangement would have 75% of the revenue going to the beneficial owner and 25% going to the agent bank.[3] Depending on the type of assets being lent and the borrowing demand, lending revenue earned by the owner of the security may completely offset custodial and clearance fees for institutional investors.

In addition to traditional custodian bank lenders, a number of specialty third-party agent lenders have entered the equity lending market over the past several years. Under this structure, the assets are lent by an agent firm who represents the beneficial owner but is not the custodian of the assets. Once a loan is negotiated between the agent lender and the borrower, the agent facilitates settlement by working with a traditional custodian bank in arranging delivery of the shares to the borrower. In comparison with custodian banks, these noncustodial lenders often offer advantages to the beneficial owner such as more specialized reporting, flexibility, and more lending revenue.

---

[3] Bargerhuff & Associates, "Securities Lending Analytics" (2nd quarter, 2000).

As an alternative to agency-lending arrangements, the beneficial owner may decide to lend assets directly to borrowers. Increasingly, owners choose to lend their assets via an exclusive arrangement, where the owner commits his assets to one particular borrower for a specific period of time. For example, in recent years, the California Public Employees Retirement System (CalPERS) has lent its portfolios through an auction system with the winning bidder gaining access to the portfolio for a predetermined period of time. This arrangement guarantees a return to the beneficial owner for loaning out the assets. Another avenue that some institutions have explored is managing their own internal lending department, therefore having total control over the lending process and keeping all of the revenues generated. Due to the large costs involved in setting up a lending department and the infrastructure needed, this option is only available to the largest institutional investors.

Lender's Rights

The owner of a stock retains beneficial ownership of the shares it lends. This status gives the owner the right to receive the value of any dividends or distributions paid by the issuing company while the stock is on loan. However, rather than being paid by the company, the dividend and distributions are paid by the borrower. This is referred to as a *substitute payment*. The beneficial owner is also entitled to participate in any corporate actions that occur while the security is on loan. For example, in the case of a tender offer, if the beneficial owner wishes to participate in the offer and the borrower is unable to return the security prior to the completion of the offer, the borrower is required to pay the beneficial owner the tender price. The only right the lender gives up when lending their assets is the right to vote on a security.[4] However, the lender generally has the right to recall the loaned security from the borrower for any reason, including to exercise voting rights.

In the event of a recall, the borrower is responsible for returning the shares to the lender within the normal settlement cycle. For example, if the beneficial owner sells a security that is on loan, the agent lender will send a *recall notice* to the borrower on the first business day after the trade date $(T + 1)$ instructing borrower that the shares need to be returned to the agent within two business days $(T + 3)$. If the shares are returned within this period, the custodian can settle the pending sell trade. If the borrower fails to return the shares by $(T + 3)$, the agent may buy shares to cover the position, therefore closing out the loan.

---

[4] For a discussion of lending and voting, see Susan Christoffersen, Christopher Geczy, David Musto, and Adam Reed, "How and Why do Investors Trade Votes, and What Does it Mean?" working paper, Wharton School of Business, University of Pennsylvania, March 2004.

Lender's Risks

There are three types of risk the beneficial owner faces when lending stock: investment risk, counterparty risk, and operational risk. *Investment risk* involves the choices that the beneficial owner or their agent makes in investing collateral. Some lenders are reluctant to take risk in their reinvestment of collateral, and they invest primarily in overnight repurchase agreements or other very low risk investments. Other lenders look to achieve extra income by investing in higher risk assets. For example, lenders can earn more return by investing in longer term investments and short-term corporate debt with lower credit ratings. It is the beneficial owner's responsibility to monitor the investment of the collateral to manage these risks. Even if there is a loss from investing the borrower's collateral, the beneficial owner is still responsible for returning the borrower's full collateral when the security is returned.[5]

Counterparty risk is the risk that the borrower fails to provide additional collateral or fails to return the security. The beneficial owner can manage this risk by approving only the most creditworthy borrowers and by imposing credit limits on these borrowers. Furthermore, the fact that collateral is marked to market daily allows lenders to buy shares to cover the loan if the borrower will not return the shares.

The last major risk to the beneficial owner is *operational risk*. This is the risk that various responsibilities of the agent lender or borrower are not met. This could be the failure to collect dividend payments, the failure to instruct clients on corporate actions resulting in missed profit opportunities, the failure to mark a loan to market, and the failure to return a security in the event of a recall. These risks can be minimized by maintaining a good lending system which tracks dividends, corporate actions, and the collateralization of loans.

BORROWERS

The largest borrowers of stocks are prime brokerage firms facilitating the short demand for their own proprietary trading desks, for their hedge fund clients, and for other leveraged investors. Trading desks often borrow stock to enable long–short trading strategies. Further-

---

[5] A recent example of this risk is provided by Citibank which, acting as an agent lender, is estimated to have lost approximately $80 million in collateral on an investment in asset-backed security issued by National Century Financial Enterprises. After this event occurred, it was unclear whether Citibank would cover the beneficial owners for this loss of collateral. See "Citibank faces NYC Dilemma," *Journal of International Securities Lending*, Q3, 2003.

more, tremendous growth in the hedge fund industry during the past decade has resulted in an increase in the use of other sophisticated strategies that require borrowing stock.[6] Because lending firms are reluctant to approve hedge funds as creditworthy borrowers, hedge funds have traditionally used prime brokers to gain access to the lending markets.

The two risks that a borrower faces are the risk of a loan recall and the risk of a decrease in rebate rates. A borrower's challenge is to find a lender that best balances these risks. *Recall risk* is the risk of the stock being recalled by the lender before the borrower is prepared to close out his position, which happens in approximately 2% of the loans in the sample of one study.[7] Borrowers would prefer to have loans lasting the duration of the short position, but guaranteed term loans are rare.[8] So, borrowers need to manage recall risk by working with a lender that is likely to be willing to loan the stock for an extended period of time. Often the most stable sources of stock loans are portfolios with little turnover, such as index funds.

There are no rules governing which loans will be recalled if a beneficial owner recalls its stock. If the agent for the lender has loaned the stock to several prime brokerage firms and some of those shares need to be returned, the lending agent has discretion in deciding which prime brokers' loans will be recalled. Moreover, if the prime broker, whose loan has been selected, has allocated these shares to several borrowers, the broker has flexibility in selecting which of the borrowers will have their shares recalled. If the borrower's loan does get recalled by the lender, it is the borrowers' responsibility to return shares to the lender either by buying shares in the market or by borrowing the shares from another lender. If the borrower fails to return the shares, the lender can use the borrower's collateral to buy shares to cover the loan, which is known as a *buy-in*. In other words, recalls can force borrowers to unwind their trading strategies suboptimally or expose the borrowers to potentially poor execution in the case of a buy-in.

---

[6] According to the SEC's September 2003 staff report, "*Implications of the Growth of Hedge Funds*, "…hedge fund assets grew from $50 billion in 1993 to $592 billion in 2003, an increase of 1084 percent…" Furthermore, the same report states: "Many hedge funds regularly engage in short selling as a major component of their investment strategy."

[7] Gene D'Avolio, "The Market for Borrowing Stock," *Journal of Financial Economics* (November 2002), pp. 271–306.

[8] For a discussion of term loans, see D'Avolio, "The Market for Borrowing Stock" and Christopher Geczy, David Musto, and Adam Reed, "Stocks Are Special Too: An Analysis of the Equity Lending Market," *Journal of Financial Economics* (November 2002), pp. 241–269.

THE DETERMINANTS OF REBATE RATES

The rebate rate, or the rate a borrower is paid on his cash collateral, effectively determines the price of a stock loan. This rate is determined by supply and demand in the market for borrowing stock. For highly liquid stocks that are widely held by institutional lenders, the borrower can expect to earn the full rebate or *general collateral rate*, on the collateral. This rate is generally 5 to 25 basis points below the Fed funds rate for each day.[9] When there is less available supply in the equity lending market, as with middle-capitalization stocks, the spread generally increases to around 35 basis points.[10]

The majority of loans in the equity lending market are made in widely held stocks that are cheap to borrow. However, on less widely held securities or securities with large borrowing demand, rebate rates may be reduced, in which case, the securities are said to be "trading special" or just "special." This means that the rebate rate is negotiated on a case by case basis, and the rate earned by the borrower on the collateral is below the general collateral rate paid on easily available securities. Only a few stocks are on special each day; a one-year sample in one study had approximately 7% of its securities on special.[11] And, the specials aren't necessarily limited to small stocks; 2.77% of large stocks were found to be on special in the same sample.[12] In rare cases, when a stock is in high demand, the rebate rate can be significantly negative. For example, shares of Stratos Lightwave, Inc. had a rebate rate more than 4,000 basis points below the general collateral rate in late August 2000, just after the firm's initial public offering.[13] In these cases, the lender is keeping the full investment rate of return on the collateral and also earning a premium for lending the securities.

Although specials are identified by their low rebate rates, the difficulty of borrowing specials goes beyond the increase in borrowing costs. Only well-placed investors (e.g., hedge funds) will be able to borrow specials and receive the reduced rebate. Generally, brokers will not borrow special shares on behalf of small investors; the order to short sell

---

[9] In a Fitch IBCA's report ("Securities Lending and Managed Funds") it is estimated that the industry average spread from the Fed funds rate to the general collateral rate on U.S. equities is 21 basis points.

[10] Bargerhuff & Associates, "Securities Lending Analytics."

[11] Geczy, Musto, and Reed, "Stocks Are Special Too: An Analysis of the Equity Lending Market."

[12] Adam Reed, "Costly Short Selling and Stock Price Adjustment to Earnings Announcements," working paper, University of North Carolina, June 2003.

[13] See Mark Mitchell, Todd Pulvino, and Erik Stafford, "Limited Arbitrage in Equity Markets," *Journal of Finance* (April 2000), pp. 551–584.

will be denied. Loans in stock specials will be expensive for well-placed investors and impossible to obtain for retail investors.

Specials tend to be driven by episodic corporate events that increase the demand for stock loans or reduce the supply of stocks available for loan. For example, initial public offerings, dividend reinvestment discount programs, and dividend payments of foreign companies often lead to an increase in borrowing demand and/or a reduction in the supply of available shares. In the case of IPOs, even though shares are available in the first settlement days, they are generally on special. At issuance, the average IPO's rebate rate is 300 basis points below the general collateral rate, but this spread from the general collateral rate falls to 150 basis points within the first 25 trading days. Similarly, the short selling of merger acquirers' stock drives specialness. Loans of merger acquirers' stock have average rebate rates 23 basis points below general collateral rates.[14] Additionally, because brokers prohibit their clients from buying stocks with prices below $5 on margin, there can be a limited supply of stock available for loan from broker dealers for these low-price shares.[15] Some factors that can improve liquidity in a stock and therefore improve its rebate rate include a secondary issue of the security, an expiration of an IPO lock-up period, and the reduction in short-selling demand as a result of the completion of a merger or corporate action.

CONCLUSION

As investors continue to become more sophisticated and new arbitrage opportunities develop, the securities lending markets will continue to expand and see new entrants. Beneficial owners have been increasing their participation in the lending markets, and they view the market as a low risk way to achieve increased return on their assets. Broker-dealers eager to attract the very profitable client base of hedge funds and other leveraged investors continue to expand their securities lending infrastructures. As a result, the securities lending markets have seen tremendous growth over the last decade. New entrants on both the lending and borrowing side combined with new technologies improving the transparency in the lending markets continue to increase the importance of this market.

---

[14] Geczy, Musto, and Reed, "Stocks Are Special Too: An Analysis of the Equity Lending Market."

[15] Broker dealers usually have the right to loan out any stock held in individual investors' margin accounts. However, shares that are paid in full cash rather than in margin accounts are generally not available to borrow from a broker dealer without consent of the owner.

CHAPTER 3

Shorting Using Futures and Options

Frank J. Fabozzi, Ph.D. CFA
Frederick Frank Adjunct Professor of Finance
School of Management
Yale University

Investors seeking to take a short position in a stock, a sector of the stock market, or the overall market are not limited to the cash market. Instead, investors can employ equity futures and options contracts to capitalize on their expectations about a decline in value of a stock or stock index. In this chapter, we describe the basic features of equity futures and options contracts, their profit and loss profiles, and how investors can use them to benefit from a decline in value.

FUTURES CONTRACTS

A *futures contract* is an agreement between a buyer and a seller wherein (1) the buyer agrees to take delivery of something at a specified price at the end of a designated period of time and (2) the seller agrees to make delivery of something at a specified price at the end of a designated period of time. Of course, no one buys or sells anything when entering into a futures contract. Rather, the parties to the contract agree to buy or sell a specific amount of a specific item at a specified future date. When we speak of the "buyer" or the "seller" of a contract, we are simply adopting the jargon of the futures market, which refers to parties of the contract in terms of the future obligation to which they are committing themselves.

17

The price at which the parties agree to transact in the future is called the *futures price*. The designated date at which the parties must transact is called the *settlement date* or *delivery date*. The "something" that the parties agree to exchange is called the *underlying*.

To illustrate, suppose there is a futures contract in which the underlying to be bought or sold is the stock of Company X and the settlement is three months from now. Assume further that Chuck buys this futures contract, Donna sells this futures contract, and the price at which they agree to transact in the future is $100. Then $100 is the futures price. At the settlement date, Donna will deliver the stock of Company X to Chuck. Chuck will pay Donna $100, the futures price.

When an investor takes a position in the market by buying a futures contract (or agreeing to buy at the future date), the investor is said to be in a *long position* or to be *long futures*. If, instead, the investor's opening position is the sale of a futures contract (which means the contractual obligation to sell something in the future), the investor is said to be in a *short position* or to be *short futures*.

The buyer of a futures contract will realize a profit if the futures price increases; the seller of a futures contract will realize a profit if the futures price decreases. For example, suppose that one month after Chuck and Donna take their position in the futures contract, the futures price of the stock of Company X increases to $120. Chuck, the buyer of the futures contract, could then sell the futures contract and realize a profit of $20. Effectively, he has agreed to buy, at the settlement date, the stock of Company X for $100 and to sell the stock of Company X for $120. Donna, the seller of the futures contract, will realize a loss of $20.

If the futures price falls to $40 and Donna buys the contract, she realizes a profit of $60 because she agreed to sell the stock of Company X for $100 and now can buy it for $40. Chuck would realize a loss of $60. Thus, if the futures price decreases, the buyer of the futures contract realizes a loss while the seller of a futures contract realizes a profit.

From this discussion it should be clear that if a futures contract in which a stock that an investor is interested in shorting is available, then selling a futures contract can accomplish the same objective as selling the stock. The advantages of using futures to short rather than shorting in the cash market will be explained later after we describe the mechanics of futures trading.

Liquidating a Position

Futures contracts have a settlement date. This means that at a predetermined time in the contract settlement month the contract stops trading, and a price is determined by the exchange for settlement of the contract.

A party to a futures contract has two choices on liquidation of the position. First, the position can be liquidated prior to the settlement date. For this purpose, the party must take an offsetting position in the same contract. For the buyer of a futures contract, this means selling the same number of identical futures contracts; for the seller of a futures contract, this means buying the same number of identical futures contracts.

The alternative is to wait until the settlement date. At that time the party purchasing a futures contract accepts delivery of the underlying; the party that sells a futures contract liquidates the position by delivering the underlying at the agreed-upon price. As explained later, for a stock index futures contract, settlement is made in cash only.

A useful statistic measuring the liquidity of a contract is the number of contracts that have been entered into but not yet liquidated. This figure is called the contract's *open interest*. An open interest figure is reported by an exchange for all the futures contracts traded.

The Role of the Clearinghouse

Associated with every futures exchange is a clearinghouse, which performs several functions. One of these functions is to guarantee that the two parties to the transaction will perform. To see the importance of this function, consider potential problems in the futures trade described earlier from the perspective of the two parties—Chuck the buyer and Donna the seller. Each must be concerned with the other's ability to fulfill the obligation at the settlement date. Suppose that at the settlement date the cash price of the stock of Company X is $70. Donna can buy the stock of Company X for $70 and deliver it to Chuck, who in turn must pay her $100. If Chuck does not have the capacity to pay $100 or refuses to pay, however, Donna has lost the opportunity to realize a profit of $30. Suppose, instead, that the cash price of the stock of Company X is $150 at the settlement date. In this case, Chuck is ready and willing to accept delivery of the stock of Company X and pay the agreed-upon price (i.e., futures price) of $100. If Donna cannot deliver or refuses to deliver the stock of Company X, Chuck has lost the opportunity to realize a profit of $50.

The clearinghouse exists to meet this problem. When someone takes a position in the futures market, the clearinghouse takes the opposite position and agrees to satisfy the terms set forth in the contract. Because of the clearinghouse, the two parties need not worry about the financial strength and integrity of the party taking the opposite side of the trade. After initial execution of an order, the relationship between the two parties is severed. The clearinghouse interposes itself as the buyer for every sale and the seller for every purchase. Thus, the two initial parties are free to liquidate their position without involving the other party in the original trade, and without worry that the other party may default.

Besides its guarantee function, the clearinghouse makes it simple for parties to a futures trade to unwind their positions prior to the settlement date. Suppose that Chuck wants to get out of his futures position. He will not have to seek out Donna and work out an agreement with her to terminate the original agreement. Instead, Chuck can unwind his position by selling an identical futures contract. As far as the clearinghouse is concerned, its records will show that Chuck has bought and sold an identical futures contract. At the settlement date, Donna will not deliver the stock of Company X to Chuck but will be instructed by the clearinghouse to deliver to someone who bought and still has an open futures position. In the same way, if Donna wants to unwind her position prior to the settlement date, she can buy an identical futures contract.

Margin Requirements

When a position is first taken in a futures contract, the investor must deposit a minimum dollar amount per contract as specified by the exchange. This amount, called *initial margin*, is required as a deposit for the contract. Individual brokerage firms are free to set margin requirements above the minimum established by the exchange. The initial margin may be in the form of an interest-bearing security such as a Treasury bill. As the price of the futures contract fluctuates each trading day, the value of the investor's equity in the position changes. The equity in a futures account is the sum of all margins posted and all daily gains less all daily losses to the account.

At the end of each trading day, the exchange determines the settlement price for the futures contract. The settlement price is different from the closing price, which many people know from the stock market and which is the price of the stock in the final trade of the day (whenever that trade occurred during the day). The settlement price by contrast is the value the exchange considers to be representative of trading at the end of the day. The representative price may in fact be the price in the day's last trade. But, if there is a flurry of trading at the end of the day, the exchange looks at all trades in the last few minutes and identifies a median or average price among those trades. The exchange uses the settlement price to mark to market the investor's position, so that any gain or loss from the position is quickly reflected in the investor's equity account.

Maintenance margin is the minimum level (specified by the exchange) to which an investor's equity position may fall as a result of an unfavorable price movement before the investor is required to deposit additional margin. The additional margin deposited is called *variation margin*, and it is an amount necessary to bring the equity in the account back to its initial margin level. Unlike initial margin, the variation margin must be in cash rather than an interest-bearing instrument. Any excess margin in the account may be withdrawn by the investor. If a party to a futures contract who is required to deposit variation margin fails to do so within a specified period, the exchange closes the futures position out.

Although there are initial and maintenance margin requirements for buying stock on margin, the concept of margin differs for stock and futures. When stocks are acquired on margin, the difference between the stock price and the initial margin is borrowed from the broker. The stock purchased serves as collateral for the loan, and the investor pays interest. For futures contracts, the initial margin, in effect, serves as good faith money, an indication that the investor will satisfy the obligation of the contract. Normally, no money is borrowed by the investor who takes a futures position.

To illustrate the mark-to-market procedure, let's assume the following margin requirements for the stock of Company X:

Initial margin $7 per contract
Maintenance margin $4 per contract

Assume that Chuck buys 500 contracts at a futures price of $100, and Donna sells the same number of contracts at the same futures price. The initial margin for both Chuck and Donna is $3,500, which is determined by multiplying the initial margin of $7 by the number of contracts, which is 500. Chuck and Donna must put up $3,500 in cash or Treasury bills or other acceptable collateral. At this time, $3,500 is the equity in the account. The maintenance margin for the two positions is $2,000 (the maintenance margin per contract of $4 multiplied by 500 contracts). The equity in the account may not fall below $2,000. If it does, the party whose equity falls below the maintenance margin must post additional margin, which is the variation margin. There are two things to note here. First, the variation margin must be in cash. Second, the amount of variation margin required is the amount needed to bring the equity up to the initial margin, not to the maintenance margin.

To illustrate the mark-to-market procedure, we assume the following settlement prices at the end of several trading days after the trade:

Trading Day	Settlement Price
1	$99
2	97
3	98
4	95

Consider Chuck's position. At the end of trading day 1, Chuck realizes a loss of $1 per contract or $500 for the 500 contracts he bought. Chuck's initial equity of $3,500 is reduced by $500 to $3,000. No action is taken by the clearinghouse because Chuck's equity is still above the maintenance margin of $2,000. At the end of the second day, Chuck realizes a further loss as the price of the futures contract has declined another $2 to $97, resulting in an additional reduction in his equity position by $1,000. Chuck's equity is then $2,000: the equity at the end of trading day 1 of $3,000 minus the loss on trading day 2 of $1,000. Despite the loss, no action is taken by the clearinghouse, because the equity still meets the $2,000 maintenance requirement. At the end of trading day 3, Chuck realizes a profit from the previous trading day of $1 per contract or $500. Chuck's equity increases to $2,500. The drop in price from $98 to $95 at the end of trading day 4 results in a loss for the 500 contracts of $1,500 and consequent reduction of Chuck's equity to $1,000. As Chuck's equity is now below the $2,000 maintenance margin, Chuck is required to put up additional margin of $2,500 (variation margin) to bring the equity up to the initial margin of $3,500. If Chuck cannot put up the variation margin his position will be liquidated.

Now, let's look at Donna's position. Donna as the seller of the futures contract benefits if the price of the futures contract declines. As a result, her equity increases at the end of the first two trading days. In fact, at the end of trading day 1, she realizes a profit of $500, which increases her equity to $4,000. She is entitled to withdraw the $500 profit. Suppose she does. Her equity therefore remains at $3,500 at the end of trading day 1. At the end of trading day 2, she realizes an additional profit of $1,000 that she also withdraws. At the end of trading day 3, she realizes a loss of $500 with the increase of the price from $97 to $98. This results in a reduction of her equity to $3,000. Finally, on trading day 4, she realizes a profit of $1,000, making her equity $4,000. She can withdraw $500.

Stock-Related Futures Contracts

There are two types of stock-related futures contracts based on the underlying:[1]

- Single-stock futures
- Stock index futures

---

[1] There is actually a third type, *exchange-traded funds futures*. However, trading volume as of May 2004 was so low that this contract will not be described in this chapter.

Single-Stock Futures

Single-stock futures are equity futures in which the underlying is the stock of an individual company. These contract received approval for trading in 2001. As of March 2004, single-stock futures are traded on two exchanges: OneChicago[2] and NASDAQ Liffe Markets (NQLX).[3]

Exhibit 3.1 lists single-stock futures traded on both exchanges as of March 2004. Exhibits 3.2 and 3.3 show the contract specification for the single-stock futures traded on OneChicago and NASDAQ Liffe, respectively. The contracts are for 100 share of the underlying stock. At the settlement date, physical delivery of the stock is required.

EXHIBIT 3.1 Underlying Stocks Traded on OneChicago and NASDAQ Liffe as of March 2004

a. Underlying Stocks Lists on OneChicago

3M Co.	Coca-Cola Co.
Alcoa Inc.	Comcast Corp.
Altera Corp.	Comverse Technology Inc.
Altria Group Inc.	Dell Inc.
Amazon.com Inc.	Dow Chemical Co.
American Express Co.	DuPont (E.I. Du Pont de Nemours)
American International Group	Eastman Kodak
Amgen Inc.	eBay Inc.
Applied Materials Inc.	Emulex Corp.
AT&T Corp.	Exxon Mobil Corp.
Bank of America Corp.	Ford Motor Co.
Bank One	General Electric Co.
Bed Bath & Beyond Inc.	General Motors Corp.
Best Buy Company Inc.	Genzyme Corp. - Genl Division
Biogen Idec Inc.	Goldman Sachs Group Inc.
Boeing Co.	Halliburton Co.
Bristol-Myers Squibb Co.	Hewlett-Packard Co.
Broadcom Corp. - CLA	Home Depot Inc.
Brocade Communications Sys	Honeywell International Inc.
Caterpillar Inc.	Intel Corp.
Cephalon Inc.	International Business Machines Corp.
Check Point Software Tech	International Paper Co.
ChevronTexaco Corp.	J.P. Morgan Chase & Co.
Cisco Systems Inc.	Johnson & Johnson
Citigroup Inc.	KLA-Tencor Corp.

---

[2] OneChicago is a joint venture of three futures and options exchanges (Chicago Board Options Exchange, Chicago Mercantile Exchange Inc., and the Chicago Board of Trade).

[3] NASDAQ Liffe Market is a joint venture of the NASDAQ Stock Market and the London International Financial Futures and Options Exchange (LIFFE) (an exchange that trades exchange-traded derivatives).

EXHIBIT 3.1   a. (Continued)

Krispy Kreme Doughnuts Inc.	Procter & Gamble Co.
Linear Technology Corp.	QLogic Corp.
Lowe's Cos. Inc.	QUALCOMM Inc.
Maxim Integrated Products Inc.	SanDisk Corp.
McDonald's Corp.	SBC Communications Inc.
Merck & Co. Inc.	Schlumberger Ltd
Merrill Lynch & Co. Inc.	Siebel Systems Inc.
Micron Technology Inc.	Starbucks Corp.
Microsoft Corp.	Sun Microsystems
Morgan Stanley	Symantec Corp.
Motorola Inc.	Texas Instruments Inc.
Newmont Mining Corp Hldg Co.	Time Warner Inc.
Nextel Communications Inc.	Tyco International Ltd
Nokia Corp. ADR	United Technologies Corp.
Northrop Grumman Corp.	VERITAS Software Corp.
Novellus Systems Inc.	Verizon Communications Inc.
NVIDIA Corp.	Wal-Mart Stores Inc.
Oracle Corp.	Walt Disney Co.
PeopleSoft Inc.	Wells Fargo & Co.
PepsiCo Inc.	Xilinx Inc.
Pfizer	Yahoo! Inc.

b. Underlying Stocks Lists on NASDAQ Liffe

Apple Computer Inc.	Flextronics International Ltd.	Nokia Corporation ADR
Barrick Gold Corp.	General Electric Co.	Nvidia Corp.
American International Group Inc.	Genzyme Corp	Novellus Systems Inc.
Advanced Micro Devices Inc.	General Motors Corp.	Oracle Corp.
Amgen Inc.	Home Depot Inc.	Pepsico Inc.
American Express Co.	Hewlett-Packard Co.	Pfizer Inc.
The Boeing Company	International Business Machines Corp.	Procter & Gamble Co.
Bank of America Corp.	Intel Corp.	PeopleSoft Inc.
Bed Bath & Beyond Inc.	Johnson & Johnson	QUALCOMM Inc.
Best Buy Co. Inc.	Juniper Networks Inc.	Qlogic Corp.
Broadcom Corp.	JP Morgan Chase & Co.	SBC Communications Inc.
Citigroup Inc.	Kla-Tencor Corp.	Schering-Plough Corp.
Cendant Corp.	Coca-Cola Co.	Schlumberger Ltd.
CIENA Corp.	Merrill Lynch & Co. Inc.	AT&T Corp.
Comverse Technology Inc.	Altria Group Inc.	Tellabs Inc.
Cisco Systems Inc.	Motorola Inc.	Texas Instruments Inc.
ChevronTexaco Corp.	Merck & Co. Inc.	Veritas Software Corp.
Dell Computer Corp.	Microsoft Corp.	Verizon Communications
eBay Inc.	Micron Technology Inc.	Wal-Mart Stores Inc.
El Paso Corporation	Maxim Integrated Products	Exxon Mobil Corp.
Ford Motor Co.	Newmont Mining Corp.	Yahoo! Inc.

EXHIBIT 3.2 Contract Specifications for OneChicago Single-Stock Futures

Contract Size	100 shares of underlying security
Minimum Price Fluctuation (Tick Size)	$0.01 × 100 shares = $1.00
Regular Trading Hours for Single Stock Futures	8:30 A.M.–3:00 P.M. Central Time
Position Limits	Apply only during the last five trading days prior to expiration: either 13,500 net contracts or 22,500 net contracts as required by CFTC regulations.*
Daily Price Limits	None
Reportable Position Level	200 Contracts
Contract Months	Two quarterly expirations and two serial months, for a total of four expirations per product class. OneChicago follows the quarterly cycle of March (H), June (M), September (U), and December (Z). The serial months traded are the two nearest months that are not quarterly expirations.
Expiration Date/ Last Trading Day	Third Friday of contract month or, if such Friday is not a business day, the immediately preceding business day
Settlement/Delivery	Physical delivery of underlying security on third business day following the Expiration Day
Depository for Underlying Security	DTCC

*OneChicago's Web site provides a downloadable list of position limits.
Reproduced from http://www.onechicago.com/030000_products/oc_030102.html.

EXHIBIT 3.3 Contract Specifications for NASDAQ Liffe Single Stock Futures

Nominal Contract Size	100 shares of the common stock or American Depository Receipts (ADRs) of selected companies whose shares are listed on U.S. securities exchanges (i.e., NYSE) or trade over-the-counter (i.e., NASDAQ).
Quotation	U.S. dollars per share
Minimum Tick Increment	$0.01 per share = $1 per contract
Delivery Months	The first five quarterly delivery months in a March, June, September, and December cycle as well as the nearest two serial months—i.e., January and February in December. This will insure that the first three calendar months will always be available for trading.
Symbols	Three character alpha-numeric product code.
Trading Hours	9:30 A.M.–4:00 P.M. EST

EXHIBIT 3.3 (Continued)

Last Trading Day	The third Friday of the delivery month.
Settlement Day and Time	10:00 A.M. EST on the next business day following the last trading day.
Settlement Price Calculation	The Settlement System will calculate the Daily Settlement Price based on reported prices in the two minute period prior to the time specified for contract settlement. The first ninety seconds of the settlement period will be used to monitor spread levels. The Settlement Price will be determined during the final 30 seconds of the settlement period, according to the following criteria: a. A single traded price during the last thirty seconds will be the Settlement Price. b. If more than one trade occurs during the last thirty seconds of the Settlement Range, the trade weighted average of the prices, rounded to the nearest tick, will be the Settlement Price. c. If no trade occurs during the last 30 seconds of the Settlement Range, the price midway between the active bids and offers at the time the settlement price is calculated, rounded to the nearest tick, will be the Settlement Price. d. In the circumstances where there is no traded price nor updated bid/ask spread during the last 30 seconds of trading, the settlement price of that contract month shall be the settlement price of the 1st quarterly delivery month plus or minus the latest observed calendar spread differential between the first quarterly delivery month and the contract month in question. In the event that the relevant spread price differential is not readily observable, in order to identify appropriate settlement prices, Exchange Market Services may take into account the following criteria as applicable 1) spread price differentials between other contract months of the same contract; and 2) price levels and/or spread price differentials in a related market.
EDSP Calculation (Exchange Delivery Settlement Price)	The official closing price of the underlying stock on the NASDAQ or NYSE, as of the latest possible period before NQLX system closing time (5:00 P.M. EST).
Delivery Size	Physical delivery of 100 shares (plus or minus the impact of corporate events per standard Options Clearing Corporation (OCC) rules and practices) made through National Securities Clearing Corporation (NSCC)/Depository Trust Corporation (DTC).

EXHIBIT 3.3   (Continued)

Delivery Process and Date	Delivery will be carried out via the NSCC 3-day delivery process. Three business days following the last trading day for the futures ($T + 3$), holders of net short positions deliver the underlying securities to holders of net long positions and payments of the settlement amounts are made. Generally, the underlying stock certificates are stored with the DTC where book entries are used to move securities between accounts. The net financial obligations for settlement are made, via wire transfers with designated banks, in single payments from the NSCC to firms with net credit positions and to the NSCC from firms with net debit positions. These transactions are cleared through the NSCC before 1:00 P.M. EST on the settlement date.
Price Limits	There are no daily price limits on Single Stock Futures. When the underlying shares cease to trade in the cash market, the Single Stock Futures based on the underlying will also cease trading in a manner coordinated with the applicable securities exchange.
Reportable Position Limits	200 contracts, equivalent to 20,000 shares of the underlying common stock/ADR. NQLX may introduce different reportable position limits for futures positions held within one month of the last trading date.

Note: These contract specifications may be modified before formal filing with the regulatory authority
Reproduced from http://www.nqlx.com/products/ContractSpec.asp.

Single-stock futures of only actively traded New York Stock Exchange and NASDAQ stocks are traded. Consequently, an investor interested in short selling using single-stock futures is limited to those traded on both the exchanges. There are three advantages of using single-stock futures rather than borrowing stock in the cash market (via a stock lending transaction) if an investor seeking to short a stock has the choice.

The first advantage is the transactional efficiency that it permits. In a stock-lending program, the short seller may find it difficult or impossible to borrow the stock. Moreover, an opportunity can be missed as the stock loan department seeks to locate the stock to borrow. After a short position is established, single-stock futures offer a second advantage by eliminating *recall risk*, the risk of the stock lender recalling the stock prior to the investor wanting to close out the short position.

A third *potential* advantage is the cost savings by implementing a short sale via single-stock futures rather than a stock-lending transaction. The financing of the short-sale position in a stock-lending transaction is arranged by the broker through a bank. The interest rate that the bank will charge the broker is called the *broker loan rate* or the *call money rate*. That rate with a markup is charged to the investor. However, if the short seller receives the proceeds to invest, this will reduce the cost of borrowing the stock.

There are factors that determine whether or not there is a cost savings by shorting single-stock futures. To understand these factors, we begin with the relationship between the price of the single-stock futures and the price of the underlying stock. The following relationship must exist for there to be no arbitrage opportunity:[4]

Futures price = Stock price$[1 + r(d_1/360)]$ + Expected dividend$[1 + r(d_2/360)]$

where

r = short-term interest rate
d_1 = number of days until the settlement of the future contract
d_2 = number of days between receipt of the expected dividend payment and the settlement date

The short-term rate in the pricing relationship above typically reflects the London Interbank Offered Rate (LIBOR). This is the interest rate that major international banks offer each other on a Eurodollar certificates of deposit (CD) with given maturities. The maturities range from overnight to five years. So, references to "3-month LIBOR" indicate the interest rate that major international banks are offering to pay to other such banks on a CD that matures in three months.

The difference between the futures price and the stock price is called the *basis*. The basis is effectively the repo rate (for the period until settlement date) adjusted by the expected dividend. The basis is also referred to as the *net interest cost* or *carry*. The buyer of the futures contract pays the net interest cost to maintain the long position; the seller of the futures contract earns the net interest cost for financing the buyer's long position.

Thus, a comparison of the cost advantage to shorting single stock futures rather than using a stock lending transaction comes down to empirically determining which has the lower net interest cost. NASDAQ Liffe examined this issue for the period May 1991 to November 2001.[5] The only time there was not an advantage to the using single stock

---

[4] The derivation is found in most books that cover futures contract.

[5] "Single Stock Futures for the Professional Trader," NASDAQ Liffe, undated.

future was around August 2001 when the Fed aggressively cut interest rates. In general, the study found that the advantage of using single-stock futures is adversely affected by low interest rates and steep yield curve environments.

Stock Index Futures

An investor may want to sell short the market or a sector of the market. Stock index futures can be used for this purpose. A stock index futures contract is a futures contract in which the underlying is a specific stock index. An investor who buys a stock index futures contract agrees to buy the stock index, and the seller of a stock index futures contract agrees to sell the stock index. The only difference between a single stock futures contract and a stock index futures contract is in the features of the contract that must be established so that it is clear how much of the particular stock index is being bought or sold.

The underlying for a stock index futures contract can be a broad-based stock market index or a narrow-based index. Examples of broad-based stock market indexes that are the underlying for a futures contracts are the S&P 500, S&P Midcap 400, Dow Jones Industrial Average, NASDAQ 100 Index, NYSE Composite Index, Value Line Index, and the Russell 2000 Index.

A narrow-based stock index futures contract is one based on a sub-sector or components of a broad-based stock index containing groups of stocks or a specialized sector developed by a bank. For example, Dow Jones MicroSector Indexes[SM] are traded on ChicagoOne. There are 15 sectors in the index.

The dollar value of a stock index futures contract is the product of the futures price and a "multiple" that is specified for the futures contract. That is,

Dollar value of a stock index futures contract = Futures price × Multiple

For example, suppose that the futures price for the S&P 500 is 1,100.00. The multiple for this contract is $250. (The multiple for the mini-S&P 500 futures contract is $50.) Therefore, the dollar value of the S&P 500 futures contract would be $275,000 (= 1,100.00 × $250).

If an investor buys an S&P 500 futures contract at 1,100.00 and sells it at 1,120.00, the investor realizes a profit of 20 times $250, or $5,000. If the futures contract is sold instead for 1,050.00, the investor will realize a loss of 50 times $250, or $12,500.

Stock index futures contracts are *cash settlement contracts*. This means that at the settlement date, cash will be exchanged to settle the contract. For example, if an investor buys an S&P 500 futures contract at

1,100.00 and the futures settlement price is 1,120.00, settlement would be as follows. The investor has agreed to buy the S&P 500 for 1,100.00 times $250, or $275,000. The S&P 500 value at the settlement date is 1,120.00 times $250, or $280,000. The seller of this futures contract must pay the investor $5,000 ($280,000 − $275,000). Had the futures price at the settlement date been 1,050.00 instead of 1,120, the dollar value of the S&P 500 futures contract would be $262,500. In this case, the investor must pay the seller of the contract $12,500 ($275,000 − $262,500). (Of course, in practice, the parties would be realizing any gains or losses at the end of each trading day as their positions are marked to market.)

Clearly, an investor who wants to short the entire market or a sector will use stock index futures contracts. The costs of a transaction are small relative to shorting the individuals stocks comprising the stock index or attempting to construct a portfolio that replicates the stock index with minimal tracking error.

EQUITY OPTIONS

An *option* is a contract in which the option seller grants the option buyer the right to enter into a transaction with the seller to either buy or sell an underlying at a specified price on or before a specified date. If the right is to purchase the underlying, the option is a *call option*. If the right is to sell the underlying, the option is a *put option*. The specified price is called the *strike price* or *exercise price* and the specified date is called the *expiration date*. The option seller grants this right in exchange for a certain amount of money called the *option premium* or *option price*. The underlying for an equity option can be an individual stock or a stock index. The option seller is also known as the option writer, while the option buyer is the option holder.

An option can also be categorized according to when it may be exercised by the option holder. This is referred to as the *exercise style*. A *European option* can only be exercised at the expiration date of the contract. An *American option*, in contrast, can be exercised any time on or before the expiration date.

The terms of exchange are represented by the contract unit, which is typically 100 shares for an individual stock and a multiple times an index value for a stock index. The terms of exchange are standard for most contracts. Exhibit 3.4 summarizes the obligations and rights of the parties to American calls and puts.

The most actively traded equity options are listed option (i.e., options listed on an exchange). Organized exchanges reduce counterparty risk by

EXHIBIT 3.4   Obligations and Rights of the Parties to American Options Contracts

Type of Option	Writer/Seller		Buyer	
	Obligation	Right	Obligation	Right
Call Option	To sell the underlying to the buyer (at the buyer's option) at the strike price at or before the expiration date.	Receive the option price.	Pay the option price.	To buy the underlying from the writer at the strike price any time before the expiration date.
Put Option	To purchase the underlying from the buyer (at the buyer's option) at the strike price at or before the expiration date.	Receive the option price.	Pay the option price.	To sell the underlying to the writer at the strike price any time before the expiration date.

requiring margin, marking to the market daily, imposing size and price limits, and providing an intermediary that takes both sides of a trade. For listed options, there are no margin requirements for the buyer of an option, once the option price has been paid in full. Because the option price is the maximum amount that the option buyer can lose, no matter how adverse the price movement of the underlying, margin is not necessary. The option writer has agreed to transfer the risk inherent in a position in the underlying from the option buyer to itself. The writer, on the other, has certain margin requirements, including the option premium and a percentage of the value of the underlying less the out-of-the-money amount.

Stock Options and Index Options

Stock options refer to listed options on individual stocks or American Depository Receipts (ADRs). The underlying is 100 shares of the designated stock. All listed stock options in the United States may be exercised any time before the expiration date; that is, they are American style options.

Index options are options where the underlying is a stock index (broad based or narrow based) rather than an individual stock. An index call option gives the option buyer the right to buy the underlying stock index, while a put option gives the option buyer the right to sell the underlying stock index. Unlike stock options where a stock can be delivered if the option is exercised by the option holder, it would be extremely complicated to settle an index option by delivering all the stocks that comprise the index. Instead, index options are cash settlement contracts. This means that if the option is exercised by the option holder, the option writer pays cash to the option buyer. There is no delivery of any stocks.

Index options include industry options, sector options, and style options. The most liquid index options are those on the S&P 100 index (OEX) and the S&P 500 index (SPX). Both trade on the Chicago Board Options Exchange. Index options can be American or European style. The S&P 500 index option contract is European, while the OEX is American. Both index option contracts have specific standardized features and contract terms. Moreover, both have short expiration cycles

The dollar value of the stock index underlying an index option is equal to the current cash index value multiplied by the contract's multiple. That is,

Dollar value of the underlying index = Cash index value × Multiple

For example, suppose the cash index value for the S&P 500 is 1,100.00. Since the contract multiple is $100, the dollar value of the SPX is $110,000 (= 1,100.00 × $100).

For a stock option, the price at which the buyer of the option can buy or sell the stock is the strike price. For an index option, the *strike index* is the index value at which the buyer of the option can buy or sell the underlying stock index. The strike index is converted into a dollar value by multiplying the strike index by the multiple for the contract. For example, if the strike index is 1,000.00, the dollar value is $100,000 (= 1,000.00 × $100). If an investor purchases a call option on the SPX with a strike index of 1,000.00, and exercises the option when the index value is 1,100, then the investor has the right to purchase the index for $100,000 when the market value of the index is $110,000. The buyer of the call option would then receive $10,000 from the option writer.

LEAPS and FLEX options essentially modify an existing feature of either a stock option, an index option, or both. For example, stock option and index option contracts have short expiration cycles. Long-Term Equity Anticipation Securities (LEAPS) are designed to offer options with longer maturities. These contracts are available on individual stocks and some indexes. Stock option LEAPS are comparable to standard stock options except the maturities can range up to 39 months from the origination date. Index options LEAPS differ in size compared with standard index options having a multiplier of 10 rather than 100.

FLEX options allow users to specify the terms of the option contract for either a stock option or an index option. The value of FLEX options

is the ability to customize the terms of the contract along four dimensions: underlying, strike price, expiration date, and settlement style.
Moreover, the exchange provides a secondary market to offset or alter
positions and an independent daily marking of prices.

Risk and Return Characteristics of Options

Now let's look at the risk and return characteristics of the four basic
option positions: buying a call option (long a call option), selling a call
option (short a call option), buying a put option (long a put option),
and selling a put option (short a put option). We will use stock options
in our example. The illustrations assume that each option position is
held to the expiration date and not exercised early. Also, to simplify the
illustrations, we assume that the underlying for each option is for 1
share of stock rather than 100 shares and we ignore transaction costs.

Buying Call Options

Assume that there is a call option on stock XYZ that expires in one
month and has a strike price of $100. The option price is $3. The profit
or loss will depend on the price of stock XYZ at the expiration date.
The buyer of a call option benefits if the price rises above the strike
price. If the price of stock XYZ is equal to $103, the buyer of this call
option breaks even. The maximum loss is the option price; there is a
profit if the stock price exceeds $103 at the expiration date.

It is worthwhile to compare the profit and loss profile of the call
option buyer with that of an investor taking a long position in one share
of stock XYZ. The payoff from the position depends on stock XYZ's
price at the expiration date. An investor who takes a long position in
stock XYZ realizes a profit of $1 for every $1 increase in stock XYZ's
price. As stock XYZ's price falls, however, the investor loses, dollar for
dollar. If the price drops by more than $3, the long position in stock
XYZ results in a loss of more than $3. The long call position, in con-
trast, limits the loss to only the option price of $3 but retains the upside
potential, which will be $3 less than for the long position in stock XYZ.

Writing Call Options

To illustrate the option seller's, or writer's, position, we use the same
call option we used to illustrate buying a call option. The profit/loss
profile at expiration of the short call position (that is, the position of the
call option writer) is the mirror image of the profit and loss profile of
the long call position (the position of the call option buyer). The profit
of the short call position for any given price for stock XYZ at the expiration date is the same as the loss of the long call position. Conse-

quently, the maximum profit the short call position can produce is the option price. The maximum loss is not limited because it is the highest price reached by stock XYZ on or before the expiration date, less the option price; this price can be indefinitely high.

Buying Put Options

To illustrate a long put option position, we assume a hypothetical put option on one share of stock XYZ with one month to maturity and a strike price of $100. Assume that the put option is selling for $2. The profit/loss for this position at the expiration date depends on the market price of stock XYZ. The buyer of a put option benefits if the price falls.

As with all long option positions, the loss is limited to the option price. The profit potential, however, is substantial: the theoretical maximum profit is generated if stock XYZ's price falls to zero. Contrast this profit potential with that of the buyer of a call option. The theoretical maximum profit for a call buyer cannot be determined beforehand because it depends on the highest price that can be reached by stock XYZ before or at the option expiration date.

Writing Put Options

The profit/loss profile for a short put option is the mirror image of the long put option. The maximum profit to be realized from this position is the option price. The theoretical maximum loss can be substantial should the price of the stock declines; if the price were to fall to zero, the loss would be the strike price less the option price.

Short Selling and Basic Option Strategies

Buying puts or selling calls allows the investor to benefit if the price of a stock or stock index declines.

Buying puts gives the investor upside potential if the price of the underlying declines. The upside potential is reduced by the option price; in exchange for the reduced upside potential due to the cost of purchasing the put option, the loss is limited to the option price. Thus, in comparison to short selling in the cash market by borrowing the stock, an investor who buys puts will realize a lower profit due to the option price if the price of the underlying declines. Effectively, the difference in profit when the price of the underlying declines is less than the option price due to the cost of borrowing the stock. In contrast to short selling in the cash market by borrowing the stock, the loss is limited to the option price if the price of the underlying increases.

In addition, buying a put option offers an investor leverage. This is because for a given amount that the investor is prepared to invest in a short selling strategy, greater exposure can be obtained. Of course, the greater profit potential by using the leverage provided by buying puts means that there is greater potential loss.

Now let's look at selling calls in comparison to selling short in the cash market by borrowing the stock. The profit from selling calls if the price of the underlying declines is limited to the option price received, regardless of how much the price of the underlying declines. However, there is no protection if the price of the underlying increases. In comparison to short selling in the cash market by borrowing the stock, selling calls has limited profit potential if the price of the underlying declines The loss should the price of the underlying increase is less for the call selling strategy because of the option price received. That is, selling calls and short selling in the cash market have substantial downside risk but the amount of the loss in the case of selling calls is reduced by the option price received.

Differences Between Options and Futures

The fundamental difference between futures and options is that the buyer of an option (the long position) has the right but not the obligation to enter into a transaction. The option writer is obligated to transact if the buyer so desires (i.e., exercises the option). In contrast, both parties are obligated to perform in the case of a futures contract. In addition, to establish a position, the party who is long futures does not pay the party who is short futures. In contrast, the party long an option must make a payment (the option price) to the party who is short the option in order to establish the position.

The payout structure also differs between a futures contract and an option contract. The option price represents the cost of eliminating or modifying the risk/reward relationship of the underlying. In contrast, the payout for a futures contract is a dollar-for-dollar gain or loss for the buyer and seller. When the futures price rises, the buyer gains at the expense of the seller, while the buyer suffers a dollar-for-dollar loss when the futures price drops.

Thus, futures payouts are symmetrical, while options are skewed. The maximum loss for the option buyer is the option price. The loss to the futures buyer is the full value of the contract. The option buyer has limited downside losses but retains the benefits of an increase in the value of the underlying. The maximum profit that can be realized by the option writer is the option price, but there is significant downside exposure. The losses or gains to the buyer and seller of a futures contract are completely symmetrical.

SUMMARY

There are alternatives to selling short in the cash market. An investor seeking to benefit from an anticipated decline in the price of a stock or stock index may be able to do so in the futures or options markets. Shorting individual stocks in the futures market requires the existence of a single-stock futures contract. Where one exists, a study suggests that it is less costly to implement a short selling strategy in the futures market. In the case of stock index futures, it is less costly to execute a short sale in the futures market. Buying puts and selling calls are two ways to implement short selling in the options market. There are trade-offs between buying puts, selling calls, and borrowing the stock in the cash market in order to sell short.

CHAPTER 4

Is Selling ETFs Short a Financial "Extreme Sport"?

Gary L. Gastineau
Managing Director
ETF Consultants LLC

Anyone who has wandered by video monitors in the windows of a ski or surf shop has seen dramatic pictures of skiers or surfers in obvious peril. A skier jumps from the edge of a cliff above the camera and disappears from view into the couleur below with no apparent chance of survival—until the scene cuts to another camera showing a "safe" landing on a 75-degree slope. At the surf shop, a surfer dude—or, with increasing frequency, a surfer girl—is tucked in the curl of a six-story wave headed for shore. Both skier and surfer lack obvious exit strategies.

At first glance, it might appear that an investor who ventures to sell *exchange-traded fund* (ETF) shares short is taking risks similar in magnitude to these extreme ski and surf enthusiasts. Whereas the short interest in the average listed common stock is about 2% of the stock's capitalization, the short interest in large ETFs is often 20% to as much as 55% of the ETF's outstanding shares. When one understands that short sales in ETFs can be executed *without a price uptick*—a trading practice that has not yet received regulatory approval for most other equity securities in the United States—the comparison of ETF short sellers to extreme skiers and surfers seems apt. In fact, however, the risks associated with ETF short selling are more in line with the risks accepted by a competent skier cruising on an intermediate trail. The ETF short seller, like the cruising skier, has to be alert and follow the rules of the road, but the risks are clear and manageable.

WHAT ARE THE MOST IMPORTANT SAFETY FEATURES PROTECTING ETF SHORT SELLERS?

Exchange-traded funds are a unique hybrid of closed-end and open-end investment companies. ETF shares trade like common stocks or closed-end funds during market hours and can be purchased or redeemed like open-end funds with an in-kind deposit or withdrawal of portfolio securities at each day's market close. In the United States, ETFs offer a unique level of capital gains tax efficiency and in most markets they offer a high level of intra-day liquidity and relatively low operating costs.

The trading flexibility and open-endedness of ETFs offer unusual protection to short sellers.

1. *It is essentially impossible to suffer a short squeeze in ETF shares.* In contrast to most corporate stocks where the shares outstanding are fixed in number over long intervals,[1] shares in an ETF can be greatly increased on any trading day by any Authorized Participant.[2] Creations or redemptions in large ETFs like the S&P 500 SPDRs and the NASDAQ 100 QQQ's are occasionally worth several billion dollars on a single day. The theoretical maximum size of the typical ETF, given this in-kind creation process, can be measured in hundreds of billions or even trillions of dollars of market value. The open-ended capitalization and required diversification of ETFs takes them out of the extreme risk category. As a practical matter, "cornering" an ETF market is unimaginable. The upside risk in a short sale is still theoretically greater than the downside risk in a long purchase, but even that risk is modified by the way ETF short selling is used to offset other risks.

2. *Most ETF short sales are made to reduce, offset, or otherwise manage the risk of a related financial position.* The dominant risk management/risk reduction ETF short sale transaction offsets long market risk with a short or short equivalent position. Unlike the aggressive skier or surfer, the risk manager who sells ETF shares short is nearly always reducing the net risk of an investment position. In contrast to extreme athletes, the risk managers selling ETFs short are more like the ski patrol or lifeguards: *They sell ETFs short to reduce total risk in a portfolio.*

---

[1] Exercise of employee stock options or public sale of new stock by the corporation can increase the number of shares outstanding from time to time.

[2] An *Authorized Participant* is a dealer that has signed an agreement with the fund's distributor to create additional fund shares by depositing baskets of securities with the fund custodian and to redeem fund shares in exchange for similar baskets of the fund's portfolio securities.

3. *Most serious students of markets consider the uptick rule an anachronism (at best).* Requiring upticks for short sales is certainly unnecessary and inappropriate for ETFs that compete in risk management applications with sales of futures, swaps, and options—risk management instruments that have never had uptick rules.

HOW DO ETFs WORK IN RISK MANAGEMENT APPLICATIONS?

Existing ETFs are all based on benchmark indices. While there are important benchmarks and there are unimportant benchmarks, benchmark index derivatives are widely used in risk management applications. For example, an investor with an actively managed small-cap portfolio might feel that superior stock selection reflected in the portfolio will provide good, *relative* returns over the period ahead, but that most small-cap stocks might still perform poorly. The investor can hedge the portfolio's exposure to small-caps while capturing its stock selection advantage by hedging the small-cap risk with a short position in a financial instrument linked to the Russell 2000 small-cap benchmark index. Available risk management tools for this application range from futures contracts and equity swap agreements—to the shares of a small-cap exchange-traded fund.

Derivative contracts have limited lives. Equity index futures contracts will usually be rolled over about four times a year in longer-term risk management applications. While risk managers could take futures positions with more distant settlements, liquidity is usually concentrated in the nearest contracts. Consequently, risk managers typically use the near or next contract and roll the position forward as it approaches expiration. Similar expiration provisions apply to most swap agreements, leaving the typical derivative transaction with considerable "roll" risk—risk of adverse market impact from rolling the hedge forward to the next expiration.

If a hedger uses ETF shares instead of futures, a risk management position can be held indefinitely without roll risk. Of course, the open-end nature of an ETF risk management or hedging position has other differences from futures and swaps. There is an implied cost associated with the expenses of the fund that may make the ETF a better short hedge, and there may be tracking error between the ETF portfolio and the benchmark index, but these are usually small considerations relative to fluctuating roll risk and recurring transaction costs in a longer-term rolling derivatives hedge.

Exhibit 4.1 illustrates two snapshot cost analyses of *long* stock index futures versus *long* ETF shares as one-year portfolio replication positions. When these analyses were prepared (at different times), they

EXHIBIT 4.1   Comparisons of Long Position Costs in iShares S&P 500 Fund and S&P 500 Futures for One-Year Portfolio Replication Applications (All numbers in basis points (bps) unless otherwise indicated)

	iShares S&P 500	S&P 500 Futures
Value as of 12/02/02	$100,000,000	$100,000,000
Based on a price of	$94.13*	$934.53**
Multiplier	1	250
No. of Shares/Index Units	1,062,361	428

December 2002	Estimated Costs (bps)		ETF Advantage
Commission (round trip)	8.70	1.70	
Bid/Offer Spread (round trip)	0.00	5.35	
Management Fee (annual)	9.50	0.00	
Mispricing	0.00	10.70	
Roll Risk	0.00	22.50	
Impact	30.00	21.40	
Total	48.20	61.66	13.46
May 2003			
Commission (round trip)	6.45	2.16	
Bid/Offer Spread (round trip)	0.00	5.40	
Management Fee (annual)	9.45	0.00	
Mispricing	0.00	21.59	
Roll Risk	0.00	21.00	
Impact (round trip)	28.90	21.59	
Total	44.80	71.73	26.93

*Price per share. **Index value.
Source: Salomon Smith Barney, Stock Facts PRO

We assume the ETF shares are being created, given the large size of the trade. The commission costs include $0.04 per share for the ETF plus the creation fee of $2,000 [$0.002 per share]. The market impact for the ETF was calculated using Stockfacts PRO and assumes a round-trip trade. Since the impact cost includes the spread of the underlying stocks, we are not including an additional spread for the ETF. For the futures, we used a commission of $5 per contract, a spread of 0.5, mispricing risk of 0.5, and 2 points in market impact for a trade of this size. As the size of this trade shrinks (e.g., to $10 million) the market impact for the futures and the iShares will both likely approach zero. From Kevin McNally and Dennis Emanuel, "ETF Insights—Institutional Uses of Exchanges-Traded Funds," *Salomon Smith Barney Equity Report*, December 4, 2002.

Comment: These analyses use iShares as an example, but, as the data in Exhibits 4.2 and 4.3 illustrate, most traders use S&P 500 SPDRs for S&P 500 futures substitute applications. See the discussion in the text of the economics of a risk manager selling ETFs short as a futures substitute.

indicated that the ETF was the low-cost replication instrument of choice for an investor who expected the position to stay in place for a year. The assumptions used in these analyses were appropriate at the times they were prepared, but any investor or hedger should evaluate current market conditions before choosing between futures or swaps and ETFs. More importantly, the risk manager needs to convert the analyses of Exhibit 4.1 from a long-side to a short-side cost comparison with specific data for the organization managing the risk. The reason the examples in Exhibit 4.1 show long positions in futures versus long positions in ETFs is that the expected costs and trading frictions associated with a long position are about the same for nearly everyone on the long side. On the short side, *the management fee works in favor of the ETF short seller*, but, more importantly, *the net cost of borrowing ETF shares varies over time and among risk managers*. In fact, a number of the costs change over time and among market participants.

In estimating the net share borrowing cost or *loan premium* for a short ETF position, we will not spend much time discussing the fund management fee. Lenders who buy ETF shares to lend them will sometimes be the marginal share lenders in the ETF market and when they are the marginal lenders they should be able to recoup the management fee as part of their securities lending revenue. When the marginal lender is an ordinary investor, the ETF loan premium will be unaffected by the management fee. The fact that the existence of the management fee favors the short seller may stimulate ETF share lending efforts by third-party securities lending agents working with brokerage firms and custodians. "Recapturing" the management fee should effectively increase the lending revenue on which agency lending fees are calculated. Generally, the larger component of the securities loan premium is the net interest-rate-linked spread which the share borrower pays. For ETF share loans, the total loan premium can range from near 10 basis points in a very low interest rate environment to a maximum of about 30 basis points if there is management fee recapture built into the loan premium. If the loan premium rises above that level, ETF short sellers will begin to switch to futures contracts and some investors will create ETF shares to lend.

The low end of this range is determined by the minimum administrative costs of setting up a large securities lending program and implementing only very large intermediate- and longer-term securities loans in this very liquid and relatively transparent market. The high end of the range *in this particular market* will probably be determined by the economics of persuading large pension funds with index portfolios to switch from direct ownership of indexed portfolios—with few individual stock lending opportunities—to, say, SPDRs with substantial and relatively consistent lending opportunities. In fact, an astute S&P 500 index manager will probably handle this transaction for its pension plan clients at no extra charge. A 30-basis point lending fee might cover the expense ratio of the ETF, any performance penalty associated with the way the ETF is managed,[3] an offset for any index outperformance the pension plan's index manager was obtaining and administrative costs.[4] The works of Gastineau,[5] Blume and Edelen,[6] and Quinn and Wang[7] help us understand how these costs can aggregate to as much as 30 basis points for an S&P 500 portfolio. The maximum lending fee might be larger for smaller cap funds if fund shares are created to lend, perhaps as much as 100–150 basis points for a Russell 2000 ETF because a good pension plan index manager should beat the Russell 2000 by a substantial margin. At a loan premium in this range, futures will be the short risk management tool of choice.

A more efficient[8] underlying large cap index than the S&P 500 could theoretically lead to a lower maximum lending fee and a tighter spread if the index were as widely accepted as the S&P 500. For now, a 20 basis point spread between low- and high-borrowing costs is as tight as it is likely to get, but smaller lenders and borrowers will often see significantly wider spreads and higher loan premiums. To see the short-side perspective on an ETF versus stock index futures comparison, the reader should modify the numbers in Exhibit 4.1 for a short ETF position by reversing the effect of the management fee (the management fee is the same as the fund's expense ratio in most ETFs) and adding an annual loan premium in the 10 to 30 basis point range to the cost of the ETF transaction.

---

[3] The economics of short selling and ETF share lending is complicated by the fact that managers of major benchmark ETFs seem to manage these funds with more emphasis on index tracking than on maximizing performance for fund investors. For a discussion of this issue, see Gary L. Gastineau, "The Benchmark Index Exchange-Traded Fund Performance Problem," *Journal of Portfolio Management* (Winter 2004), pp. 196–203.

[4] If pension funds become important participants in ETF lending, we would expect competition to make net ETF lending fees largely independent of interest rate levels and dependent primarily on index popularity and fund management efficiency.

[5] Gary L. Gastineau, "Equity Index Funds Have Lost Their Way," *The Journal of Portfolio Management* (Winter 2002), pp. 55–64 and Gary L. Gastineau, *The Exchange-Traded Funds Manual* (Hoboken, NJ: John Wiley & Sons, 2002).

[6] Marshall Blume and Roger M. Edelen, "On Replicating the S&P 500 Index," working paper, Wharton School of Business, University of Pennsylvania, 2002; and Marshall Blume and Roger M. Edelen, "S&P 500 Indexers, Delegation Costs and Liquidity Mechanisms," working paper, Wharton School of Business, University of Pennsylvania, 2003.

[7] James Quinn and Frank Wang, "How Is Your Reconstitution," *Journal of Indexing* (Fourth Quarter 2003), pp. 34–38.

[8] In terms of index change transaction costs.

WHO OWNS ETF SHARES?

In contrast to the obvious relevance of this question when it is asked about a common stock in the context of short selling, who owns the ETF shares outstanding should not matter very much to the ETF investor or to the risk manager who would sell ETF shares short. The opportunity to increase ETF shares outstanding, literally at a moment's notice, makes current ETF shares outstanding largely irrelevant from a trading or risk management perspective. Nonetheless, knowing something about the composition of the shareholder population and the effect of short sales on share ownership can help traders better understand the ETF market and ETF share-borrowing and -trading costs.

A typical large-capitalization common stock without significant insider holdings may show institutional investors accounting for 70% to 80% of its share capitalization. This institutional shareholder data can be accumulated from 13-F reports and similar filings with the Securities and Exchange Commission. The institutional share of ETF ownership varies widely among the funds, but most ETF 13-F summaries show institutional shareholdings in the 20–40% of ETF capitalization range, far below the institutional holdings in most of the U.S. common stocks held by the typical ETF.[9]

When the ETF institutional shareholder numbers are viewed relative to the typical large ETF's short interest, the relatively low ETF institutional ownership is almost surprising. With the short interest running about 2% of shares outstanding in the average common stock, it is not important that 2% of shares may be reported twice because one institution has lent its shares to a short seller and the shares have been purchased by another reporting institution. With a two percent short interest, double counting all or part of the short interest in the 13-F reports does not affect the reported institutional ownership of most common stocks very much because the short interest is such a negligible part of the total stock capitalization. However, the large short interest in many ETFs affects the reports considerably because *all shares that have been sold short appear as long positions in two investor portfolios.* Consequently, the ETF institutional ownership percentage reflected in the 13-F reports is *overstated* as a percentage of total shares. For example, if the short interest is reported at, say, 55% of capitalization, *the number of shares shown on the books of all holders of the ETF's shares will total 155% of the number of shares outstanding.* If the 13-F reports show that institutions hold 45% of the shares outstanding in the ETF,

---

[9] Of course, the advisors of each ETF report the ETF's *stock* positions as institutional holdings on 13-F reports.

that is actually 45% out of 155% or only about 29% of the shares that all investors combined show long in their accounts.

Huge ETF short interests also mean that short sellers play important roles in the size of an ETF's assets and in its trading activity. Specialists and other market makers have frequently maintained significant inventories of ETF shares to lend to short sellers. These market makers hedge their positions and obtain a fee from the securities lending operation, making creation of ETF shares for securities lending a modestly profitable business activity at times. In the summer of 2003, many market makers substantially reduced these ETF lending positions, apparently because interest rates were so low that ETF share lending was no longer profitable for them.[10]

The departure of some dealers from the business of buying and hedging ETF shares for the securities lending market has not led to a shortage of shares available to short sellers.[11] As the increase in many of the *short interest percentages* (SIPs) in the largest ETFs listed in Exhibit 4.2 suggests, the ETF share borrowing needs of short sellers have been readily accommodated by institutional ETF holders, by brokerage firms carrying retail margin accounts and by other dealers. When market makers reduced their participation in the ETF share-lending business, they redeemed the shares they had been lending. This reduced the funds' shares outstanding, but had no negative effect on the short interest that actually grew in most large ETFs. In fact, the same lower interest rates that reduced the attractiveness of ETF share lending to market makers also reduced the effective cost of ETF borrowing and short selling by risk managers. The reduction in the cost of borrowing ETF shares made ETF short sales more attractive relative to short futures positions in comparisons like those illustrated in Exhibit 4.1. Consequently, short ETF positions gained risk management market share from short-stock index futures positions.

With or without market makers' ETF-lending portfolios, substantial numbers of ETF shares have been made available to short sellers by institutions and by brokerage firms from their retail investor accounts—which typically exceed the size of institutional ETF holdings.[12] Broker-

---

[10] The fees associated with net securities lending are partly a function of short-term interest rates. When interest rates are low, net securities lending fees also tend to be low.

[11] We call this lending activity by market makers, *covered lending*. The term should carry no connotation that this process affects market risk exposure. It should suggest only that the holding is linked to the securities loan.

[12] Statements about the size of retail ETF holdings are hard to verify because there is no formal reporting of retail positions comparable to the 13-F filings by institutional investors. Note also that there are important restrictions on a brokerage firm's right to lend retail customer securities.

EXHIBIT 4.2 Short Interest and Short-Interest Percentage (SIP) for Ten Largest U.S. Equity ETFs (all shares in thousands)*

ETF	Symbol	Jul-02	Oct-02	Jan-03	Apr-03	Jul-03	Oct-03	Jan-04
S&P 500 SPDR	SPY							
Shares Outstanding		303,835	381,288	453,441	458,745	397,048	359,252	380,806
Short Interest		42,044	73,567	44,580	66,496	96,335	107,463	114,033
Short Interest Percentage		13.8%	19.3%	9.8%	14.5%	24.3%	29.9%	29.9%
NASDAQ 100 Index	QQQ							
Shares Outstanding		763,400	740,250	674,250	738,850	630,400	608,200	607,250
Short Interest		164,008	178,098	167,090	151,786	260,147	333,759	320,456
Short Interest Percentage		21.5%	24.1%	24.8%	20.5%	41.3%	54.9%	52.8%
iShares S&P 500	IVV							
Shares Outstanding		40,150	41,650	52,600	57,750	64,550	64,400	70,650
Short Interest		543	4,982	1,518	2,077	4,681	3,335	2,782
Short Interest Percentage		1.4%	12.0%	2.9%	3.6%	7.3%	5.2%	3.9%
DJIA DIAMONDS	DIA							
Shares Outstanding		40,453	49,504	58,205	66,256	61,907	63,058	63,861
Short Interest		11,070	19,505	11,751	16,277	21,388	19,566	28,334
Short Interest Percentage		27.4%	39.4%	20.2%	24.6%	34.5%	31.0%	44.4%
S&P 400 MidCap SPDR	MDY							
Shares Outstanding		75,205	63,258	63,258	56,334	55,836	56,762	60,913
Short Interest		6,102	5,148	4,502	4,385	5,636	7,768	8,768
Short Interest Percentage		8.1%	8.1%	7.1%	7.8%	10.1%	13.7%	14.4%

*Largest Equity ETFs based on assets of August 15, 2003.

EXHIBIT 4.2   (Continued)

ETF	Symbol	Jul-02	Oct-02	Jan-03	Apr-03	Jul-03	Oct-03	Jan-04
iShares MSCI-EAFE	EFA							
Shares Outstanding		35,800	20,600	20,600	20,200	24,800	28,400	42,800
Short Interest		270	328	576	836	970	1,265	1,446
Short Interest Percentage		0.8%	1.6%	2.8%	4.1%	3.9%	4.5%	3.4%
iShares Russell 2000	IWM							
Shares Outstanding		34,750	27,700	26,850	26,100	33,350	38,350	39,000
Short Interest		6,658	7,329	5,794	8,304	7,175	13,811	18,673
Short Interest Percentage		19.2%	26.5%	21.6%	31.8%	21.5%	36.0%	47.9%
Vanguard Total Market VIPERS	VTI							
Shares Outstanding		12,636	16,441	16,441	17,506	20,179	21,444	24,173
Short Interest		35	86	451	1,380	91	432	394
Short Interest Percentage		0.3%	0.5%	2.7%	7.9%	0.4%	2.0%	1.6%
iShares Russell 1000	IWB							
Shares Outstanding		8,850	16,350	16,350	19,850	32,400	31,100	32,350
Short Interest		377	585	1,597	886	1,048	650	1,323
Short Interest Percentage		4.3%	3.6%	9.8%	4.5%	3.2%	2.1%	4.1%
iShares S&P SmallCap 600	IJR							
Shares Outstanding		11,200	11,250	13,600	11,550	13,850	13,900	15,350
Short Interest		309	988	1,146	864	1,644	1,353	1,726
Short Interest Percentage		2.8%	8.8%	8.4%	7.5%	11.9%	9.7%	11.2%

Data source: American Stock Exchange. Reflects revised data up to January 23, 2004.

dealers, both in their roles as market makers and for their own risk management operations, are also substantial holders, lenders and short sellers of ETF shares. There is little published data to help us quantify all these participations.

WILL IT ALWAYS BE POSSIBLE TO BORROW ETF SHARES AT LOW-COST FOR RISK MANAGEMENT APPLICATIONS?

Clearly, when short-term interest rates increase from 2003 levels, the attractiveness of securities lending should increase for dealers who create and hold hedged positions in ETFs while lending the ETF shares to short sellers. Their activity should assure a supply for ETF share borrowers. However, an interesting change in the U.S. Federal Tax Code will certainly change the dynamics of ETF securities lending and short selling even if it does not change the economics very much.

The 2003 Tax Act, formally the Jobs and Growth Tax Relief Reconciliation Act of 2003, cut the tax rate for individual investors on *qualified dividends* from certain equity securities (including most ETFs) to 15%. The Internal Revenue Code distinguishes between various kinds of dividend and interest income, on the one hand, and payments in lieu of such dividend and interest income, on the other hand. This distinction can be significant for municipal bonds, for example, where *payments in lieu of municipal interest are not exempt from federal and certain state income taxes*, while the actual interest payment or an interest passthrough from municipal bond funds will qualify fully for tax exemption. Similar provisions apply to *Treasury interest*, which is *generally exempt from state income taxes, but payments in lieu of Treasury interest* on securities lent out *do not qualify for tax exemption*.

Under the 2003 Tax Act, dividends can be affected by a similar distinction between actual or passed-through dividends and payments in lieu of dividends. Corporations have had to exercise care that the "dividends" they have received on common and preferred stocks have qualified for the tax code's corporate tax dividend-received deduction by being *actual dividend payments or pass-throughs rather than payments in lieu*. Most individual investors have not had to worry about the character of such payments until now. For 2003, the new tax act provides that as long as an individual investor has no reason to believe that what he or she is receiving is a payment in lieu, the taxpayer can assume dividend payments from a brokerage firm or other custodian that holds the taxpayer's stocks, equity mutual funds or equity ETF shares are qualified dividends. New Treasury rules dictate that financial intermediaries report dividend qualification status for 2004 and subsequent years. *Payments in lieu of ETF dividends from securities lenders will not qualify for the special dividend tax rate in 2004 and later years.* While some observers have suggested that the lower dividend tax rate for individuals may increase the cost of borrowing dividend-paying securities, it is more likely that there will be a modest change in *where* the shares will be borrowed.

Some current ETF share lending may dry up. For example, brokers carrying ETFs in individual investor's accounts will not be able to certify the ETF dividends as eligible for the 15% tax rate if they lend out the shares. Institutional investors may have a more complex tax calculation to make. Mutual funds, for example, often use ETFs to equitize small cash balances. In fact, mutual funds probably account for a substantial fraction of reported ETF institutional ownership.[13] Some mutual funds may not be willing to loan their ETF shares as freely in 2004 and later years because *any payment in lieu of dividends that they receive from the borrower will not be distributable as qualifying dividends to their taxpaying individual shareholders.* However, the provisions of Internal Revenue Code § 854 will govern the eligibility of fund dividend distributions for the 15% tax rate. This section was written to cover eligibility of dividends for the dividend-received deduction and it, in effect, applies nonqualifying income to expenses first, leaving qualified dividends to be distributed. Assuming the same treatment under the new law, only funds with very low expense ratios or very large share lending programs, will risk distributing payments in lieu of dividends when they loan out ETF shares.

Any tax-exempt account will lend shares readily. Lending opportunities might draw in the pension plans we described as potential ETF lenders in the previous section. Long ETF positions held by a broker-dealer in its risk management activities will be lendable because the broker-dealer cannot take advantage of the special 15% dividend tax rate. Long positions held by a dealer to hedge an equity swap transaction where the broker-dealer pays the *return on an ETF* as a swap payment in return for receiving the *return on a stock position* should also be lendable without incurring disadvantageous tax treatment. The swap payments are already payments in lieu and, hence, the position held by the dealer would be lendable without disturbing any individual investor's receipt of a qualified dividend.

The net effect of this provision of the tax law on who lends ETF shares and under what circumstances or with what promises as to the

---

[13] Many ETFs trade until 4:15 P.M. Eastern Time, making them readily tradable by a fund facing a last-minute cash purchase or sale of its shares. However, because reports to the SEC usually show total holdings for the accounts of a reporting investment advisor, it may be difficult to distinguish mutual fund holdings from other accounts managed by an advisor.

nature of the cash flows involved, may not be as great as the economic effect of interest rate changes on securities lending. In most recent interest rate environments, lending ETF shares created specifically for the purpose of lending has been a moderately attractive business opportunity for specialists and other market makers. As short-term interest rates move up from recent extremely low levels, ETF share lending could become an attractive business activity for dealers once again. Of course, the need for more extensive record keeping to meet requirements the Treasury may impose could affect the economics of short selling and securities lending in unpredictable ways. Pension plan ETF share lenders should be able to avoid most such record-keeping costs.

As an aside, the QQQs—with their 55% of capitalization short interest in December 2003—pay only a tiny dividend. Ironically, however, the new dividend tax treatment has encouraged many firms to begin paying dividends or to increase their dividends, so the possibility of a larger QQQ's dividend cannot be ignored. Realistically, any QQQ's dividend is not likely to be large enough to affect the lending of QQQ shares anytime soon.

WHAT IS THE EFFECT OF SHORT SELLING AND RISK MANAGEMENT ACTIVITY ON ETF TRADING VOLUME AND TRADING COSTS?

The facts that QQQs are the most actively traded equity security in the world (in terms of *number of shares*) and that SPDRs are the most actively traded securities (in terms of *trading value*) are not the result of frenetic trading by the *average investor* in these fund shares. That the total number of SPDR and QQQ shares outstanding turns over every few weeks simply reflects that these ETFs have become extremely popular risk management instruments, and have taken significant risk management market share from futures contracts. The effect of these hedging applications on trading spreads and share volume makes the nature of the markets in a few actively traded ETFs with large short interests very different from the markets in less active ETFs and more traditional securities.

At first thought, widespread use of ETFs in risk management applications should not have a material effect on the quality of the markets in the ETF shares. Other things being equal, the bid/asked spread that an investor or trader faces in an ETF should be largely a function of spreads in the markets for the underlying basket of securities that make up the ETF portfolio. However, if the ETF's portfolio becomes a standard portfolio or basket trade and if ETF market makers experience a high level of trading activity in the ETF shares, they may trade the ETF at a tighter spread than an investor trading in a similar basket or less active ETF would experience. A benchmark index portfolio basket, whether for the S&P 500, the QQQs or the Russell 2000, is a standard basket and will trade more cheaply as a basket than an investor or trader can trade the individual securities separately. If an ETF is extraordinarily active like the SPDRs and QQQs, a consistent high level of trading activity in the ETF shares may further reduce trading costs.

Tight spreads on these baskets and on some of the related ETFs are not just the result of a large number of orders interacting. In today's markets, the presence of a number of market centers—on exchanges, on NASDAQ, and on the trading books of a variety of electronic communication networks (ECNs)—permits some market participants who can access multiple market centers to trade the most active ETF shares at very low cost.

The interaction of multiple ETF market places with futures contracts on the ETFs themselves and, more importantly, with futures contracts on the indices underlying the ETFs, leads to active trading in what we call an index "arbitrage complex" that facilitates active trading on tight spreads for online traders and traders at hedge funds and broker-dealers. As the pattern of growth and decline in capitalization reflected in the shares outstanding for each of the 10 largest ETFs listed in Exhibit 4.2 illustrates, the number of shares an ETF has outstanding is not stable. Short selling and other risk-management-related ETF activity varies greatly in importance depending, in large measure, on how widely the underlying index for the ETF is used in risk management applications. Ultra-tight trading spreads from the interaction of competing markets and competing instruments have had a major effect only on the S&P 500 SPDRs and the QQQs. The growing short interests for the DIAMONDS, based on the Dow Jones Industrial Average, and the iShares Russell 2000 fund suggest that these funds might ultimately experience some similar trading effects.[14]

Two funds based on the same underlying index—the S&P 500 SPDR, the largest ETF in terms of assets, and the iShares 500 ETF, the third largest ETF in terms of assets—vary greatly in trading activity, and in the absolute and relative size of the funds' short interests. This particular case is interesting because the iShares 500 has a very slightly lower expense ratio than the 500 SPDR. Also, the two funds have had very similar performance for most of the period they have competed, with the SPDRs showing the better performance earlier and the iShares 500 fund having done a little

---

[14] Significant recent activity in single stock futures (SSF) contracts on the DIAMONDS and the iShares Russell 2000 ETFs may be contributing to this change. Some of these multimarket effects on trading activities are described in Chapter 8 of Gastineau, *The Exchange-Traded Funds Manual*.

better more recently. Trading activity and the short interest are concentrated in the S&P 500 SPDR, probably because it was the first ETF on the market and its trading and risk management applications are better established. The short interest in the 500 SPDRs is worth nearly twice as much as the value of all shares outstanding in the iShares 500 fund.

As Exhibit 4.2 illustrates, short interest, a good indicator of risk management applications for an ETF, varies considerably over funds and indices and over time. Substantial differences in short interests also will be found among smaller ETFs. In smaller ETFs, measurements like the short interest or the percentage of institutional ownership may be determined by a few large shareholders or large short sellers. For example, it is theoretically possible for securities lending and relending to lead to a short interest in excess of the share capitalization of a fund. Furthermore, in at least one case, (the iShares MSCI Taiwan Fund) institutional ownership reported under rule 13-F once accounted for more than 100% of the shares outstanding as a result of securities lending among a few large institutional investors combined with dealer trading facilitation.

ARE RISK MANAGEMENT APPLICATIONS AND HEAVY ETF SHARE TRADING DESIRABLE FOR FUND SHAREHOLDERS AND FUND ADVISORS?

From the viewpoint of a fund shareholder who might want to trade fund shares from time to time,[15] the tighter the market spread and, other things being equal, the more active trading in the fund shares becomes, the easier and cheaper it will be to trade shares in the fund. However, significant effects of a fund's membership in an index arbitrage complex and trading in different market centers competing to tighten trading spreads are still confined to two funds: the S&P 500 SPDRs and the QQQs. Shareholders in funds with at least $100 million in assets and a conscientious exchange specialist are not likely to be at a significant trading cost disadvantage to multibillion dollar funds with more trading activity, but no active futures contract. Trading has to expand very dramatically before trading activity *per se* has a significant effect on ETF trading *costs*.[16]

---

[15] In contrast to a buy-and-hold investor.

[16] Unfortunately, the indices used in benchmark index funds tend to be relatively inefficient, increasing embedded transaction costs associated with index changes. These costs penalize longer term investors in the funds to a much greater degree than a long-term investor will benefit from lower share trading costs. See Gary L. Gastineau, "Equity Index Funds Have Lost Their Way," *The Journal of Portfolio Management* (Winter 2002), pp. 55–64; and Quinn and Yang, "How Is Your Reconstitution."

Great popularity in the market for risk management instruments is not necessarily an advantage to an ETF's investment advisor. ETF short sales supported by market-maker-share inventories held to lend to short sellers have a positive effect on an ETF's shares outstanding. These market maker activities, in fact, foster the creation of lendable fund shares that pay fees to the fund advisor, increasing the assets under management and, together with the increase in trading activity, create an appearance of success for the fund that might have the effect of attracting additional assets. On the other hand, if the recent trend to less-covered lending by specialists and other market makers, who create shares to lend them, and more lending by other holders of ETFs becomes the dominant pattern, short selling will reduce *an ETF's shares outstanding*. A short seller needs a buyer. If shares are easy to borrow, that buyer is likely to be a market maker who will sell the shares back to the fund and shares outstanding will decline. It matters very much to fund advisors whether shares are created to lend or lending is an incidental activity of ETF investors and replaces shares issued by the fund.

To put the impact of short selling ETFs in an economic perspective, if all open short positions in the QQQs in December 2003 were covered by share borrowing from traditional investors, the shares supplied by the short sellers reduced the fund's assets by approximately $12.5 billion. At the fund's 20 basis point expense ratio, this represents forgone fee revenue of approximately $25 million annualized. There is little question that the large benchmark ETFs are more actively traded as a result of risk management applications. Short sellers can meet the needs of ETF buyers with shares borrowed from traditional investors rather than shares created to be loaned. This pattern is certainly not attractive to the fund's advisor. Of course, without the effect of active trading, the funds might be much smaller, making the net effect of a large-short interest unclear.

WHAT IS THE SIGNIFICANCE OF THE SHORT INTEREST FOR GROWTH IN ETF ASSETS?

An interesting aspect of fluctuations in ETF shares outstanding and fluctuations in the short interest, is the fact that growth in assets committed to ETFs reflects an entirely different process than growth in assets committed to conventional mutual funds. With trivial exceptions, it is not common practice to sell shares in conventional mutual funds short.[17] If

---

[17] There is limited short selling in the shares of the Fidelity Select (sector) Portfolios, but we are not aware of much other short selling of conventional mutual fund shares.

creation of ETF shares to lend for a short sale is fully replaced by borrowing from traditional investors, each share sold short supplies an additional long share that appears in some investor's account but does not increase the fund's shares outstanding. ETF shares credited to investors' accounts consist of the total fund shares outstanding on the fund's books plus the short interest. The short selling mechanism leads to more ETF shares "owned" in shareholder accounts than there are shares outstanding. This phenomenon merits careful consideration by all ETF users. If you do not understand this, reread the prior three paragraphs until you do.

The most widely circulated data on ETF assets focuses on the current market value of each fund's recorded outstanding shares.[18] This weekly ETF market report places no emphasis on *changes in the number of shares outstanding in each ETF.* Investors looking at this report perceive growth or decline in the value of ETF portfolios as more a function of market price changes in underlying portfolios than of net investment or disinvestment by fund share holders.

Aggregate ETF net investment and redemption data reflecting the value of changes in shares outstanding is published monthly by the Investment Company Institute (ICI). These reports translate share changes into net purchases and sales at the prices of the actual purchases (creations) and sales (redemptions). The ICI data compilation shows and prices the changes in shares outstanding appropriately, but it cannot take into account the fact that changes in an ETF's short interest substitute for shares purchased or redeemed with the fund.[19] In Exhibit 4.3, we average the sums of the shares outstanding and the short interest for each of the 10 largest equity funds for the middle of the months December 2002 and January 2003 and compare that average with the same data for the middle of December 2003 and January 2004.[20] Three of the larger ETFs, particularly the S&P 500 SPDRs and the QQQs, experienced *declines* in shares outstanding from the end of 2002 through 2003. When the general increase in ETF short interests over

---

[18] A weekly summary compiled by the American Stock Exchange and distributed by e-mail to anyone who requests it.

[19] See http://www.ici.org/stats/etf/index.html.

[20] The ranking of the 10 largest equity funds is based on assets in mid-August 2003, as reported by the American Stock Exchange. The reason for averaging December and January is that the short interest and the contemporary shares outstanding are mid-month figures. The short interest is published only on a mid-month settlement, not a month end, which would be the usual way to judge growth or decline in the funds from year end 2002. The data in Exhibits 4.2, 4.3, and 4.4 comes from the American Stock Exchange's data website, www.amextrader.com.

EXHIBIT 4.3 Largest Equity ETFs Shares and Equivalents Held in Long Accounts—Year End 2002 to Year End 2003

ETF	Symbol	Dec-02	Jan-03	Average	Dec-03	Jan-04	Average	% Change Shares Outstanding	% Change Share Equivalents
S&P 500 SPDR	SPY								
Shares Outstanding		421,691	453,441	437,566	377,506	380,806	379,156	−13.35%	
Short Interest		62,315	44,580		127,092	114,033			
Total Share Equivalents		484,006	498,021	491,014	504,598	494,839	499,719		1.77%
NASDAQ 100 Index	QQQ								
Shares Outstanding		719,500	674,250	696,875	633,950	607,250	620,600	−10.95%	
Short Interest		163,473	167,090		350,113	320,456			
Total Share Equivalents		882,973	841,340	862,157	984,063	927,706	955,885		10.87%
iShares S&P 500	IVV								
Shares Outstanding		47,450	52,600	50,025	68,850	70,650	69,750	39.43%	
Short Interest		3,369	1,518		1,468	2,782			
Total Share Equivalents		50,819	54,118	52,469	70,318	73,432	71,875		36.99%
DJIA DIAMONDS	DIA								
Shares Outstanding		58,304	58,205	58,255	64,509	63,861	64,185	10.18%	
Short Interest		14,575	11,751		23,063	28,334			
Total Share Equivalents		72,879	69,956	71,418	87,572	92,195	89,884		25.86%
S&P 400 MidCap SPDR	MDY								
Shares Outstanding		63,358	63,258	63,308	60,688	60,913	60,801	−3.96%	
Short Interest		6,214	4,502		8,831	8,768			
Total Share Equivalents		69,572	67,760	68,666	69,519	69,681	69,600		1.36%

EXHIBIT 4.3 (Continued)

ETF	Symbol	Dec-02	Jan-03	Average	Dec-03	Jan-04	Average	% Change Shares Outstanding	% Change Share Equivalents
iShares MSCI-EAFE	EFA								
Shares Outstanding		21,800	20,600	21,200	36,400	42,800	39,600	86.79%	
Short Interest		1,440	576		1,761	1,446			
Total Share Equivalents		23,240	21,176	22,208	38,161	44,246	41,204		85.53%
iShares Russell 2000	IWM								
Shares Outstanding		27,250	26,850	27,050	37,700	39,000	38,350	41.77%	
Short Interest		7,209	5,794		16,962	18,673			
Total Share Equivalents		34,459	32,644	33,552	54,662	57,673	56,168		67.41%
Vanguard Total Market Vipers	VTI								
Shares Outstanding		16,404	16,441	16,423	22,763	24,173	23,468	42.90%	
Short Interest		562	451		694	394			
Total Share Equivalents		16,966	16,892	16,929	23,457	24,567	24,012		41.84%
iShares Russell 1000	IWB								
Shares Outstanding		14,800	16,350	15,575	30,950	32,350	31,650	103.21%	
Short Interest		622	1,597		1,319	1,323			
Total Share Equivalents		15,422	17,947	16,685	32,269	33,673	32,971		97.61%
iShares S&P SmallCap 600	IJR								
Shares Outstanding		11,950	13,600	12,775	14,750	15,350	15,050	17.81%	
Short Interest		1,761	1,146		1,347	1,726			
Total Share Equivalents		13,711	14,746	14,229	16,097	17,076	16,587		16.57%

Data Source: American Stock Exchange. All figures are mid-month.

55

this period is added to shares outstanding, only the S&P MidCap SPDR showed a decline in its net share position—a very small one—over that interval. If the reduction in shares outstanding was due primarily to market makers withdrawing from ETF share lending, substantial net ETF purchases by the public have been accommodated by short sellers and, hence, net long ETF investment has been much more robust in 2003 than some observers have suggested.[21]

Exhibit 4.4 illustrates how changes in an ETF's short interest can distort interpretations of that ETF's popularity with (long) investors. A number of analysts have noted that the third largest U.S. ETF, the iShares S&P 500 fund, enjoyed an increase in shares outstanding in 2003 while the older and massively larger S&P 500 SPDR had fewer shares outstanding at the end of 2003 than at the beginning. Exhibit 4.4 shows what happens when we add the short interest to the outstanding shares of each of the funds. The 2003 increase in shares held by long investors in SPDRs was still less than the net increase in long positions in the iShares S&P 500 fund. The SPDR, held long did increase, however. From an analytical perspective, the large and fluctuating size of many ETF short-interest positions, year-end tax motivated transactions by dealers, and uncertainty about where the shares sold short are borrowed make any statement about short-term changes in investor interest in ETFs of dubious validity.

CONCLUSION

ETF short interests have been growing dramatically while the short interest in the typical common stock has declined slightly. We see no particular reason to expect a continuation of the rapid growth in the short interest of many ETFs, but there is also no particular reason to expect ETF short interests to decline, especially for ETF shares used widely in risk management applications. On balance, short selling contributes to the trading efficiency of a few of the more actively traded ETFs. Even more importantly, it contributes to the efficiency of various index arbitrage activities and, consequently, to overall market efficiency.

---

[21] Of course, observers who have looked only at the total value of ETF shares outstanding have also been misled by a rising stock market. For many purposes the ICI analysis of ETF investments and disinvestments is the appropriate measure of ETF growth or decline; but Exhibit 4.2 indicates that ETF analysts should also monitor and evaluate changes in ETF short interests. Data on ETF institutional ownership and short interest reports are difficult to interpret consistently over time.

Investors need not examine or even care about the short interest in an ETF they choose for longer-term investment. The large or small size of its short interest has no implications for a fund's suitability for long-term investment purposes. Fund analysts and active traders should understand the significance of short selling in the ETF market place, both for its trading cost implications and its sometimes misleading effect on the statistics for share ownership and ETF investment in the aggregate. The ETF short interest is important, but it requires careful interpretation.

Theory and Evidence on Short Selling

Restrictions on Short Selling and Exploitable Opportunities for Investors

Edward M. Miller, Ph.D.
Research Professor of Economics And Finance
University Of New Orleans

Mainstream finance theory is developed in a highly abstract world in which, among other assumptions, investors are assumed to be as willing and able to sell short as to take a long position. This is obviously unrealistic. Most institutional investors are not permitted to go short. Most individual investors are afraid to make short sales. There are various institutional obstacles to short selling (uptick rules, the need to borrow the stock, etc.). Even for the investor who would never go short, the optimal investment strategies in a market with restricted short selling proves to be quite different from in a textbook market with free short selling.

In this chapter it will be shown that in a world with restricted short selling that:

1. Markets are unlikely to be efficient and stock picking can pay.
2. The inefficiencies more often take the form of there being overvalued securities that can be identified by analysis.
3. This asymmetry implies a case for conservative accounting.
4. Successful investors often win by avoiding losing.
5. The best strategy is to analyze intensively a few stocks rather than searching for a few big winners.
6. Knowing when to sell is a better route to investment success than seeking winners to buy.

7. The effects of obstacles to short selling are stronger for events in the distant future.

This chapter will develop the implications for practitioners of a world where there is little short selling and where there are some uninformed, overoptimistic investors. These assumptions seem more plausible than the assumptions in mainstream finance theory, that investors can make short sales as easily as they take long positions, and that there are no uninformed investors.

Textbooks sometimes deduce that security prices should be efficient by assuming homogeneous beliefs. Obviously people disagree about all sorts of things including sports, politics, and securities. It is also true that sometimes investors are mistaken and they are often mistaken about things that are a matter of public record. The standard theory has argued that such mistakes could not lead to incorrect pricing because better informed investors would trade against the less informed investors in a way that would prevent incorrect pricing. It will be shown in this chapter that while the standard theory is correct about the absence of grossly underpriced securities, it is incorrect with regard to the existence of overpriced securities.

The inability of informed investors to eliminate overpricing of securities arises from their inability to make short sales as easily as standard theory assumes. In most cases the informed investors will not hold enough of the overpriced stock for their selling to eliminate the overpricing. For their selling to eliminate the overpricing, they would have to sell short. However, various obstacles prevent them from making the required short sales. This implies (contrary to standard theory) that there will be some overvalued stocks that can be identified with publicly available information.

The discussion of markets with restricted short selling will start by considering the case where there is divergence of opinion and one group of investors can be identified as right and one group as wrong using publicly available information. This should make it clear that analysts can add value, and how investors can use their analysis to avoid overvalued stocks. In Chapter 6, I will consider the case where there is a multiplicity of opinions and it is not clear which is correct.

DEMAND AND SUPPLY CURVES ARGUMENTS

The essence of the argument can be shown in the demand-and-supply diagram shown as Exhibit 5.1. Here there are only two opinions about a stock. One group of investors has a higher estimate and will be referred to as the *optimists*. The other group has a lower estimate and will be referred to as the *pessimists*. Later the types of errors that might be made will be discussed. For simplicity, each investor who desires a security in his port-folio will be assumed to buy a certain quantity of that security. (This ignores the intensive margin in which the more that is bought the more optimistic an investor is about a security.) As can be seen in Exhibit 5.1, the demand curve for a security then consists of two horizontal lines. With the assumption of no short selling, the supply curve is a vertical line at the number of shares issued by the company. By the standard argument, the equilibrium price is where the supply and demand curves intersect.

The interesting question is whether the intersection will occur at the higher or the lower price. Is the price set by the optimistic or the pessimistic investors? The length of the higher line is the product of the number of optimistic investors multiplied by the number of shares each purchases. If this exceeds the number of shares outstanding, the price is equal to the willingness to pay of the optimistic investors. Otherwise, it equals the willingness to pay of the pessimistic investors.[1]

Should we think of prices as typically being set by the optimists or the pessimists? Notice that the market value of any stock in current markets is just a small fraction of the market value of all stocks, and

EXHIBIT 5.1   Demand and Supply Curves Argument

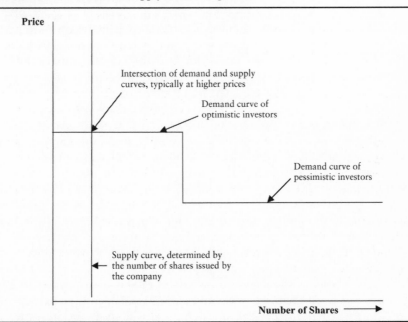

---

[1] In the very unlikely case that the supply curve intersects the demand curve in its vertical section, the price is indeterminate.

that the typical investor has a position in only a small fraction of the large number of stocks that are available. The result is that typically the intersection occurs on the upper horizontal line, so that the prices typically reflect the opinions of the more optimistic investors.

As an illustration of the relevant type of arithmetic, imagine a company has a total market value of $1 billion dollars and 10 million shares outstanding, implying a market price of $100. If each investor holds as little as one round lot (100 shares), it will take 100,000 investors to absorb the full supply of the stock issued by the firm. If there are more than 100,000 investors who are optimistic about the stock, the upper horizontal line will extend beyond the vertical line indicating the supply, and the price will be at the upper value.

Typically, with two types of investors (optimists and pessimists) the price will be set by the optimists if the percentage of optimists exceeds the percentage of all investors who own the shares. Given that typically only a small percentage of investors will own any particular share, this condition appears to be commonly met. Thus, the optimists set the price. Obviously, this example requires that the average size of holdings be the same for the pessimists and the optimists, but this seems a reasonable first assumption. Likewise, dividing investors into only two groups is usually a gross simplification (which can be relaxed without altering the essence of the argument).

That prices are set by optimists is not the same as the textbook statement that the price reflects the opinion of the average or typical investor.

We can expect that some optimistic investors are unaware of publicly available information or misinterpret it. These can be referred to as overoptimistic investors, and they can be expected to set some prices. With some prices set by the overoptimistic investors, it follows that there will be some overpriced stocks. The demonstration that, with restricted short selling and divergence of opinion, there could be overvalued stocks identifiable from publicly available information is, of course, inconsistent with efficient markets. This implies that it is possible to use security analysis to beat the markets (i.e., outperform indices on a risk-adjusted basis).

That there are obstacles to short selling is critical to the argument because if the pessimists were willing and able to sell short, their short selling would eventually saturate the demand of the optimists.

Since in a short sale the buyer of the shares gets ownership of the shares issued by the company (and the certificates if any exist), these shares still exist. However, the lender of the shares retains the right to call back his shares and sell them. He will still receive the dividends he expects (the borrower will pay these). The stocks he lent will show up on his list of holdings. Indeed, if he is a retail investor he will never know the shares were lent. Thus, the lender of the shares will act as if he still owned them. In effect, the short seller has created new shares that are identical to the old shares (except for voting rights). In a portfolio these new, synthetic shares are a perfect substitute for the shares lent. The market acts as if the total quantity of shares in existence is the sum of the shares issued by the company, and the shares created by short sellers. Thus, in the Exhibit 5.1, the extra shares created by short selling can be recognized by altering the supply curve. In this simple case, the number of shares is shown as increased.[2]

Because the quantity of stock sold short is typically very small, usually less than 1%, allowing for realistic quantities of short selling does not change the conclusion that prices are set by the optimists.

Ofek and Richardson[3] find that in February 2000, studying 3,946 non-Internet firms with prices over $10, that the mean short interest was only 1.8%. For the Internet firms the mean was only 2.8%. Even for the top 5% of the 273 Internet firms, the short interest was only 10.6% of the shares outstanding (versus 7.85% for the non-Internet firms).

Asquith and Meulbroek[4] analyzed the data for firms listed on the U.S. major exchanges (the New York Stock Exchange and the American Stock Exchange) for 1976–1993 as a percentage of the number of shares outstanding. The short interests showed a strong tendency to increase over time. Most firms have very low short interests. For 1993, the median short interest was only 0.82%. The mean was only 1.78%. However, a few firms were found to have appreciable short interest. Ten percent had over 4.46% short interest. Five percent had over 6.93% short interests. The top 1% has short interests of 12.92%. For the time period studied, the peak of the top 1% short interests was in 1990, when it was at 14.04%.

These are all relatively small numbers. Even for the most heavily shorted firms (the top 1%) the quantity of stock available for holding is increased to only 115% of the quantity issued by the company. Thus, as a first approximate model where the quantity of stock available for purchase equal that issued by the company are quite realistic. Thus, only a small percentage of investors can absorb the full supply of stock on the market. Models of the academic type where unlimited shorting is permitted can result in total quantities of stock available for investors that are many fold the number issued by the company. These are further from the truth than

---

[2] While not relevant to this discussion, since the number of shares sold is expected to increase as the price increases, the effect is to replace the vertical supply curve by one with a slope. This makes slightly more likely the possibility that the supply curve intersects the demand curve in between the prices set by the optimists and the pessimists. Then the price is above the valuation of the pessimists, but below that of the optimists. This complexity does not change the basic point being made.

[3] For an academic view, see Eli Ofek and Matthew Richardson, "Dotcom Mania: The Rise and Fall of Internet Stock Prices," *Journal of Finance* (June 2003), pp. 1113–1138.

[4] Paul Asquith and Lisa Meulbroek, "An Empirical Investigation of Short Interest," working paper, Harvard Business School, Harvard University, 1995.

the approximation that the stock available for purchase is only that issued by the company. Models where the only stock available for purchase is that issued by the company are the models with no short selling.

Recognizably Overpriced Stocks Can Exist

This simple observation that prices are set by the optimistic investors and that these are sometimes wrong is useful. It can explain why there do appear to be overvalued stocks that are widely agreed to be overvalued.

Lamont and Thaler present evidence of gross mispricing in some technology carve-outs in which the IPO exceed the value of the original firm.[5] These appear to be clear errors that were not arbitraged away because of the costs of shorting.

The classic example is the recent Internet boom. Most observers were saying the stocks were overvalued, but yet they stayed at these high levels. For instance, in 1999, Perkins and Perkins wrote a book showing why the Internet stocks were overpriced.[6] An appendix to their book provided estimates of how fast the companies would have to grow over the next five years to justify the current (June 11, 1999) prices. At that time, this portfolio had a market value of $410 billion dollars based on combined sales of $15.2 billion (most of that from only AOL and Qwest), and with whopping losses of over $3 billion. Only 22 of these companies actually showed profits. The Perkins closed their book with an open letter to investors entitled, "Sell now." Here they say Internet stocks are overvalued and urge, "If you hold any of these stocks, it is time to sell." Their advice proved correct.

Similar arguments revealing the overpricing could have been found in many magazines and newspaper articles. Textbook and mainstream academic finance theory argues such overpricing is impossible since trading by informed investors would eliminate it. The problem for financial theory has been to explain how such obvious overpricing could have survived. A review article of mine summarizes it and explains how the Internet bubble was possible.[7] In essence, enough short selling did not emerge to prevent the optimists from bidding the prices up to these levels.

Ofek and Richardson interpret the Internet boom in terms of the theory of this chapter.[8] They document substantial short sale restric-

---

[5] Owen Lamont and Richard Thaler, "Can the Market Add and Subtract: Mispricing in Tech Stock Carve-Outs," working paper, University of Chicago, 2001. Also see Chapter 7 in this book by Lamont.

[6] Anthony N. Perkins and Michael C. Perkins, *The Internet Bubble* (New York: Harper Business, 1999).

[7] Edward M. Miller and M. Imtiaz A. Mazumder, "The Internet Bubble," *Journal of Social, Political, and Economic Studies* (Winter 2001), pp. 683–689.

[8] Ofek and Richardson, "Dotcom Mania: The Rise and Fall of Internet Stock Prices."

tions, for Internet stocks using evidence on short sales, short sale rebate rates, and option pairs (situations where put-call parity was violated). They also show a link between heterogeneity of opinions and price effects on Internet stocks.

Most interesting they show that the expiration of lockups on Internet stocks is associated with substantial declines in prices. They show that by the summer of 2000 almost $300 billion of shares had been unlocked in a short time. They argue this had much to do with the ending of the Internet bubble. They describe the large number of investors (insiders, venture capitalists, institutions, and sophisticated investors) who were freed by the expiration of lockup agreements to sell their Internet shares.[9]

The idea of the investors who value something most setting the price is widely accepted in the art market. We may agree that the average per-

---

[9] The only weak point in the argument is "that to the extent these investors did not have the same optimism about payoffs that existing investors had, their beliefs would now get incorporated into stock prices." The problem is that the selling by most of these investors need not be caused by less optimism about returns (although this was probably true of some), or even about risk in some absolute sense, but merely by a desire for diversification. The incremental effect of a share of the risk of a portfolio is greater when there is already much of the stock in the portfolio than when there is little. The result (using Markowitz optimization or something similar) is that the premium (often called a *risk premium*) over the return on other stocks needed to retain the share in the portfolio is much greater for these undiversified investors than for diversified investors. One can easily imagine a company founder, other insider, or an angel investor being undiversified, and hence being willing to sell to a diversified investor who is actually more pessimistic. The company founder might expect 13% on a stock that he thinks has a beta of 1.2 but rationally sell to a diversified investor who expects 10% and believes the beta to be 1.4. However, even if the sellers are actually more optimistic than average, the only way the increased supply resulting from their sales can be absorbed is for the price to fall. The sloping demand curve here arises from there being divergence of opinion and restrictions on short selling.

Of course, some of the sellers following a lockup expiration may indeed be more pessimistic. This is especially likely for the institutions and others who have had shares from venture capitalists distributed to them. These are probably well diversified, so their selling would be due to pessimistic views rather than merely seeking diversification. Since the venture capitalist rather than the institutions had decided to buy the stocks originally, these receiving institutions are likely to have opinions much closer to the mean. Because the mean valuation is usually lower than that of the optimists (especially for stocks with a wide divergence of opinion), it is very likely that these new holders were indeed more pessimistic than the current marginal investors. Finding the stocks overvalued, they would have sold. It is also plausible that many insiders (having access to the information on costs, sales projections, and an understanding of the size of the market and the strength of the competition) had more pessimistic views than the previously price setting optimists. In these cases, the expiration of the lockups would indeed cause the incorporation of more pessimistic views into the marketprice.

son will pay very little for a picture of a soup can to hang on his wall. However, we understand that if there is an auction, and one person is willing to pay several million dollars for that painting, that will be the market price. Likewise, many do not like Picasso prints, but if there are a hundred originals of a print, the price is the amount needed to induce the person with the 101st highest valuation to sell. No one tries to argue that average opinion sets prices in the art world.

If there are some overpriced stocks that can be identified by publicly available information, it will pay to hire analysts and do analysis of publicly available information. Such investing has the potential to outperform the market and index funds.

When the Pessimistic Investors Are Uninformed

Of course, in some cases the uninformed investors will not be the optimistic investors. The pessimistic investors will be the ones instead who do not realize the potential of a security. This situation is depicted in Exhibit 5.2.

EXHIBIT 5.2   Exhibit with Pessimistic Investors

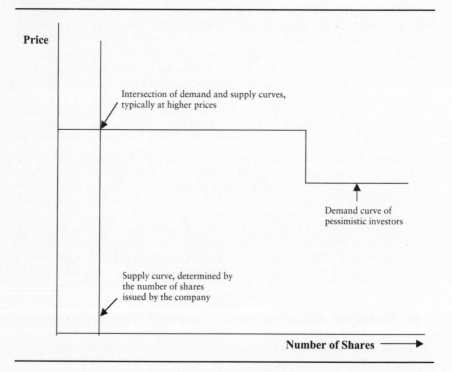

Notice for the uninformed investors to set the price, in this case there must be a very large number of uninformed investors. If the purchasing power of the informed investors is greater than the market value of the stock, the informed investors will set the price. In the above example of a company with 100 million shares, if each informed investor purchases a round lot (100 shares), the uninformed investors can only set the price if there are less than a million informed investors. With the average being 1,000 shares (allowing for institutions), 100,000 investors are needed.[10]

Notice that the more shares the average informed investors are willing to purchase on average, the smaller the number of informed investors that are needed to eliminate the underpricing. If the informed investors will purchase an average of 1,000 shares, it takes only 100,000 to eliminate the underpricing. Of course, the more extreme the underpricing, the greater the potential returns. The greater the potential returns, the greater the proportion of his wealth an investor will commit to an investment opportunity. Increasing the proportion of wealth committed to an opportunity reduces the number of investors who can recognize an undervaluation before it is eliminated. In the extreme, one investor with sufficient resources could act on an idea (by taking over the company), and eliminate the underinvestment. Thus, it is very unlikely there will be grossly undervalued stocks that can be easily recognized.

As discussed below, this suggests a strategy of trying to win, not by searching for grossly undervalued stocks, but by trying to identify and avoid the overpriced ones. The case for this strategy is made stronger when it is realized that while good information is readily disseminated, there are obstacles to the dissemination of negative information.

Informational Considerations

In considering the likelihood of a hundred thousand people being unaware of a factor that should raise the price of a stock (which includes an analysis which puts together information already available), remember that there are strong incentives to publicize good news.

Because of stock options, the threat of takeovers, and the like, corporate managements prefer higher stock prices. They can be expected to draw attention to any information that they think has been neglected by the markets (new products in development, an expected upturn in business with the business cycle, the pending solution of an operational

---

[10] This 100,000 is a long-term number based on their being a buyer for every lot of stock owned by the more pessimistic investors. In practice, most investors do not constantly monitor the market, and a much smaller number is needed to purchase any stock coming on the market on a particular day and to bid the price up to the fair value by competition among themselves.

problem, bad luck that has temporarily depressed earnings, and so on). Virtually never will a firm publicize facts like the obsolescence of their products, the products' lack of durability, or the stupidity (or senility) of their management. Just imagine what the sales reps for the competition could do with statements such as "Competitor X has a better product," "Our product is obsolete," or "We have found unexpected durability problems with our product." A plaintiff's lawyer would love to have a statement on record saying, "Our product is unsafe."

If analysts or brokers identify a stock that is underpriced, they can be expected to publicize the information that make them believe it is undervalued. They, and their firm, could get an order to purchase the stock by informing investors of the information. Just as an example, a recent news story states, "Keane's nod carries some punch as his advice reaches 12,000 retail stock brokers at Wachovia Securities."[11] If each broker keeps only nine investors informed, the word has reached 108,000 investors, more than the 100,000 investors discussed above.

In contrast, even when short selling is allowed, few investors will place short sale orders. Only a few investors will own any given stock, so phone calls saying the stock is over valued will typically be greeted with "That's interesting, but I don't own any." In many cases, if the stock is actually owned, it is because the broker making the call sold it to the investor. There are real problems in calling a client up and explaining why the stock you previously urged him to buy should now be sold. Even those who own a stock are unhappy at brokers and analysts who draw attention to a stock's problems, since this forces its price down, making current owners poorer. The current owner usually has an ego investment in the stocks he owns, and telling him that these stocks are overvalued is to question his good judgment.

The brokerage firms that employ analysts are also investment banking firms that bring out new issues. Publicizing bad news about a firm does not help attract investment banking business from that firm.

Other investors (once they have accumulated a position) have an incentive to publicize the case for making an investment. If others follow them, the price may be bid up, making their own positions more profitable. The quicker any underpricing is eliminated by others learning of the investment's merits, the quicker profits can be taken (i.e., the higher the annualized rate of return from the investment) and the funds invested elsewhere. Also, it is pleasant at social gatherings to demonstrate your brilliance by talking about why the stock you just bought is

---

[11] Mark Davis, "Local Stocks: Analyst's Optimistic Rating Pushes Up DST Stock," *The Kansas City Star* Web site (September 30, 2003), posted at http://www.kansascity.com/ mld/kansascity/business/6891701.htm.

a good buy. Admittedly, short sellers have the same incentive to publicize negative information, but because there are so few of them relative to the longs (see above), their impact is much less.

Even the press is likely to assist in eliminating underpricing. Most business press stories are inspired by press releases. It is much easier to take a press release and write a story out of it than to do investigative work from scratch. Negative stories often eliminate the cooperation from the company that is needed for future stories. Because of the incentive that companies have to raise their stock prices, their press releases and the stories based on them have an optimistic bias.

The disincentive to publicize bad news has been offered as one reason for the profitability of momentum strategies.[12]

There is also a behavioral aspect here. Investors are reluctant to admit to themselves, their spouses, or their bosses that they have made a bad investment. Selling a stock means admitting to a mistake. A much better psychological strategy (even if a bad investment strategy) is to find reasons why the stock that has gone down is still a good investment and will come back. One study found that stocks above their purchase price are 50% more likely to be sold than stocks that are below their purchase prices.[13] Because of this bias, more analytic attention to stocks where there is not obvious bad news may unearth publicly available information that can be acted on profitably. The information may have been disseminating slowly enough so that prices have not fully adjusted yet. A stock that has fallen without an obvious explanation may be one that should be looked into further.

When we combine the obstacles to short selling with the asymmetry in the ease with which positive versus negative information is disseminated, we discover that there will be very few grossly underpriced securities that can be discovered from publicly available information, while there will be some overpriced securities that can be identified. As will be seen below, this observation has strong implications for investment strategy and for how a firm should allocate its analytical resources.

Accounting Implications

The above argument shows how in the absence of short selling, mistakes on the high side (those which cause investors to raise their estimate of the value of a stock) tend to raise stock prices, while those on the negative side do not. Thus there is an important asymmetry here. Accounting conven-

---

[12] Harrison Hong, Terence Lim, and Jeremy Stein, "Bad News Travels Slowly: Size, Analyst Coverage, and the Profitability of Momentum Strategies," *Journal of Finance* (February 2000), pp. 265–295.

[13] Terrance Odean, "Are Investors Reluctant to realize Their Losses?" *Journal of Finance* (October 1998), p. 1786.

tions which cause naive investors to overestimate the value of the company do more harm than those which cause naive investors to underestimate a stock's value. This analysis of investing as a loser's game provides an argument for conservative accounting.[14]

Probably the most important number for investors that comes out of the accounting process is earnings per share. This argument suggests that conventions that often overstate earnings should be avoided even if alternative conventions understate earnings. Overstated earnings often lead to overpriced stocks. Even if many analysts understand the true situation, there are likely to be enough who are misled for the stock to be overpriced. In contrast, suppose a convention produces misleadingly low earnings, but the information is available to compute a better measure. In this case, there are likely to be enough analysts who recognize the true situation for the price to reflect their evaluations. It follows that errors that understate earnings are likely to be less damaging than errors that overstate earnings. Thus, when a rule cannot be devised that is certain to be correct, it is probably best to err on the conservative side.

There is a social cost from stock prices that do not reflect value. Calculated costs of capital are partially based on their stock price.[15] Hence, if the stock is overpriced, then the cost of capital for that firm will be underestimated, and the firm may overinvest. If stock in a particular industry becomes overvalued (as happened with Internet stocks during the late 1990s), there may be overinvestment. Capital can be easily attracted when stock prices are high. Thus, the conclusion is that accounting methods should be biased towards the conservative side.

As an example, consider whether to expense an item such as research or to permit it to be capitalized. Although it is recognized that most research will be valuable over a number of years, it is difficult to know how many years. This difficulty has kept research from being capitalized and then amortized. Suppose a firm was free to amortize research expenditures over a number of years, even if the research had yielded very little. This would make the reported profits higher. Some investors might realize the research had yielded little, and value the company at a lower price. However, there would probably be enough investors who took the company's accounting at face value for the stock price to reflect their higher valuations. However, if the research is expensed when done (the current procedure), there will probably be some investors who do not realize the research expenditures have long-term value. However, there

---

[14] Edward M. Miller, "Why Overstated Earnings Affect Stock Prices But not the Reverse," *Journal of Accounting, Auditing, and Finance* (Fall 1980), pp. 6–19.

[15] See a standard text such as Anthony F. Herbst, *Capital Asset Investment* (New York: John Wiley & Sons, 2002).

are likely to be enough investors who recognize the value of the research (or at least intelligently estimate it), to raise the firm's stock price. These investors will be the optimists who set prices.

An example can be provided by convertible bonds. The drug company, Cephalon, issued convertible bonds with a zero interest rate. Why would anyone buy bonds that do not yield anything? The answer is that the conversion option is valuable. Cephalon's stock price could go up a lot, especially if its antidrowsiness drug, Provigil, is approved for new uses. Since the proceeds from the bond sales will be invested at a profit, the earnings per share should go up. If the bond holders get a valuable conversion option from the convertible feature, should not that be reflected in the accounts?

A little background may be useful. At one time the earnings per share for stocks were based just on the number of shares outstanding. This was misleading because there would be more shares outstanding if the convertible securities were converted. Firms could get their earning per share up by selling convertible securities and using the proceeds to purchase profit-earning assets (or using convertible securities to buy other companies). The interest charges were low because of the conversion feature. However, until converted there was no dilution on the books. Investors tended not to convert till required because of the lower risk of bonds than equity, and the fact that the interest rate usually exceeded the dividend rate (which was often near zero). The ability of outstanding convertible bonds to raise stock prices was eventually reduced by requiring earnings per share to be reported on a fully diluted basis.

Does making a conversion adjustment in the accounting affect the stock price? Many would argue that it should not because investors can find out about the convertible securities and calculate their own numbers. If the accountants did not do the calculation, surely many, perhaps most (weighted by size of portfolio), investors would do so. If investors make such adjustments, the price will reflect the adjustment. It then appears that what the accounting rules will have little impact on the stock price or economic efficiency.

However, the above analysis with restricted short selling makes it very likely the accounting treatment will make a difference. Due to lack of time or lack of skill, there are many investors who will not make the required adjustments for potential dilution. Thus presenting diluted earnings per share earnings will be useful.

A more complex example is provided by the current controversy over contingent convertible bonds.[16] These are convertible bonds that provide

---

[16] David Henry, "The Latest Magic in Corporate Finance," *Business Week* (September 8, 2003), pp. 88–89.

for conversion only if a contingency has occurred, such as the price reaching a considerably higher value than the conversion value. Under standard accounting rules, the earnings per share are adjusted for full conversion of convertible securities that could be converted. However, with a high contingent price that must first be reached, this conversion need not be reflected in the accounts until the higher price is reached.

With contingent convertible bonds, the conversion adjustment is avoided until the contingency occurs, which is usually further in the future. For recent Cephalon contingent convertible bonds, there was a potential 15% dilution. Failure to make allowance for dilution makes a stock appear more attractive. The investors who fail to make the adjustments will be the optimistic investors that tend to set the price. This applied to the original question of whether to make any adjustments for potential dilution and to the current issue of whether firms should be allowed to avoid adjusting for dilution when a contingency provision is involved.

Another example is the current controversy over whether and how to expense employee options. Clearly these options are of value to employees and frequently are used in recruiting and retaining valued employees. Employees consider them part of the compensation package. It is also clear that they typically cost the shareholders something through potential dilution. If they could be easily valued, there would be no dispute about the desirability of including them as an expense. However, there is considerable dispute about how to value them and agreement that any formula will be frequently misleading. For instance, Hewlett-Packard claimed that its profits would have been cut 64% had it treated stock options paid to employees and executives as a compensation expense, while Cisco Systems said the proposed rule would have reduced 2002 earnings 80%.[17]

There will be some investors who fail to recognize that the profitability of firms making heavy use of options for compensation is overstated. These investors will be willing to pay more for the stocks in question. They are likely to be overrepresented among the optimistic investors who set the price. Now suppose a conservative formula was used that often overstated the value of the compensation. Many informed investors would recognize the understatement of income. These more optimistic investors would be the price-setting investors. Thus, this argument suggests that, if the goal is to have market prices reflect values, we would include the cost of options as employee compensation. Admittedly, those that think technology (especially startup firms) should be encouraged (at the expense of the less informed investors) oppose option expensing. Thus, the obstacles to short selling even have implications for accounting.

---

[17] "FASB Delays Stock-Option Proposal," *Mercury News Wire Services* (September 12, 2003), Posted at http://www.bayarea.com/mld/mercurynews/business/6753519.htm.

THE PATTERN OF STOCK PRICES OVER TIME WITH UNINFORMED INVESTORS

The previous section used demand and supply curves to make some simple points about markets with no short selling. Of necessity such a discussion leaves out the time dimension. It is also a little extreme. In the United States short selling is legal, even if relatively rare (but remember there are many markets where short selling is forbidden). Although in the United States short selling is possible, it is not nearly as simple as many mathematical models would make it. In these models, short positions are equivalent to long positions with a negative sign. Someone who sells short can just take the money and invest it elsewhere (just as someone with a long position can sell it and invest the funds elsewhere). This, of course, is not what really happens in a short sale.

The lender of the stock which is sold short needs assurance that the stock will be returned. This is traditionally done by providing a cash deposit equal to the value of the stock sold short (and marked to market as its price changes). For most individuals, no interest is paid on these proceeds (the cases where interest is paid will be discussed later). Considering this case provides some useful insights.

The simplest case can be shown with the aid of Exhibit 5.3. Suppose there is a nondividend paying company that is going to liquidate at a

EXHIBIT 5.3   Price Limits when Short Sellers Receive No Interest on the Proceeds

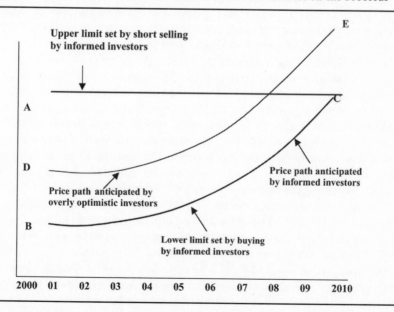

future date, say 2010. One might imagine it as a mining company that will liquidate when the deposit is exhausted (or when it's right to mine the deposit lapses). The well-informed investors analyze the company and estimate the liquidating dividend, C, in the exhibit. To decide how much to pay for the security, the informed investors discount this liquidating dividend at the appropriate risk-adjusted rate, and arrive at a value for each earlier date. Curve BC shows this price as a function of time. An informed investor should follow a simple rule: Buy the stock if its price is less than the value on line BC. The logic is simple. When the security can be bought at a price below BC, it is priced to yield more than other securities of equivalent risk.

It is easy to argue that in a market with many well-informed investors that the price will never fall below the line BC. This is because if it did, the informed investors would place buy orders for the stock and bid it back up to the line BC. If all investors were well informed, it would be obvious that the prices at all times would be on the line. But as pointed out earlier, there are likely to be quite a few badly informed investors. A harder problem is whether the price could be held above the line by uninformed investors.

The textbook answer to the problem of uninformed investors possibly bidding the price up is similar to why the price could not be below the line BC. Just as informed investors would buy if it was below the line, informed investors would sell if it was above. This selling would force the price back to the line.

However, the argument has a flaw. The informed investors may not even own the stock they predicted to sell. If there are no informed investors who own the stock, how could selling by informed investors force the price down to the right level?

This counter argument is usually met with a casual assertion that a stock not owned would be sold short. The rule for profiting in short selling is the same as for profiting from going long, "buy low, sell high." When an investor fails to receive prompt use of the proceeds, a short sale is profitable only if the stock can be sold now for more than the cost of later repurchasing it. Under the best of conditions (where the short seller can put up stocks already owned as margin and there are no dividends being paid), only stocks anticipated to decline in price are profitable short sales.

Now consider a stock below line AC but above the lower line, say at point D. Since price D is below the liquidation price, purchasing and holding the stock till liquidation will prove profitable. However, since line BC was calculated to yield a normal (risk-adjusted return), any stock above that line will yield a below market return. For concreteness, imagine stock D is priced to yield 1% per year. This clearly should not be held since the investor can do better with other assets.

With reason this stock can be said to be overpriced. Although many defenders of the efficient market hypothesis assert overpriced stocks are short sales candidates, this stock is not a short sale candidate. Because stock E will rise in price, it is not a short sale candidate. Investors lose money by shorting stocks that subsequently rise in price. The advice, "buy low, sell high," applies to short sales.

The example points out that an overpriced stock is not necessarily a short sale candidate. This is a mistake frequently made by efficient market proponents who casually assert that overpriced stocks will be sold short. (The usual definition of an overpriced stock is one that is expected to have a return below that on securities of comparable risk.)

Sometimes short selling is plausible. If the price is above line AC, informed investors could potentially short the stock and make a profit. Since line AC is the liquidation price, a stock sold now and bought back just before the company is liquidated would be profitable (if there are no carrying costs for the short sale). Of course, there could be a wild ride before the profit was realized.

Notice is that the upper limit (set by short selling) and the lower limit (set by buying) can be quite far apart. The lines are far apart when there will be several years before the uncertainty about the true value is resolved (which happens here when the company is liquidated). Between the two lines, the rule for informed investors is "sell, if owned." Since line BC shows the price increase required for the stock to show a normal return, if the price is above this line, the appreciation will be below that needed to justify holding it. Thus, the stock should be sold if owned.

Admittedly, whether or not short sales of overpriced stocks are made is not critical as long as investors are considered to all have the same expectations (homogeneous expectations). If all investors agreed that a fair price for the stock lay along the curve BC, they would regard any price above the line as a signal to sell the stock, and their selling would force the price back to the line. Thus, with homogeneous expectations (which textbooks tend to assume), efficient market pricing is insured regardless of the institutional arrangements for short selling.

Pricing with Uninformed Investors

The argument presented above needs not hold if there are some uninformed investors. Suppose many investors believe the liquidating dividend will be E. Their current willingness to pay will be D (i.e., the present value of E). If there are enough such investors to absorb the entire supply, the market price will be D. As the price rises above B, the informed sell to the less informed. The informed investors drop out of the market once their stock holdings are exhausted, and competition among the optimistic investors bids the price up to D.

As long as there are sufficient overoptimistic investors, the price will be at D. A sufficient number of overoptimistic investors need not be a very high number. For instance, if the company has 100 million shares outstanding and each investor typically takes 1,000 shares, only 100,000 investors need be optimistic about the stock to sustain the price at D. If there are a total of 10 million investors in the economy, this would require that only 1% be overoptimistic for the stock to be overpriced.

The above argument shows that in the presence of uninformed investors, there could be some overpriced stocks that could be identified by analysis of publicly available information, contrary to a well known implication of the efficient markets hypothesis. This is the same conclusion that was reached earlier, but now we are showing it holds even if all investors are able to sell short, but are required to surrender the proceeds of the shorts sale as a security deposit on which they do not earn interest, a situation that is true for most individual investors.

Investors Who Can Receive Use of the Proceeds

Up to this point, the theory has been developed on the assumption that investors can never receive use of the proceeds of a short sale. This is the situation for most individual investors. However, in the United States this rests on custom, not legal prohibition. Institutions and brokerage houses can frequently borrow certificates using procedures that give them some return on the proceeds. As a practical matter, the ability of the institutions to borrow shares under circumstances where they receive part of the proceeds is of only limited importance, since most institutions are operating under constraints that prevent short selling. However, some institutions (such as hedge funds, long–short investment companies, certain mutual funds, and other investment companies) may sell short and other large players (brokerage houses) may arrange to receive a return on the proceeds of a short sale. Thus this case should be considered.

There are several procedures that permit receiving some return on the security provided against loan of the certificates Hanson and Kopprasch once reported 75% of brokers' call is standard.[18] In other cases, borrowers of the shares deposit either other securities as security (in which case the return on these securities is still available to the short seller), or a bank letter of credit. They pay the lender an explicit fee for each day the shares are loaned. This fee offsets the earnings from the proceeds, in

---

[18] See H. Nicholas Hanson and Robert W. Kopprasch, "Pricing of Stock Index Futures," in Frank J. Fabozzi and Gregory M. Kipnis (eds.), *Stock Index Futures* (Homewood, IL: Dow Jones-Irwin, 1984) pp. 72–73.

effect causing the proceeds to earn less than the market rate. Much of the lending apparently comes from index funds that maintain a large inventory of most securities and are more than happy to get some incremental revenue from lending securities. Securities that are not held by index funds, or for which there is a heavy demand for shorting, will be harder to borrow, and the interest an institution receives will be less. In some cases, it may be necessary to pay a per day fee to borrow a scarce stock.

D'Avolio got data from one of the largest lenders of securities in the world for the period from April 2000 to September 2001.[19] The borrowers of the stock were usually brokerage firms borrowing either for themselves or for institutional short sellers (hedge funds, short selling funds, long-short funds). The collateral for borrowing is cash 98% of the time (the rest of the time it is Treasury securities). In most cases, this security lender paid interest on this collateral at a rate that is referred to in the industry as the *rebate rate*. As noted above, this rebate is not normally passed on to the retail customer. On "nuisance loans" for under $100,000 in securities, no rebate was paid. D'Avolio calculated an implicit fee as the difference between the Federal funds rate and the rebate rate. In the few cases where Treasury securities were used as collateral, an explicit fee would be charged. For most stocks, the implicit fees were always under 1%. In a few cases, there is a shortage of shares to be borrowed and the implicit fees are higher. These stocks are referred to as being on "special" by practitioners. In even fewer cases, the implicit fee is large enough so the rebate rate is negative. The interest earned varies according to demand and supply for the securities.

The majority of stocks (91%) were not on special (referred to as "general collateral") on any given day. For these stocks the value-weighted mean fee was only 17 basis points per year. The vast majority of the dollar value of stocks appeared to be available for borrowing. For most of these stocks, the borrowing would be done at a nominal fee. The stocks that appeared to be possibly unavailable (i.e., not listed by this lender), tended to be very low capitalization stocks and often too small or too low priced to be of institutional interest. (Since most lending was coming from institutions, this is not surprising.)

On average 8.75% of stock loans were specified as "special." The value-weighted mean loan fee was much higher, at 4.69%. There was an average of six stocks on any given day for which the rebate rate was negative (i.e., the borrower of the stock did not receive interest on the collateral and had to pay money to the lender as well). For these, the

---

[19] Gene D'Avolio, "The Market for Borrowing Stock," *Journal of Financial Economics* (2002), pp. 271–306.

implied fee averaged 19%. (The highest was 55% once for Krispy Kreme and 50% for Stratos Lightwave).

Exhibit 5.4 shows the situation of a short seller who can receive interest on the proceeds of a short sale (see below). The upper limit is then a curved line growing at the interest rate earned. Unless the interest earned on proceeds of short sales equals the competitive rate of return earned on long positions, the two curves will differ by an amount that increases with the period of time until the uncertainty is resolved. Because the competitive rate of return on stocks (averaging about 10%) is much higher than the Federal funds rate (at the historically low rate of 1% at the time of writing), there would still be an appreciable gap between the two curves, even if the full Federal funds rate was paid.

The large gap between the upper and the lower limits arises because a short seller does not receive full use of the proceeds of his short sale. Instead a short seller deposits the proceeds as a security deposit with the lender of the shares, where he either receives no interest (individuals) or less than market interest (institutions). When the short seller does receive

EXHIBIT 5.4   Price Limits when Short Sellers Receive Interest on the Proceeds

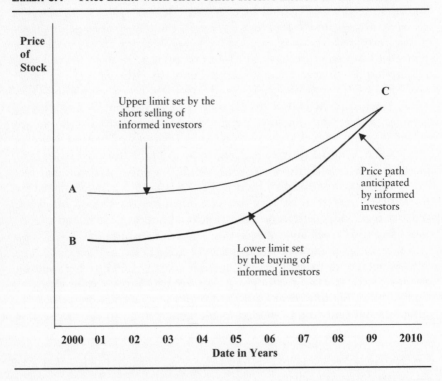

interest on the proceeds, it is possible to lose money on the short sale proper and still be financially ahead. The earnings from investing the proceeds can offset a loss on the stock as long as the rate of return on the stock is below the rate earned on the proceeds. In these circumstances, it is possible to violate the "buy low, sell high," rule and still make money. For instance, suppose a nondividend paying stock is sold short at $100 and bought back at $99 two years later. The short position has lost money. However, if the $100 received for the stock could be invested at even 1%, it would have grown to slightly more than $100. The $2 earned from investing the proceeds of the sale is greater than the $1 loss on the short sale, and the maneuver is profitable.

The violation of the "buy low, sell high" principle would be more striking if the short seller actually got use of the proceeds, and could invest it at the typical rate earned on equity, as is traditionally assumed in theoretical finance. However, a sum approximately equal to the proceeds is deposited as collateral (usually the sum is actually 102% of the market price to provide a safety margin for intraday fluctuations). This sum is marked to market.

So far the implications of systematic risk have been ignored. The beta of a short position is the negative of the beta of a long position, and is hence normally a negative number. In the capital asset pricing model, the required rate of return for an investment depends on the correlation of the return from the investment with the other securities in the portfolio, a characteristic that can be measured by its beta. Because of the negative beta of short positions, rational investors will often be willing to accept a lower return than they otherwise would, possibly even a negative return. Thus, the return a stock must earn if it is not to be sold short is higher for high beta stocks. This effect moves the line AC in Exhibit 5.4 downwards. However, high beta stocks also require a higher return for inclusion in a portfolio on the long side. If both buyers and short sellers use the capital asset pricing theory, the beta adjustment in the rate of return for the upper limit and the lower limits are equal, and the percentage difference in the rate of return is unchanged. The implication still remains that the distance between the two curves increases with time until resolution of the uncertainty.

Whether or not the effective upper limit to a stock price will be set by those institutional short sellers (who are both not constrained from selling short and able to receive a return on use of the proceeds), or by individuals not able to receive use of the proceeds, depends on the relative numbers of the two groups of investors and the strength of the buying by the overly optimistic investors. Often, (especially for the smaller capitalization stocks not widely traded by institutions) there will be too few potential short sellers able to receive use of the proceeds. In this case, the price will be bid up by optimistic investors to levels where further rise is limited by short selling by individuals (and possibly not even by them). When this happens, those short sellers who can receive use of the proceeds will be able to earn abnormal returns that cannot be earned by individuals.

Since some institutional investors do get use of the proceeds, and they are likely to have the analytical talent and expertise to identify good short candidates, individual investors who do not get use of the proceeds (or get even worse terms) should be very careful about short selling. It is plausible that competition between the hedge funds and other institutional investors has reduced the rate of return on short selling candidates to a negative number, making short sales profitable only for those who can earn interest on the proceeds of the sale.

On the long side, institutions have no such advantage. Individuals and institutions earn the same return from a long position. In fact, individuals trading in smaller amounts may even be able to avoid the price impact that many institutions experience when they trade in large quantities. However, because some institutions are willing to engage in short selling, those who can borrow stocks on favorable terms may find the opportunities desirable. Since much of the cost of the required expertise will be required to take long positions, the marginal cost of the research required for short selling may be low. Someone who is already following an industry may come across short candidates as a byproduct. For instance, a money manager may follow firm A and the outlook for its new products. However, firm A's success may be at the expense of firm B. If the market price does not yet reflect this fact, a short sale candidate has been identified at very little cost. If the investment process is computerized (a quant shop), the cost of identifying the short candidates may be very low. Once the stocks have been ranked by expected return (and the tops stocks bought), the low ranked stocks with negative returns can then be sold short.

If the money manager is unwilling to go short, he might spend no further analytic resources on a firm once he had been decided that it was not a candidate for purchase. If short sales are allowed, some additional research into a firm may be needed to determine if the short sale will be profitable. Thus, the research for the short selling opportunity is relatively cheap, but probably not free. Even then, in a "bounded efficient market" justifying the short sale may require recognizing that its negative beta permit taking a riskier long position (i.e., instead of holding some bonds to moderate risk, equities are held and short positions are used to protect against a market decline). In other cases, the short sale may permit taking a larger position in the same industry on the long side, or being more aggressive in holding firm A. (This leads to paired trading.)

A money management firm that has mostly long-side clients may find it profitable to introduce one or more short side (or long–short) funds since the marginal cost of managing them will be low.

Other Obstacles to Short Selling

The example used above in Exhibits 5.3 and 5.4 to develop the theory was highly unrealistic. It was designed to provide a very favorable case for short sellers' ability to provide a lid to stock prices even in the presence of less informed investors. Remember, the example involved a company that was scheduled to liquidate at a known date in the distant future. A liquidation date means that just before that date the stock has to sell at the expected liquidation value. This makes the stock act like a zero-coupon bond.

However, bonds typically have maturity dates, but not common stocks. In practice, very few companies have a known, planned liquidation date.[20] If one tries to project the price in 2010, one is really guessing what will the market expectations be in 2010 about the future of the company and about the dividends to be paid well after 2010. This infinite life makes short selling riskier, and implies that short positions will seldom be entered into for stock believed to be overvalued except when the overvaluation is very extreme and the holding period is short.

To a professional fund manager, the idea expressed in Exhibit 5.3 that a stock would be a short sale candidate because it could be sold short now for $101, and bought back in 2010 for $100 would be laughable. Why wouldn't he take that deal since it would be extra profit? One reason was given above. It would tie up part of his margin limit, preventing him from exploiting what could be much better opportunities to sell short other stocks or to buy stocks on margin.

Another reason is that one must comply with maintenance margin rules. A stock that is slightly overpriced today could be much more overpriced next year. On the way to $100, the stock now priced at $101 could go to $200 or $300. This would cause margin calls that could force the short position to be closed out at a very large loss. During the Internet boom, many investors correctly concluded certain stocks were grossly overvalued. They also correctly concluded they would eventually return to much more reasonable levels. Surely, making a short sale now with the intention of buying back the stock later should have been profitable. What actually happened was that the overpriced stocks became more overpriced and investors were forced to close out their positions at a large loss.

---

[20] The major exception is companies being taken over or selling their assets to other companies and then liquidating, paying the proceeds out as a liquidating dividend. These resemble the case in Exhibit 5.3, except that the period of time till liquidation is usually measured in months rather than years.

Aware of this risk, many smart investors (perhaps most) will not take a short position in overpriced stocks when it may be years before the overpricing is eliminated, or where the overpricing could easily get much worse before it is corrected. They limit their shorting to situations where the stock's overpricing will be corrected within a relatively short time frame (ideally by the company filing bankruptcy). Asensio's book on his shorting selling experience contains many accounts of shorting grossly overpriced stocks, but describes no attempts to hold positions for years.[21] Academics have recently discovered this problem, producing the limits to the arbitrage literature.[22]

This is a fundamental difference with long positions. If one is certain a stock will have a much higher price in the future (sufficiently higher to provide a suitable risk-adjusted rate of return), a long-term investor can buy it in confidence and expect to end up with a profit even if the stock's price falls before it starts rising. (This assumes he is not trading on margin.) This is not true for short positions. Even in the absence of maintenance margin requirements, those considering lending stocks would still require security deposits. There would be limits on how large positions investors could take. A mark-to-market provision is needed to protect the stock lenders. Such a provision means short sellers can be forced to cover even if they are right about the stock's long-run value.

Also because the standard stock lending agreement provides for the stock to be returned on demand, a short seller is always concerned not only with whether he can borrow the stock, but with whether he can keep it borrowed (normally if the lender wants the stock certificate returned the short seller can borrow it from another lender, but this is not guaranteed). Short squeezes have occurred. Many other potential short sellers are deterred from making short sales in thinly traded stock because of a justified fear that the stock will be called away from them before the position has proved profitable. Because index funds are not active traders, borrowers can borrow stock from them with less worry about having the certificates recalled because the original owner wishes to sell the stock. This makes them preferred lenders.

The research of D'Avolio shows that this risk of recall is real, but perhaps not as serious as some feared during the time period he studied.[23] During the 18 months of his study, about 105 of stocks would have been subject to a recall. In the few cases where buyers were forced to cover, the

---

[21] Manuel P. Asensio, *Sold Short: Uncovering Deception in the Markets* (New York: John Wiley & Sons, 2001).

[22] Andrei Shleifer and Robert W. Vishny, "The Limits of Arbitrage," *Journal of Finance* (March 1997), pp. 35–55.

[23] D'Avolio, "The Market for Borrowing Stock."

average returns were apparently negative on the day of the forced covering (−0.7%). The most likely reason for this is that the supply of stock for shorting was reduced because the main lenders (institutional investors) were selling. In the simplest case, a large institution decides to sell. This forces a recall of the stock lent out. Fortunately, the selling by the institution forces the price down and the short seller can cover on a down day. D'Avilio documents that in the quarter following recalls, the institutional ownership declines.

Typically, the shortage of stock to be borrowed resolves itself, and after an average of 23 days there appears to stock available again for borrowing. By incurring some transaction costs, the short position could be reestablished. The mean daily return during the period when the stock was unavailable for borrowing was −0.2%. Thus, the short seller forced to close out his position and then reestablish it experiences not only added transactions cost (spread, market impact, commissions) but also an opportunity cost in that he has lost part of the potential profits from the short position. When the short was part of a hedge, the short seller loses his hedge for this time period.

In the United States there is an uptick rule in which short sales on exchanges can only be made on an uptick. The regulatory goal seems to prevent short selling from driving prices down. If this goal was achieved, it could be argued that it made it harder for market prices to reflect all opinions, including the negative ones. However, this is probably not a major problem over the long run. Even what looks like a steady decline is usually interrupted by upticks on which short sales could be made. To the extent this is done, short sales may interrupt attempts at price recoveries and result in lower prices. Still, the need to sell on an uptick probably means that short sellers get worse executions in setting up their positions and this lower their returns. This is one more obstacle to short sales.

Regardless of how long the positions are open, United States income tax law treats profits from short sales as short-term capital gains and taxes them at higher rates than long-term gains. This lowers the profits for taxable investors and is one more obstacle to taking long-term short positions.

Legal obstacles should not be forgotten. In many countries short sales are prohibited. In Chapter 13, Bris, Goetzmann, and Zhu provide a table showing which countries permit short selling and some details. As of December 2001 the countries prohibiting short selling included Colombia, Greece, Indonesia, Jordan, Pakistan, Peru, Singapore, the Slovak Republic, South Korea, Taiwan, Venezuela, and Zimbabwe. In another group of countries short selling was prohibited for some period during the 1990s. These included Hong Kong, Norway, Sweden, Malaysia, and Thailand. Then there was a group of countries where short selling was allowed but apparently rarely practiced, including Argentina,

Brazil, Chile, Finland, India, Israel, New Zealand, the Philippines, Poland, Spain, and Turkey. In China the short sales restrictions are binding for the A shares (domestic), but not for the B shares (for foreigners).[24] While the countries without short selling tend to be the smaller emerging market ones, it is a rather long list and, in the aggregate, economically important.

In the United States there are obstacles for most institutions. Since short selling is traditionally considered speculative and prudent men do not speculate with other people's money, endowments, trust funds, and certain others appear very reluctant to make short sales. Almazan et al. report that 70% of investment managers are precluded by charter and strategy restrictions from short selling.[25] Fewer than 10% of those eligible actually make short sales. Admittedly, options could be used to create the equivalent of short positions and might even be at a lower cost. However, Koski and Pontiff find in a study of equity mutual funds that 79% make no use of derivatives, even though these are more likely to be permitted and may be the most efficient means of placing bets against a stock.[26]

Textbooks and academic articles are filled with "arbitrage" portfolios in which there are long positions and short positions of the same value, and no net investment. The long positions are financed by the short positions. As usually stated this idea is ridiculous. If anyone approaches a broker and asks to purchase a portfolio with zero investment he would be laughed at. In the United States such an arrangement would be illegal because it would violate the Federal Reserve margin rules.[27] Unfortunately, the otherwise excellent Elton and Gruber text

---

[24] Lianfa Li and Belton M. Fleisher, "Heterogeneous Expectations and Stock Prices in Segmented Markets: Applications to Chinese Firms," working paper, Ohio State University, 2002.

[25] A. Almazan, K. C. Brown, M. Carlson, and D. A. Chapman, "Why Constrain Your Mutual Fund Manager?" working paper, University of Texas at Austin, 2000.

[26] J. L. Koski and J. Pontiff, "How are Derivatives Used: Evidence from the Mutual Funds Industry," *Journal of Finance* (1999), pp. 791–816.

[27] Actually, there is one case in which this portfolio may be a useful conceptual device. Imagine a large institutional investor that in the absence of beliefs would hold an index portfolio with all the stocks of interest in it. He could overlay on this portfolio a zero investment arbitrage portfolio where there were negative weights on many securities. The proceeds from selling the securities that were labeled short in the "arbitrage" portfolio could then be used to increase the long positions in other securities. If not carried too far, there would be no actual short positions and the earnings of the new portfolio would be the sum of the index earnings plus the arbitrage portfolio earnings.

Given that many large institutions seem to be closet indexers, the outcomes of studies using the arbitrage portfolio approach could actually be useful to them.

illustrates Markowitz optimization with a exercise in which the portfolio takes long and short positions totaling many millions with only a small initial investment.[28] This violates the Federal Reserve margin rules.

Of course, if I could persuade you to lend me some stocks on my promise to return them in a few years, I could sell the stocks and invest in others. If my security selection was good, I would earn enough to buy the stocks I needed to repay you and leave a profit for me.

Alas, in practice it is very hard to get friends to lend you a few dollars for a short term need. It is unlikely a friend would lend you stocks worth thousands or millions merely upon your promise to repay them. In practice, lenders of securities require collateral so that they are not taking an appreciable risk. This collateral is at least the market value of the securities (and usually 102% of this value in the United States and 105% for international securities). Since the lender is holding the collateral, it is not available for taking long positions. In practice this collateral is virtually always cash, although Treasury bonds are sometimes used. The theoretical case of using the long securities as collateral (probably with an excess deposit for safety to the lender) is apparently not observed, although it is not clear to me why it is not done.

Thus, as a practical matter, a decision to hold a short position comes along with a decision to hold an equivalent dollar amount as cash. As discussed above, interest close to the risk free rates may be earned on this collateral for institutional investors. A natural question is, "How important is this as an obstacle to short selling?" It clearly eliminates the possibility, liked by theoreticians, in which a single informed arbitrageur forces securities into a correct pricing relationship by opening a very large self-financing position.

How serious the obligation to maintain a cash deposit as collateral presumably depends on whether the investor would normally hold cash. In a capital asset pricing model framework where cash is the risk-free asset, investors would often be holding some of the risk-free asset for risk reduction. Transferring this to the collateral account probably does not hurt. However, when the short positions are eliminating most systematic risk (as in the textbook arbitrage example), the investor may find he has more cash than desired.

However, the rate of return on cash is different from the rate on long-term bonds. It is usually presumed that the bond rate will be higher (in a rational expectations model with no risk it will not be). Presumably, most long-term investors would prefer bonds to cash for the risk-free part of their portfolio, if any. This may not make a big difference

---

[28] See Edwin J. Elton and Martin Gruber, *Modern Portfolio Theory and Investment Analysis* (New York: John Wiley & Sons, 1995).

since Treasury securities can be used as collateral (with an explicit fee paid for borrowing the stock to sell short). However, there remains a high possibility that the investor is still forced to hold more low risk assets than he would prefer.

Especially, for the investor who would like to hold matched long and short positions that essentially eliminate market risk, this need to hold collateral does reduce the attractiveness of long–short portfolios. Suppose the investor has discovered a strategy that earns 3% over the risk-free or the bond rate, and has diversified away all nonmarket risk. With the collateral requirements, his earnings are now 3% above the risk-free rate (with the zero-coupon bond rate taken to be the risk-free rate for investors whose horizon equals the maturity of the bonds).

Is this attractive? If the investor would otherwise hold bonds or cash, it is. In asserting it is, I have disregarded the residual risk which is always in long-short portfolios. However, for investors who believe the equity risk premium is positive (and the evidence is that over the long-term stocks have outperformed bonds by a big margin), 3% above the bond rate would still be unattractive because they would do better with a pure long portfolio. Those investment managers who have expertise in equities are normally hired by investors who want to earn equity level returns. For these investors, short positions with a need to post collateral may reduce returns (even risk-adjusted returns), even though the managers can identify stocks that will underperform on a risk-adjusted basis. In these circumstances, there is no reason to believe short selling will always be able to eliminate overpricing that is identifiable on the basis of publicly available information.

There is one possible class of investors for whom the need to post collateral will not be a major problem. These are broker dealers who hold a large inventory of customer's securities in margin accounts. The standard margin agreements permit these to be lent out (and contain no provision for crediting the owners with any profits earned). If these are used for making short sales, the broker brings in cash which is available for other purposes. Because such brokers normally are heavily indebted to banks for the money to finance short positions, they in effect earn the broker's call rate on this money.

Broker-dealers are often those best positioned to convert calls into puts by selling puts, buying calls, and then hedging by selling the stock short. In theory, puts may be priced to reflect their costs of operation and may provide a more attractive way for individuals and others who do not get use of the proceeds from a short sale to act on any negative beliefs they have. Of course, since puts are usually short-term instruments, the cost of rolling them over in commissions and spreads again makes placing long-term short bets unattractive.

The implication in Exhibit 5.3 that investors would short sell any stock whose price exceeds AC leaves out dividends. In the example, a stock that is certain to be selling for slightly less than it is selling for today would be sold short. If the stock is dividend paying, the short sellers must pay the dividends. A profit is not earned on a stock that went down by less than the dividends paid. Thus, a short-selling candidate is one whose expected total return (capital gains plus dividends) is negative for the investor who does not receive interest on the collateral.

While it might be thought that prices normally drop by the amount of the dividend when a stock goes ex-dividend, this is not quite true. The reason is that taxable investors prefer capital gains (less so than it used to be before the reduction in the tax rates on dividends) and prefer to delay buying till after the dividend, and to do selling just before. The result is that the need to pay dividends is an additional drag on the profits from short selling a dividend paying stock.

Another obstacle to short selling in the United States is that it must be made in a margin account, and short sales are counted against the Federal Reserve Rule margin limits (except for broker dealers, or those large investors who avoid this restriction by booking transactions overseas). Investors with a given amount of capital can be expected to rank their opportunities in the order of return. After ranking, investors will find that they can only accept investments whose estimated excess return annualized is much higher than $x\%$, where x is perhaps 5% (just for illustrations). This would mean accepting for long positions stocks that will yield more than 5% over an index (or over the prediction of the capital asset pricing model or other model specifying minimum risk-adjusted returns). For short positions this would mean stocks whose total return is less than minus 5% (i.e., a nondividend paying stock whose price declines by over 5% per year). Shown in Exhibit 5.5 the upper limit is then much higher, and thus is higher the further the position is from planned liquidation. In practice, many of the good analysts and hedge funds managers will generate more profitable ideas than they can exploit with the funds available to them. Thus, this constraint will be binding.

There are probably many individual investors who have a very good knowledge of a narrow set of companies (probably because they are in the relevant industry or in one that deals with them). As individuals, they are likely to be capital limited (with risk consideration limiting the fraction of their wealth they are willing to invest in their ideas) and rather frequently a good long idea may displace a good short idea.

One other restriction on short selling should be noted. Insiders are forbidden to sell short (at least not without refunding any profits to the company). This probably has little effect on most stockholders who are classified as insiders because of the size of their holdings. They can just

EXHIBIT 5.5   Price Limits for Stocks on Special

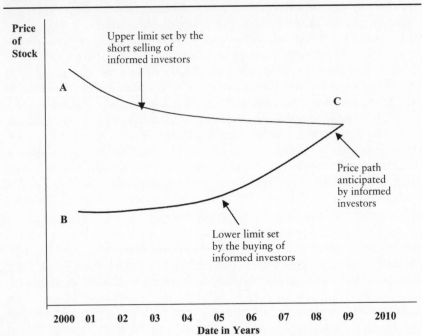

reduce their long positions. However, there probably are many officers and directors who are prevented from taking short positions by this prohibition. Because these individuals must keep up to date on public information relevant to their companies, they may sometimes be aware of factors that when correctly analyzed show their company's stock to be overvalued. Once they have reduced their own positions to zero, they are not allowed to go short. However, if without using nonpublic information they conclude their company is a buy, they are allowed to buy. Admittedly, those closely involved in a venture are sometimes overoptimistic about its future and believe their own propaganda.

The obstacles to short selling are large enough so that there are probably profitable opportunities to be exploited by those who are legally free to make them, and large enough to get use of the proceeds. It may be easier to identify a profitable short than a profitable long. It may be cheaper to do so if much of the overhead cost of becoming familiar with an industry must be incurred to intelligently take long positions.

The existence of such short selling opportunities suggests that there is merit to the idea of hedge funds (which try to take both long and short positions), and to mutual funds that take both long and short positions.

While a single short sale is risky, the addition of a short position to the typical institutional portfolio reduces total risks rather than raising it. One suspects adding short selling (or managing funds that permit short selling) to the services offered by an investment management firm can provide a nice incremental return on its staff and analytical resources.

Thus, on close analysis the standard efficient market fails because of the restrictions on short selling make it likely that divergence of opinion will result in some stocks being overvalued, and overvalued in such a way that they can be identified from publicly available information.

If short selling does not eliminate identifiable overpricings, the situation is one of "bounded efficient markets." Let us return to the implications for practitioners of there being overvalued securities that can be identified by using publicly available information.

THE BOUNDED EFFICIENT MARKETS HYPOTHESIS

The above example critiques the efficient market hypothesis by showing that trading by informed investors cannot prevent certain stocks from being overpriced, causing the upper limit to stock prices to be above the lower limit.

Exhibits 5.3 and 5.4 shows the upper and lower limits grow steadily further apart as time increases. This is the usual effect of compound interest. The two curves differ by the present value of the proceeds of a short sale compounded at the difference between the competitive market rate and the rate earned on the proceeds of short sales (often zero). The longer the period in which these have to compound, the greater the price difference that can arise without providing profitable opportunities for trading by informed investors (unless they already have positions).

Many have tried to extend, without examination, a belief that the "market imperfection" of commissions and other transactions costs did not prevent markets from being "reasonably" efficient to a belief that problems with short selling (dismissed as a friction) cannot prevent markets from being "reasonably" efficient. Unfortunately, no matter how broadly "reasonably" is defined, the power of compound interest is such that over a long enough period of time, overly optimistic investors can cause prices to deviate by more than a specified amount from the efficient market level.

Often, the assumption of prompt and full use of proceeds of short sales is not made explicitly in efficient market arguments, but it is considered an implication of the perfect market assumption. This is unfortunate because such a key and incorrect assumption should be explicitly made.

Incidentally, other market frictions, such as commissions and spreads, can be incorporated into the model by recognizing that the two curves can differ by the typical costs of arbitrage, without anyone being able to profit from arbitrage. This merely moves one of the limits by the costs of arbitrage. Then, instead of the two lines converging over time, the gap at zero time is the cost of arbitrage.

The above argument has led the author to propose replacing the standard efficient markets argument with a bounded efficient markets model.[29] The theory is called *bounded efficiency* because it is a generalization of the traditional efficient markets model. Instead of prices being constrained by informed investors to be at a single "efficient" level, they are constrained to be within upper and lower bounds. In the limit where the upper and the lower limits are the same, the two models are identical.

The Evidence Regarding Bounded Efficiency

There have been numerous tests for abnormal profits available from information relevant to long periods of time. Evidence is accumulating that markets may not be fully efficient against some such long-term information.[30]

The now well-known small-firm anomaly is an example since it may be years before the error (if it is one) of avoiding small firms shows up in investment returns.[31] The evidence that returns on small capitalization stocks have been abnormally high and those on large stocks abnormally low is consistent with there being no stocks identifiable from publicly available information that can be profitably sold short.

Suppose someone realized that large firms promised subnormal returns, and hence concluded that they were overpriced (as they may be). If he responded by selling short a diversified portfolio of large capitalization stocks following a buy-and-hold strategy, he would have lost a fortune. For instance the Lustig-Leinbach study suggests a small firm effect from 1931–1979.[32] Since the smallest quintile of stocks are outside of the S&P 500

---

[29] Edward M. Miller, "Bounded Efficient Markets: A New Wrinkle to the EMH," *Journal of Portfolio Management* (Summer 1987), pp. 4–13.

[30] For early evidence see Donald B. Keim, "The CAPM and Equity Return Regularities," *Financial Analysts Journal* (May/June 1986), pp. 43–48; or Bruce J. Jacobs and Kenneth N. Levy, "Disentangling Equity Return Regularities: New Insights and Investment Opportunities," *Financial Analysts Journal* (May/June 1988), pp. 18–44 for a summary and references.

[31] This was originally publicized in Donald B. Keim, "Size Related Anomalies and Stock Return Seasonality: Further Empirical Evidence," *Journal of Financial Economics* (June 1983), pp. 13–32.

[32] Ivan L. Lustig and Philip A. Leinbach, "The Small Firm Effect," *Financial Analysts Journal* (May/June 1983), pp. 46–49.

universe, selling the S&P 500 short in 1931 would be the strategy for someone thinking large capitalization stocks were overvalued.

Of course, this would have been a money losing strategy. The actual return from the beginning of 1931 to the end of 1979 for the S&P 500 was +9.1% according to the Ibbotson and Sinquefield data. Such a prolonged short position would have been a disaster. Investors who knew of the overvaluation of large firms at the beginning of the period wouldn't have made the short sales called for in the usual argument in support of the efficient market hypothesis. If the market has been efficient with regard to firm size, the mechanism keeping it so has almost certainly not been short selling of overpriced firm size categories.

There appear to be higher returns on stocks neglected by analysts and lower returns on widely followed stocks, a finding inconsistent with efficiency.[33] A similar comment could be made for low price to earnings ratio stocks.[34]

In a series of papers, Fama and French have argued that returns can be predicted using market indices, a measure of capitalization, and a measure that identifies value stocks (they prefer book to value, but price earning ratios and cash flow to price also work).[35] While they have chosen to interpret their results as being explained by risk considerations, most observers interpret this as evidence that certain types of stocks have tended to outperform the market. Because of the strong uptrend in the market, it appears that one who thought growth stocks or large stocks were overvalued and shorted them would have lost money. Similar comments could be made for the use of momentum variables, and for many other variables which have been shown to have some long-term predictive power.[36]

---

[33] Avner Arbel, Steven Carvell, and Paul Strebel, "Giraffes, Institutions and Neglected Firms," *Financial Analysts Journal* (May/June 1983), pp. 57–63.

[34] See S. Basu, "Investment Performance of Common Stocks in Relation to Their Price-Earnings Ratios: A Test of the Efficient Markets Hypothesis," *Journal of Finance* (June 1977), pp. 663–682; or Jeffrey Jaffre, Donald B. Keim, and Randolph Westerfield, "Earnings Yields, Market Values, and Stock Returns," *Journal of Finance* (March 1989), pp. 135–148.

[35] Eugene F. Fama and Kenneth R. French, "The Cross-Section of Expected Stock Returns," *Journal of Finance* (1992), pp. 427–465; Eugene F. Fama and Kenneth R. French, "Common Risk Factors in Returns on Stocks and Bonds," *Journal of Financial Economics* (1993) pp. 3–56; and Eugene F. Fama and Kenneth R. French, "Value Versus Growth: The International Evidence," *Journal of Finance* (December 1998), pp. 1975–1999.

[36] Narasimhan Jegadeesh and Sheridan Titman, "Returns to Buying Winners and Selling Losers: Implications for Stock Market Efficiency," *Journal of Finance* (March 1993), pp. 65–91.

Implications for Arbitrage Pricing Theory

Inability of a short seller to earn the market rate of return on the proceeds of a short sale is a powerful argument against the particular efficient market model called *arbitrage pricing theory*. An actual arbitrage portfolio (where the proceeds of the short sale were not received until the position was closed out) would not be profitable for an individual unable to get use of the proceeds unless the inefficiencies in pricing were extreme. Again, the author would propose a bounded arbitrage theory where there are upper and lower limits with arbitrage preventing prices from moving outside these limits.[37] The limits would be smaller if there were institutions or brokerage firms able to earn a return on the proceeds of short sales. The longer it is until disagreement about a factor is resolved, the further apart the upper and lower limits are.

Having argued that bounded efficiency is a better description of real world markets than full efficiency, let us look at some of the implications for security analysis and portfolio management.

The Incentive to do the Analysis Needed for Bounded Efficiency

Portfolios which have benefited from a detailed analysis of the securities (and elimination of those that appear overvalued) should earn the competitive rate of return. This rate will be somewhat above the rate earned by investing in the indices. In a bounded efficient market it pays to do analysis, at least if one has a large portfolio. In turn, this analysis, and the resulting buying and selling by the informed investors, keeps the market bounded efficient.

Suppose the return on unmanaged portfolios is about 10% per year. Suppose analysis that reduces the number of avoidable mistakes is an extra 2% per year, making an achievable goal 12% per year. If these figures are of the right order of magnitude, they explain why we find analysts available for hire. The common question of one purporting to be an expert analyst is "If you're so smart, how come you are not rich?" In a bounded efficient market where there are no grossly undervalued securities, even the best analysts do only a little better than random selection. Thus, they cannot become rich just by investing and managing their own money (although they may insure a comfortable retirement). Thus, if they are to enjoy a high standard of living they must sell their services.

The bounded efficient markets model also explains why analysts' services are bought. For even a 100 million dollar pension fund, an extra 2% is an extra 2 million dollars, and this will justify hiring quite a

---

[37] Edward M. Miller, "A Problem in Textbook Arbitrage Pricing Theory Examples," *Financial Management* (Summer 1989), pp. 9–10.

few analysts. Thus, it is not surprising to find that much analysis is done, since those with the skills have the incentive to work and those with funds to invest can benefit from hiring them. This ongoing analysis (and the associated buying and selling) keeps markets efficient, but only within certain bounds.

There is a fundamental paradox in mainstream efficient markets theory. If markets are truly efficient, the optimal strategy is not to expend resources in trying to forecast returns, but to merely buy a portfolio designed to duplicate an index. However, if everyone follows such a passive strategy, there is no mechanism to keep the markets efficient and the passive strategy quits working. In the above model there is enough incentive for analysis to keep the market bounded efficient, thus resolving the paradox.

Implications for Analysts' Research Strategy

Of course, in many cases the uninformed overoptimistic investors will either not exist at all, or not be numerous enough to cause a particular stock to be overpriced. Thus, most stocks will be priced to fall along the curve BC in Exhibits 5.3 and 5.4. The rate of return earned by these stocks will be that earned by a stock moving along line BC, which will be referred to as the "competitive rate of return." This rate should vary with the systematic risk of the stock, but since this complication is not essential to the argument, it will not be further developed.

Although most stocks will be priced to yield the competitive rate of return, there will be a few stocks priced to yield less. These are the stocks that lie at points such as D. The return on an index is an average of the returns on the efficiently priced stocks and the stocks priced above efficient levels (which yield less than a competitive rate). Because the average includes some stocks priced to yield less than the competitive rate and few or none priced to yield more than the competitive rate, it follows that the index should yield less than the competitive rate. An investor who purchases an index fund or who purchases randomly should thus earn less than the competitive rate. This implies the competitive rate is above the indices.

An investor who researches stocks thoroughly before buying should be able to earn the competitive rate. In spite of the sales pitch of many advisors, active management probably does not succeed through identifying stocks that will grossly outperform the averages. Instead, the usefulness of analysis is that every so often it identifies stocks which have been bid up to a level where they promise to yield less than a competitive rate.

Some game analysts have divided games into two groups.[38] Some are won by a brilliant performance, such as golf or track. These are "winner's games." There are other games won merely by avoiding mistakes until the opponent makes a mistake. These are "loser's games." Tennis is a classic loser's game since you win by not missing a shot before your opponent does.[39] The analysis above shows that investing is basically a loser's game.[40]

Investing as a "losers' game" has implications for how to do analysis and for the number of stocks analyzed. Most institutional portfolio managers look at hundreds of separate stocks. They receive suggestions from their industry experts, from an army of brokerage experts, and then add insights obtained from the business press. With this many companies to be analyzed, either each stock receives a cursory analysis, or a fortune is spent on analysis.

The analysis of investing as a losers' game shows there are few, if any, stocks priced low enough to yield above competitive returns. Once a suitable set of stocks have been identified (enough stocks for the desired diversification), there is little to gain from examining additional stocks. At most, identifying additional competitively priced stocks permits slightly greater diversification or a small return improvement.

Since including an overpriced stock in a portfolio involves a substantial loss, enough securities should be studied to permit eliminating those overpriced securities that can be identified from publicly available information. The initial choice of securities might be random, might be the result of a simple screening routine, or might involve drawing a sample designed to leave the final portfolio well diversified (such as examining two companies from each industry).

This is opposite to the way many investment organizations act. There is no shortage of investment ideas. There is a constant stream of phone calls from brokers and faxed reports. It is very easy to spend most of the work day looking at these reports, and not have any time left over to thoroughly analyze any of the purchase candidates. It is often more fun to talk to a salesman (who was hired to be charming) than to do a tedious spread sheet analysis.

The above search strategy is similar to one that might be employed for any other good which frequently has hidden defects (and seldom has

---

[38] Charles D. Ellis, *Investment Policy: How to Win at the Loser's Game* (Homewood, IL: Dow Jones Irwin, 1985).

[39] Obviously a little oversimplified since good players hit the ball in such a way that the opponents have trouble returning it.

[40] Edward M. Miller, "How to Win at the Loser's Game," *Journal of Portfolio Management* (Fall 1978), pp. 17–24.

hidden virtues of similar magnitude). Since some buyers will not discover these problems, the posted prices are likely to be based on what these careless buyers will pay.

Consider the problem of buying apples from a pile in a store. Experience shows most are good, but a few may have worms. Once you have eliminated the ones with worms, it makes little difference which ones are bought. Someone who examines everyone in the store wastes time. Someone who picks out half a dozen apples without careful examination (the index fund strategy), risks biting into a worm. Optimally one apple is selected, inspected, and then bought if found worm free. One then goes on to the next. When the shopping basket contains the desired number of good apples, the shopper stops. Someone who thought it necessary to look at all apples, but lacked the time to examine each carefully, could easily be the shopper who buys the shiny but wormy apple.

Buyers of used cars do not normally try to obtain full information, and then make their choice. This would involve having a mechanic inspect every car in the lot. Instead, they make a tentative choice based on easy established characteristics such as color, age, price, make, and so on. After they have made a tentative choice, they then hire a mechanic to check it for hidden defects. Experience shows that one should not buy without a full knowledge of the car being bought, because there frequently are overpriced cars with hidden defects. (The price gets set high because some buyers, unaware of the hidden defects, will pay it). The market for houses has similar characteristics, with a termite inspection and title search frequently being the last things done before buying.

Of course, the stocks that are most worthy of an intense look are those already in the portfolio. Frequently stocks that seemed fairly valued (or even undervalued) at the time of purchase come to be overvalued. This may be because the industry becomes fashionable again, or something makes the particular firm attractive. In any portfolio much of the profit will come from such good fortune, or apparent luck. It is unwise to buy on the "greater fool theory" ("Yes, I think it is overpriced, but a greater fool will buy it from me for even more"). However, much money may be made from fools. When mass foolishness hits the market for a stock, one should be equipped to recognize it, and sell to the "fool" offering to buy it. Indexing does not offer this potential for profit.

Index funds benefit from some lucky picks, but being an index fund, they do not sell them when they become overpriced. The index fund follows them down again as they return to a fair valuation. In a "bounded" efficient market, a good active manager sells these lucky picks when they become too overpriced and hence beats the index fund.

The above argument suggests that the difference between the less successful managers and the more successful may not be so much in what they choose to buy, but in their skill at deciding when to sell. Both good and bad managers benefit from a certain number of lucky picks, but the bad ones ride them up and then ride them back down. They fail to recognize when they have become overvalued, or alternatively suffer from a psychological inability to admit to themselves that they were wrong (and suffer possible embarrassment), and keep holding on hoping to get up even.

In addition to stocks that rise unexpectedly in price, there will be some stocks that are headed for trouble whose impending problems can be recognized in time to sell them. Of course, to benefit from selling such stocks one must recognize the problem while there are still others who are willing to buy them at a good price (which usually means they do not yet recognize the problem).

One example was the introduction of radial tires. They were recognized as longer lasting and superior. Car manufacturers were putting them on cars and tire manufacturers were making good money. All this was being pointed out in the business press. Yet, because the radial tires were longer lasting, one could forecast an eventual fall in the replacement market. Smarter managers might have used this knowledge to get out of tire manufacturers.

Errors that Can Lead to Overpricing

Another question is what types of mistakes are likely to lead to the overpriced securities that should be avoided.

The compounding of the opportunity costs of being short suggests that the errors that are likely to lead to significant overpricing are those where the mistake won't be apparent for several years. While the illustration was initially constructed with the uncertain event being the magnitude of a liquidating dividend, the basic argument applies to any uncertain future event, or series of future events.

Consider a case where some investors are overoptimistic, and this will become apparent in a month. Perhaps the question is whether a particular lawsuit will be won, whether a contract will be awarded, or what next quarter's earnings will be. If the long-run rate of return is 1% per month, the stock can be overvalued by only 1% (plus the commissions and transactions costs) before a short sale becomes profitable. Short selling by those who have done their analysis could prevent appreciable overvaluation from occurring when the uncertainty will be resolved in the near future.

Transactions costs are a major obstacle to exploiting short-term inefficiencies. A model which shows a high annualized rate of return for the next month (say 24%) actually implies a price increase of about 2%. Buying now and selling next month could easily eat up 2% of that. The inevitable errors of execution, trading on effects that no longer exist, or merely appeared to exist because of data mining, will further reduce the profits. Haugen[41] in his books draws attention to the high potential returns he found in the work he did with Baker.[42] However, Hanna and Ready report that after a sophisticated adjustment for transaction costs, most of these abnormal profits disappear.[43] The apparent reason is excessive transactions.[44] For taxable accounts, strategies that involve exploiting short-term mispricing involve paying short-term capital gains taxes.

Thus, the sort of overvaluation which might arise from near horizon errors is probably not exploitable at a profit (unless one would be buying or selling the stock anyhow and the analysis is used only to improve the timing). Hence, for practical purposes one may wish to act as if information that would be impounded in stock prices in the near future is efficiently impounded, and not devote large amounts of analytic talent to predicting events that will occur in the near future. Notice this is the opposite of what most analysts do. Vast amounts of effort are devoted to forecasting the next year's earnings with relatively little devoted to looking several years ahead.[45]

Now consider an event that won't occur for years. As shown in Exhibit 5.3 and 5.4, the power of compounding is such that failure of short sellers to receive full use of the proceeds for many years results in an appreciable difference between the upper and the lower bounds for stock prices. Stocks may exist that well-informed analysts would conclude will have essentially zero returns for the next few years. An investor aware of them would sell them if owned and invest the proceeds in

---

[41] Robert A. Haugen, *The New Finance: The Case Against Efficient Markets*, 2nd ed. (Upper Saddle River, NJ: Prentice Hall, 1999); and Robert A. Haugen, *The Inefficient Stock Market: What Pays Off and Why*, 2nd ed. (Upper Saddle River, NJ: Prentice Hall, 2001).

[42] Robert A. Haugen and Nardin L. Baker, "Commonality in the Determinants of Expected Stock Returns," *Journal of Financial Economics* (July 1996), pp. 401–439.

[43] J. Douglas Hanna and Mark J. Ready, "Profitable Predictability in the Cross-section of Stock Returns," working paper, University of Wisconsin—Madison, July 28, 2003.

[44] Admittedly, the Hanna and Ready procedure seemed to focus on staying in the top decile of stocks and selling them when the model no longer had them in the top decile (or in some versions six months later). More realistic strategies would probably retain stocks until they dropped into much lower decile. Haugen uses optimization models that restrict trading and reports that the system showed profits even after a 2% round-trip cost. Hanna and Ready indicate the trading tended to be in the smaller, less liquid stocks where his more sophisticated model of transactions costs found them to be higher.

[45] For descriptions of the role of analysts, see Mitch Zacks, *Ahead of the Market* (New York: Harper Business, 2003).

other stocks. However, as pointed out repeatedly, they are unlikely to be good short sale candidates.

Plausible Sources of Overpricing over the Long Run

What are some of the mistakes that could lead to long-term exploitable pricing errors? There is a very large literature now on behavioral finance, showing the various biases to be expected in investor decision making.[46] While most of these biases are clearly likely, there is much debate about just how typical they are. However, as long as a reasonably large fraction of investors make the mistakes they describe, they are likely to cause at least some overpricing of stocks, with the investment implications discussed above.

One of the lessons of the analysis at the start of this chapter is that it is not necessary for even the average investor to be subject to these biases. Even if a substantial minority make the mistakes, overpricing is likely. To argue for overpricing occurring, it is not necessary to argue that the typical investor will make a mistake. Here is where the analysis of this chapter is useful, since it is more likely that a substantial minority will make a mistake than that the typical investor will. This makes more plausible various inefficiencies.

One possibility is extrapolating growth too far forward. It is difficult to accurately project growth for several years into the future and investors frequently make overoptimistic projections. The price will be set by the investors with the most optimistic projections. The most optimistic investors will often be those who extrapolate growth rates far forward, failing to recognize such things as coming market saturation, new competition, perhaps lower cost overseas firms getting into the business. Companies will often put out press releases about their own new products, new models, or cost reductions. As pointed out, these are usually sufficiently well publicized that the information is promptly reflected in prices of the company putting out the press releases. However, success for one company often implies reduced sales or price com-

---

[46] For examples, see Gary Belsky and Thomas Gilovich, *Why Smart People Make Big Money Mistakes and How to Correct Them: Lessons from the New Science of Behavioral Economics* (New York: Fireside, 2000); Haugen, *The New Finance: The Case Against Efficient Markets*; Haugen, *The Inefficient Stock Market: What Pays Off and Why*; Hersh Shefrin, *Beyond Greed and Fear: Understanding Behavioral Finance and the Psychology of Investing* (New York: Oxford University Press, 2002); Andrei Shleifer, *Inefficient Markets: An Introduction to Behavioral Finance*, Clarendon Lectures in Economics (New York: Oxford University Press, 2000); and Robert J. Shiller, *Irrational Exuberance* (Princeton, NJ: Princeton University Press, 2000) among others.

petition for another. Naturally, the other company does not put out press releases about how their products are now obsolete or overpriced (just imagine what fun the competitor's salesmen could have with such press releases). Large numbers of investors (enough to keep the price up) are probably valuing the stock using naive formulas (such as extrapolating growth) that can lead to overpricing.

Although it seems plausible that the earnings growth of a firm for next year will be similar to the earnings growth for last year, numerous studies show that the actual serial correlation is very low.[47] Since this fact is not well known, it is likely that many extrapolate earnings growth forward, and then are willing to overpay for a stock. Fuller, Huberts, and Levinson show that there is essentially no correlation between the previous four year's growth rate in earnings per share and the next four year's growth rates.[48] There are probably enough investors making this error to cause some securities to be overpriced.

Most textbooks present the Gordon valuation model. This shows that the present value of a perpetually growing stream of earnings is $CF/(i - g)$, where CF is the end of year cash flow, i is the interest rate, and g is the growth rate. In exercises, this formula is used to derive stock values for growth stocks from the historical rates of growth. Students are left with the impression that one can safely extrapolate growth rates far into the future.

Textbooks do recognize that this formula can not be used to value rapidly growing companies, and propose using a period of super normal growth followed by a long-term growth rate. The period of super normal growth is often quite long. One book illustrates the procedure with an example with 13% for six years, followed by five years of a constantly declining growth rate, finally reaching 8%. These growth rates are far higher than historical evidence justifies. Again, the impression is left that growth rates can be safely extrapolated forward.

Work by Bauman and Dowen shows that investments in companies projected to have high earnings growth have yielded poor investment results.[49] Zacks showed that from October 1987 to September 2002, the fifth of stocks with the highest projected analyst consensus earnings

---

[47] See for instance I. M. D. Little and A. C. Rayner, *Higgledy Piggledy Growth Again* (Oxford, Basil Blackwell, 1966); Richard A. Brealey, *An Introduction to Risk and Return from Common Stocks* (Cambridge, MA: M.I.T. Press, 1983); and Russell J. Fuller, Lex C. Huberts, and Michael J. Levinson, "Returns to E/P Strategies, Higgledy Piggledy Growth: Analysts' Forecast Errors, and Omitted Risk Factors," *Journal of Portfolio Management* (Winter 1993), pp. 13–24.

[48] Fuller, Huberts, and Levinson, "Returns to E/P Strategies, Higgledy Piggledy Growth: Analysts' Forecast Errors, and Omitted Risk Factors."

[49] W. Scott Bauman and Richard Dowen, "Growth Projections and Common Stock Returns," *Financial Analysts Journal* (July/August 1988), pp. 79–80.

growth (3–5 years forward) were actually money losing investments, averaging total returns of –0.6%, versus 9.0% for the S&P 500 over the same period.[50] This would be consistent with the theory put forward here. Dechow and Sloan[51] document that analysts' long-term growth forecasts are almost three times realized growth and show that high analysts' forecast growth is very powerful in predicting below normal returns five years in the future.[52]

High price to earnings ratio stocks are frequently those with high growth prospects. It has been repeatedly documented that the high-price earnings ratio stocks have underperformed the market.[53]

Closely related to the high returns on low price to earning ratio stocks, are the high returns on high book value to price stocks. In the well-known Fama and French work on the cross section of stock returns,[54] they found that high book-to-market value companies had had higher returns. The Haugen and Baker results confirmed these.[55] Later when Hanna and Ready reexamined these two methods for picking stocks, they found similar results using later data.[56]

There seem to be at least two reasons companies with high projected growth have proved poor investments. One is that growth frequently slows down as a market is saturated—a fad ends. The other occurs when new competition enters. Fast growing, highly profitable businesses attract new entrants and the resulting competition lowers the growth rates for firms already in the business.

---

[50] Zacks, *Ahead of the Market*, p. 217.

[51] P. Dechow and R. Sloan, "Returns to Contrarian Investment Strategies: Tests of Naive Expectations Hypothesis," *Journal of Financial Economics* (January 1997), pp. 3–27.

[52] Dechow and Sloan, "Returns to Contrarian Investment Strategies: Tests of Naive Expectations Hypothesis," Table 5.

[53] For a discussion with earlier references, see Basu, "Investment Performance of Common Stocks in Relation to their Price-Earnings Ratios: A Test of the Efficient Markets Hypothesis;" and Jaffre, Keim, and Westerfield, "Earnings Yields, Market Values, and Stock Returns."

More recently see Dechow and Sloan, "Returns to Contrarian Investment Strategies: Tests of Naive Expectations Hypothesis," and Fuller, Huberts, and Levinson, "Returns to E/P Strategies, Higgledy Piggledy Growth: Analysts' Forecast Errors, and Omitted Risk Factors."

[54] Fama and French, "The Cross-Section of Expected Stock Returns."

[55] Haugen and Baker, "Commonality in the Determinants of Expected Stock Returns."

[56] Hanna and Ready, "Profitable Predictability in the Cross-section of Stock Returns."

Also, when a growth company disappoints by suffering a decline in earnings, or even a slow down, it frequently loses its status as a growth company and the resulting high price-earnings multiple. A fast-growing company projected to have a next year's earning of $1 and a price earning ratio of 40 would be a $40 stock. However, it may disappoint and earn only $0.50. If this happens, it typically loses its growth company status and comes to be priced at perhaps 20 times earnings. The stock is hit with a double whammy, lower earnings and a lower multiple. This makes its price fall to $10 (20 × $0.50), only a quarter of what it had been. This is a real investment disaster. Such events seem regularly to occur, and only a few such disasters in a growth portfolio will cause it to underperform a value portfolio. The value portfolio may benefit from the opposite, a value stock's experiences increase earnings and this causes some investors to view it as a growth stock, worthy of a higher multiple.

It is not necessary for the average investor to make the mistake of overpaying for growth (although they may). If a substantial minority of investors overpay for growth, the stock will be overpriced and better informed investors can benefit. Given the large number of mutual funds and management companies that use the word growth in their titles, the existence of enough investors seeking stocks with high forecast growth to cause overpricing is very plausible. The historically poor performance of such stocks makes it seem even more likely that the above errors have repeatedly occurred.

Another possibility would be underestimating the probability of a rare negative event. The extreme example of underestimation would of course be setting the probability at zero. With only limited time for analysis, the easiest approach is to use the most likely outcomes. The possibility of certain negative developments is simply not considered. This can result in treating the mode (the most likely outcome) as the mean, a common mistake. A major product liability case, an expensive marketing mistake, a major fraud, etc. may be excluded from the analysis, even though each year such events happen to some firms. The intervals between such events are large for any one company, and it may be years before the error of ignoring such low frequency events is revealed by one of them happening. If the price of the stock is set by those who do not consider these possibilities, good analysis may be able to identify stocks rationally expected to underperform the market.

An event whose probability may be frequently underestimated is the entry of new competition into an industry. A standard way of forecasting a firm's future profits is to forecast the sales of its industry, its share of these sales, and its profit margin per unit. Its current market share and per unit margins are often forecast to continue. This procedure often forecasts high growth for firms with strong market positions or monopolies in growing industries. Yet economic theory and experience both show that rapidly growing, highly profitable industries often attract entry. The prices of certain stocks are set by those using these extrapolation techniques. Analysis should be able to avoid at least some unfortunate purchases of such securities. Examples would be Xerox or IBM, when conventional wisdom forecast their continued dominance of their industries.

It was noted earlier that stocks with high market values relative to book value tended to underperform. When entry is possible (and it usually is), a high ratio of market value to book implies that the market values the assets in that business very highly. A relatively small investment by another firm would be expected to result in a large increase in the value of the entering firm. The managers of other firms desire higher stock prices, and one can be expected to eventually enter the industry.

If the high market-to-book value firm has a more reasonable price to earnings ratio (i.e., the stock price does not seem unreasonable given the level of earnings), this implies it has a high rate of return on equity (and usually on assets also). Such a high rate of return is often the result of a business that is highly profitable. Again, such a business tends to attract entry, and the entry eventually forces the profit margins back to more normal levels, reducing the stock prices.

When the high market-to-book price goes along with a high price-earnings ratio, it is probably a high growth firm, which as described above tends to disappoint. One reason is that the growth potential seen by the market is also seen by competitors. They naturally rush to exploit such highly visible opportunities.

While this behavior by businesspeople is taught in every economics course and understood by many investors, there will be substantial numbers of investors who do not recognized how it applies to a particular case. Their buying can cause the stock to be overpriced, providing someone for the better informed and more intelligent investors to sell to.

Sometimes the high earnings are merely temporary due to luck or the business cycle. This will usually be recognized by competitors, and entry will not occur. However, when the temporarily high earnings revert to normal, the stock price drops, again making these investments poor ones.

Admittedly, there are barriers to entry of various types, and occasionally entry into a highly profitable business is hard. Occasionally, the high ratio is due to the assets being valued at a historical cost that is well below current prices (such as timberland or mineral deposits bought many years ago). There are valuable patents and hard to duplicate business organizations that complicate entry. If not asked, managers tend not to mention the possibility of entry. If asked, they naturally exaggerate the barriers to entry. If you are in a highly profitable business that others could enter, you do not wish to publicize the ease of entry.

Instead, you try to scare potential entrants off by talking about the barriers and how high they are. Your patients are very strong. You certainly don't want to announce to the world how weak they are, or that there is an alternative technology that doesn't infringe on them.

Your high profits are due to an excellent management, marketing, and research team that no other competitor could duplicate. You may even imply, or the public relations firm (whose continued employment depends on the CEO's goodwill) may even state that the high profits are due to the CEO's genius. While a new entrant may be able to hire away some of your talent, you are certainly not going to reveal that. Historically, key talent has often broken off to create new firms. Key managers often realize just how profitable a business is, and know how to duplicate the organization. Of course, emphasizing the barriers to entry is just another example of managers putting out information that tends to increase or sustain the price of their stock, and not mentioning or concealing information that tends to lower it.

Again, there are lots of smart investors out there who recall enough economics to know that high profits (and high market-to-book ratios) attract entry and tend not to last for this or other reasons. However, there are enough others who neglect this possibility for a stock to become overpriced. These are who the better informed investors sell to.

Although history shows that in a new industry or a highly profitable industry, new competition is common, it is difficult for an analyst to put this in a report. If he writes a report that shows the three leading firms will drop from say 90% of an industry to 50% (based on what has happened in other industries), his boss will note that this implies that the market share of smaller players will grow rapidly. The boss, thinking of the profits from buying into the firms that will gain this market share, will naturally want to know who these successful firms will be. An analyst who cannot answer this very difficult question (many of the new entrants have not announced, or even formulated their plans yet) looks bad. Much better is to just allocate the projected growth in sales among the existing firms, setting the investors up for disappointment when the new competition enters.

Thus, bounded efficient markets theory not only predicts profitable opportunities for analysis in a market with many informed investors, but also gives some guidance as to useful types of analysis. The analysis should be focused on making better estimates of events that will occur years in the future using nonobvious information or analysis.

Portfolio Construction Implications

It was argued above that there is a major asymmetry here. Stocks that will grossly outperform the market will be very hard to find (just as efficient market theory argues), while there are some that will underperform. One might be tempted to say that publicly available information is only useful for identifying stocks that will underperform the market. However, as a logical point, if some will underperform, it follows that others must overperform. However, because there are many smart investors with good access to information, such stocks will outperform by only a small amount. It turns out that this model has implications for how portfolios are constructed and how stocks are chosen for analysis.

If you believe in a bounded optimization model, you believe that securities that will vastly outperform the market cannot be identified. As a result, if an analyst (or a model) predicts returns that exceed by more than a small amount those that you think should exist, you reduce the estimates to a plausible value. For instance, if you believe that a security of average risk should earn 10%, you might not believe estimates of returns over 12%. Thus, if using a formal optimization model, you never enter very high estimates into the model. If 12% is all that you find plausible, all estimates are capped at 12%. If you believe certain risks require higher returns in the market, perhaps the upper limit varies a little with risk. If you believe beta should be priced, your estimates might be constrained to never exceed the capital asset pricing model estimates plus 2%.

In a model with many very smart competing investors, there are few opportunities to identify securities that will grossly outperform. If you use high estimates, the most likely outcome is a sacrifice of diversification for what proves to be only a small level of outperformance. An obvious implication for portfolio construction is that only small bets are placed on those that appear likely to outperform the market. Large bets sacrifice diversification for only small expected gains. In a formal Markowitz analysis, a constraint on the maximum weight for each holding might be used to prevent over optimism about a stock from leading to under diversification.

In practice, an upper limit of the estimates put into a model, and an upper limit on the weights may produce very similar portfolios. Thus, the issue of which to use will not be discussed further here.

Interestingly, with upper limits on holdings, lower limits set by no short positions, and a very large number of securities to select from, most securities will have a weight of zero in the portfolio. The securities held will typically be at the maximum weights set for diversification. The portfolios chosen will often be the minimum number needed for diversification with the securities chosen held at the maximum percentage, and others at zero. For instance, if the maximum is set at 4% of the portfolio (to prevent under diversification due to over optimism, as theory suggests is wise), one would expect 25 securities to held, each at 4% of the portfolio, and hundred or thousands of other securities held with weights at 0%. Note, whether the optimization program was given 35, 500, or 5,000 securities, one would expect this outcome. However, providing estimated returns (especially good estimates of returns) on more securities raises analysis costs without raising expected returns. Thus, the number of securities analyzed should be only enough to insure that the program will be able to find 25 whose expected return is high enough to justify purchase. This merely repeats the point made earlier on limiting the number of securities analyzed.

The logic of bounded efficient markets implies a trade off between return and diversification that is likely to cause many portfolios to be less than fully diversified. The reason is that if there are overpriced securities that can be discovered by analysis, it will pay to do analysis. Increasing the number of securities also increases the costs of doing the analysis required to avoid holding overpriced securities. It is likely (as a first approximation) that the analytical costs are proportional to the number of securities followed. Since analysis (especially analysis good enough to uncover negatives others have missed) costs money, there is a limit to the number of securities that can be followed efficiently.

Of course, decreasing the number of securities held decreases diversification. However, the increase of risk (measured by variability of returns) from dropping a security increases as the number of securities decreases. Thus, an actively managed portfolio has an optimal number of securities. Too many securities reduce returns (due to inadequate analysis) by more than can be offset by any increased diversification.

In contrast, in a fully efficient market, there is always a reduction in risk to be obtained from adding another security. Thus, the textbooks conclude that every investor should hold the market portfolio. (The market portfolio is one that includes every asset.) If one modifies the textbook model to include certain fixed costs of holding a security (custodial costs, auditing costs, collection of dividends etc.), there is an upper limit to the number of securities. However, the implied portfolios will still be very large. These portfolios will be indexed portfolios.

Paradoxically, although modern investment theory includes the assumption that every investor will use Markowitz optimization, there is actually very little need for it in an efficient market, since the simple procedure of mixing the "market portfolio" (or an index approximating it) with the risk-free asset provides a portfolio that cannot be beaten with regard to either return or risk.

However, in a bounded efficient market (as in other inefficient markets) there is a case for using Markowitz optimization or similar optimization methods. As discussed, it will pay to hire analysts (to avoid overpriced securities). Of course, analysts are hired to actively manage portfolios. Actively managed portfolios in a bounded efficient market will have a small enough number of securities so that they are not fully diversified. This can create an opportunity for formal optimization even in a model where the securities held do not differ much in return.[57] The optimization may be useful in minimizing risk even if it does not increase returns. In particular, all 25 security portfolios that have the same return may not have the same risk.

There are several possible uses for optimization. Since the use of optimization for obtaining the best possible combination of risk and return is well known, it will not be discussed here. If there are few securities with returns much above the competitive level, choosing securities to maximize return is likely to be less critical (once the poor performers have been eliminated).

A less obvious application is for determining the optimal portfolio size. If one can estimate how much better the estimates of return are with analysis, experiments can be conducted to determine the risk return combinations that are possible. Suppose at a cost of $100,000 per stock analyzed, it is possible to exclude stocks that will under perform by enough to cause them to be excluded from the portfolio. Imagine the effect of this is to raise the portfolio return by 2% before expenses, at the expense of excluding a fifth of the stocks examined. Imagine a billion dollar portfolio. The gross improvement possible in returns is 2%, or $20,000,000 per year. This is the return before expenses. An active strategy appears worthwhile. If 200 stocks are studied (at $100,000 each), the analytical costs are $20 million. These consume the whole of the potential increase in return. Thus, 200 stocks is the outer limit to the number of stocks to be studied. This will result in about a 160-stock portfolio. (This large a portfolio can be rejected because the return is the same as an indexed portfolio, but the diversification is less). If 100 stocks are analyzed (which implies an 80 stock portfolio), the costs will be $10,000,000 per year (which is 1% of the portfolio value). In these examples, the selected portfolio always earns 2% more than the index (because of the implicit assumption that one can find stocks yielding 2% over the index, but competition prevents finding any yielding more than that). This means there is a net improvement in returns of 1% possible (the $10,000,000 in increased returns is divided by the billion dollars in the portfolio) over the benchmark index, but with the sacrifice in diversification of going from the market portfolio to 80 securities. If 50 stocks are followed, the analytical cost drops to $5 million. The improvement in net return is 1.5%, but there is

---

[57] Of course, where the securities held differ in returns, getting the right trade off between risk and return is complex enough so that there is a case for formal optimization.

increased risk because the size of the portfolio is reduced to 40 stocks (50 are studied and a fifth eliminated, leaving 40). With 25 stocks studied, the increase in return would be 1.75% and the expected portfolio size 20 stocks. Thus, a risk return tradeoff can be derived, and an optimal number of securities to study determined.

Notice the decision variable is the number of stocks to study, with the number of stocks in the portfolio being those in the group studied that are not rejected after the detailed study. To assist in further discussion, imagine the decision is to study 25 stocks intensively.

While one could measure the risks of the various sized portfolios (that result from analyzing different numbers of securities) from the risk of randomly selected portfolios of that size, consideration might be given to using the risk of an optimally designed portfolio instead. In general, a portfolio with optimally selected weights will have a lower risk than an equally weighted portfolio with the same stocks. The difference becomes important for smaller portfolios. As the above analysis shows, the optimal size of portfolio results from a tradeoff between excess return and risk.

Once one has decided on the number of stocks for analysis, the issue becomes how to pick the stocks for initial analysis (and then for inclusion in the portfolio). Picking the number of stocks needed for adequate diversification, and putting the same percentage in each is one plausible approach. For instance, 25 stocks for initial analysis might be believed (after analysis as above) to provide the proper trade-off between risk and return. (As discussed, this implies expecting a 20-stock portfolio.)

Using random selection risks that the final portfolio would be less diversified than it could be. By luck alone, one industry might be over represented. Simple rules, like selecting no more than two stocks from each of the industries might be used to reduce this risk.

Another approach might be to select multiple lists of stocks with the required number of stocks and then use an optimization program to select weights to minimize the risk. (The inputs would be a covariance matrix and a set of returns.) The set of stocks used to construct the portfolio with the smallest variance might be used as an initial list for analysis. Such a procedure is virtually assured to give a portfolio with a lower risk than a randomly selected portfolio.

These would then be studied to see if they were overvalued. A few would probably be rejected. If time permitted, the excluded securities might be replaced and new securities restudied.

Of course, the idea of using a screening program to decide which stocks are subject to intensive analysis is common. However, the usual screening programs are aimed at identifying potentially high return stocks. In the approach urged here, the screening program is used to find candidate stocks that would be most useful in reducing risk. The argument is that one's a priori belief is that the return characteristics of stocks are similar in an efficient market, but their risk reduction potential is likely to vary (and to be specific to the portfolio to which they are added).

While these 20 stocks might be equally weighted, a lower risk could probably be obtained by explicit optimization. Even if the original 25 stocks had been such that equal weights were optimal (as could easily result from using the optimization idea suggested below for initial selection), after about five had been excluded, equal weights might not be optimal (imagine for instance that all the stocks dropped were growth stocks).

Once the initial portfolio had been established, analytical resources would be devoted to following these stocks, plus a small number selected by one of the methods discussed below as candidates for addition to the portfolio.

An interesting issue is how to choose (from thousands of possible stocks) a few not owned to be intensively studied. Part of the decision might be based on the probability that analysis will unearth securities with expected returns better than random. Plausibly, the best opportunities will be found for smaller stocks, and for those not followed by analysts. Many have argued that undiscovered stocks that will outperform are more likely to be found in the smaller stocks. However, it is likely that there are enough other investors searching these stocks for great bargains that few are to be found. However, even if not a bargain when bought, one may be more likely to profit from an unwarranted run up in price that gives you a change to get out at a profit. It is known that smaller capitalization stocks are more volatile. If a certain percentage of run up are not justified by facts (as ascertained after thorough analysis), the profit potential in small stocks may be greater.

Besides this, the small stocks need fewer optimistic investors to be bid up in price. Since some of these investors are likely to be uninformed, there will likely be some run-ups in price that one can benefit from by selling after the run-up if your analysis says it is unwarranted. A single product company may have a boost in profits from a fad affecting that product, or from a temporary competitive advantage, or from any of the other reasons discussed above. The number of investors who need to make a mistake to raise the price is smaller for such stocks. Your chance of discovering the mistake is greater while there is still someone to sell to is greater for the smaller stocks. Thus, small stocks may provide good opportunities for active managers.

Less obvious, in picking stocks for analysis, risk reduction potential might be given considerable weight. Once the portfolio has been launched, the relative weights for the stocks in it are known. Random sets of about five stocks can be considered for inclusion in the portfolio with the expected return set either at the values for the stocks already selected (possibly with adjustments for how one believes the market to price the associated risk). The set that gives the greatest reduction in risk might then be chosen to be those analyzed for possible addition to the portfolio.

If formal optimization is not used, one might look for stocks that filled holes in the portfolio with regard to industry mix or exposure to certain factors. These may be in the same industry as the stocks rejected for inclusion in the original portfolio or, at least, in industries with similar factor exposures.

With fluctuations in prices over time, portfolios will tend to become even less diversified over time. One possible corrective action is rebalancing from time to time (trying to maintain fixed percentages in each security held). However, the sales required will raise transactions costs, and raise taxes paid by taxable portfolios. To minimize transaction costs, the weights might be allowed to deviate from those originally chosen as market prices changed, subject to an upper limit to enforce diversification.

The cheapest way of controlling risk (interpreted as variability in return) and achieving diversification is likely be to use cash inflows to purchase new securities that provide desired exposures. There will normally be new money, dividends, and proceeds from sales of securities discovered to be overpriced coming into the portfolio. Since the suggested strategy involves sales of overvalued securities, the new money coming in will be larger than with indexing. Some of the available money would be used for increasing holdings of securities that have desirable risk properties. Some might be used for adding new securities that had passed the screening. In practice, an optimization program with constraints (maximums) on estimated returns will not buy the existing holdings that have gone up appreciably in price, but will use cash flows to add to those securities where price declines have left them underweighted (or their class of securities underweighted).

If a couple of unlucky initial picks of stocks for analysis had led to the two retail stocks analyzed being excluded, the next stock considered for purchase might be a retail one. Of course, this stock would be carefully studied to be sure it was not overpriced. If it proved to be fairly priced it would be bought. If considered overpriced, another retail stock would be looked at. The same would apply to categories such as growth stocks.

Once a portfolio has become less than optimally diversified due to changing prices (or possibly it started out less than optimally diversified because some stocks failed to survive the initial analysis), some additions to it will restore diversification better than others that have the same expected returns. Prior to doing expensive analysis, one's presumption may be either that all securities have the same expected returns, or that these returns are those predicted from a simple risk model. (As discussed above, the major exception may be among stocks of different sizes.) Thus, selection among possible additions to the portfolio (especially of the same size) cannot be based on anticipated returns. However, the contributions to diversification (and risk reduction) are likely to differ between securities.

Markowitz optimization may be useful in identifying possible risk reducing additions to the portfolio. This procedure is cheap if historical data are used in deriving the covariance matrix (with sophisticated methods used to reduce the large random element in historically derived portfolios[58]). Normally, candidates for analysis can be identified this way at low cost. If they prove after analysis not to be overpriced, they may be purchased. Hopefully, by repeating this process, diversification can be maintained at low transactions costs. Only if this procedure fails would sales for the purpose of maintaining diversification be done.

It is conceivable that the optimal portfolio strategy is to combine analyzed stocks with unanalyzed ones. This might happen if certain categories were believed to have such efficiently priced securities as not to justify any analysis, and other categories had less efficiently priced securities. The most plausible example of this would be where there were believed to be opportunities for analysis in small stocks, while certain large stocks were so well studied that one did not expect to be able to uncover information not reflected in the prices. Yet, diversification might require some exposure to large capitalization stocks. One optimization exercise might combine studied small stocks expected to earn a competitive 12%, with other stocks selected by simple rules and expected to yield 10%. There are firms now that offer to provide completeness portfolios at low cost to provide diversification and exposure to types of securities one does not maintain expertise in.

Optimization can help decide whether extra expenses should be incurred in analyzing additional securities. Suppose it was believed that after analysis the chosen securities had an expected return of 12%, when randomly selected securities would have a return of 10%. One could add in different sets of randomly selected securities and then compute the expected return and variances for the newly optimized portfolios. In general, the portfolios with these additional securities would show lower expected returns (since the additional securities were expected to have a return of only 10%) and also lower risks (as measured by the variance). The best set of additional securities could be identified, and the sacrifice of return to get a reduction in risk estimated.

---

[58] For methods of obtaining a covariance matrix that are superior to brute force calculation from historical data see Edwin J. Elton and Martin Gruber, *Modern Portfolio Theory and Investment Analysis* (New York: John Wiley & Sons, 1995).

It is possible that the risk reduction (increased diversification) benefits of additional securities would justify adding unanalyzed securities.

Suppose one believes that, after analysis, four-fifths of the stocks appear to have no major overpricing. However, a fifth show major overpricing, such that an optimization program reduces the weight to zero (for simplicity, I have left out the intermediate alternatives). One may then be able to add the alternative of spending the $100,000 to study an additional stock and using the information to decide on whether or not to include that stock. If the stock is included with an estimated return of 12%, one had achieved a reduction in risk for a cost of $100,000. Since all the included stocks are presumed to have a 12% expected return, there is no increase in expected return before expenses and a $100,000 reduction in expected return after expenses. If the candidate stock proves to be overpriced, one forgoes the added diversification benefit. Of course, after the analysis is done the $100,000 is already spent and the portfolio return reduced by this amount. At least conceptually, with knowledge of the client's trade off between expected return and risk, whether analyzing an additional stock was worthwhile can be determined.

In doing such an analysis notice the only inputs to Markowitz optimization (and similar procedures) are expected returns and a covariance matrix. The size of the firm does not enter into the calculations. If one believes it will be cheaper to analyze a small firm (perhaps because it is in only one line of business), the ratio of added benefit to the portfolio from identifying a suitable security to the cost of analysis will be greatest for the smaller stocks.

In practice, one usually cannot purchase the required analysis of an additional stock at short notice. The difficulty is not finding someone to take your money and give an opinion. It is not even finding someone whose opinion you think is worth $100,000. The difficulty is being sure the new analysis is comparable with the analysis done by your own staff. Thus, the information on the benefits of analyzing an additional stock is most useful in deciding on how large an analytic budget to incur.

In practice, the cost of an analytic staff is fixed in the short run. Procedures such as discussed above aid in determining the budget for analysis and the number of stocks to be followed. In the example above, a budget of $2,500,000 per year would permit following 25 stocks. The expected portfolio size would be 20 stocks (allowing for a fifth to be rejected). These 20 would be in the portfolio (with perhaps weights chosen by an optimization program) and the analytic resources devoted to following these 20 stocks, plus five more as candidates for purchase and to replace any that became overpriced. Analyses of this type would be done form time to time to determine if the staff size was optimal. There is a role for consultants, because managers are likely to be always in favor of a larger budget. The larger budget implies higher fees for outside managers, and more staff for inside managers.

While formal optimization using historical data is cheap, it is an open question whether it is better to use optimization for risk control, or to use traditional rules such as target exposure to industries.

Multiple Opinions Case

The discussion here dealt with the case where there were only two opinions, one of which was right and one was wrong. We presumed that we knew which was right (a strong assumption). With these assumptions we were able to derive many interesting and useful conclusions. The two opinions case was adequate for developing these conclusions, which do hold for more realistic models. However, normally there are many different opinions about the value of a security. This situation will be referred to as a divergence of opinion. It is discussed in Chapter 6.[59]

CONCLUSIONS

Because of restrictions on short selling, many overvalued stocks will be excluded from portfolios by being sold if owned or, otherwise, not bought; however, they will not be sold short. This is because stocks that promise less than a competitive rate of return should be excluded from portfolios but often are not good short sale candidates, especially for those who do not receive use of the proceeds.

It follows that prices are set by the most optimistic investors, not by the typical investor. In many cases the most optimistic investors are also the over optimistic investors. The result is sometimes overpriced stocks that can be identified by good analysis.

Because of the ease of a minority of investors purchasing enough stock to cause it to be overpriced, accounting rules should err on the conservative side. Conservatism will seldom lead to underpricing since there will usually be enough well informed investors to keep the stock priced at least competitively. However, if the accounting sometimes exaggerates profits, there are likely to be enough poorly informed investors for the stock to become overpriced.

The obstacles to short selling, especially failure to receive full use of the proceeds or to receive a market return on them, are more important when the errors in pricing will occur years in the future than when they will be revealed in the near future. Exploitable opportunities to avoid

---

[59] See Chapter 7.

overpriced stocks are most likely when the overpricing is due to various factors that will be typically revealed only years in the future. Possible opportunities arise from things like extrapolating growth too far in the future, not allowing for new entry or market saturation, leaving out numerous low probability adverse events that in the aggregate have an appreciable effect, and the like. Looking for such events several years out probably has a higher return than trying to forecast next year's earnings, which is where so much effort is expended.

Since competition makes it very difficult to identify stocks that are grossly undervalued, investment success comes from avoiding losers rather than finding great winners. Investing is a loser's game. If great winners will be very hard to find in a competitive economy, analytic effort should be focused on a small number of stocks which can be extensively studied, rather than on an extensive search for stocks that will double in a year. Typically, investment managers try to follow far too many stocks, frequently failing as a result to uncover relevant negative information about certain stocks.

This yields a theory of bounded efficient markets in which there are upper and lower bounds for stock prices, with most stocks at the lower bound, priced to yield a competitive return. However, the competitive return is higher than the average return. This difference is small enough so that it is probably not worthwhile for individual investors to attempt to pick stocks. However, a small percentage advantage applied to a large sum of money does justify analysis in institutions. It is this analysis that keeps markets close to efficient.

CHAPTER 6

Implications of Short Selling and Divergence of Opinion for Investment Strategy

Edward M. Miller, Ph.D.
Research Professor of Economics and Finance
University of New Orleans

Mainstream finance theory is developed in a highly abstract world in which, among other assumptions, investors are assumed to be as willing and able to sell short as to take a long position. This is obviously unrealistic. Most institutional investors are not permitted to go short. Most individual investors are afraid to make short sales. There are various institutional obstacles to short selling (uptick rules, the need to borrow the stock, and so on). Even for the investor who himself would never go short, the optimal investment strategies in a market with restricted short selling proves to be quite different than in the textbook markets with free short selling. I had earlier proposed an alternative theory which is updated for use here.[1]

It will be shown here that in a world with restricted short selling that

1. Divergence of opinion tends to raise prices.
2. Thus profits can be improved by avoiding stocks with high divergence of opinion, including those analysts disagree about.
3. When the divergence of opinion drops, stock prices tend to decline.

---

[1] Edward M. Miller, "Risk, Uncertainty, and Divergence of Opinion," *Journal of Finance* (September 1977), pp. 1,151–1,168.

4. Since the divergence of opinion on initial public offerings declines as they become seasoned, these stocks tend to underperform the market.
5. Since risk correlates with divergence of opinion, the return to risk, both systematic and nonsystematic, is less than the typical investor would require to invest in risky stocks.
6. Thus, the typical investors should overweight the less risky stocks in his portfolio.
7. There is a winner's curse effect in the stock markets such that you tend to purchase the stocks you erred in evaluating. This holds even if every single investor is, on average, unbiased in his or her valuations.

This chapter will develop the implications for practitioners of a world where there is little short selling and where investors disagree about the merits of securities. Both seem at least as plausible as the alternatives, that investors trade in perfect markets and always agree on the values for all relevant variables (and successfully do the complex calculations required to construct an optimal portfolio).

Textbooks sometimes deduce that security prices should be efficient by assuming homogeneous beliefs. This is obviously wrong since people disagree about all sorts of things including sports, politics, and securities. A more sophisticated version recognizes that investors do disagree about future returns and risks of a security but argues that their beliefs are unbiased (i.e., are correct on average). This, combined with prices reflecting average opinions, implies that the prices will be unbiased estimates of fair values.

However, with substantial divergence of opinion some investors are likely to believe the security has a negative expected return. This implies that they expect a price decline. The logical action for an investor expecting a price decline is to short the security. It follows that where short selling is prohibited, that such negative opinions will not be fully reflected in stock prices. This implies (contrary to standard theory) that there will be some overvalued stocks that can be identified with publicly available information.

Chapter 5 discussed markets with obstacles to short selling in which one group of investors can be identified as right and one group as wrong using publicly available information. This showed how analysts can add value and how to use their analysis to avoid overvalued stocks.

However, normally there are many different opinions about the value of a security and it is not clear which is correct. It will initially be assumed that there is no short selling. Later the case will be discussed where short selling is merely restricted.

With divergence of opinion (and restricted short selling), lowering the price of a security not only causes investors who already own the security to buy more, but it also causes investors who previously would not have bought the security at all to buy. There is then a marginal investor who will only buy if the price is at or below some level. Much of this section will be developing the implications of the marginal investor for portfolio management.

From a purely logical viewpoint, divergence of opinion implies that at least one of the opinions (and perhaps all of them) is wrong. To make it possible to compare this theory with the efficient market theory, the assumption will be made that investors all have unbiased expectations. Of course, this is just an exposition device. The behavioral finance literature shows that all sorts of biases exist. Unbiased expectations means that if all the opinions were averaged, the average would be the correct value. Incidentally, it may even be true that each investor is on average correct when his estimates are averaged over all the stocks he follows, even though he is sometimes high and sometimes low. Finally, the implications of divergence of opinion for value additivity, closed-end funds, and spin-offs will be developed.

INTERACTION OF DIVERGENCE OF OPINION AND SHORT SELLING RESTRICTIONS

A distribution can be represented in either probability density form or cumulative form. The first bell-shaped curve in Exhibit 6.1 shows the distribution of investors' opinions about the security's maximum value. This is the price at which the security just enters into their portfolios. At lower prices they may hold more of the security, although this effect cannot easily be shown in the exhibit (since it has only two dimensions).

EXHIBIT 6.1   Number of Investors with Various Estimates of Value

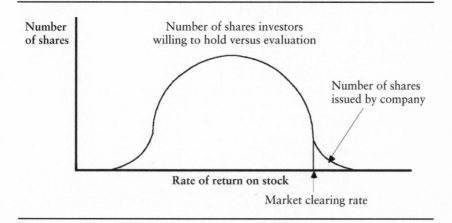

The same information can also be shown as a cumulative distribution as shown in Exhibit 6.2. The vertical axis is the price and the horizontal axis shows the number of investors whose willingness to pay for a security is at, or below, that level.

For expositional convenience, imagine that investors buy one share if they decide to include a security in their portfolios and no shares otherwise. (The argument can easily be generalized to where each investor buys a certain number of shares depending on his wealth and diversification requirements.)

The vertical line in Exhibit 6.2 shows the number of investors needed to absorb the total quantity of the stock in existence (which at one share per investor is also the number of shares issued). The equilibrium price is at the intersection of the cumulative probability distribution and the vertical line. If the price was higher, investors who thought the stock was worth at least that price would not be willing to hold all of the stock that exists. The excess stock would be offered for sale, causing the price to drop.

If the price was below the point of intersection, there would be more investors who thought the stock was worth at least that amount. Some investors who thought the stock was worth including in their portfolio would find

EXHIBIT 6.2   Cumulative Distribution of Investor's Valuations

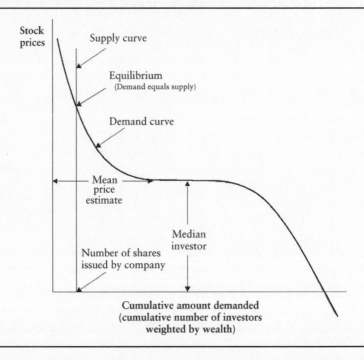

none to purchase at the prevailing prices. These disappointed investors would bid the price up until it reached the equilibrium price.

Exhibit 6.2 is actually a demand/supply diagram. The demand curve is simply the cumulative valuation curve as long as each investor purchases one share. The supply curve is simply the number of shares outstanding, a number determined by the company. The theory of price determination offered is that the price is set at the level where demand equals supply. In a more general formulation the demand curve is the summation of all investors' demand curves.

In the exhibit the supply curve was shown as simply the quantity of stock issued by the company. A short sale is essentially the issuance of new stock by the short seller. The volume of short sales increases with the price causing the total quantity of shares to increase. Thus the supply curve has a slightly upward slope. However, since the volume of shares issued by short sellers is just a small fraction of the number issued by the firm itself, the argument is little altered if realistic amounts of short selling occur. Boehme, Danielson, and Sorensen, as part of a larger study (discussed later), report that the mean short interest as of July 1, 1999, was only 1.454% of the number of shares held.[2] Even looking at the top 1% of firms, the short interest was only 15.6%. One would expect much higher ratio if there were not obstacles to short selling, whether institutional or psychological.

Equilibrium Prices Do Not Equal Consensus Value Estimates

Several simple points emerge from the above analysis. Probably most important is that there is nothing to insure that the demand and supply curves intersect at a price representing the consensus valuation of all investors. The consensus is at point A, the value where half of the investors think the stock is worth more and half think it is worth less. Only by coincidence would this consensus value be the market determined price.

Normally only a small fraction of investors can absorb a security's total floating supply. Consider a small company with ten million shares outstanding. Suppose each investor purchases 1,000 shares. Only 10,000 investors need think the stock is worth holding to absorb the whole supply of the stock. The stock will be priced at the level that is just adequate to induce the marginal investor, the ten thousandth investor, to hold it.

Normally, much less than half of the investors can absorb the floating supply of a stock, with the result that the marginal investor's evaluation is far above the valuation of the median investor or the average investor. An alternative way to express the argument so far is that the

---

[2] Rodney D. Boehme, Bartley R. Danielson, and Sorin M. Sorescu, "Short Sale Constraints and Overvaluation," working paper, American Finance Association 2003 Annual Conference, January 2003.

price is set by the optimistic investors (as was shown in Chapter 5, "Bounded Efficient Markets"). Notice that this result is quite consistent with every investor making unbiased estimates of the value of each security. By saying that the estimates are unbiased, it is asserted that if the true values were known, the average of the investors' opinions would equal this true value. Unbiased evaluations can still contain errors. If these errors differ from individual to individual, divergence of opinion will be observed and the effects discussed here will occur.

As an empirical observation, any one stock is normally owned by only a minority of investors. For individuals, breadth is very low with the typical investor owning only a few stocks

Chen, Hong, and Stein examined "breadth," which they defined as the percentage of investors who own a security.[3] The investors for whom they had data were mutual funds, which are representative of other institutional investors (which account for most trading on the exchanges). They found that over all U.S. stocks (on the NYSE, AMEX, and NASDAQ) the mean breadth was only 1.29%. Even for the largest quintile of firms (size breaks based on the NYSE), the average breadth was only 7.09%. For the next quintiles, the values in order were 2.56%, 1.43%, 0.76%, and 0.25%.

Individual investors, having smaller portfolios, are usually much less diversified than institutions. Barber and Odean found that the mean household's portfolio contains only 4.3 stocks and the median portfolio 2.3.[4] If this few stocks are held in the typical portfolio out of the thousands that could be held, it follows that only a small fraction of investors can have holdings in a typical stock. This implies that breadth is even smaller for stocks that are held predominantly by individuals.

This explains why equilibrium will be reached on the right hand side of the distribution, with the optimists setting the price.

Varying the Divergence of Opinion

While the basic mechanism of price determination is best understood using a cumulative distribution, the effects of changing the distribution can best be understood using probability density diagrams. Consider Exhibit 6.1. The number of investors who believe the stock will earn at least a certain percentage is represented by the area to the right of the value.

Now let us consider increasing the divergence of opinion while holding the average opinion constant. In the exhibit, this widens the dis-

---

[3] Joseph Chen, Harrison Hong, and Jeremy C. Stein, "Breadth of Ownership and Stock Returns," *Journal of Financial Economics* (2002), pp. 171–205, Table 1.
[4] Brad M. Berber and Terrance Odean, "Trading is Hazardous to Your Wealth: The Common Stock Investment Performance of Individual Investors," *Journal of Finance* (April 2000), pp. 773–806.

tribution while holding its center fixed. As can be seen, as long as only a fraction of the investors find the security attractive, a wider distribution of opinion raises the price above which enough investors can be found to absorb the fixed supply of a particular stock. Thus, the greater the divergence of opinion, the higher the price can be expected to be.

One implication of Exhibit 6.3 is that the more investors are required to absorb the supply of a security, the further to the left on the diagram will be the equilibrium. This implies a lower price. Holding the future dividends constant, a lower price implies a higher rate of return. If we define breadth to be the percentage of investors that include a long position in their portfolios, the implication is that stocks with a high ownership breadth will have higher returns. Chen, Hong, and Stein have derived the implication that change in breadth should help predict price changes, and found that it was supported.[5] Those stocks whose change

EXHIBIT 6.3 Effect of Changing the Divergence of Opinion

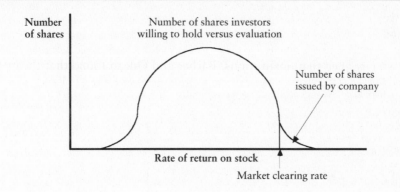

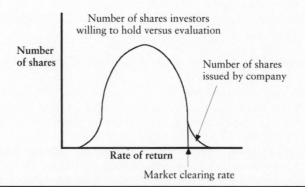

---

[5] Chen, Hong, and Stein, "Breadth of Ownership and Stock Returns."

in breadth is in the lowest decile of the sample underperform those in the top decline by 6.38% in the 12 months after formation. After adjusting for size, book–to-market, and momentum, they find the value to be 4.95%, and still statistically significant.[6]

There is one unrealistic implication of a model where every investor looks at every stock and then buys those he or she thinks are best. Imag-

---

[6] There is some question about whether the effect found here is really a divergence of opinion effect as predicted by Exhibit 6.1. In a long-term equilibrium with everything held constant, the stocks with high breadth will have a lower price, which (assuming the same dividends) implies a lower return on average. Thus, in a cross-sectional regression one would expect breadth to go along with return. However, in a time series context, if one increases the breadth holding everything else constant, the price should drop. Thus, I would have predicted change in breadth to be inversely correlated with return, the opposite to what they found.

Instead, I have a suspicion that they found it takes time to accumulate or reduce large institutional positions and that, as a result, when extra new funds are added to the list of holders, they frequently are still in the process of accumulating the stock, and this accumulation continues in the next few quarters. Likewise, when some funds have reduced their holdings to zero, there are other funds that are in the process of reducing their holdings and this produces continued selling. There may also be a degree of herding among institutional investors such that after one fund has accumulated a position it then talks it up, inducing other funds to go into it.

Analyzing changes in breadth while holding the number of shares constant implies that the intramarginal investors are changing their holdings of the stock, or that there is a change in the fraction of potential investors who are bothering to examine a stock. If existing investors are changing their holdings of the stock (the depth), one needs to explain why. One possibility is that a few large investors (members of founding families typically) are choosing to reduce their holdings. While their rationalization may be diversifying their own portfolios, the timing is likely to avoid periods when their inside information says it is best to continue to hold the stock and, at worse, to be when their actual inside information tells them the price is likely to decline. The increase in breadth is offset by a decrease in depth by the informed investors. Of course, rational investors, upon reading of such insider sales, are likely to deduce that the future is not bright. This effect would be likely to lower return.

Another possibility is that the shape of the distribution of opinion changes. If the optimistic investors become less optimistic, while still remaining optimistic enough to hold the stock, they could generate net selling that result in an increase in breadth. The problem is that this is a change in the information set that is likely to make it harder to untangle the effect of pure breadth. In particular, this would be a change in the average expectations that changed the average opinion. This would tend to lower the future returns while the breadth increase was increasing them.

In Markowitz optimization, the limits to accumulating a stock with a high return is set by the increased risk to the portfolio. The higher the standard deviation (risk) of the stock, the quicker this limit is reached. Thus, an increase in risk could generate increased selling by existing holders that leads to an increase in breadth.

ine investors all make estimates of returns (subject to errors of course) and then feed the data into a Markowitz optimization program. They then purchase the portfolios chosen. Suppose the divergence of opinion does not vary with firm size. In Exhibit 6.1, the price is set by going from right to left on the bell shaped curve until the available supply of stock is absorbed. For a small company with only a few shares outstanding, the estimated return required by the marginal investor will be higher than for a large company. This predicts that the breadth will be smaller for the smaller companies. Also, they will be more overpriced than the large companies. Such overpricing predicts that in turn small stocks will have a lower return than large stocks. This is the opposite of what has actually been observed in the data. Small capitalization stocks have earned higher returns than large capitalization stocks. Where does the above model go wrong?

The error is in the implicit assumption that all investors look at all stocks. In practice, investors use two-stage decision making in which they look at only a fraction of the available securities. The probability of a stock being looked at is probably roughly proportional to size, so that the above bias becomes less of a problem. Merton has developed a model in which investors only invest in securities with which they are familiar.[7] Investors are less familiar with the smaller firms.

There is a possibility for bias. Firms that are well known to consumers, to investors (say serving the New York market or providing investor services), or that receive a lot of free publicity in the media (such as media firms, and drug and other technology firms that frequently make news by bringing out improved newsworthy products) will be more often looked at. It is likely that some fraction of the investors looking at a firm will decide to buy it, thus causing these firms to be bid up. In contrast, firms that are in prosaic businesses that seldom make the news (say cement) or that serve populations that are too poor to have many investors (rural areas perhaps) may not be looked at very often. If only a few investors look at a firm, it has to be priced so that a higher proportion of those that look will choose to buy. This implies that these neglected firms will provide on average higher returns. This theory has been set out in detail elsewhere.[8]

Technology can change the number of firm's investor's look at. Premodern computer technology, small firms (especially those located out of money market centers) failed to come to the attention of many inves-

---

[7] Robert C. Merton, "A Simple Model of Capital Market Equilibrium with Incomplete Information," *Journal of Finance* (July 1987), pp. 483–510.
[8] Edward M. Miller, "Can the Neglected Stock Effect be Explained by Two Stage Decision Making?" *Review of Business and Economic Research* (Fall 1989), pp. 64–73.

tors. Now computer screening tools are widely available. A screen is just as likely to show up a small firm as a large one (assuming size is not being used as a screen and set to automatically exclude the small firms). If this results in more small firms being viewed, the marginal investors for small firms could now be even further to the right than large firms. This might imply that their returns going forward would be below normal. This speculation also predicts that during the period in which screening programs were coming into use, more and more small firms would be "discovered" and have their prices bid up. This would cause an overperformance of small firms during the period when computerized screening was coming into use.

The above argument shows that prices will be higher and returns lower if there are both constraints to short selling and divergence of opinion. Both of these preconditions appear to be true.

The Winner's Curse

The stocks for which the investor succeeds in out-bidding other investors will be those for which the investor has overestimated the value. The above effect is what has become known as the "winner's curse" in the competitive bidding literature. Early descriptions of this effect as applied to bidding are in Capen, Clapp, and Campbell[9] and in Miller.[10] A firm is more likely to submit the winning bid in "a high bid wins" contest when it overestimates the value. There will be a correlation between the magnitude of the errors made and the probability of winning. This causes the overestimation, conditional on having won, to be positive. The winner typically experiences a "good news/bad news" situation where the good news is that he has won, and the bad news is that he would have been better off if he had not won. The winner's curse implies that the winner will typically be disappointed in the profit from winning, and may even experience a loss.

Any market where prices are set at the highest, or the highest of so many bids (and in which perfect short selling does not occur), risks winner's curse behavior.

Although not normally pointed out in the winner's curse literature, the argument depends on the absence of short selling. For oil leases, real estate, and similar unique objects, a short sale is not possible. If short sales were readily made, the winning price would not be influenced by the disagreement among the bidders and the effect would disappear.

---

[9] E. Capen, R. Clapp, and W. Campbell, "Competitive Bidding in High-Risk Situations," *Journal of Petroleum Technology* (June 1971), pp. 641–653.
[10] Edward M. Miller (principal investigator and author of most of study), *Study of Energy Fuel Resources*, Vol. 1 (Cambridge, MA: Abt Associates, 1969).

Consider an auction where a bidder sees the price rise above what he things something is worth. In discussions of the winner's curse it is assumed he simply drops out of the bidding (reduces his demand to zero). However, if short selling was possible, he would offer to sell short. The price would then reflect the average valuation. If the average bidder was correct in his valuation, the price would reflect this and there would not be a winner's curse.

The author originally worked out the winner's curse effect for a study of the sale of federal oil and gas leases, and then later realized the effect could be extended to other markets where true values were uncertain and prices were set by competitive bidding.[11] The stock market is such a market.

In a market that exhibits winner's curse behavior, investors are typically disappointed with the outcomes of their investment even if their original estimates were unbiased. Divergence of opinion implies that at least some investors' estimates contain errors. In a model where the security ends up being owned by the optimistic investors with the highest valuations, there is a positive correlation between the error in an estimate and the probability of the security being included in the portfolio. Thus the expected error conditional on a security's inclusion in the portfolio is positive. This implies that the securities selected perform worse than anticipated.

An important point should be appreciated. Of potential investor's estimates of returns are considered to be unbiased estimates of the actual returns, this does not imply that the estimates of the investors that actually hold the asset are unbiased estimates.[12] Only some investors hold any single stock in their portfolio, and these are the investors with the higher estimates. The estimates of the investors holding a stock are more likely to reflect positive mistakes, mistakes that overestimate the returns. When the errors made by investors are weighted (difference between estimated return and the actual value for the expected mean of the return distribution) by the size of their positions in each stock, we will find that the stocks with positive errors have higher weights than the stocks with negative errors (for which the weights will typically be

---

[11] Miller, *Study of Energy Fuel Resources.*

[12] In this model, the potential (but not the actual) investor's estimates of the rates of return are presumed to be unbiased estimates of the returns actually to be earned. This is to say that if every investor's estimate of all returns are averaged, and the experiment is repeated many times, the average will approach the correct value. This is probably the most favorable assumption that could be made for the efficient market hypothesis. Notice, it is being presumed that errors are being made, but that for every positive error there is an equally common negative error.

zero, since they do not hold these stocks about which they have negative estimates).[13] This is a general problem in decision-making.

One solution to this problem is to reduce return estimates for the expected error before choosing the optimal portfolio. This problem has had some discussion in the bidding literature and in the capital budgeting literature where it has been referred to as the problem of "uncertainty induced bias."[14] The amount of the reduction increases with the uncertainty in the return estimates. While the paper proposing this made the list of the 25 most-cited financial management papers,[15] the idea has yet to make it into textbooks. However, explicit solutions have not been worked out for investment applications. The need for this correction for uncertainty induced bias is not generally appreciated, and examination of textbooks will show the recommended procedure is to make the best estimate of expected return and risk that is practical, and then to compute an optimal portfolio using these as inputs. The textbooks do not even point out the problem.

It is necessary to correct for the winner's curse effect. I have discussed how to do this in the capital budgeting literature under the subject of uncertainty induced bias.[16] Using a decision tree argument, it can be shown that even with unbiased estimates that net present value is the wrong criteria. This happens whenever there are more poor projects than good ones. This situation is normally to be expected in competitive markets. Of course, security selection is one type of capital budgeting problem, presumably one that might benefit from this approach.

Sources of Divergence of Opinion

The discussion in the previous section has left unclear the assumption that investors differ in their beliefs and in their valuations. Clearly a major reason for the differences of opinion is differences in information. Some investors know things other investors do not. Given the limits on

---

[13] Keith Brown, "A Note on the Apparent Bias of Net Revenue Estimates for Capital Investment Projects," *Journal of Finance* (September 1974), pp. 1215–1216. See also, Keith Brown, "The Rate of Return of Selected Investment Projects," *Journal of Finance* (September 1978), pp. 1250–1253.

[14] Edward M. Miller, "Uncertainty Induced Bias in Capital Budgeting," *Financial Management* (Fall 1978), pp. 12–18. See also, Edward M. Miller, "The Competitive Market Assumption and Capital Budgeting Criteria," *Financial Management* (Winter 1987), pp. 22–28.

[15] Kenneth A. Borokhovich, Robert J. Bricker, Terry L. Zivney, and Srinivasan Sundaram, "Financial Management (1972–1994): A Retrospective," *Financial Management* (1995), pp. 42–53.

[16] Miller, "Uncertainty Induced Bias in Capital Budgeting." See also, Miller, "The Competitive Market Assumption and Capital Budgeting Criteria."

human brain power and constraints on time, it is virtually certain that no one person will know everything that is available to be known. It is also plausible that people differ in which information they know and do not know. It is easy to imagine a case where some individuals have an informational advantage. Because of occupation, education, and location some people acquire relevant information at virtually no cost (in terms of cost of seeking the information for investment purposes) while others have to actively search out the same information. For instance an engineer may know things from his job can be easily applied to evaluating a semiconductor investment, while another investor would have to consciously educate himself on these issues to understand. Those whose occupations are in medicine, engineering, law, and the like may in the course of the business learn things about companies and their products that the professionals employed by institutions learn only later. Another source of divergence of opinion is that some investors have inside information and others do not.

Investment Implications

There is a large body of theoretical literature on the asymmetric information and how investors may make deductions from observing others' trading as to what information they have. Alternatively, they may make deductions from observing market prices as to how other investors value a security. This is not the place to review this literature, but in some models investors adjust their beliefs with the aid of information they obtain from observing other investors.

If everyone has different information and the information is combined in the way discussed in this chapter, it was shown that the investor who purchases a security will be disappointed (i.e., the return will be less than expected). If one plays with Markowitz optimization routines, one will find that putting in expected returns for one security that are appreciably higher than required for it to be included in the portfolio will result in that security having a weight that is a multiple of that security's weight in the market portfolio. As a rule of thumb, the further your estimate is from the average estimate, the more likely you are to suffer from the winner's curse effect. One common solution is to adjust the estimates (or the estimates from a staff member) to correct for them. When an adequate record is available, a regression of estimated errors (for securities actually purchased) on the estimate's deviation from the average might be used to improve estimates.

Because the higher the percentage of ones portfolio the computer says to put into a stock, the higher the likely error is in your estimates, diversification requirements serve to limit the effect of these errors. If your computations suggest putting 30% of a portfolio into a situation, error is likely (possibly because you lack information others have). A requirement that no more than say 5% of an institutional portfolio be in any one security helps protect against this. Logically, this argument for diversification is different from the usual volatility reducing argument, which is also valid.

Psychological research shows that people are usually overconfident in their estimates in the presence of uncertainty. This limits the extent to which they make adjustments of this type. Individuals with limited experience who have never studied market history would be especially prone to fail to adjust for the above uncertainty-induced bias effect. This is especially likely since the need to adjust for uncertainty-induced bias is not taught in schools.

Indexing represents an extreme correction for uncertainty-induced bias. If an investor knows he has virtually no information that others lack, he may decide to just hold some of everything. If there were no grossly overoptimistic investors out there, this might be optimal. It is even more likely to be optimal if there are known to be insiders trading in the market. "Buy and hold" is a sensible strategy against a market where there are known to be better informed investors. If one tries to buy low and sell high, one may just be buying when prices incorrectly appear to bargains. The prices are low because the insiders or other better informed investors are selling. When you decide to sell because they appear high, it may be they appear high only because you lack the information held by better informed investors.

In Chapter 5, the companion chapter to this one, I argued that markets were bounded such that there were few (possibly no) undervalued securities that could be identified from publicly available information while there could be overvalued securities. The optimal strategy is to do analysis to avoid the overvalued securities. However, as discussed above, if in the course of the analysis one convinces oneself that a security is grossly underpriced, one is likely to be wrong. Since the undervalued securities are likely to be only a little undervalued, the optimal percentage in a portfolio is likely to be low. A tight limit on the amount of any one security held in a portfolio is a logical implication of the above analysis. High diversification is a result.

Theoretical Objections

Since my original "Risk, Uncertainty, and Divergence of Opinion" paper was published in 1977, there has been considerable discussion. The original paper and the exposition above provide a simple diagrammatic exposition of the effects of divergence of opinion with short selling restricted.

After I published the argument, Figlewski[17] and Jarrow[18] provided a more mathematical treatment. Jarrow also correctly points out there could be investor disagreement about the risk properties of securities that exactly counterbalanced the effects of the investor disagreements about expected returns, leaving each investor's demands for securities unchanged.

Working in a general equilibrium framework, Jarrow also gives a counter example in which with multiple stocks subject to short sales constraints, the imposition of the short selling constraints on all risky assets leads to lower prices for one of the assets. Imagine there is a group of investors who is much more optimistic about stock A than stock B, and another group who have the opposite view, preferring B to A, but less strongly. Before trading each group has all of its wealth in the stock they think will do best. A short selling restriction prevents them from making short sales of the less preferred stock and using the proceeds to purchase the more preferred stock. In the theoretical model with full short selling, the first group would sell short B and use the funds to buy A. The other group would short sell A and use the funds to buy B (this provides the buying of B that is needed for the first group to sell). However, because the group buying B prefers B less strongly than the other group prefers A, the new set of prices have B at a lower price and A at a higher price. Thus, removing short selling constraints does not raise the prices of all risky assets since one price went down. No real world example of this effect was pointed out.

In a general equilibrium, results contrary to what I proposed appear theoretically possible when there are strong substitution effects among securities. However, given the large number of securities that are available to modern investors, substitution effects are unlikely to reverse the conclusion that (all other things being equal) increasing divergence of opinion in the presence of short sales constraints will raise the price of a particular security and lower its returns.

Jarrow discusses the extreme case where investors agree on a diagonal covariance matrix, but disagree on the variances. He shows restricting short sales will raise prices.

Jarrow refers to a multiperiod model of Williams in which investors start off disagreeing about the covariance matrix and expected returns.[19]

[17] Steve Figlewski, "The Informational Effects of Restrictions on Short Sales: Some Empirical Evidence," *Journal of Financial and Quantitative Analysis* (1981), pp. 463–476.

[18] Robert Jarrow, "Heterogeneous Expectations, Restrictions on Short Sales, and Equilibrium Asset Prices," *Journal of Finance* (December 1980), pp. 1105–1113.

[19] Joseph Williams, "Capital Asset Prices with Heterogeneous Beliefs," *Journal of Financial Economics* (November 1977) pp. 219–239.

In a steady state they end up agreeing on the covariance matrix, but still disagree about the mean returns. Intuitively, as time passes more and more evidence accumulates about covariances and eventually the investors come to agree. As Jarrow puts it, "they agree about the expected return required to hold the asset in their portfolios." In this circumstance Jarrow's conclusion regarding the effects of restricting short selling are, "If they agree upon the covariance matrix of next period's asset prices, relative risky asset prices will always rise."

With new information constantly arriving, investors clearly do not agree completely on the covariance matrix of all securities (and of course most investors do not even use explicit covariance matrices in decision making). However, their opinions about the risk properties of securities probably differ less than their opinions about the securities' expected returns. Most investors try to limit the effect of large covariances among pairs of securities by trying to diversify across industries, and often by diversifying across categories of stocks strongly exposed to certain factors (growth versus value, small versus large, cyclical versus defensive, etc.). In practice, investors are likely to disagree more about expected returns than about questions such as the firm's industry, or whether it is a cyclical or a defensive stock.

The few investors who use explicit estimates of covariances typically derive them from historical data. This is because the vast numbers of covariances needed for a full Markowitz optimization make any other procedure infeasible. While there are many alternative ways of using historical data, they are likely to give somewhat similar estimates.[20] More importantly, for well-diversified portfolios (i.e., institutional ones), the measure of risk will be the correlation of a particular security with the whole of the portfolio. Since institutional portfolios resemble each other, the relevant measures of risks will be similar to each other and similar to a beta calculated with regard to a diversified U.S. index. In the textbook capital asset pricing model, the required return on a stock is $= R_f +$ beta $(R_m - R_f)$, where R_f is the risk-free rate and R_m is the return on the market. Stocks that fall above this security market line should be bought, and those that fall below it not bought, and sold if owned. Short selling constraints can bind because a particular investor believes a stock to be overvalued because of his estimates of beta as well as his estimates of return.

Of course investors can disagree on betas as well as on expected returns. Investors with a sufficiently high estimate of beta, but a conven-

---

[20] See Edwin J. Elton and Martin Gruber, *Modern Portfolio Theory and Investment Analysis* (New York: John Wiley & Sons, 1995) for a description of many ways of using historical data. Better results are often obtained by multifactor models or averaging data than by simply computing a covariance matrix from historical data.

tional estimate of the expected return would often wish to short the stocks in the absence of short sale constraints. The short would provide a hedge against market declines, permitting a greater investment in other risky securities without increasing total portfolio risk. With short sale constraints, those who have low estimates of beta buy more of that stock, while selling is limited by the difficulties in reducing the weight below zero.

Varian, in "Divergence of Opinion in Complete Markets: A Note" (the phrase complete markets implies no obstacles to short selling) concluded that for plausible parameters of risk aversion that dispersion of opinion should lower asset prices.[21] As the reference to complete markets in the title shows, he is explicitly assuming full ability to make short sales (or the equivalent). As he pointed elsewhere, the effect on price of changing the divergence of opinion should depend on the curvature of the demand curve.[22]

It is useful to consider changing divergence of opinion in the context of Markowitz optimization. Imagine a large number of identical investors that have initial identical beliefs and risk preferences. Consider a security that has a higher return and a higher risk than the rest of the portfolio. For each of these investors the weight of every security has been chosen so that the effect of purchasing another share would lower utility because the increase in expected return would not offset the increase in risk. Likewise, buying one less share would lower utility because the loss in utility from lower return would more than offset the increase in utility from lower risk. All of the other securities than the share in question can be grouped into a portfolio and treated as a single security. As the weight of this security is increased in the portfolio, the risk (variability) of the portfolio increases at an increasing rate. The reason it increases at an increasing rate is that the covariance between the return on this security and the rest of the portfolio (which already includes some of this security) increases steadily.

Now imagine one investor raises his (or her) estimate of the return from the security by 1% and another lowers it by 1%. This increases the divergence of opinion while holding the mean opinion constant. Return increases linearly with w (the weight). However, because portfolio risk increases at an increasing rate as w goes up, the investor with the raised estimate of return raises his w for the security by less than the one with the lowered return estimate lowers his w. Since we assumed that the two

---

[21] Hal R. Varian, "Divergence of Opinion in Complete Markets: A Note," *Journal of Finance* (March 1985), pp. 309–317.

[22] Hal R. Varian, "Differences of Opinion in Financial Markets," in Courtenay C. Stone (ed.), *Financial Risk: Theory, Evidence and Implications* (Boston: Kluwer Academic Publishers, 1989).

investors had the same wealth, the effect of the increased dispersion of return estimates was a decrease in the average w. If price was to be unchanged, this would imply net selling. However, equilibrium can be maintained if the price drops, raising the return and hence causing all investors to have slightly higher return expectations. Thus, without short selling restrictions, we might expect increased dispersion of opinion to sometimes result in lower prices and higher returns.

One can imagine a security where the dispersion of return estimates was small enough so that no one wished to short it. The more pessimistic investors simply underweight it in their portfolios. Thus, if the short constraint binds on sufficiently few investors, changing the divergence of opinion could lower the price rather than raise it.

However, since the above effect depends on the curvature in the demand curve (which in turn results from the covariance of a security with a portfolio increasing as the weight of that security in the portfolio increases), I would expect it to be relatively minor compared with the effect of preventing investors from reducing the holdings below zero.

One would expect this effect to be strongest for the securities which typically compose a large proportion of a portfolio. If one is thinking of investors as being basically similar, the large stocks that have a high weight in the "market portfolio" must typically have a high weight in individual portfolios also. It is for such stocks that the price lowering effect of increasing divergence of opinion would be most powerful.

EMPIRICAL TESTS

There are two obvious ways to test the divergence of opinion theory prediction that increased divergence of opinion lower returns in the presence of restrictions on short selling. One is to see if constraints on short selling affect returns. The other is to see if high divergence of opinion stocks have lower returns.

Evidence on Short Sales Constraints

The level of short interest can be interpreted in several ways. If short sales are observed, some short selling is possible. Since the major reason for short sales is because one expects the stock to underperform, the level of short interests can be interpreted as a measure of the strength of the belief that the stock will underperform. Sometimes this underperformance is merely relative to certain other securities. In this case, the short sale is usually part of a hedge of some type. In other cases, the investor expects the stock to actually go down, or at least to go up by less than what he or she will earn on the short sale proceeds. Because of short selling costs (in the form of failure to receive use of the proceeds or receiving a low rate of return on the proceeds), short sellers can be presumed to have an appreciably lower expectation for future returns than those that hold long positions. With this interpretation, the size of the short interest relative to the long interest becomes a measure of the divergence of opinion regarding the stock's value. When there is little divergence of opinion, there will probably be few whose views are sufficiently negative to lead them to short the stock. When the divergence of opinion is large, not only will there be some who believe the stock will underperform, but many of these will be sufficiently pessimistic to believe the stock will underperform by enough to make a short sale profitable. Thus, at any given level of short selling cost, the greater the short interest, the greater the divergence of opinion. Therefore, the divergence of opinion theory suggests that the stocks with the greatest short interest (relative to the number of shares outstanding) will underperform other stocks. This has been shown by several studies.

In the twenties and early thirties there was actually a loan crowd on the floor of the New York Stock Exchange where stock loans were arranged, and the interest rates paid on the proceeds were quoted in the *Wall Street Journal*. Jones and Lamont collected data on the rates charged to borrow stocks for 1926 to 1933 and on the returns to shorted stocks.[23] For hard to borrow stocks, the rates were sometimes negative (i.e., the borrower of the stock not only got no interest on the proceeds of the security deposit, he or she paid additional sum to the lender of the stock). They found that the higher the fee paid for borrowing stocks, the lower the return on the stocks. In other words the short sellers seemed able to identify stocks that would underperform the market. It appears that when there was little interest in shorting stocks, the demand could be met by brokers lending out the shares already in their possession. However, when the demand for shares to be shorted grew, brokers were forced to go to the loan crowd to find shares to borrow. Noticing there was interest in borrowing stocks, the *Wall Street Journal* then added coverage of that stock to its list of stocks whose borrowing fees were reported. This story suggests those stocks that were added to the list were those with a high interest in being borrowed (which was confirmed by observing that the fees for these stocks were usually higher when they were added to the list). These newly listed stocks were found to underperform the market after listing by 1–2% per month. Even after paying the fees, shorting

---

[23] Charles M. Jones and Owen A. Lamont, "Short-Sale Constraints and Stock Returns," *Journal of Financial Economics* (2002), pp. 207–239. See also Chapter 7 in this book.

these stocks would have been profitable. Because addition to the short borrowing list was observable and the fees charged were reported, the possibility of earning abnormal returns is inconsistent with the efficient markets model. The correlation of high short costs and low returns is predicted by the divergence of opinion, restricted short selling model.

Early studies showed an inconsistent relationship between short interests and future returns. Desai et al. suggest that this was because of the small numbers of stocks studied and the fact that only a minority of stocks have large short interests, introducing much noise into the studies.[24] For instance, Brent et al. studying 200 stocks for each year from 1981–1984, found changes in short interest to be of little use in predicting returns.[25] The only statistically significant result was that for 1981 the returns for the months following increases in short interest were 1.1% greater than for the months with decreases in short interests.

Figlewski showed that the return on stocks with relatively high short interest was lower than on other stocks for the 414 of the S&P 500 stocks for which he could obtain data for January 1973 through June 1979.[26] Stocks were classified into portfolios, using January to June of each year for classification, and the next 12 months to measure performance. After adjusting for beta, the alphas for the half of the decile portfolios with the lowest short interest were all positive, and the alphas for the decile portfolios with the highest short interest were all negative. The rank order of the portfolios was statistically significant. His study showed that the short interest information could be used to improve performance in choosing stocks for long positions. It also appeared useful for identifying stocks likely to earn less than required by their risk. The latter would normally be candidates for sale if owned. However, because the returns were still positive for all portfolios, following the short sellers would prove an unprofitable investment strategy unless one got some returns on the proceeds, or unless the short sales served to reduce risk by hedging another investment. Because the divergence of opinion effect is probably greatest on the smaller stocks, Figlewski's use of S&P stocks and practice of value-weighting within portfolios probably reduced the effects. Likewise, his use of six months of data to identify the short interest and a 12-month holding period probably reduced

---

[24] Heman Desai, K. Ramesh, S. Ramu Thiagarajan, and Bala V. Balachandran, "An Investigation of the Informational Role of Short Interest in the NASDAQ Market," *Journal of Finance* (October 2002), pp. 2263–2287.

[25] Averil Brent, Dale Morese, and E. Kay Stice, "Short Interest: Explanation and Tests," *Journal of Financial and Quantitative Analysis* (June 1990), pp. 273–289.

[26] Figlewski, "The Informational Effects of Restrictions on Short Sales: Some Empirical Evidence."

the returns available judging from the more impressive results obtained in the Desai et al. study discussed next, which rebalanced monthly.

Desai et al. investigated the effect of short interest on returns on NASDAQ using data for June 1988 to December 1994.[27] They document that NASDAQ stocks with short interest of over 2.5% of the shares outstanding have negative (and statistically significant) abnormal returns of −0.76% per month in the next month. The returns are calculated relative to a factor model with the Fama-French factors (where the factors reflect the market, the firm size, and the book-to-market ratio) and a momentum factor. For firms with a short interest of at least 10%, the return is a −1.13% per month.

These are economically significant results and serve to show that information on relative short interest can be used to make investment decisions. This result is contrary to the efficient market model. There are obvious implications for stock selection. Take long positions in stocks with small short interests. Stocks with large short interests should be avoided. Since in the Desai et al. sample the mean level of short interest is only 0.85% and the median 0.11%, they show that very few investors sell short (whether due to legal restrictions, unwillingness to do so, cost, or lack of opportunities is not clear). The 90*th* percentage of short interest for the Desai et al. sample was 2.09%, so their evidence relates to desirability of avoiding a relatively low percentage of all firms. Unfortunately since no information is given as to the market returns during this period, or the rebates available from the interest on the collateral offered, there is little evidence as to whether the short seller made money, or whether the data on relative short positions could be used to identify profitable shorts. However, at least for the stocks with over 10% short interest, the underperformance of 1.13% is large enough to suggest that profitable short sales could have been identified by using the available data.

Asquith and Meulbroek using a large sample of NYSE/AMEX firms for 1976 to 1993 also found a strong negative relationship between short interest and subsequent abnormal returns.[28] They document abnormally low performance for firms that are sufficiently heavily shorted to appear in the top 5% or top 1% of all exchange-listed firms. Their data shows that the publicly available short interest data could have been used to identify stocks that would underperform the market, and probably stocks that could be profitably sold short. The study is very impressive in that 40,000 individual observations were manually checked in comparing the various

---

[27] Desai, Ramesh, Thiagarajan, and Balachandran, "An Investigation of the Informational Role of Short Interest in the NASDAQ Market."
[28] Paul Asquith and Lisa Meulbroek, "An Empirical Investigation of Short Interest," working paper, Harvard Business School, Harvard University, 1995.

databases in an effort to eliminate errors and that they compare the heavily short sold stocks with other stocks in a number of different ways, consistently finding that the heavily shorted stocks underperformed.

Dechow et al. in a study that uses the Asquith and Meulbroek database for 1975 to 1993 find that firms with a zero short interest position have a one-year abnormal return (calculated relative to an equal weighted average for the NYSE and AMEX) of 2.3%.[29] For those firms with over 5% shorted, the abnormal return was −18.1%. They then document that stocks with high ratios of accounting numbers to prices (that generally indicate value stocks) including book value, cash flow, earnings, and a constructed measure of "value" had higher than average returns. Those with low ratios had negative abnormal returns. They show that short sellers tended to concentrate on the groups with low ratios. Within the decile with the lowest ratios they looked at the abnormal returns for those with low short interest (under 0.5%, which is a half of 1%) and those with high short interest (above 0.5%). Consistently, the high short interest stocks had lower returns, consistent with divergence of opinion theory.

For instance, for the low earnings-to-price sample (high P/E), the abnormal returns were −6.0% for the low short interest stocks and −11.8% for the high short interest ones. For the low book-to-price ratio firms, the low short interest stocks had a abnormal return of −7.0% versus −11.1% for the high short interest stocks. For the low cash-flow-to-price stocks the figures were −5.9% for the low short interest stocks, and −16.6% for the high short interest stocks. That the numbers are negative for both groups reflects the tendency for "growth" stocks to underperform. The obvious implication for growth stock investors is that within the category of growth stocks, those with high short interests should be avoided. Of course, these numbers also suggest avoiding growth stocks since they were underperforming so badly. The results are consistent with divergence of opinion theory.

Similar results were found for the value stocks with the low short interest stocks outperforming the high short interest stocks. For instance, the high earnings-to-price stocks had an abnormal return of 6.4% if low short interest and −2.7% if high short interest. Again, within value stocks, avoiding high short interest stocks would pay.

In the United States, short sale data come out only once a month, making it hard for investors to act on this information. In Australia, short sale data is made available to interested parties (which include investors) on the Australian Stock Exchange's information system almost

---

[29] Patricia M. Dechow, Amy P. Hutton, L. Meulbroek, and R. Sloan, "Short Sellers, Fundamental Analysis, and Stock Returns," *Journal of Financial Economics* (2001), pp. 77–106.

immediately after they are made. There, short sales can act to lower stock prices as soon as they are announced.[30] In particular, a market short sale produces a cumulative abnormal return of –0.20% (20 basis points) within 20 trades of being made. The effect of limit-order short sales is much less (about –0.05% with 20 trades). The abnormal return was measured relative to regular sales in the same stock of the same size (and also matched for time of day and day of the week and for uptick or zero-tick status). Thus, the abnormal returns show the differential effect of a short sale over a regular sale. The much greater effect for market orders is one that would be expected if those with time sensitive information use market orders (as they logically should). They also show that the effect is greatest for short sales within a day of significant company announcements (which produce trading halts on the exchange). These are the ones which would be expected to be informational.

I do see one statistical problem. This is that under Australian rules short sales have to be made on an uptick or zero tick. As the authors point out, "the order can clear out a price step but cannot trade down to the next price step." It is possible that short sales frequently do clear out the price step (and traders know they do). If the short sale has just cleared out the limit order to buy, one might expect the bid to drop almost automatically and the stock to trade down mechanically. This could happen even if no one was watching the short sales and no one responded. Imagine a case where there is a 2,000 share short sale order. At the allowed transaction price there are 1,000 shares to be bought. There would then appear on the record a 1,000 share sale marked as a short sale. There would be no more limit orders to buy at that price. The bid should drop automatically. The next market order would be filled automatically at the lower bid. Indeed, the remains of the short sale order might be entered again, and could be filled once the next market order had been placed. The sequence could repeat itself until the short seller had sold what he wished (or the price had become unattractive to him).

Regular sales may leave unfilled limit orders. Thus, a 2,000-share sale would go through the 1,000-share limit order and perhaps take out only part of the next limit order. A second sell order would then be at the same price, rather than at a lower price. Thus, if we compare records of 1,000-share transactions, the short sales would have many cases where they clear out the limit orders, while the other sell orders would not clear the limit orders nearly as often.

---

[30] Michael J. Aitken, Alex Frino, Michael S. McCorry, and Peter L. Swan, "Short Sales are Almost Instantaneously Bad News: Evidence from the Australian Stock Exchange," *Journal of Finance* (1998), pp. 2205–2223.

For the ask price to move, I presume someone would have to change it. However, even then some of the changes in the ask price could merely reflect someone observing that the bid had dropped and then deciding to lower the ask price to keep the spread at a desired level. It is interesting that the effect measured bid-to-bid for market orders is –0.111 versus –0.077 for the ask-to-ask for the 15-minute time interval (their Table II). This is consistent with the above story.

Admittedly, for limit short sales the bid and ask effects are similar. However, I would presume the limit short sale becomes a limit order that can only be executed when another trade had been done earlier. Then a market order to buy would produce a short sale. However, one might expect many market orders to be less than for the short sale quantity, leaving a part of the short sale in effect. There would be no automatic drop in the bid in many of these cases.

Especially, if short sale orders (or intended short sales) are relatively large compared to the size of the limit orders on the book, I would expect this to be a problem. Given that few individuals are willing to sell short, I might expect the short sellers (probably being big players such as institutions and hedge funds) to sell in relatively large quantities, producing the above effects.

In spite of this problem, it is extremely plausible that the professionals who are watching the market (including making a market in a stock) do notice short sales, and interpret a short sale as evidence that an informed investor is negative enough on the stock to sell short. An obvious policy question is whether such short information should be made available to U.S. investors.

Many of these authors writing on the informational effects of short sales seem unaware (judging from the citations) of the expectation that stocks with high divergence of opinion (which can be evidenced by a high short interest) should underperform the market. They interpret their results as being consistent with short sellers possessing private information. Of course, the short sellers may possess adverse private information. One source of divergence of opinion is that people have different levels of private information and those with negative information that suggested a price decline are likely to either short the stock, buy puts, write calls, or avoid owning it.

Danielson and Sorescu figured out a way to examine changes in the strength of short sale constraints.[31] When options exist, negative bets can be placed using them, such as by buying puts. These often indirectly

---

[31] Bartley R. Danielson and Sorin M. Sorescu, "Why Do Option Introductions Depress Stock Prices? A Study of Diminishing Short-Sale Constraints," *Journal of Financial and Quantitative Analysis* (December 2001), pp. 451–484.

result in short selling as option dealers and others make short sales in the course of placing hedges. The professional dealers can often make short sales easier and at lower costs than can individuals or institutions. They can get use of at least part of the proceeds of short sales and are often in a much better position to borrow the required shares. Thus, the short sale constraints should be relaxed when options are introduced.

If divergence of opinion combined with short selling constraints tends to raise prices, reducing the constraints should be accompanied by a lowering of the stock price, and the magnitude of this lowering should be larger when the divergence of opinion is greater. Examining abnormal returns (residuals from a market model) around the time of option introductions, Danielson and Sorescu found the typical effect was a highly significant drop in returns. A lowering of the stock price, of course, implies abnormal returns. Using standard deviation of returns, standard deviation of abnormal returns (from market model), volume of trading (divided by number of shares), and divergence of analysts' estimates of future earnings, they found that each had a tendency to increase in magnitude the (negative) abnormal return around the introduction of options. One puzzle was that for option introductions before 1981 the effects were often the opposite of that predicted by the model.

Danielson and Sorescu produce a model that they describe as being in the Jarrow-Miller theoretical framework, which they contrast with the prediction of Diamond and Verrecchia that divergence of opinion has no effect on security prices.[32] The Danielson and Sorescu model predicts that short interest will increase with the introduction of options. Their empirical results confirm this.

The Danielson and Sorescu model also predicts that with the introduction of short selling, high beta stocks will have a greater increase in short interest and the price of high beta stocks will decline more than the price of low beta stocks. The predicted effect of beta was found.

Finally, the Danielson and Sorescu model predicts that the stocks that have the greatest increase in short interest will also evidence the largest price declines. This result was also found. I am not aware of a theory other than divergence of opinion theory that predicts this set of effects.

Evidence on Varying the Divergence of Opinion

The above theory of divergence of opinion with restricted short selling implies that when divergence of opinion changes, prices should change. In particular, when divergence of opinion declines, prices should decline.

---

[32] Douglas W. Diamond and Robert E. Verrecchia, "Constraints on Short-Selling and Asset Price Adjustment to Private Information," *Journal of Financial Economics* (1987), pp. 277–311.

This should produce below normal rates of return. This effect can be seen from Exhibit 6.3 where the divergence of opinion is changed while leaving unchanged the mean opinion. Just compare the top panel with a large divergence of opinion with the bottom panel where the divergence of opinion is less.

The theory concerning divergence of opinion in the presence of restricted short selling also implies lower rates of return when divergence of opinion is high (a level effect rather than a change effect). Because testing this prediction is greatly complicated by the tendency of risk and divergence of opinion to vary together, the testing of this implication will be discussed after changes in the diversion of opinion have been discussed.

The Low Return to Initial Public Offerings

The prediction that declining divergence of opinion should produce declining prices (all things being equal) can explain the low returns to *initial public offerings* (IPOs). When a company is new, there is often great uncertainty about its future. Some investors will be much more optimistic than others. The optimistic investors will be expected to set the price. As the company acquires an operating history, it becomes easier to forecast its future earnings and dividends. The divergence of opinion shrinks. This lowers the price relative to well-seasoned stocks.

As an illustration, consider a company with a drug to cure cancer. At startup it may have only an idea, perhaps based on academic research. One can legitimately disagree about the future of the company. Somebody might assume a high probability of actually curing cancer and then look at how much patients (or their insurance companies) would pay. Even with discounting, the potential value of the firm is high. Others would be much more pessimistic, seeing almost certain bankruptcy.

One can imagine a cohort of such companies. For each one, the price is set by the more optimistic investors. Over time, research reduces the uncertainty and the divergence of opinion. With animal experiments, certain drugs are shown to work to cure animal cancers. For others, the animals die, unacceptable side effects are found, or the cancers just keep on growing. Eventually human trials are begun. Thus, as time passes, uncertainty and divergence of opinion decline. Eventually, one drug may be shown to work and the product introduced. After a year or so, the drug's price and typical annual sales are known. There are still optimists (who see price increases easily obtained or other sources of growth) and pessimists who foresee slower growth. However, the divergence of opinion is much reduced.

As the cohort of companies develops, the average divergence of opinion will decline. Much of the reduction in average divergence of opinion comes not from the successful companies whose research stays on schedule, but from those whose business plans fail. When the single product of a one-product company fails (say the mice die from side effects), the only disagreement between the optimists and pessimists is likely to be the liquidation value of the used laboratory and office equipment. Even the optimists can not give a very high value to these. When all the companies in this hypothetical cohort are averaged, the divergence of opinion declines over time. Thus, these stocks should under-perform the market.

Many studies (Aggarwal and Rivoli,[33] Aggarwal, Leal, and Hernandez,[34] Brav and Gompers,[35] Carter, Dark, and Singh,[36] Dawson,[37] Finn and Higham,[38] Ibbotson,[39] Kunz and Aggarwal,[40] Levis,[41] Loughran,[42] Loughran and Ritter,[43] Loughran, Ritter, and Rydqvist,[44] Ritter,[45] Stern

---

[33] Reena Aggarwal and Pietra Rivoli, "Fads in the Initial Public Offering Market?" *Financial Management* (1990), pp. 45–57.

[34] Reena Aggarwal, Ricardo Leal, and Leonardo Hernandez, "The Aftermarket Performance of Initial Public Offerings in Latin America," *Financial Management* (1993), pp. 42–53.

[35] Alon Brav and Paul A. Gompers, "Myth or Reality? The Long-Run Underperformance of Initial Public Offerings: Evidence from Venture and Nonventure Capital-Backed Companies," *Journal of Finance* (1997), pp. 1701–1821.

[36] Richard Carter, Frederick H. Dark, and Ajai K. Singh, "Underwriter Reputation, Initial Returns, and the Long-Run Performance of IPO Stocks," *Journal of Finance* (1998), pp. 285–311.

[37] Steven M. Dawson, "Secondary Stock Market Performance of Initial Public Offers, Hong Kong, Singapore and Malaysia: 1978–1984," *Journal of Business Finance and Accounting* (1987), pp. 65–76.

[38] Frank J. Finn and Ron Higham, "The Performance of Unseasoned New Equity Issues-Cum-Stock Exchange Listings in Australia," *Journal of Banking and Finance* (1988), pp. 333–352.

[39] Roger G. Ibbotson, "Price Performance of Common Stock New Issues," *Journal of Financial Economics* (1975), pp. 235–272.

[40] Roger M. Kunz and Reena Aggarwal, "Why Initial Public Offerings are Underpriced: Evidence from Switzerland," *Journal of Banking and Finance* (1994), pp. 705–723.

[41] Mario Levis, "The Long Run Performance of Initial Public Offerings: The UK Experience 1980-1988," *Financial Management* (1993), pp. 28–41.

[42] Tim Loughran, "NYSE vs. NASDAQ Returns: Market Microstructure or the Poor Performance of Initial Public Offerings," *Journal of Financial Economics* (1993), pp. 241–260.

[43] Tim Loughran and Jay R. Ritter, "The New Issues Puzzle," *Journal of Finance* (1995), pp. 23–51.

[44] Tim Loughran, Jay R. Ritter, and Kristian Rydqvist, "Initial Public Offerings: International Insights," *Pacific-Basin Finance Journal* (1993), pp. 165–199.

[45] Jay R. Ritter, "The Long-Run Performance of Initial Public Offerings," *Journal of Finance* (1991), pp. 3–27.

and Bernstein,[46] Stoll and Curley,[47] and Uhlir[48]) have shown that IPOs do worse than the general markets, in spite of their higher risks.

Ritter examined the returns from 1,526 initial public offerings from 1975 to 1984.[49] The three-year return was 34.47%. In contrast, his control sample of 1,526 firms (matched for industry and size) returned 61.86% over the same period. This is a striking finding because the IPOs were much riskier than the comparison stocks, whether or not risk is measured as a single stock variability, or as beta.

For instance, Ritter reports that the beta averaged 1.39 for the first year, 1.24 for the next year, and 1.14 for the third year, showing the IPOs to have high systematic risk. Part of these higher betas probably reflected the industry and size of the firms, since the betas for the matched firms were 1.14, 1.13, and 1.04 respectively. However, the betas for IPOs still appear to be higher than for seasoned firms.

Note the tendency for risk as measured by beta to decline over time. Similar results were reported by Clarkson and Thompson[50] for the United States and by Finn and Higham[51] for Australia. It is unlikely that the economic risk of the business declines as rapidly as the beta does. This reduction in beta reflects a process of seasoning.

Beta is defined as the correlation coefficient of the stock's return with the market's return multiplied by the ratio of the stock's standard deviation to the market's standard deviation. The decline with seasoning of initial public offerings is probably due to a decline over time in the variability of the stock price (instead of a change in its correlation with the market). As a company develops, there is a decline in uncertainty and in divergence of opinion.

The above also shows a conflict with the capital asset pricing model in two ways. The higher beta should cause IPOs to have higher returns than the market, while they actually have lower returns. Also, the capital asset pricing model would predict that these declines in beta with

---

[46] R. L. Stern and Peter Bernstein, "Why New Issues are Lousy Investments," *Forbes* (1985), pp. 152–190.

[47] Hans R. Stoll and Anthony J. Curley, "Small Business and the New Issues Market for Equities," *Journal of Financial and Quantitative Analysis* (1970), pp. 309–322.

[48] Harald Uhlir, "Going Public in the F.R.G.," in R.M.C. Guimaraes, B.G. Kingsman, and S.J. Taylor (eds.), *A Reappraisal of the Efficiency of Financial Markets* (New York: Springer-Verlag, 1988).

[49] Ritter, "The Long-Run Performance of Initial Public Offerings."

[50] Peter M. Clarkson and Rex Thompson, "Empirical Estimates of Beta when Investors Face Estimation Risk," *Journal of Finance* (1990), pp. 431–454.

[51] Frank J. Finn and Ron Higham, "The Performance of Unseasoned New Equity Issues-Cum-Stock Exchange Listings in Australia," *Journal of Banking and Finance* (1988), pp. 333–352.

time would be accompanied by increases in prices. This effect alone would cause initial public offerings to outperform the market, which is the opposite of what is observed.

If the variability in the stock price is interpreted as a measure of the divergence of opinion, the prediction is that the price will decline over time with the variance. This is what is observed. If the underperformance of initial public offerings is due to their divergence of opinion declining over time, we would expect to find the standard deviations of their returns to decline over time. Shah calculates the standard deviation of returns as a function of the days from the start of trading for a large sample of Indian IPOs.[52] He shows that the returns are much more variable for the first few days of trading.

Gao, Mao, and Zhong test the theory that the poor performance of IPOs is due to divergence of opinion in the presence of short selling.[53] They use volatility immediately after the offering as a surrogate for divergence of opinion. They argue that short selling stock immediately after an IPO is unusually hard. They use the 20-day excess volatility (above that of NASDAQ) as a measure of divergence of opinion, and find that the coefficient for excess volatility is statistically significant in both univariate and in a multivariate equation (with other variables that are believed to affect IPO returns). For each 1% increase in excess volatility, their sample underperforms the NASDAQ index by 2.44%, 6.38%, and 9.45% over 1-year, 2-year, and 3-year horizons respectively. Even stronger results were obtained when they used a multivariate procedure to decompose excess volatility into "intrinsic volatility" and "residual volatility." This involved adjusting the volatility estimates for sector, log of issue size, book to market, and leverage. Only the residual volatility is regarded as a surrogate for divergence of opinion. The residual volatility proved to be even more powerful in this formulation.

These results may be a little on the conservative side since issue size, price to book, and underwriter rank (variables controlled for) are probably also correlated with divergence of opinion. As discussed below, the smaller firms tend to be the startup IPOs where (in the absence of a good track record) there is "hope" for the business's future. There is plausibly considerable disagreement about how much "hope" is worth. The issue's price to book ratio is probably also related to the amount of hope. The high price-to-book (at issue) companies are those where investors are paying much for an intangible asset (such as patents, good

---

[52] A. Shah, "The Indian IPO Market: Empirical Facts," working paper, Centre for Monitoring Indian Economy, Bombay, India, 1995.

[53] Yan Gao, Connie X. Mao, and Rui Zhong, "Divergence of Opinion and IPO Long-Term Performance," working paper, May 28, 2003.

will, management, brand names, a good business plan, etc.). There is much more scope for disagreement about the value of these various intangibles than there is about the value of tangible assets (valued at historical cost minus depreciation).

The divergence of opinion (with restricted short selling) theory is capable of explaining not only the long run underperformance of initial public offerings, but also which offerings will underperform the most. Certain IPO characteristics correlate with long-run underperformance. Most appear to be surrogates for the extent of divergence of opinion about a firm's prospects. No other theory seems to be able to predict the extent of underperformance. It explains why the greatest underperformers are those with a short operating history, low sales, low prestige underwriters, low institutional ownership, high volatility, high underpricing at the time of issuance, regional exchange listing, and are in certain industries.

Price and return volatility measure risk and uncertainty, surrogates for the divergence of opinion. One way that divergence of opinion can lead to greater variability is that greater divergence of opinion increases the slope of the demand curve. The steeper the demand curve, the more price fluctuates with random buying and selling. Thus price and return volatility can serve as surrogates for divergence of opinion. Carter, Dark, and Singh have found that the standard deviation, calculated over the first 225 days commencing 6 days after the offer, of 2,292 (1979–1981) IPOs predicts 3-year underperformance.[54]

As the story about new cancer firms suggests, the greatest divergence of opinion should be about a startup firm, with some investors believing the new venture has a bright future, and others seeing it as having a much poorer future. There are other firms that have a long operating history when they go public. These firms may be going public only because the founding families want to diversify. The future profitability of such firms is more easily predicted. There will be less divergence of opinion about the value of such firms. Thus, it is not surprising the IPOs of the youngest firms show the worst performance (Ritter[55] and Fields[56]).

The startup stage firms are likely to be the smallest ones, the ones with the least sales, and the lowest market values. Such firms have been

---

[54] Carter, Dark, and Singh, "Underwriter Reputation, Initial Returns, and the Long-Run Performance of IPO Stocks."

[55] Ritter, "The Long-Run Performance of Initial Public Offerings."

[56] Laura Fields, "Is Institutional Investment in Initial Public Offerings Related to the Long-Run Performance of These Firms?" working paper, University of California Los Angles, 1995.

found to have the worst performance (Loughran and Ritter,[57] Brav and Gompers,[58] and Keloharju[59]).

Simon found that IPOs offered from 1926 to 1933 listed on regional exchanges showed substantial underperformance over 60 months.[60] This was not true for IPOs listed on the New York Stock Exchange. Why did the exchange of listing make a difference? The most likely reason is that the New York Stock Exchange had listing and disclosure requirements, but the regional exchanges did not. These requirements forced the most speculative IPOs off of the New York Stock Exchange and onto regional exchanges. In particular, startup firms with only a short operating history would have been eliminated by the New York Stock Exchange's requirements for historical data. Also, even if the firms were similar before listing, the information disclosed for a New York listing probably reduced the divergence of opinion for these IPOs. The difference in performance with the type of exchange disappeared after the imposition of regulations by the Security and Exchange Commission. Thus, this effect can be explained by restrictions on short selling interacting with divergence of opinion.

Even reputation effects can be explained. Carter, Dark, and Singh[61] and Nanda, Yi, and Yun[62] have shown that initial public offerings underwritten by higher-prestige underwriters have better long-run performance than those underwritten by others. The reason is that the underwriters with better reputations have more to lose from a failed underwriting, and as a result they refrain from underwriting IPOs that they think may fail. In practice, avoiding embarrassment is likely to mean avoiding those companies whose futures are very uncertain with hard to predict returns. Thus, the underwriter's reputation reflects the quality of the available information and the divergence of opinion. Thus, the IPOs underwritten by lower-reputation underwriters would be expected to underperform.

---

[57] Loughran and Ritter, "The New Issues Puzzle."

[58] Brav and Gompers, "Myth or Reality? The Long-Run Underperformance of Initial Public Offerings: Evidence from Venture and Nonventure Capital-Backed Companies."

[59] Matti Keloharju, "The Winner's Curse, Legal Liability, and the Long-Run Price Performance of Initial Public Offerings in Finland," *Journal of Financial Economics* (1993), pp. 251–277.

[60] C. Simon, "The Effect of the 1933 Securities Act on Investor Information and the Performance of New Issues," *American Economic Review* (1989), pp. 295–318.

[61] Carter, Dark, and Singh, "Underwriter Reputation, Initial Returns, and the Long-Run Performance of IPO Stocks."

[62] Vikram K. Nanda, J. Yi, and Y. Yun, "IPO Long-Run Performance and Underwriter Reputation," working paper, University of Michigan, 1995.

Evidence on Divergence of Opinion and Returns

Now look at the evidence on whether high divergence of opinion stocks tend to have lower returns. Here we are looking at the effect of the level of divergence of opinion rather than the effect of changes. The most readily available measure of divergence of opinion has been analysts' forecasts of future earnings. Early studies on the correlation of this measure of divergence of opinion and returns from stocks were mixed, often not supporting the theory. However, as will be seen, more recent studies have supported it.

Cragg and Malkief (the earliest study) collected earnings and growth estimates from both buy- and sell-side firms for 1961 to 1968 with the goal of using expectations data to test asset pricing models.[63] Unlike later work, which focused on the projections of next year's earnings, they focused on the long term (three to five year) growth rate estimates. Since they lacked explicit forecasts of percentage returns, they assumed the expected returns were the five-year growth rate plus the dividend yield. They tried beta and various risk factors suggested by arbitrage pricing theory to explain the differences in expected returns with some success. However, when the variance in growth rate projections was used, it was found to be highly significant and a more powerful variable. The firms the analysts disagreed about the most were found to have the highest estimated returns.

They then tried to explain price-earnings ratios (where earnings were a normalized value), which theory suggests should be explained by the forecasted long-run growth rate, the dividend payout ratio, and a measure of risk. They found that the standard deviation of forecasted growth rates always had a negative sign in explaining price earnings ratios. This led Cragg and Malkiel to conclude: "the variance of analysts' forecast may represent the most effective risk proxy available."[64] They interpreted it as a measure of systematic risk (it seemed to work better than beta), although they conceded it could be interpreted as specific risk. I choose to interpret it as a measure of uncertainty about the estimates and hence risk. Not surprisingly, it appears that investors in the 1960s (preacceptance of the capital asset pricing model and the idea of systematic risk) chose to pay less for stocks about whose future growth had the greatest uncertainty.

---

[63] John Cragg and B. Malkiel, *Expectations and the Structure of Share Prices* (Chicago: University of Chicago Press, 1982).

[64] Cragg and Malkiel, *Expectations and the Structure of Share Prices*, p. 165.

Arnott[65] and Carvell and Stredbel[66] found that stocks with high disagreements among analysts had higher returns in the future. This suggests that the tendency for divergence of opinion to lead to higher prices is not large enough to completely overcome investors' risk aversion.

It is possible that some of these early studies suffered from a bias in studies using the I/B/E/S data discovered by Diether et al.[67] The standard version of this data set tends to understate the dispersion in forecasts for the rapid growing companies that have split their stock. Also, these early studies involved only the largest companies, which later studies showed to have the weakest divergence of opinion effects. Later studies, that had access to analysts' data for more companies have found a divergence of opinion effect in the direction predicted by divergence of opinion theory.

Brennan, Chordia, and Subrahmanyam use stock returns from 1977 to 1989 to investigate the role of dispersion of analysts' opinion (measured by coefficient of variation) on stock returns.[68] In their simplest model, when they controlled for many other variables, they found a statistically significant inverse relation between the analysts' dispersion and returns. An interesting plot (not discussed in their paper) of the cumulative return versus dispersion shows the effect was strong and negative from 1979 to 1983, but that there was little effect for the rest of the period. Because they estimate a number of other models (critiqued by Haugen), they chose to interpret their data as that the dispersion of analysts' opinions lacks a significant effect.[69]

In contrast, Jacobs, Starer, and Levy reported a statistically significant negative relationship between returns and analysts' disagreement in earnings forecasts for the 11 non-January months of the year and a statistically significant positive relationship for January.[70] Controlling for

---

[65] R. Arnott, "What Hath MPT Wrought: Which Risks Reap Rewards," *Journal of Portfolio Management* (Fall 1983), pp. 5–11.
[66] S. Carvell and P. Strebel, "A New Beta Incorporating Analysts' Forecasts," *Journal of Portfolio Management* (Fall 1984), pp. 81–85.
[67] Karl B. Diether, Christopher J. Malloy, and Anna Scherbina, "Differences of Opinion and the Cross Section of Stock Returns," *Journal of Finance* (October 2002), pp. 2113–2141.
[68] M. Brennan, T. Chordia, and A. Subrahmanyam, "Cross-Sectional Determinants of Expected Returns," working paper, University of California Los Angeles, October 2, 1998.
[69] Chapter 13 in Robert A. Haugen, *The Inefficient Stock Market: What Pays Off and Why*, 2nd ed. (Upper Saddle River, NJ: Prentice Hall, 2001).
[70] Bruce I. Jacobs, David Starer, and Kenneth N. Levy, "Long-Short Portfolio Management: An Integrated Approach," *Journal of Portfolio Management* (Winter 1999), pp. 23–32.

other measures of risk with a multiple variable model, the correlations were not statistically significant.

Barry and Gultekin, using data from 1976 to 1985, also found a measure of analysts' diversion of opinion—the coefficient of variation in estimates divided by the square root of the number of analysts—that produced positive return in January, but negative returns in other months.[71] Since Tinic and West reported high return in January for high beta stocks, and Barry and Gultekin report that high dispersion of opinion stocks are high beta, the high returns in January may indicate that for January the risk surrogate effect of the divergence of opinion measure dominates.[72] Unfortunately, more recent researchers have not analyzed their data by month.

Because analysts normally prepare earnings estimates only for large companies of institutional interest, and estimates from several analysts are needed to measure the analysts' dispersion of opinion, the correlations calculated in the above studies are related only to the small fraction of all companies that are well researched by institutional analysts.

Han and Manry provide a powerful demonstration of how dispersion of opinion leads to lower returns.[73] For 1977–1990 they calculated the dispersion of analysts' forecasts of earnings (divided by stock price to put them on the same scale) for the coming fiscal year. These were divided into ten deciles. The returns in excess of the average returns for the size decile that the firm was a member of (an attempt to eliminate the effect of firm size on returns and to eliminate the price movements during this time) were calculated. These returns were then accumulated and plotted for the next 100 weeks for each decile. It appears that the abnormal returns were largest for the firms about which there was the least divergence of opinion. The top decile (lowest dispersion of opinion) had a 2-year cumulative excess return of 9.13% (significant at the 0.001 level). In contrast, the decile with the greatest dispersion of opinion had an excess return of 4.37% over the two years. This is a 13.5% difference. The graph of the results showed that the difference in return appeared to be still growing at the end of 100 weeks.

---

[71] Christopher B. Barry and Mustafa N. Gultekin, "Differences of Opinion and Neglect: Additional Effects on Risk and Return," in John B. Guerard, and Mustafa N. Gultekin (eds.), *Handbook of Security Analyst Forecasting and Asset Allocation* (Greenwich, CT: JAI Press Inc., 1992).

[72] Seha M. Tinic and Richard R. West, "Risk and Return: January and the Rest of the Year," *Journal of Financial Economics* (1984), pp. 561–574.

[73] B. H. Han and David Manry, "The Implication of Dispersion in Analysts' Earnings Forecasts for Future ROE and Future Returns," *Journal of Business Finance & Accounting* (January/March 2000), pp. 99–126.

Han and Manry state that results were similar when cumulative returns were computed after controlling for beta (both historical and future, size, and book-to-market ratio). In all cases, they report that a highly significant negative association between dispersion and future returns was found. This is a striking result since dispersion of opinion is a surrogate for risk, and one might have expected the riskiest stocks to have the highest returns.

Besides conventional risk, dispersion of analysts' opinions measures a type of risk to an institutional manager's career. If a stock is bought about which analysts disagree strongly about future earnings, it is very likely that at least one analyst's report advised avoiding the stock. If the stock turns out badly, someone can point to that analyst's report (or the data and arguments used) to say that it was obvious that this stock should not be bought. If the manager buys a stock that the analysts agree on, there is less likely to be ammunition for his opponents to critique his decision. Instead, he will be able to argue that any earnings disappointments (a very common cause for poor price performance) were something that could not have been anticipated, since no one did anticipate them. If institutional investors and investment advisors are avoiding a stock for the above reason of career safety, it would be expected that the price would have to be sufficiently lower so that other investors were attracted by the probability of higher returns.

Han and Manry also ran a regression in which cumulative abnormal returns were explained by the log of the dispersion of analysts' opinions, the log of size, and beta (estimated with future data). The log of the dispersion of analysts' opinions was still negative and statistically significant at the 0.001 level. Essentially the same result was obtained when the log of size was replaced by the log of the number of analysts (which is sufficiently correlated to size that they did not wish to include both in one statistic). They report (in a footnote) that results were qualitatively similar when controlling for return on equity and the book-to-market ratio.

A very interesting finding comes from the Zacks organization.[74] They studied 3,300 companies with analysts' estimates for October 1987 to September 2002 (excluding those not expected to show a profit). Then they calculated an earnings uncertainty measure by dividing the standard deviation of analyst's earnings estimates for the coming fiscal year by the average earnings estimate. The stocks were divided into five portfolios. The average returns (which correspond to an equally weighted portfolio rebalanced monthly) ranged from 5.6% for the fifth of stocks that had the highest uncertainty to 14.3% for the

---

[74] Mitch Zacks, *Ahead of the Market* (New York: Harper Business, 2003), p. 235.

stocks with the lowest uncertainty (with the remaining quintiles having averages of 11.9%, 12.3%, and 9.9% in order of increasing uncertainty). Since the stocks with the greatest divergence of opinion are likely to be those with the highest risk, standard theory would suggest they would have higher returns rather than lower returns, yet the lower returns are actually found.

The Zacks organization made an interesting finding.[75] The approximately 10% of the 3,300 stocks that were projected to have losses for the coming fiscal year had an average return of −9.8%, while the other stocks (expected to be profitable) had an average return of 11.1% (an equally weighted average of all stocks for October 1998 to September 2002 earned 9.0%). Since companies that fail to earn profits for a series of years go bankrupt, typically making the stock worthless, the companies that are projected to lose money in the next year would appear to be unusually risky. Thus standard theory would predict that these stocks of risky, money losing companies would have above average returns However, the opposite happened. The theory presented in this chapter can explain what is happening. Those who are most optimistic about a stock are likely to be those who think a company's problems are only temporary (which may or may not be true). They are the ones who set the price, and on average, they are too optimistic.

A contributing factor comes from behavioral finance where it has been noticed that many investors are reluctant to sell at a loss. The reason for this is that selling at a loss forces one to admit to oneself that a mistake has been made (and maybe to admit to a boss or client). Much better for self esteem (and possibly for job protection) is to come up with a list of reasons why the stock is still a good buy. With the many losing investors unwilling to sell, the effective supply on the market is reduced, and it does not take as much buying from the optimistic investors to maintain the price.

A recent and important paper is by Diether, Malloy, and Scherbina.[76] Using data from January 1983 to November 2000 and measuring divergence of opinion by the coefficient of variation of analysts' forecasts, they divided stocks into five quintiles and then calculated returns for the next month. Returns decreased monotonically from 1.48% per month for those with low divergence of opinion to 0.69% per month for those with the highest divergence of opinion. To see if the effect was somehow related to size, stocks were classified into five size quintiles and the experiment repeated. In all size quintiles, firms with

---

[75] Zacks, *Ahead of the Market*, p. 88.
[76] Diether, Malloy, and Scherbina, "Differences of Opinion and the Cross Section of Stock Returns."

the highest dispersion of opinion had lower average returns than the firms with the lowest dispersion of opinion. For the three smallest quintiles, the decline was monotonic with the difference between those with the greatest and the least dispersion statistically significant. Especially striking were the results for the smallest quintile, where there was a monotonic decline in monthly returns from 1.52% per month (the highest of any of the 25 size and dispersion of analysts' forecasts cells) to 0.14% per month for the firms with the greatest dispersion of analysts' forecasts. The authors note this is an enormous 16.4% per year difference depending on dispersion.

To be sure, results were not influenced by the value-growth stock choice, stocks were classified in three book-to-market groups and then into three size groups within each category. Finally, there were three dispersion groups within each of the other nine groups. In all nine categories, there was a monotonic tendency for the mean return to drop as the dispersion increased. The dispersion effect appeared greater in the value stocks (high and medium book-to-market) than in the growth stocks, as well as in the small stocks in all book-to-market groups.

Another 9-way sort was done by momentum categories based on returns from 12 months earlier to 2 months earlier (i.e., winners versus losers), then by size, and finally by dispersion. Dispersion effects were not statistically significant among the winner portfolios. They were in the predicted direction among the loser portfolios and among those that were in neither the winner nor loser categories. The differences between low-dispersion and high-dispersion portfolios showed a statistically significant advantage for the low-dispersion portfolios in the small capitalization category within the loser category and in the neither loser nor winner categories. Thus the dispersion effect is not just a surrogate for the momentum effect (high-momentum stocks had previously been shown to outperform). Dispersion seemed especially powerful among the loser groups, possibly due to the large difference in dispersion within that group. The optimists and the pessimists appear to differ greatly among this group of stocks, possibly because some analysts were much quicker than others to recognize negative developments (or to view them as permanent rather than as temporary).

Tests were also run in a regression format to see if a 3-factor model (market, smallness, and book-to-market) explained the returns on equal-weighted portfolios formed on the basis of dispersion. This model left an unexplained negative residual for the portfolio of stocks with the highest dispersion. Similar results were obtained for a 4-factor model with the above factors plus momentum.

Dispersion of opinion was found to have a significant correlation with a number of risk measures including beta, the standard deviation of return, and the standard deviation of earnings per share. Thus, financial theory (where investors avoid risky stocks) would suggest that high divergence of opinion stocks would have to have higher returns to compensate for their higher risk. That instead they had lower returns, suggests that the winner's curse effect resulting from high divergence of opinion is strong enough to overpower the risk effects.

When turnover (which is correlated with dispersion of opinion) is included in a regression equation along with dispersion of opinion, the divergence of opinion was statistically significant while turnover was not.

Investors who are planning to use dispersion of analysts' forecasts in investing (the rule is to avoid stocks with a high divergence of opinion) should worry about the possibility that their data is stale. Examining the returns for different time periods from the formation of the portfolios showed that the abnormal returns declined over time. After five months the advantage of the lowest dispersion portfolios over the highest dispersion firms was no longer statistically significant. Experiments with different holding periods showed that the longer the holding period, the smaller the excess profits (before transactions costs). The dispersion of 2-year forecasts of earnings showed similar results to those using the dispersions of 1-year forecasts, although the effect was not as strong.

Diether et al. report important time differences. The divergence of opinion return difference was significant for all size quintiles for the period from 1983 to 1991. For 1992 to 2000 it was significant only for the smallest size quintile. They attribute this to several causes, including a reduction in obstacles to short selling.

One of the implications of dispersion of opinion theory is that any overpricing will be eliminated when the uncertainty is resolved. For the smaller stocks, Scherbina showed that between 11% and 33% of the return differential between low- and high-dispersion stocks falls in a 3-day window around the earnings announcement dates.[77] She classified stocks into five size quintiles and three analysts' forecast dispersion groups. In the high-dispersion third, the smallest of the five size quintiles has statistically significant abnormal returns for the three days around the announcement of earnings. In the middle-dispersion group, the smallest quintile has statistically significant negative abnormal returns. It appears, as predicted by theory, that the resolution of uncertainty lowers price as the average valuation of the optimists is reduced.

---

[77] Anna Scherbina, "Stock Price and Differences of Opinion: Empirical Evidence that Prices Reflect Optimism," working paper, Northwestern University, April 2001.

Scherbina later expanded on the idea that analysts with poor forecasts for earnings simply stop coverage rather than put out bad news.[78] She presents empirical evidence that this happens. The average earnings surprise (reported quarterly earnings minus average of the analysts' estimates) is negative and correlated with the dispersion of opinion. She estimates a measure of bias in earnings for the case where the number of analysts following a stock declines by assuming they would have estimated earnings one cent lower than the lowest estimate. This estimate of bias turns out to highly significant in predicting the earnings surprise. As in previous studies, the earnings surprise is related to the past quarter revision in earnings forecasts (i.e., analysts do not adjust their estimates as much as they should, probably to minimize sharp changes). High market equity-to-book equity (i.e., a measure of growth stocks status) predicts negative earnings surprise. This means that the analysts overestimated earnings for growth stocks to a larger degree.

When examining the abnormal earnings around the announcements of earnings (i.e., whether they did better than the average stock during the three days around the announcement), she showed that when used in isolation, dispersion of earnings had a statistically significant negative effect. This meant that stocks with a high dispersion of opinion about earnings tended to decline in price when the earnings were announced, presumably because the announcement reduced some of the dispersion of opinion. As might be expected from the above finding that analysts do not adequately adjust their estimates, the previous quarter's revision has a powerful effect on the abnormal returns. If analysts have been revising returns upwards, the abnormal returns will be larger.

Interestingly, when this variable is in the equation the measure of dispersion of opinion remains negative, but it is no longer statistically significant. This indicates a possible statistical problem. Since analysts revise their estimates at different times, when there is a trend in analysts estimates (presumably because new information is coming out), the dispersion in analysts' opinions may be related to the (absolute) value of this trend. Thus, on the positive side, for revisions, the two could be correlated for statistical reasons. On the negative side, there could be some additional negative correlation.

Scherbina shows that an estimate of the effect of the missing analysts' forecasts is statistically significant in predicting abnormal returns when used alone, but its effect becomes insignificant when the last quarter's revisions are included.

---

[78] Anna Scherbina, "Analysts Disagreement, Forecast Bias and Stock Returns," working paper, Harvard University, September 2003.

Ackert and Athanassakos had earlier found that the bias in analysts' forecasts increases with the dispersion in earlier analysts' forecast for 1980–1991.[79] Their explanation is that analysts are under pressure to be optimistic (for instance to win favor with companies and potential investment banking clients). The greater the uncertainty about the prospects for the company's earnings, the easier it is for them to be optimistic without risking too much embarrassment. Assuming that investors base investment decisions equally on all analysts (or on the mean of their opinions), stocks with optimistic earnings estimates (relative to what will actually happen) will perform worse. They test this by calculating the standard deviation of analysts' estimates of earnings (apparently not standardized). After grouping firms into quartiles they find that the quartile with the lowest dispersion of estimates outperforms the quartile with the highest dispersion of estimates by the equivalent of 11.35% per year. The effect is slightly less at 10.16% when adjusted for beta, indicating the high dispersion of opinion stocks are higher beta ones. These results are similar to those obtained from dispersion of opinion theory combined with restrictions on short selling.

It should be noted, however, that they do have an alternative theory to explain the inverse correlation between divergence of opinion and future returns. In their model, the underperformance results from uncertainty (measured by the standard deviation of analysts' estimates) which permits analysts to produce biased earnings estimates that then affect investor behavior. The work of Scherbina supports part of this model showing that there is a price decline around the earnings announcement that increases with the divergence of opinion.[80] This would logically be expected to be accompanied by increasing divergence of opinion in the period until the next announcement. By using a 60-day window following the announcement to calculate drift, they exclude the informational content of the earnings announcements. Thus, though appearing to interpret their work as supporting Varian rather than Miller, their work is compatible with both theories. Empirical work on the effect of divergence of opinion should include both the earnings around earning announcements and the period between announcements.

Boehme, Danielson, and Sorescu, using data from January 1988 to July 1999, examined the effect of short sale constraints and divergence of opinion on returns.[81] The data sample was composed of all firms for

[79] Lucy F. Ackert and George Athanassakos, "Prior Uncertainty, Analyst Bias, and Subsequent Abnormal Returns," *Journal of Financial Research* (Summer 1997), pp. 283–273.

[80] Scherbina, "Stock Price and Differences of Opinion: Empirical Evidence that Prices Reflect Optimism," cited in Diether et al.

[81] Boehme, Danielson, and Sorescu, "Short Sale Constraints and Overvaluation."

which short interest data were available in electronic form, which meant using New York Stock Exchange data from 1988 and NASDAQ data from 1993. Their measure of short sales constraints was the relative short interest (the monthly short interest divided by the number of shares outstanding). They rely on research by D'Avolio to support this.[82] He showed that the costs of shorting stock (except for the least shorted stocks) rose with the short interest. Boehme et al. noted that using analysts' earnings estimates to estimate divergence of opinion excluded the smallest firms, which were the ones where short constraints were the most likely to be binding and divergence of opinion effects the strongest. Thus they chose to use volatility and turnover as measures of divergence of opinion.

Two proxies for divergence of opinion were used. One was the standard deviation of error terms from a market model estimated over the previous 100 days. They justify this by reference to theoretical models correlating belief dispersion with asset time-series volatility. They quote the Peterson and Peterson evidence of a positive relationship between return volatility and the dispersion of I/B/E/S forecasts.[83] As described above, there are other studies that show a positive correlation between return volatility and the dispersion of analysts' forecasts.

Using volatility as a surrogate for divergence of opinion in testing the Miller prediction that, all things equal, dispersion of opinion raises stock prices and lowers returns, puts the Miller hypothesis at a disadvantage. This is because volatility is a direct measure of risk, and risk is generally regarded as undesirable and something that investors will avoid. As described below, divergence of opinion creates a situation in which nonsystematic risk should be priced.

The other proxy used for divergence of opinion is turnover (trading volume over a 100-day period divided by number of shares outstanding). The argument is apparently that most trading consists of one who is relatively optimistic about a security selling to one who is more pessimistic, and thus the extent of turnover proxies for divergence of opinion.

They do not use analysts' divergence of opinion about earnings. One argument is that it is available only for the larger firms, and in their study they wanted to include smaller firms, firms too small to have opinions available on them. The two proxies for divergence of opinion used, turnover and standard deviation of error terms from a market model, can be calculated for all firms, including the smallest.

---

[82] Gene D'Avolio, "The Market for Borrowing Stock," *Journal of Financial Economics* (2002), pp. 271–306.

[83] P. P. Peterson and D. R. Peterson, "Divergence of Opinion and Return," *Journal of Financial Research* (1982), pp. 125–134.

Their basic methodology was to calculate monthly deviations in returns from a four factor model in which three of the factors were those used by Fama and French, plus a momentum factor.[84] The three Fama and French factors reflected the influence of the market (i.e., the traditional return to beta), the return to small size, and the return to high versus low book-to-market stocks. The momentum factor was suggested by Carhart,[85] and supported by evidence[86] that this addition was needed to the Fama-French model. This is a relatively stringent test. These four factors are given the first chance to explain returns, and to the extent these factors are related to either constraints on short selling or divergence of opinion, the measured effect of the variables of interest are reduced.

The abnormal returns relative to the four-factor model were calculated resulting in 555,436 observations. For each month the stocks in the database (i.e., those with short interest data) were sorted into 64 mutually exclusive portfolios with four size categories, four categories of relative short interest, and four categories of a surrogate for divergence of opinion (volatility or turnover). Each of these 64 categories constituted a separate portfolio. Statistically significant negative abnormal returns were interpreted as evidence of overvaluation. As predicted, the most overvalued portfolios were those that were expensive to short (small size and being in the highest quartile of relative short interest) and possessed high (in the highest quartile) dispersion of investor beliefs, whether measured by volatility or turnover.

The statistically significant effects were focused on firms outside of the quartile of the largest stocks. Firms in these categories were then combined into one portfolio for further tests. The reported results used volatility as the measure of divergence of opinion. The returns to these portfolios were abnormally negative (relative to the four-factor model) and statistically significant. For a one year horizon, the portfolios underperformed by monthly amounts equivalent to between 10.4% and 19.6%. For a one-month holding period the abnormal return was equivalent to −26.9% annually. For the practical investor, this procedure seems able to identify stocks that should be avoided, and possibly even sold short.

---

[84] Eugene Fama and Kenneth French, "Common Risk Factors in Returns on Stocks and Bonds," *Journal of Financial Economics* (1993), pp. 3–56.
[85] Mark Carhart, "On the Persistence in Mutual Fund Performance," *Journal of Finance* (1997), pp. 57–82.
[86] Eugene Fama and Kenneth French, "Multifactor Explanations of Asset Pricing Anomalies," *Journal of Finance* (May 1996), pp. 55–84

Further work showed that the effect required both high short interest and high dispersion of opinion as theory predicted. Both high relative short interest and high volatility are relatively poor predictors of overvaluation, but are powerful when combined.

The authors also show the results for the raw returns. The point estimates showed the returns to be negative over a one-month period, and to be less than the risk-free rate over a one-year period. These return differences were statistically significant when compared to a portfolio with high short sales constraints, and low volatility over one-month and one-year periods. They were also significant when compared with a portfolio with both low short sales constraints and low dispersion of investors' beliefs. Over one month this desirable value weighted portfolio earned 1.07%, while the short sale constrained, high diversity portfolio lost 1.38%. This is an economically significant difference.

While Boehme et al. interpreted turnover (volume divided by number of shares) as a measure of diversion of opinion and found that it lowered return for many classes of firms, there is another study that reached what appears to be a different conclusion.[87] Garfinkel and Sokobin argued that volume could be used as a measure of divergence of opinion.[88] In particular, they devise two measures of abnormal turnover around earnings announcements, which they plausibly argue measures divergence of opinion. They then examine the earnings drift after the announcement of earnings. Earlier research had established that there was a tendency for stocks experiencing unexpected earnings increases or decreases to continue moving in the same direction, an effect that is called "drift." They were curious how this drift was affected by divergence of opinion as measured by abnormal volume. Their result was that abnormal volume was accompanied by positive drift, and that the higher the abnormal volume the more positive the drift. They interpreted this as consistent with Varian's work that interpreted divergence of opinion as a measure of risk, which should be rewarded by a higher rate of return.[89] Clearly that is possible, and it is indeed plausible that the higher divergence of opinion stocks are indeed riskier.

However, there is another interpretation in terms of Miller's theory that divergence of opinion in the presence of short selling can raise prices.[90] In the short and medium run, that theory predicts that rising divergence of opinion should raise prices, and falling divergence of

[87] Boehme, Danielson, and Sorescu, "Short Sale Constraints and Overvaluation."

[88] John A. Garfinkel and Jonathan Sokobin, "Volume, Opinion Divergence and Returns: A Study of Post-Earnings Announcement Drift," working paper, August 2003.

[89] Varian, "Divergence of Opinion in Complete Markets: A Note."

[90] Miller, "Risk, Uncertainty, and Divergence of Opinion."

opinion should lower them, all things equal. Consider a stock where most of the relevant information about its value comes every quarter when the earnings (along with an income and balance sheet statement and management commentary) are released. This is believed to be plausible, especially for smaller companies. Of course, there is some other information (general economic data, etc.), and there is considerable uncertainty about just what future earnings will be. It is to be expected that there will be divergence of opinion about the value of this company and about future earnings. Each time earnings are announced some of this uncertainty is resolved, but there are always new events occurring that different investors interpret differently. Thus, we would expect that the divergence of opinion about the value of this stock would decline at the time of each earnings announcement and then gradually increase (as hard to interpret information became available). Prices should decline when earnings come out and then drift upwards. The greater the divergences of opinion, the greater this drift. The prediction of divergence of opinion theory is thus supported by this paper.

Since the period from earnings announcement to earnings announcement averaged 90-plus days, the 60-day window of Garfinkel and Sokobin excludes the period immediately before a new earnings announcement. Other studies show that prices typically react before the announcement of earnings, and that such movements are in the direction of the unexpected component of the coming earnings announcement.[91] This is probably due to some combination of inside information leaking out and investors reacting to such information as other firms publishing quarterly and annual statements before the firm in question.

Ideally, one paper would study the effect of divergence of opinion on returns over a period, and then break that down into the effect when earnings were announced, during the period between announcements, and just before announcements. Such a paper would combine the work of Garfinkel and Sokobin with that of Scherbina.[92] While it is intellectually interesting to break returns down into the earnings announcement reaction, a drift period, and a prenew announcement period, most investors will hold their positions for a long enough period to include all three periods. However, even if transaction costs prevent investors from planning to buy and sell within one period, having a little knowledge of

---

[91] Richard J. Rendleman, Jr., Charles P. Jones, and Henry A. Latane, "Empirical Anomalies Based on Unexpected Earnings and the Importance of Risk Adjustment," *Journal of Financial Economics* (1982), pp. 269–287.

[92] See both Scherbina, "Stock Price and Differences of Opinion: Empirical Evidence that Prices Reflect Optimism;" and Scherbina, "Analysts Disagreement, Forecast Bias and Stock Returns."

returns over the next few days may help in timing transactions that would be made in any case. Such knowledge might help investors decide whether to trade before or after the next announcement, the details of which they cannot anticipate.

It might be nice to control for the availability of nonearnings information. One surrogate might be how early in the earnings season earnings were announced (frequently a guess can be made at earnings from knowing what was announced by other firms in the industry). Another might be whether the firm was in an industry where there were monthly or weekly announcements of industry sales. A third might be whether there were frequently warnings or other announcements given (obviously this study would be more labor intensive).

In an appendix, Garfinkel and Sokobin report that they found the tendency reported by others for stocks with high analysts' divergence of estimates to have lower returns, and that their abnormal volume measures worked best for stocks without analysts forecasts (which tended to be smaller companies).

In considering the wisdom of avoiding stocks with high volatility, it should be recalled that volatility is usually considered an aspect of risk and hence something to be avoid. In spite of the finance theory holding that there is tradeoff between risk and return, it appears that there is a strategy that is both higher return and lower risk, buying stocks with low dispersion of beliefs.

The measure of volatility used (interpreted as a measure of divergence of opinion) was the residual from a market model. Thus, it measures what financial theorists call diversifiable (or nonsystematic risk). In theory such risk should not affect returns because investors can and have diversified it away. In practice, most institutional investors may be diversified enough to have diversified away most of this risk. Even this conclusion presumes that the institutions have not exposed themselves to a type of nonsystematic risk which has not been diversified away (such as a heavy emphasis on growth stocks or those exposed to another factor).

Many individual investors are very poorly diversified, holding only a few individual issues. They are very definitely exposed to this volatility risk. For them, avoiding high dispersion of opinion stocks should both increase return and lower risk.

Boehme, Danielson, and Sorescu did a second study.[93] The data ended in July 2000, slightly later than in their other study. The major

---

[93] See both, Rodney D. Boehme, Bartley R. Danielson, and Sorin M. Sorescu, "The Valuation Effects of Dispersion of Opinion: Premium and Discount," working paper, February 20, 2003, presented at FMA in October, 2003; and Boehme, Danielson, and Sorescu, "Short Sale Constraints and Overvaluation."

addition is considering the effect of options. As discussed above, Danielson and Sorescu had earlier shown that options served to make short sales constraints less binding.[94] In this study they added the availability of options as an additional indicator of whether the short sales constraint was binding.

They contrast the effects of divergence of opinion in the model of Miller where there are short sale constraints with the models of Merton and Varian, which they interpret as predicting that prices will be lower and returns higher in the presence of divergence of opinion. In Merton's model investors only invest in securities they are familiar with, and thus hold nondiversified portfolios.[95] Thus, investors demand compensation for nonsystematic risk in their securities. In a market without obstacles to short selling, this results in higher returns for the high divergence of opinion stocks. Varian concluded that for plausible parameters of risk aversion that dispersion of opinion should lower asset prices in a complete market.[96] Presumably, the effects he considered could outweigh the effects of restrictions of short selling.

Boehme et al. argue that the hypotheses of Merton, Varian, and Miller should be regarded as complementary. They argue that stocks differ in both the degree of divergence of opinion, and in the severity of their short sale constraints, and that the relative strength of the effects should depend on the stocks. They argue that for stocks with a high dispersion of opinion, the Miller effect should dominate where there are strong constraints on short selling and the Merton-Varian ones where short selling is relatively unconstrained. As an indicator of the strength of short sale constraints they use size, the presence of options, and relative short interest (the percentage of a firm's shares that are short). It is argued that the costs of borrowing the stocks to deliver in a short sale rises as the number of shares borrowed increases. Thus, the level of short interest is viewed as an appropriate proxy for the marginal cost of shorting a security. The stocks of large firms are viewed as easier to borrow because there is more stock available. If options on a stock are available, trading these (especially puts) provides an indirect equivalent to a short sale without borrowing the stock. Because of the way the option markets work, the result of a negative bet in the options market is often that an option dealer sells the stock short, but these dealers can

---

[94] Bartley R. Danielson and Sorin M. Sorescu, "Why Do Option Introductions Depress Stock Prices? A Study of Diminishing Short-Sale Constraints," *Journal of Financial and Quantitative Analysis* (December 2001), pp. 451–484.
[95] Merton, "A Simple Model of Capital Market Equilibrium with Incomplete Information."
[96] Varian, "Divergence of Opinion in Complete Markets: A Note."

do this more cheaply than other investors. Thus, short selling is less constrained for stocks with options.

One of the interesting results was that relative short interest helped predict returns. The higher the relative short interest, the lower the returns. When returns are expressed as deviations from the predictions of the four factor model, it was found that the quartile of firms with the highest relative short interest had statistically significant lower returns (by 0.394% per month) and the quartile with the lowest relative short interest had statistically higher than average returns (by 0.273% per month). These are large enough differences to be useful to investors. Because even the most heavily shorted stocks had positive returns, individual short sellers who typically do not get use of the proceeds, would lose money by shorting the most heavily shorted stocks. However, investors could improve their returns by being long in the stocks with the lowest relative short interest. These results are similar to those found by other studies using short interest figures. The authors state that the negative abnormal returns for highly shorted firms are driven by the highly negative returns among these stocks with high divergence of opinion.

Although these authors interpret high short interest as evidence for relatively high costs to shorting, it can also be interpreted as direct evidence for divergence of opinion. Because of the costs of shorting, including the failure to get a market rate of the proceeds of short sales, only investors who expect the returns on a stock to be much lower than normal will short the stock. In fact, short sellers (except for those involved in some type of hedge) are typically selling short stocks that they expect to actually decline in price. As the divergence of opinion about the returns from a stock increases, the fraction of the investors who expect negative returns (or returns below any other low level) increases. Thus, the relative short interest is also a surrogate for divergence of opinion.

In their main tests, the authors attempt to identify a set of stocks which are relatively short sale constrained. These are the stocks with no options (which make them likely to be among the smaller capitalization stocks) and are also among the quartile of firms with the highest relative short interests. They also identified a set of relatively short interest unconstrained stocks. These were the companies with options traded which were also in the highest quartile for capitalization. All other firms were in an unconstrained class. The reader may immediately note that the sizes of the highly constrained (primarily small firms) and the unconstrained firms (large firms) are quite different. If absolute returns were being studied, this might be a problem since a size effect could be confused with a short sales constraint-related effect. However, since the primary measure of returns was the deviation from the returns predicted by a 4-factor model (one of which factors was size), this appears to be less of a problem.

Using volatility (standard deviation of the residuals from a market model for the last 100 days) as a measure of divergence of opinion, the abnormal returns (relative to a 4-factor model) were then calculated. For the unconstrained set of firms, the returns increased with the volatility surrogate for divergence of opinion. They interpret this as being consistent with the prediction of the Merton-Varian theory. The simplest interpretation is that volatile firms are riskier, and the investors will only hold them if they get a higher return. This higher return is estimated at about 1% per month for the quartile of the most volatile firms. This is an important effect because most of the market value is in these relatively large firms.

Logically, the presence of a reward to risk does not disprove that the prices are still not being set by the most optimistic investors, with the less optimistic investors holdings being at zero rather than the negative value a strict Markowitz optimization would imply. Remember these firms are in the least short sold group, which may imply that many holders simply choose not to sell short.

Another factor is that these are likely to be relatively large firms in which a significant fraction of institutional investors have taken a position. Working from the extreme right hand of the bell curve, one has to go further toward the average opinion to find sufficient investors to absorb the supply of stock. This would make the price-raising effect of divergence of opinion weaker (but not nonexistent) with a correspondingly small return lowering effect.

One other possibility is that during the period in question (1992–July 2000 for NASDAQ, 1988–July 2000 for the NYSE) unusually volatile large capitalization stocks with options is a category that would pick up many of the large capitalization growth stocks that were doing very well during this period. Possibly the results would be different if the sample had been extended on either side. However, since the abnormal return was measured relative to the predictions of a multifactor model, including factors designed to control for growth versus value and size, this is less of a concern.

The results for the highly short sale constrained firms were found to be consistent with Miller's divergence-of-opinion theory. As the divergence of opinion increased the return declined. The short constrained firms with high divergence of opinion underperformed by 140 basis points per month. As Boehme et al. point out, this is a striking confirmation of Miller's predictions. Although they do not point it out, since volatility is usually considered a risk measure, to get such abnormally low returns, the divergence of opinion effects must overwhelm a strong risk effect. If potential investors note the high volatility (which can be calculated from publicly available information and probably approximated from observing a chart of the stock), they are likely to regard the stock as highly risky. They will be willing to invest in it only if they expect a high enough return to compensate them for this risk. For them not only to fail to earn the required risk premium, but to actually underperform the market by this much, is a striking effect.

The firms that were in neither the highly constrained nor in the unconstrained group show no significant effect of the volatility surrogate for divergence of opinion.

The results reported above were for a 1-year holding period. For a 1-month holding period, the highly constrained portfolio had abnormal returns that were even more negative. The results also held for months 2 through 12. This shows that even with some lag in getting the data, the effect would be useful for investment purposes.

Similar results were obtained with turnover (volume divided by number of shares outstanding) as the measure of divergence of opinion. Several authors (Harris and Raviv[97] and Varian[98]) have presented models in which difference of opinion leads to more trading. For their short-sale-unconstrained portfolio, the difference between the fourth and first quartiles with regard to turnover was statistically significant at the 10% level, with the higher turnover firms showing the higher returns. Because high turnover firms are regarded as more liquid, and the effect is in the opposite direction, it is apparently not due to a liquidity effect (investors should be expected to accept a little lower expected return in exchange for greater liquidity).

When they turned to the highly short-sale-constrained stocks, the results were more striking. The high divergence-of-opinion stocks had the lower returns. The return on a hedge portfolio (difference between the high divergence of opinion and the low divergence quartiles) of –0.45% per month was statistically significant at the 5% level. This led the authors to conclude "there is relatively unambiguous evidence of the Miller hypothesis."

Since high short interest can also be interpreted as evidence of high divergence of opinion, it should be noted that the very low abnormal returns earned by the portfolios with stocks that were classified as highly constrained (no options, high short interest) and above average (top two quartiles) in either volatility or turnover can be interpreted as support for the effect of divergence of opinion. These often have t statis-

---

[97] Milton Harris and Artur Raviv, "Differences of Option Make a Horse Race," *The Review of Financial Studies* (1993), pp. 473–506.
[98] Varian, "Differences of Opinion in Financial Markets."

tics as high as 6. These are clearly the types of stocks to avoid, or even sell short if some use of the proceeds are received, or it is part of a hedge. For instance, the combination of highly short-sale-constrained stocks and fourth quartile for turnover had an abnormal return (relative to a four-factor prediction) of –1% per month and a t statistic of –6.93.

The Qu, Starks, and Yan Model

Qu, Starks, and Yun have devised a simple model in which divergence of opinion leads to volatility even in the absence of restrictions on short selling (and presumably the same effect occurs where there are restrictions), but only if the precision of estimates differ.[99] Investors are presumed to make their initial investment decisions based on their own estimates of returns. After investors place their orders, the market aggregates them and a new price is determined. Investors realize other investors may have information or expertise they lack. Hence, when an investor sees the new market price, he (or she) adjusts his own estimates to reflect it. This changes his desired holding of the security and the prices. The result is there is more volatility in the stocks with greater divergence of opinion.

In the extreme case, where everyone agreed, the start of trading would reveal no information. No one would be forced to change opinions, and the price would not change. In the case where one group of investors holds to their opinion more strongly (higher precision), they change their demand curves relatively little when they see the trading of others. The group with less confidence in their estimates changes their willingness to pay when they see others who they presume to know more, and this feedback makes the prices more volatile.

As a simple example, suppose you know little about a company and believe the price should be 20 times the earnings. If everyone agrees on this reasoning and the inputs (say, historical earnings), they all arrive at the same estimate of value and no volatility is created.

Now suppose there is a smaller group that has a different estimate (say a higher one), and these are believed to have information you lack. Their estimates are much higher than yours and similar investors'. They do not reveal their estimates before trading (to prevent you from trading on them). However, their very act of buying reveals information. You, knowing your estimates do not reflect what they know (or can figure out), adjust your estimates to incorporate the probability they are right. This makes you willing to pay more (or buy more). This induces additional buying from you. All things being equal, this would cause the price to rise.

---

[99] Shiseng Qu, Laura Starks, and Hong Yan, "Risk, Dispersion of Analysts Forecasts and Stock Returns," working paper, University of Texas, September 30, 2003. Presented at the FMA meeting in 2003.

However, the other group of investors is also adjusting their estimates to reflect what they learned about your willingness to pay (and hence the information you have). Because your estimates are lower than theirs, they adjust their estimates downwards.

Suppose each group of traders has the same wealth and are otherwise identical. They also have the same confidence in their information. In this case, the divergence of opinion does not lead to a price change after the start of trading. The reason is that their selling upon learning you disagree is exactly equal to your buying upon learning their opinions. Each of you have adjusted your estimates and traded on them. This had led to trading, with the previously more pessimistic becoming more optimistic and placing buy orders, and the previously more optimistic becoming more pessimistic and placing sell orders. However, because you held your opinions with equal confidence, and had equal buying power, the opening of the market is accompanied by much trading, but the price is unchanged. The divergence of opinion has not led to volatility in the second period.

Now suppose one group is known by everyone to have better information (this is reflected in their model by a higher precision for the estimates). One possibility is those with the higher precisions estimates are "insiders," and everyone agrees their estimates are better. For concreteness, imagine that they are more optimistic (i.e., willing to hold more at any price). At the start of trading, they learn that they are more optimistic than the other investors. However, knowing that they have the better information, they adjust their estimates very little (or even leave them unchanged). The other investors, seeing the market price is now higher and knowing there are insiders in the market with better information, adjust their estimates very much upwards. The result is that these relatively uninformed investors are now willing to buy more. The additional amounts they are willing to buy are greater than the amounts the inside investors are willing to sell at the current price. Thus, the price must move up. This move in the price constitutes second period volatility. The result is that divergence of opinion now leads to volatility.

Their model is only a two-period model, where there is trading after people form their expectations, and then they use the price to improve their estimates. However, it might be extended to a multiperiod model where investors are always forming new estimates using the nonmarket information they have, and then revising their estimates from how the market acts. When people's confidence in their estimates differ, buying and selling are not equal at the old prices. The magnitude of price moves after the information disclosure increase with divergence of opinion.

As a simple example, when new earnings are announced an investor uses them to adjust his future earning estimates. (Is this just a temporary change, or is it permanent?) He (or she) places his trades based on his beliefs. If the market does not act in a way consistent with his beliefs, he considers the possibility that he is wrong and adjusts his estimates. This leads to further trading (usually reversing part or all of his previous position if the market does not confirm his interpretation). If everyone holds his opinions with equal confidence, the market moves immediately to a new equilibrium price reflecting the new information. Once it has moved, there may be further trading as some revise their expectations (now they have seen how the market acted) upwards and some downwards. However, if all are equally confident, this additional trading is neutral as to price. All that happens is that brokers make money. However, when one group is more confident than the other, the price moves to reflect their opinions.

Suppose for instance relatively uninformed investors read the news of an earnings increase overnight (from $1.00 to $2.00 per year). Possibly this could be because some shipments were made this year that would otherwise have been made next year. In this case, the estimate of long-run average earnings should not be changed and your demand curve (including the price at which you are willing to buy) should be unchanged. You retain your previous demand curve (which means you start buying at $20). However, it is possible that the company has moved to a new long-term level of earnings and they will now be $2.00. This calls for adjusting the demand curve and becoming a buyer at $40. Imagine a call market in which everyone submits their demand curves and a clearing price is selected and trades made.

Suppose the average analysts (and the investors who follow them) adjust his long-term estimate of earnings by only half of the change (they now expect $1.50 per year). However, there is considerable divergence of opinion. While $1.50 was the average of the estimates, there is a range of estimates (say from $1.00 to $2.00). If everyone uses the nice simple formula for a demand curve such that purchases start at 20 times estimated annual earnings, the price rises from $20 to $30. In simple models this price change occurs even though some with higher estimates bought and those with lower estimates sold (imagine an auction market where they send in a demand curve based on their estimates and then these demand curves were aggregated by computer and a clearing price announced). In such a model with unbiased investors, the new and old prices reflect average opinions of all traders.

The first trade reveals that some people's estimates are higher or lower than the average. The investors who find they disagree with the average presume that the new price reveals some information and adjust their estimates. This leads to additional trading. If all are equally confident in their estimates, the resulting buy orders equal the sell orders and there is no further change in price. The divergence of opinion has lead to trading, but not to volatility.[100]

However, if some investors are more confident than others, price could further adjust after the first round of trading. In the simple two-version model, where there were only $1.00 estimates (the long-run level of dividends is not changed, and the extra money paid out now will be taken back with the next announcement) and $2.00 estimates (this is a new level of dividends that will continue forever), everyone revises their estimates towards the $1.50 average (which was deduced by dividing the new price of $30 by 20). With the new estimates, there is a new round of trading, but buying and selling are equal in volume and the price would not change.

However, imagine that the informed investors stick with their estimate of $2.00. They do not change their estimates at all. The less confident investors (perhaps knowing they are not well informed) have little confidence in their estimates. They revise them substantially when they discover their evaluation differs from that of the average. In the second round of trading the demand curves for these investors have moved upwards, but the demand curves for the other groups have not moved. The result is a further change in price after the new price is revealed. Thus, it can be seen that divergence of opinion leads to both trading and also to volatility, but only if investors differ in their confidence.

In the Qu, Starks, and Yan model, the price movement after the first trade contains information not only on what other investors know, but on how confidently they hold their opinions. If they are weakly held, they are revised in the next round and prices move in the direction of those with the strongest opinions. While confidence in an opinion and the rightness of it are not the same (we all know people who are wrong, but do not even recognize the possibility of being wrong), there probably is a correlation since a rational person should know whether he is better or worse informed than others. In their model it is really the relative strengths of the opinions that determine which opinion is adjusted most in the second round. Someone that has inside information, or even real expertise, will probably know he has an advantage and adjust his opinion less than others. Technical traders know they lack fundamental information and are

---

[100] Notice with no divergence of opinion, every investor might make the same shifts in his demand curve. Then the market clearing price could change, but there would be no actual trades made. In classic theory where everyone uses Markowitz optimization with the same inputs, the new price is the price at which the representative investor is just willing to hold the stock in the quantity he holds. At the price where he wishes to neither buy nor sell, there is a new equilibrium. The price has changed without trading.

(or should be) willing to adjust their opinions as the market provides more information.

If it is assumed that the estimates are made by analysts and published (but only after their clients have acted on them), it can be seen that volatility should be related to divergence of opinion, and analysts' divergence of estimated earnings is a surrogate for the investors' estimates. The assumption of divergence of opinion seems very plausible (especially since analysts are known to differ in their estimates). It is also plausible that at least some investors are aware that others may have better information and hence revise their estimates upon seeing price action in the market. If nothing else, insiders are known to have better information and to sometimes make investment decisions based on this information.[101] Thus it is rational for noninsiders to adjust expectation by price action seen in the market.

It also appears there are "technicians" who know they do not possess all fundamental information, and trade on market action. Thus, it seems plausible that divergence of opinion could lead to volatility. Conversely, volatility could be used as an indicator of divergence of opinion.

If divergence of opinion tends to lead to lower returns, and volatility indicates high divergence of opinion, the implication is that returns will be lower from more volatile stocks, all things being equal. Of course, all things are not equal, and volatility over the period is a risk.[102] Since theory suggests investors dislike risk, they would require a higher return from more volatile stocks.

The above story also implies that trading volume and dispersion of opinion will be correlated. It will be recalled that such a correlation was assumed by Boehme et al. when they used turnover as a measure of divergence of opinion.[103] This correlation has been found.[104] Because risk in finance is usually measured by volatility of returns, it also implies a correlation between risk and dispersion of opinion as I argued in

---

[101] As discussed elsewhere, contrary to popular opinion, while trading on inside information is illegal, failing to trade is not illegal, and a decision not to trade can legally be based on inside information.

[102] If stocks follow a random walk, short-term volatility leads to long-term volatility. Thus, even if the investors are trying to avoid only long-term volatility (say in the level of retirement consumption), they would require higher expected returns from the stocks that exhibited more short-term volatility.

[103] See Boehme, Danielson, and Sorescu, "Short Sale Constraints and Overvaluation" and also, Rodney D. Boehme, Bartley R. Danielson, and Sorescu, "The Valuation Effects of Dispersion of Opinion: Premium and Discount."

[104] Bipin B. Ajinkya, Rowland K. Atiase, and Michael J. Gift, "Volume of Trading and the Dispersion in Financial Analysts' Earnings Forecasts," *Accounting Review* (April 1991), pp. 389–401.

1977. Qu et al. after developing their theory, examined empirically the relationship between divergence of opinion by analysts (standardized by dividing by the previous year's price) and stock returns for 1983–2001.[105] In the sample of firms with at least two analysts' opinions, they found that the average realized returns (value weighted) fell as the divergence of opinion increased (going from 1.46% to 1.15% for the quintile of firms with the greatest divergence of opinion). They also found firm size (capitalization) decreased as divergence of opinion increased. Thus, they divided the firms into five quintiles by capitalization and repeated the calculation within the size categories. In all size classes there was a tendency for the quintile of firms with the greatest divergence of opinion to underperform the market. However, the divergence of opinion effect was relatively small for the two quintiles of the largest firms. Among the smallest (lowest capitalization) firms the returns dropped from 1.775% for the ones with the least divergence of opinion to 0.93% for those with the highest dispersion. For these small firms, the difference between the high and low divergence of opinion quintiles was statistically significant. (It was not for the other size categories or for all sizes combined.)

The divergence of opinion effect was larger when they repeated the study using a different method of standardizing the divergence of opinion. Here the divergence of opinion was measured after dividing it by the average forecast earnings (creating a coefficient of variation). Now the average return dropped from 1.465% for the largest firms to 1.15% for the firms with the greatest divergence of opinion. Again the divergence of opinion effect was relatively small for largest two quintiles of firms. In the quintile with the smallest firms the returns dropped monotonically from 1.98% for the firms with the least divergence of opinion to 0.685% for the firms with the greatest divergence of opinion. The divergence of opinion effect was statistically significant for the two smallest quintiles, and for all firms combined.

From this data the winning strategy for investors was to buy firms in the smallest quintile with the lowest divergence of opinion. This yielded 1.98% per month for 1984 to 2001 when divergence of opinion was standardized by average earnings and 1.77% when standardized by share price. This suggests that for investors the standardization by average earnings was the more useful. It should be noted that this method of standardization gives the highest divergence of opinion measure for firms with very low forecast earnings. For instance, consider a company whose sales per share was about $10 with earnings estimated at $1.00

---

[105] Qu, Starks, and Yan, "Risk, Dispersion of Analysts Forecasts and Stock Returns."

in normal times and analysts' estimates are plus or minus $0.10. However, the country is in a recession and the analysts' forecasts average sales of $8.00 with average earnings of $0.10 with a range of $0.01 to $0.20. The divergence of opinion may not be particularly large when viewed in relation to sales or normal earnings. However, because the earnings are so low, the coefficient of variation measure is large. This is why these authors do not like this measure. It should be noticed that the firms that are high on this divergence of opinion measure probably include many whose earnings are abnormally depressed, and that these firms are unusually risky (if earnings fall much lower they may go bankrupt). Furthermore, this risk is systematic in that a recession would badly hurt most of these firms. Thus, this measure of divergence of opinion would be expected to be correlated with risk.

Note standard financial theory states that investors would avoid unusually risky firms unless they expect to be rewarded by higher returns. Thus, these unusually risky and high divergence of opinion firms would be expected to have higher than normal returns.

However, in spite of theoretical prediction that the small firms with a high coefficient of variation in earnings forecasts should have high abnormal returns, their returns of 0.68% per month were actually the lowest of the 25 size-divergence-of-opinion classifications. This result is contrary to mainstream theory, but easily explained by divergence of opinion theory.

Anderson et al. also found that for 1991 to 1997 there were negative returns to a dispersion of analysts' forecasts of earnings, but a positive return for a dispersion of analysts' growth estimates.[106]

Qu et al. also repeated their analysis limiting themselves to firms which had estimates from at least five analysts.[107] There was still a divergence of opinion effect, but it was reduced.

As Qu et al. note, this screen and the requirement that firms have prices above $5.00 and at least 10 monthly statistics within a calendar year imply that "it is unlikely that our sample is dominated by extremely small or illiquid stocks that face severe short sale constraints." However, it is likely that the remaining short sale restrictions (including a simple unwillingness to sell short) explain their results. Their results would probably be even stronger if they had not eliminated low-priced stocks, stocks with poor data, and stocks followed by less

---

[106] Evan W. Anderson, Eric Ghysels, and Jennifer L. Juergens, "Do Heterogeneous Beliefs and Model Uncertainty Matter for Asset Pricing?" working paper, June 13, 2003.

[107] Qu, Starks, and Yan, "Risk, Dispersion of Analysts Forecasts and Stock Returns."

than two analysts (or less than five for most of their work). The smallest stocks are usually followed by few or no analyst, and it is among these stocks that the divergence of opinion effect is likely to be strongest.

Qu et al. also performed various other tests. Their statistics show that the exposure to market risk or beta is greatest for the portfolios with the highest dispersion of analysts' forecasts. Later in this chapter the fact that high dispersion of analysts' opinion stocks tend to be high beta stocks will be used to explain the fact that returns to increasing beta risk are less than predicted. The high dispersion of analysts' opinion stocks also tends to be the smaller ones and the value stocks.

A divergence-of-opinion risk factor calculated as the divergence in returns between the quintile with the greatest divergence of opinion and the quintile with the lowest had a 0.26% return during the period of the study, although it was not statistically significant. They also performed experiments in which book to market and size (capitalization) were controlled for by constructing portfolios. They found that a dispersion factor (the return to the quintile with the highest dispersion minus the return to the quintile with the lowest dispersion) helped explain returns to stocks within a single size book-to-market category (their Table 6).

The idea of a dispersion-of-opinion factor suggests that the return to dispersion of opinion varies over time. This is not a primary prediction of divergence-of-opinion theory, although the effect could differ in strength over time. This should be a caution to investors planning to invest on the basis of the effect, since there may be times when it is weaker than average, or even negative. The high standard deviation (their Table 5) for the factor returns suggests it rather frequently had negative returns.

A possible explanation for the strength of the divergence-of-opinion factor differing is that when divergence of opinion drops, prices should drop. Such a drop would affect the high divergence-of-opinion stocks more than others and the return to high divergence of opinion would then be negative. When divergence of opinion rises, the returns to the stocks should rise. High divergence-of-opinion stocks are probably affected more by fluctuations in the level of divergence of opinion than low divergence-of-opinion stocks. Another possibility is that the high divergence of opinion stocks have certain characteristics in common, including industry mix. When the stocks of this type are declining, high divergence of opinion stocks are declining.

Qu et al. also constructed a standard deviation of divergence-of-opinion estimate, which helped to explain returns. In the divergence-of-opinion model, changing the divergence of opinion alters the price. Hence, the more often the divergence of opinion changes, the more prices will fluctuate. Because stocks with fluctuating prices (high volatility) are usually considered risky, there is no problem in considering the standard deviation of diversion of opinion as a risk measure. Investors should rationally avoid stocks with such fluctuations in the divergence of opinion. This should raise the return on these stocks. That is what they found, although the average return to accepting this risk was a relatively small 0.08% per month. This was not statistically significant. It should be noticed that the return to the divergence-of-opinion factor and the return to the standard deviation of dispersion of opinion were positively correlated (with a relatively high 0.78). Because in standard divergence-of-opinion theory divergence of opinion should lower return and fluctuating divergence of opinion should raise it, there may be a statistical problem here.[108]

Insider Information

A major source of divergence of opinion is that some investors are insiders and others are not. As noted above, insiders are likely not only to be better informed, but will be believed to be better informed by others. Insiders will also be more confident in their information than others.

It is impractical (and usually illegal) for insiders to use their information on the short side. It may be thought that it is illegal for insiders to use their information on the long side. However, this is incorrect as long as the insiders do not make trades based on their inside information. Consider a company founder who now has a $200 million position in his company and few other assets. Any financial adviser would urge him to diversify by selling much of his position (or giving it to a charity). If he has inside information that is negative for the stock it is clearly illegal to sell on that information (although proving he did so is a problem). However, if his inside information says the company best times are still in the future, he is legally free to postpone his diversification program. Thus, anyone trading the stock may be buying it from someone who knows there is no undisclosed good news.

Seyhun reports on a massive study of the ability of insider trading from 1975 to 1994 to predict U.S. stock returns.[109] He documents that they have useful information and that following them results in improved returns.[110]

---

[108] Miller, "Risk, Uncertainty, and Divergence of Opinion."

[109] Nejat H. Seyhun, *Investment Intelligence from Insider Trading* (Cambridge, MA: MIT Press, 1998).

[110] I made this point about not trading in a book review that also summarizes some of his results. Edward M. Miller, "Investment Intelligence from Insider Trading," *Journal of Social, Political, and Economic Studies* (Winter 1999), pp. 477–484.

Fortune published in 2002 a study that looked at selling by insiders after 1999.[111] They show that executives took out $66 billion from the 1035 companies that met their criteria (market caps of at least $400 million and fallen by at least 75% from the highs they reached during the bubble years). These are not trivial sums. Since there were not prosecutions for insider trading, let us presume all were legal. While the article gives several cases, the largest dollar amount illustrates my point. Phil Anschutz chairman of Qwest sold almost $1.6 billion of stock to Bell-South in May 1999. I would assume he had a portfolio that essentially consisted of stock in Qwest. It was obviously undiversified. His company, like most of those discussed in the article, were companies that most financial observers would have been labeled as highly risky. *Highly risky* means there was an excessively large chance the firm's stock could decline greatly or even disappear. Textbook advice would be to diversify.

One can easily imagine public information that led to return estimates that would make a diversified investor purchase stock in such a company while the undiversified insider should sell. A mutual belief that the stock would earn normal returns would probably make a trade in the interests of both parties. For insiders, selling logically required only that they not expect extraordinarily high returns from holding longer. They could have easily postponed their sales legally if they had any inside information that the stocks would be worth more once that information was out. This consideration would make an insider trade informative. It is also possible that as smart people, well informed (presumably part of why they had the jobs they did) and forced to be close observers of the industry in which they worked, they deduced their stocks were overpriced without using any inside information (very high prices relative to earnings, book value, cash flows, and knowledge that there were strong competitors might have let to that conclusion without using inside information). Of course, it is possible that some of the selling in that $66 billion was based on real insider information. In either case, there probably was real diversity of opinion among different investors.

The story also mentions a few cases of executive buying. For instance, Gateway founder Ted Waitt, after having been a seller, had recently been a buyer of Gateway stock when he returned to the company after an absence. Let us assume he was buying only on public information. However, if upon returning to the company he had become aware of big, undisclosed problems, he could have legally refrained from buying. The article mentions other examples of insiders buying stock in their own companies.

---

[111] Mark Gimein, "The Greedy Bunch: You Bought. They Sold," *Fortune* (August 11, 2002).

Likewise, there are many company executives with options that would be profitable to exercise. To exercise and then sell because the insider has information that prices will someday be lower is illegal (although again enforcement may be a problem). However, the insider may choose not to exercise if he has reason to believe the stock is overvalued, or to delay exercise until certain uncertainties have been resolved. A corporation that already has a large enough ownership position in a company to be an insider may not be able legally to purchase the remainder on inside information. However, if the firm would be a good strategic fit, and on the basis of the inside information, it knows there are no major undisclosed problems; it may proceed with an offer. It is traditional in friendly mergers for companies to give potential purchasers access to its books (i.e., inside information). While I presume it would be illegal for the potential purchaser to make an offer on the basis of undisclosed favorable information, it is certainly free to refrain from making an offer if after this "due diligence" it discovers problems that worry it. Thus, one source of divergence of opinion is differences in insider status.

CONCLUSIONS

Mainstream financial theory has been built on unrestricted short selling along with substantive rationality in which all investors are aware of all potentially relevant facts, and are able to do the optimal analysis. Among other things, this implies that investors will agree on measures of expected return and risk (homogeneous expectations). An alternative is that investors are merely procedurally rational, collecting data and using complex analytic methods only when the apparent benefit exceeds the costs. In this case investors will exhibit divergence of opinion.

Interesting effects emerge when divergence of opinion is combined with real world obstacles to short selling. Many investors will choose not to hold any of most stocks. The demand curves will slope not merely because investors buy more of each stock as the prices come down, but because more investors decide to include the security in their portfolios. The marginal investor will usually be among the more optimistic investors. The equilibrium price will not be the consensus value but something higher. The greater the divergence of opinion about a stock, the higher the price. Winner's curse behavior will appear. Investors who do not correct for this effect will find a gap between the anticipated investment returns and the average returns earned.

Extensive empirical studies reviewed in this chapter support divergence of opinion theory, and the implications that high divergence of opinion stocks should be avoided. In the presence of some uninformed investors and overoptimistic investors, prices need not reflect the valuations of informed investors, and markets need not be efficient. Stocks with high divergence of opinion or high short positions should be avoided. Investors should make a correction for uncertainty induced bias.

CHAPTER 7

Short Sale Constraints and Overpricing

Owen A. Lamont, Ph.D.
Professor of Finance
Yale School of Management
and
Research Associate
NBER

Short sale constraints can allow stocks to be overpriced. Constraints include various costs and risks of shorting as well as legal and institutional restrictions. If these impediments prevent investors from shorting certain stocks, these stocks can be overpriced and thus have low future returns until the overpricing is corrected. By identifying stocks with particularly high short sale constraints, one can identify stocks with particularly low future returns.

This chapter is based on the following papers: with Charles M. Jones, "Short Sale Constraints and Stock Returns," *Journal of Financial Economics* (November 2002); and with Richard H. Thaler, "Can the Market Add and Subtract? Mispricing in Tech Stock Carve-Outs," *Journal of Political Economy* (April 2003); "Go Down Fighting: Short Sellers vs. Firms," working paper, November 2002; discussion of "Perspectives on Behavioral Finance: Does Irrationality Disappear with Wealth? Evidence from Expectations and Actions," by Annette Vissing-Jorgensen, *NBER Macroeconomics Annual 2003*, edited by Mark Gertler and Kenneth Rogoff; with Richard H. Thaler, "Anomalies: The Law of One Price in Financial Markets," *Journal of Economic Perspectives*, forthcoming. I am grateful to my coauthors, Charles M. Jones and Richard H. Thaler, for their permission to use material from our joint work.

Consider a stock whose fundamental value is $100 (i.e., $100 would be the share price in a frictionless world). If it costs $1 to short the stock, then arbitrageurs cannot prevent the stock from rising to $101. If the $1 is a holding cost that must be paid every day that the short position is held, then selling the stock short becomes a gamble that the stock falls by at least $1 a day. In such a market, a stock could be very overpriced, yet if there is no way for arbitrageurs to earn excess returns, the market is still in some sense efficient. Fama describes an efficient market as one in which "deviations from the extreme version of the efficiency hypothesis are within information and trading costs."[1] If frictions are large, "efficient" prices may be far from frictionless prices.

In this chapter, I discuss evidence that supports the overpricing hypothesis. I start by briefly reviewing the various constraints that impede short selling. Since other chapters cover the mechanics of short selling and securities lending in more detail, I focus on some nonstandard constraints, including the political and legal harassment of short sellers through the ages. I then discuss the predictions of the overpricing hypothesis, reviewing the literature and the various variables that one might be able to use to identify short sale constraints and overpricing. Then I review three striking cases in which extremely high short sale constraints lead to extremely high overpricing and thus extremely low subsequent returns. These three cases are: short selling in the 1920s and 1930s; fights between short sellers and the companies they short; and Palm/3Com in the year 2000. I conclude with a discussion of the tech stock mania of 1998–2000, and whether the entire market (and especially the tech sector) was identifiably overpriced.

SHORT SALE CONSTRAINTS

Many things constrain investors from going short. First, there are mechanical impediments to short selling due to the poor functioning of the securities lending market. Second, more generally, there are a variety of institutional and cultural factors that discourage short selling.

Mechanical Impediments to Shorting

To be able to sell a stock short, one must borrow it, and because borrowing shares is not done in a centralized market, finding shares can sometimes be difficult or impossible. In order to borrow shares, an

---

[1] Eugene F. Fama, "Efficient Capital Markets: II," *Journal of Finance* (December 1991), pp. 1575–1617.

investor needs to find an institution or individual willing to lend shares. Financial institutions, such as mutual funds, trusts, or asset managers, typically do much of this lending. These lenders receive a fee in the form of interest payments generated by the short-sale proceeds, minus any *interest rebate* that the lenders return to the borrowers.

This rebate acts as a price that equilibrates supply and demand in the securities lending market. In extreme cases, the rebate can be negative, meaning investors who sell short have to make a daily payment to the lender for the right to borrow the stock (instead of receiving a daily payment from the lender as interest payments on the short sale proceeds). This rebate apparently only partially equilibrates supply and demand, because the securities lending market is not a centralized market with a market-clearing price. Instead, rebates reflect individual deals struck among security owners and those wishing to short, and these actors must find each other. This search may be costly and time-consuming.

The securities lending business can be dysfunctional at times. In some respects, it is actually harder to borrow stock today than it was in 1928. (I will discuss details later.) The good news is that it appears to be getting somewhat better in the past decade, and there have been some recent attempts towards creating a more centralized market. For the time being, the lending market does not work perfectly. Being simply unable to short is particularly likely for individual retail investors, although there is extensive anecdotal evidence of institutional investors unable to short no matter how much they are willing to pay for the ability to borrow shares. "Getting the borrow" (that is, obtaining the stock loan) can be difficult, because the securities lending market is some combination of a bureaucracy and a market. Favored customers stand a better chance of getting the borrow. There have been reports of short sellers exchanging drugs and sex in order to get the borrow.[2] (I do not recommend this procedure.) This is a good clue that prices are not fully equilibrating this market.

Once a short seller has initiated a position by borrowing stock, the borrowed stock may be recalled at any time by the lender. If the short seller is unable to find another lender, he is forced to close his position. This possibility leads to *recall risk*, one of many risks that short sellers face.

There are several reasons that a shareholder might refuse to lend stock, or might withdraw his shares from the stock lending market. First, if the lender sells his stock, he must recall his stock loan so that he can deliver his shares to the buyer. Second, shareholders may refuse to lend their stock because they fear that by helping short sellers, they will be helping drive stock prices down (I discuss these cases later). Third, for

---

[2] Jon Friedman, "The Business Nobody Wants To Talk About," *Business Week* (September 25, 1989), p. 196.

individual investors, brokers typically only have the ability to lend out of margin accounts, not cash accounts. Fourth, some institutions do not have stock lending programs at all, perhaps because they feel their holdings are too small and the income generated by lending would not be enough to compensate for the fixed cost of setting up a lending program.

Generally, it is easy and cheap to borrow most large cap stocks, but it can be difficult to borrow stocks which are small, have low institutional ownership, or which are in high demand for borrowing. A somewhat paradoxical description of the stock lending market is that it usually works very well, except when you want to use it, in which case it works terribly. By this I mean that it can be difficult or expensive to short stocks that many people believe are overpriced and many people want to short. Of course, this point is the essence of the overpricing hypothesis: Stocks are only overpriced when informed investors are unable or unwilling to short them. No one would want to short them if they weren't overpriced, and they wouldn't be overpriced if they weren't hard to short.

Other Short Sale Constraints

In addition to the problems in the stock lending market, there are a variety of other short sale constraints. U.S. equity markets are not set up to make shorting easy. Regulations and procedures administered by the SEC, the Federal Reserve, the various stock exchanges, underwriters, and individual brokerage firms can mechanically impede short selling. Legal and institutional constraints inhibit or prevent investors from selling short (most mutual funds are long only). We have many institutions set up to encourage individuals to buy stocks, but few institutions set up to encourage them to short. The growth of hedge funds is a welcome correction to this imbalance.

In addition to regulations, short sellers also face hostility from society at large. Policy makers and the general public seem to have an instinctive reaction that short selling is morally wrong. Short selling is characterized as inhuman, un-American—and against God. (Proverbs 24:17: "Do not rejoice when your enemy falls, and do not let your heart be glad when he stumbles.") Hostility is not limited to America. In Malaysia in 1995, the Finance Ministry proposed mandatory caning as the punishment for short sellers. Governments often restrict short selling in an attempt to maintain high security prices. Meeker reviews the attempts by a colorful cast of characters (from Napoleon to the New York state legislature) to ban short selling.[3]

---

[3] J. Edward Meeker, *Short Selling* (New York: Harper & Brothers Publishers, 1932).

Short sellers face periodic waves of harassment from governments and society, usually in times of crisis or following major price declines as short sellers are blamed. Short sellers are often thought to be in league with America's enemies. The general idea seems to be that short selling is bad, and when bad things happen (such as war) it probably involves short sellers in some way. For example, the New York Stock Exchange (NYSE) imposed special short selling regulations during World War I (in November 1917) in response to both a substantial market decline and a fear that the Kaiser would send enemy agents to drive down stock prices.

Jones and Lamont discuss the crackdown on short selling after 1929.[4] Short sellers were extremely unpopular in 1930, and many politicians, journalists, and investors blamed them for the stock market crash. Press accounts in October 1930 contain reports that officials of the NYSE were quietly discouraging stock lending and that the lenders themselves (such as investment trusts) wanted to discourage short selling. President Herbert Hoover met with Richard Whitney, president of the NYSE, to discuss the situation. The FBI's J. Edgar Hoover was quoted as saying he would investigate the conspiracy to keep stock prices low. Numerous antishorting regulations stem from this period, such as the uptick rule and the Investment Company Act of 1940 that placed severe restrictions on the ability of mutual funds to short. Political and legal antishorting pressure, which arises periodically after major market declines, seem essential to understanding why we have so few institutions developed to allow shorting.

The events following September 11, 2001, are consistent with this pattern. Following a major terrorist attack on the United States, the SEC and various other regulatory bodies investigated the claim that terrorists had shorted stocks or had bought puts, armed with foreknowledge of the attacks. This investigation turned up no evidence of terrorist shorting. As far as I know, there is no evidence that Osama Bin Laden, the Kaiser, Stalin, or any other major villain ever shorted stock. Enemies of freedom (for example, Napoleon) are more interested in suppressing short selling along with other forms of free expression.

More generally, the decline in equity prices in the early 2000s led governments to limit short selling. Press reports indicate that authorities in Britain and Japan have sought to discourage shorting and securities lending. A major lender of European stocks announced it was ceasing securities lending and urged others to do the same.

In addition to hostility from governments, short sellers also face hostility from the firms they short. Managers of firms don't like people

---

[4] Charles M. Jones and Owen A. Lamont, "Short Sale Constraints and Stock Returns," *Journal of Financial Economics* (November 2002), pp. 207–239.

who short sell their stock, especially if the short sellers are accusing the firms of fraud and even more especially when the fraud accusations are true. Consequently, sometimes companies fight with their short sellers. (I detail these actions later.)

In extreme cases, short sale constraints can include violence and intimidation. There are various reports of short sellers receiving death threats, requiring bodyguards, and arming themselves. In at least one case, someone may have been killed because of short selling. The case involves the Tel-Com Wireless Cable TV, whose official spokesperson was Ivana Trump. On 12/14/1998, *Barron's* reported that "several terrified investors told *Barron's* and the police that their families had been threatened by convicted criminals who accused the investors of selling short." A year later, 11/01/1999, *Barron's* reported that one of the threatened individuals had been found murdered, execution-style, in Colts Neck, New Jersey.

THE OVERPRICING HYPOTHESIS

Short sale constraints can prevent negative information or opinions from being expressed in stock prices, as initially discussed by Edward Miller in 1977.[5] Although constraints are necessary in order for mispricing to occur, they are not sufficient. Constraints can explain why a rational investor fails to short the overpriced security, but not why anyone buys the overpriced security. To explain that, one needs investors who are willing to buy overpriced stocks. Thus two things, trading costs and some investors with downward sloping demand curves, are necessary for substantial mispricing. This willingness to hold overpriced stocks can be interpreted either as reflecting irrational optimism by some investors, or rational speculative behavior reflecting differences of opinion.

A Rational Story: Harrison and Kreps

In 1978, Harrison and Kreps constructed a model with rational investors where differences of opinion, together with short sale constraints, create a "speculative premium" in which stock prices are higher than even the most optimistic investor's assessment of their value.[6] Short sale

---

[5] Edward M. Miller, "Risk, Uncertainty, and Divergence of Opinion," *Journal of Finance* (September 1977), pp. 1151–1168. An updated and expanded discussion of Miller's model is described in Chapters 5 and 6.

[6] J. Michael Harrison and David M. Kreps, "Speculative Investor Behavior in a Stock Market with Heterogeneous Expectations," *Quarterly Journal of Economics* (May 1978), pp. 323–336.

constraints generate a pattern of overpriced stock leading to subsequent low returns.

Here I give an example that illustrates the model of Harrison and Kreps. In the model of Miller, short sale constraints cause stock prices to reflect only the views of the optimists. The Harrison and Kreps story goes beyond Miller to say that the stock can be priced even higher than the most optimistic assessment of its true value. In their model, everybody agrees that stocks are overpriced but are still willing to hold stocks.

Suppose investor A and investor B have different beliefs about the prospects for the level of NASDAQ. Each one knows what the other one believes, but they agree to disagree, so there is no asymmetric information. Assume a simple set up with three dates, date 0, 1, and 2, and for simplicity assume risk neutral agents behaving competitively, a discount rate of zero, and there are sufficient numbers of type A and type B investors for each type to hold all of NASDAQ by themselves. Suppose it is currently date 0 and both A and B believe that NASDAQ is worth 2,000 today. Specifically, they both believe that at date 2 it will be worth 3,000 with 50% probability and 1,000 with 50% probability. However, A thinks that at date 1 some news will arrive that will resolve all uncertainty, while B thinks there will be no relevant news released until date 2. This belief about when news gets released is the only disagreement between A and B (it is not necessary to state who, if either, is right in their beliefs). The Harrison and Kreps model has the remarkable property that in the presence of short sale constraints, both A and B would be willing to hold NASDAQ at 2,500 at date 0, despite the fact they both think it is only worth 2,000.

To get to this result, work backward from date 1, using the principle that with short sale constraints the optimist always sets the price. At date 1, if good news has arrived then A will value NASDAQ at 3,000 while B still thinks it is worth 2,000, thus the price will be 3,000, A will hold all the asset, B will hold none of it. If bad news arrives at date 1, the price will be 2,000 and B will hold all of it. Since these two states happen with 50-50 probability, the date 0 expected price for date 1 is 2,500. Thus at date 0, both A and B are willing to hold NASDAQ at a price of 2,500. Although everyone thinks it is overvalued at date 0, they are willing to buy at date 0 because they believe they are following a dynamic trading strategy that will take advantage of the other guy. This example formalizes the notion of the "greater fool" theory of asset pricing. Note that in this example, everyone agrees that long-term expected returns between date 0 and date 2 are low (as the value is expected to fall from 2,500 to 2,000), and thus a buy-and-hold strategy is a bad idea.

There are several ways to describe this result. First, you could say that the reason NASDAQ trades at 500 above fundamental value at date 0 is that both A and B think there is a 50% chance they will be able to sell it at date 1 for 1,000 more than it is worth. Equivalently, you could say that there is a valuable resale option that is bundled in with the security. Short sale constraints are crucial for this story. If traders were allowed to short at date 1, the price would no longer be set only by the optimist, so that there is no longer a 50% chance that one can sell the asset for 1,000 more than it is worth.

Several predictions emerge from the Harrison and Kreps story. First, if you took an opinion survey at date 0, both A and B would say NAS-DAQ was overvalued relative to date 2 but fairly valued relative to date 1. Both would say it is overvalued but not likely to fall in the near term. Second, volume is a key part of the story. Since everyone is following a dynamic trading strategy, you see lots of trading at date 1 as traders try to take advantage of one another. Without volume, there would be no overpricing. Volume indicates differences of opinion; more precisely, volume indicates changes in differences of opinion, as some switch from being the optimist to being the pessimist.

Third, securities that are less liquid will be less overpriced, and you might see apparent mispricings between seemingly identical securities. Suppose you introduced a derivative security (say, a bundle of puts and calls) that trades at date 0, doesn't trade at date 1, and gives exactly the same payoff at date 2 as NASDAQ. This security will be priced at 2,000 at date 0. Thus there will appear to be a violation of the law of one price—assets having identical payoffs should have identical prices, but they do not. The derivative security is cheaper because it is less liquid, although this effect is not a "liquidity premium" in the traditional sense. Rather, it reflects the fact that you cannot follow a dynamic trading strategy with the derivative security, and so cannot try to exploit the other traders who disagree with you.

An Irrational Story: Overconfidence

In the Harrison and Kreps story, investors agree to disagree. Is this rational? There is a large literature in economics, starting with Aumann, debating this point.[7] Under some circumstances, it can never be rational for investors to agree to disagree: even if they have different information, they must reach a consensus if they are rational. This consensus reflects the fact that I know that other people have information that I do not have. Thus if they disagree with me, I infer that they have information that contradicts my information. So the mere fact that we observe

---

[7] Robert Aumann, "Agreeing to Disagree," *The Annals of Statistics* (November 1976), pp. 1236–1239.

strong disagreement—and resulting trade—between investors suggests that someone is not behaving rationally.

One form of irrationality that generates disagreement is overconfidence. There is ample evidence from the cognitive psychology literature that individuals overestimate their own abilities and tend to think they are above average. Thus overconfident traders are perfectly willing to disagree with other investors (since they think they are smarter than their trading partners), and to buy stock that others believe is overpriced. So this is one motivation for the Harrison and Kreps story.

More generally, moving beyond the specific dynamic story of Harrison and Kreps, irrational traders might make other errors that can lead to overpricing in the presence of short sale constraints. They might get overexcited about certain stocks that have an interesting and dramatic story, or be beguiled by optimistic projections made by the issuers of the stock. Generally, short sellers like to target "fads, frauds, and failures." If irrational investors are swept up in fads, bamboozled by frauds, or ignoring the possibility of failure, then they will buy overpriced stock.

Evidence

A variety of empirical evidence confirms the prediction that binding short sale constraints lead to low returns, although much of the evidence is circumstantial because it is hard to observe the level of short sale constraints for different stocks. Looking across stocks, the prediction is that when constraints bind more tightly, subsequent returns will be lower. One can test this hypothesis either by finding stocks with higher constraints (if constraints vary across stocks), or finding stocks with higher unexpressed shorting demand (if the demand for shorting varies across stocks). The basic idea of looking at shorting demand is that some investors want to short a stock but are impeded by constraints, thus the stock is overpriced. If one can estimate the size of this group of investors, one can measure the extent of overpricing. In practice, measures of shorting constraints and shorting demand tend to be highly correlated since both are reflecting the same mechanism that constraints prevent informed investors from immediately correcting overpricing.

One measure of shorting demand is *short interest*, that is, the level of shares sold short. Unfortunately, using short interest as a proxy for shorting demand is problematic, because the quantity of shorting represents the intersection of supply and demand. Demand for shorting should respond to both the cost and benefit of shorting the stock, so that stocks that are very costly to short will have low short interest. Stocks that are impossible to short have an infinite shorting cost, yet the level of short interest is zero. Thus it could be possible that short interest is negatively correlated with overpricing (we will see this issue arise below in the 3Com/Palm case). The problematic nature of short interest leads to weak empirical results.

An alternative measure of shorting demand is breadth of ownership. If short sale constraints prevent investors from shorting overpriced securities, then all they can do is avoid owning overpriced stocks. With dispersed private information or differences of opinion, overpriced stocks will tend to be owned by a few optimistic owners. Chen, Hong, and Stein find evidence in favor of this hypothesis.[8]

Overpricing is most likely when investors disagree most. Diether, Malloy, and Scherbina examine one measure of disagreement, dispersion in analyst forecast about future profits.[9] They find the stocks with high analyst disagreement have low subsequent returns, consistent with the overpricing hypothesis.

COSTS OF SHORTING

Jones and Lamont study a direct measure of shorting costs, coming from the securities lending market.[10] Stocks that are expensive to short, as reflected in the rebate rate, should have low subsequent returns. It is difficult to test this hypothesis, however, because data on rebate rates are difficult to find. To test for overpricing, ideally one needs many years of data. Recently, several financial economists have begun collecting data on rebate rates from proprietary sources, but so far only a few years of data have been collected.

Fortunately, there is a historical source that is publicly available. Jones and Lamont introduce a unique data set that details shorting costs for NYSE stocks from 1926 to 1933. In this period, the cost of shorting certain NYSE stocks was set in the "loan crowd," a centralized stock loan market on the floor of the NYSE. A list of loan crowd stocks and their associated loaning rates was printed daily in the *Wall Street Journal* (WSJ).

From this public record, we collected eight years of data on an average of 90 actively traded stocks per month, by far the most extensive panel data set on the cost of shorting ever assembled. There is substantial variation in the cost of shorting, both in the cross section and over

---

[8] Joseph Chen, Harrison Hong, and Jeremy C. Stein, "Breadth of Ownership and Stock Returns," *Journal of Financial Economics* (November 2002), pp. 171–205.

[9] Karl B. Diether, Christopher J. Malloy, and Anna Scherbina, "Differences of Opinion and the Cross-Section of Stock Returns," *Journal of Finance* (October 2002), pp. 2113–2141.

[10] Jones and Lamont, "Short Sale Constraints and Stock Returns."

time for individual stocks. Furthermore, new stocks periodically appear in the loan crowd, and we are able to track the behavior of these stocks both before and after they first appear on the list. Stocks appear on the list of loan crowd stock when shorting demand cannot be met by normal channels, and when stocks begin trading in the centralized borrowing market, they usually have high shorting costs. Thus the list conveys important information about shorting demand.

It is important to emphasize that these stocks are generally extreme cases representing only a small part of the universe of stocks. They are the stocks everyone wants to short. In our sample, a few of the stocks were astronomically expensive to borrow, with negative rebates and shorting costs of more than 50% per year. Modern equivalents would be highly controversial, highly priced, difficult-to-short stocks such as (in recent years) Krispy Kreme, Prepaid Legal, or Palm. These modern examples also had very negative rebates and shorting costs of up to 79% a year. D'Avolio reports that in modern data, just a handful of stocks have extreme negative rebates.[11]

Rebate rates reflect supply and demand of shares to lend. Stocks go on special when shorting demand is large relative to the supply of shares available for lending. Thus, specific stocks can be costly to short either because there is a large demand or a small supply. No matter what the reason for the high shorting costs, however, the consequences of the costs are clear. Stocks that are expensive to short can be overpriced since it is expensive to correct the overpricing. Thus, we do not need to identify the reason for the low rebate rate in order to test whether it results in overpricing.

Exhibit 7.1 shows the time pattern of market/book ratios for stocks entering the list. The figure shows the change in a stock's market/book compared to when that stock is not on the loan list. Quarter zero is the quarter that the stock first appears on the list. Looking at the figure, the time pattern of market/book is exactly what is predicted by the overpricing hypothesis. In the period prior to entering the loan rate list, market/book ratios rise, peaking at 30% above average in the quarter just before appearance on the loan list. After appearing on the loan list, market/book ratios fall, going down to just 5% above average three quarters later. This pattern suggests that stocks become overpriced over the course of several months, they are identified as overpriced by short sellers, and the demand for short selling rises. Stocks appear on the loan list due to this demand, and subsequently fall as the mispricing is corrected.

---

[11] Gene D'Avolio, "The Market for Borrowing Stock," *Journal of Financial Economics*, (November 2002), pp. 271–306.

EXHIBIT 7.1   Abnormal Market/Book of Firms Entering Loan Crowd

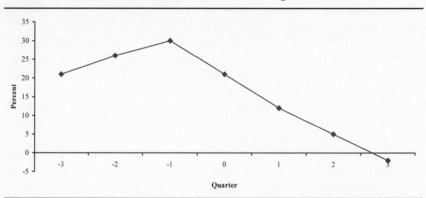

Looking directly at the stock returns subsequent to appearing on the list, Jones and Lamont find that stocks that are expensive to short or which enter the loan list have low subsequent returns, consistent with the hypothesis that they are overpriced. Stocks that newly enter the borrowing market exhibit especially substantial overpricing. By itself, this return predictability is important because it shows that transactions costs keep arbitrageurs from forcing down the prices of overvalued stocks. However, we also find that loan crowd entrants underperform by more than the costs of shorting, so it appears that shorting these stocks is a profitable strategy even after paying the associated costs. Thus not only are these stocks overpriced, they are more overpriced than can be explained by measured shorting costs alone. It must be that unwillingness to short (perhaps due to some other unobserved shorting cost) is partially responsible for the low returns on stocks entering the loan crowd for the first time.

Put another way, a rational investor would not be willing to buy these stocks since they would not generate sufficiently high income from lending the stock out. Even if the magnitude of the returns was quantitatively equal to the shorting costs, in equilibrium all shares must be held by some investor who is not lending them out. Thus some investors were voluntarily buying stocks with extremely low subsequent returns, despite the fact that the high shorting costs were publicly observable in the *Wall Street Journal*, and high shorting demand might be inferred by the first appearance of these stocks in the *Wall Street Journal*'s list. Why these investors were willing to buy these overpriced stocks is a mystery.

The magnitude of the effect is huge, reflecting the fact that this is a very special sample of extremely overpriced stocks that have extremely low returns. In the period 1926 to 1933, loan crowd entrants have (in the year following their first appearance) average returns that are 1% to 2% per month lower than other stocks of similar size. So over the next year they underperform by about 12–24% in total. While this effect might seem implausibly large, it has recently been reproduced with modern data. Ofek, Richardson, and Whitelaw look at a sample of stocks with negative rebate rates (high shorting costs) 1999–2002, and find similar underperformance.[12] In addition, similarly huge effects are seen in the next two sections: companies fighting with short sellers and tech stock carve outs.

GO DOWN FIGHTING

Yet another form of short sale constraints are those deliberately engineered to hurt the short sellers. Lamont studies these cases.[13] Firms—either management or shareholders—can take a variety of actions to impede short selling of their stock. Firms take legal and regulatory actions to hurt short sellers, such as accusing them of illegal activities, suing them, hiring private investigators to probe them, and requesting that the authorities investigate their activities. Firms take technical actions to make shorting the stock difficult, such as splits or distributions specifically designed to disrupt short selling. Management can coordinate with shareholders to withdraw shares from the stock lending market, thus preventing short selling by causing loan recall. These battles between short sellers and firms can be extraordinarily acrimonious. The following statement from the sample used in Lamont gives a flavor of attitudes toward short sellers: "Your activities are mean, shameful and loathsome. They are motivated by appalling avarice and greed, and they will not be permitted to go unanswered."

An example of the various antishorting strategies used by firms is provided by Solv-Ex, a firm that claimed to have technology for economically extracting crude oil from tar-laden sand. Short sellers claimed that Solv-Ex was a fraud. On 2/5/96, the management of Solv-Ex faxed a letter to brokers and shareholders: "To help you control the value of your investment…we suggest that you request delivery of the Solv-Ex certificates from your broker as soon as possible." This suggestion was essentially an attempt at market manipulation. The letter was an attempt to orchestrate a short

---

[12] Eli Ofek, Matthew Richardson, and Robert F. Whitelaw, "Limited Arbitrage and Short Sales Restrictions: Evidence from the Options Markets," *Journal of Financial Economics*, forthcoming.

[13] Owen A. Lamont, "Go Down Fighting: Short Sellers vs. Firms," working paper, 2002.

squeeze using the stock lending system. One might think that such an attempt to manipulate prices would be illegal, but it is not. Things that hurt short sellers tend to be legal, because short sellers are a despised minority.

Any shareholder heeding Solv-Ex's suggestion would have withdrawn his shares from the stock lending market, potentially forcing short sellers to cover their positions. On 2/2/96, before the letter, Solv-Ex's price was at $24.875. By 2/21/96, the price had risen to $35.375, perhaps due to Solv-Ex's attempted squeeze. Solv-Ex took other action against short sellers as well. Later in 1996, Solv-Ex said that it had hired private investigators to find out who was (supposedly) spreading misinformation about the firm, and subsequently it filed suit against a well-known short seller, claiming he had spread false information.

However, in this case it was Solv-Ex which was engaged in illegal activities, not the short sellers. Solv-Ex delisted at 7/1/97 at $4.25, amid an SEC investigation of whether Solv-Ex had defrauded investors. It entered Chapter 11 bankruptcy in 1997, and in 2000 the court ruled that the firm had indeed defrauded investors. In this case, the evidence is consistent with the idea that Solv-Ex was overpriced in February 1996, since it subsequently fell sharply.

Lamont looks at long-term returns for a large sample over 25 years of 270 similar firms who threaten, take action against, or accuse short sellers of illegal activity or false statements. The sample is constructed using publicly observable actions from news reports and firm press releases. It turns out that (as in the Solv-Ex case) sample firms have very low returns in the year subsequent to taking antishorting action. Abnormal returns are approximately –2% per month in the subsequent year, and continue to be negative in subsequent years. Thus the evidence is consistent with the idea that short sale constraints allow very substantial overpricing, and that this overpricing gets corrected only slowly over many months.

An alternate interpretation of the results are that anti-shorting actions are a signal that insiders know that the firm is overvalued, so that the low returns reflect inside information instead of short sale constraints. While it is certainly true that anti-shorting actions may reveal negative inside information, this story does not explain why it takes so long for the information to be reflected in stock prices. With no frictions, the information should be immediately incorporated. In contrast, short sale constraints provide an explanation for the slow reaction of prices to information. Since the effect persists for years, the low returns are not primarily a short-term under-reaction to bad news. Rather, the low returns reflect persistent overpricing.

What should an investor do if he or she sees a firm taking an anti-shorting action? The evidence cannot say whether it is a good idea to short this stock. Although one can make large gross returns on average if one is able to maintain a short position for months, maintaining the short position might be difficult or expensive. Even if there are no problems borrowing the stock, a short seller may need to spend time and money dealing with lawsuits and investigations. It is unclear how these costs and benefits net out. It is clear, however, that it is a bad idea in general to own stock in a firm that is taking these actions. Investors seeking high returns should look elsewhere.

A notable feature of the data is that many of the sample firms are subsequently revealed to be fraudulent. The evidence on subsequent stock returns suggests that in public battles between short sellers and firms, short sellers usually are vindicated by subsequent events. The evidence suggests that short sellers play an important role in detecting not just overpricing, but also fraud.

3COM/PALM

A third example of clear overpricing comes from 3Com/Palm, studied in Lamont and Thaler.[14] In this case, the driving force is not fraud but rather overoptimistic investors. Again, having some investors overoptimistic is not a problem, as long as there are more rational investors who can correct their mistakes by short selling. But add overoptimistic investors and short sale constraints together, and the result is overpricing.

On March 2, 2000, 3Com (a profitable company selling computer network systems and services) sold a fraction of its stake in Palm (which makes hand-held computers) to the general public via an initial public offering (IPO) for Palm. In this transaction, called an *equity carve-out*, 3Com retained ownership of 95% of the shares. 3Com announced that, pending an expected IRS approval, it would eventually spin off its remaining shares of Palm to 3Com's shareholders before the end of the year. 3Com shareholders would receive about 1.5 shares of Palm for every share of 3Com that they owned.

This event put in play two ways in which an investor could buy Palm. The investor could buy (say) 150 shares of Palm directly, or he could buy 100 shares of 3Com, thereby acquiring a claim to 150 shares of Palm plus a portion of 3Com's other assets. Since the price of 3Com's

---

[14] Owen A. Lamont and Richard H. Thaler, "Can the Market Add and Subtract? Mispricing in Tech Stock Carve-Outs," *Journal of Political Economy* (April 2003), pp. 227–268.

shares can never be less than zero (equity values are never negative), the price of 3Com should have been at least 1.5 times the price of Palm. Since 3Com held more than $10 a share in cash and securities in addition to its other profitable business assets, one might expect 3Com's price to be well above 1.5 times the price of Palm.

The day before the Palm IPO, 3Com closed at $104.13 per share. After the first day of trading, Palm closed at $95.06 a share, implying that the price of 3Com should have jumped to at least $145 (using the precise ratio of 1.525). Instead, 3Com fell to $81.81. The "stub value" of 3Com (the implied value of 3Com's non-Palm assets and businesses) was minus $63. In other words, the stock market was saying that the value of 3Com's non-Palm business was minus $22 billion!

This example is puzzling because there is a clear exit strategy. This spin-off was expected to take place in less than a year, and a favorable IRS ruling was highly likely. Thus, in order to profit from the mispricing, an arbitrageur would need only to buy one share of 3Com, short 1.5 shares of Palm, and wait six months or so. In essence, the arbitrageur would be buying a security worth at worst worth zero for –$63, and would not need to wait very long to realize the profits. Exhibit 7.2 shows the actual time pattern of the stub value of 3Com. As can be seen, the stub returned to a more rational level after several months. If one had been able to costlessly short Palm and buy 3Com, one could have made very substantial returns. Lamont and Thaler find abnormal returns for 3Com/Palm and five other similar cases to be about 10% per month.[15]

EXHIBIT 7.2   3Com/Palm Stub: 3/2/00–9/18/00

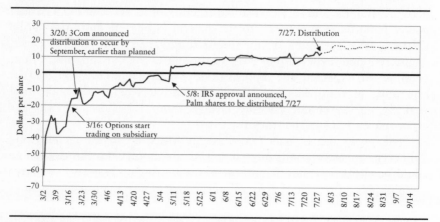

---

[15] Lamont and Thaler, "Can the Market Add and Subtract?"

This mispricing was not in an obscure corner of capital markets, but rather took place in a widely publicized initial public offering that attracted frenzied attention. The nature of the mispricing was so simple that even the dimmest of market participants and financial journalists was able to grasp it. On the day after the issue, the mispricing was widely discussed, including in two articles in the *Wall Street Journal*, one in the *New York Times*, and it even made *USAToday*!

The Palm/3Com episode is not unique. Lamont and Thaler provide other examples during the 1998–2000 stock market bubble.[16] These mispricings often involved technology and internet stocks, with the more exciting internet stock being overpriced and the more traditional stock underpriced. A somewhat older example comes from the 1920s. In 1923, a young man named Benjamin Graham, later to coauthor a classic book on security analysis, was managing money. Graham noticed that although Du Pont owned a substantial number of General Motors (GM) shares, Du Pont's market capitalization was about the same as the value of its stake in GM. Du Pont had a stub value of about zero, despite the fact that Du Pont was one of America's leading industrial firms with other hugely valuable assets. Graham bought Du Pont, shorted GM, and profited when Du Pont subsequently rose.

Shorting Palm during this period was either difficult and expensive, or (for many investors) just impossible. Those who were able to borrow Palm paid a high price; D'Avolio reports maximum borrowing costs of 35% (in annual terms) for Palm in July 2000.[17]

Exhibit 7.3 shows data on short interest (expressed as a percent of total shares issued) and stub value (expressed in dollars per parent company stock price) for Palm (ignore the other line for now). The figures show that as the supply of shares available grows via short sales, the stub value gets more positive. One might interpret this pattern as roughly tracing out the demand curve for Palm. As the supply of shares grows via short sales, we move down the demand curve of irrational investors and Palm's price falls relative to the parent.

At its peak, short interest in Palm was an amazing 147.6% of all shares issued. More than all the floating shares had been sold short. This is possible if shares are borrowed, then sold short to an investor who then permits the shares to be borrowed again. This multiplier-type process takes time to operate, due to frictions in the securities lending market. This peak level of short interest for Palm was reached on 7/14/00, two weeks before the announced distribution, at a time when the stub was positive but rising. Exhibit 7.3 shows why short interest is at best a

---

[16] Lamont and Thaler, "Can the Market Add and Subtract?"
[17] D'Avolio, "The Market for Borrowing Stock."

EXHIBIT 7.3   3Com/Palm: Actual Stub, Synthetic Stub, and Short Interest: 3/3/00 to 7/21/00

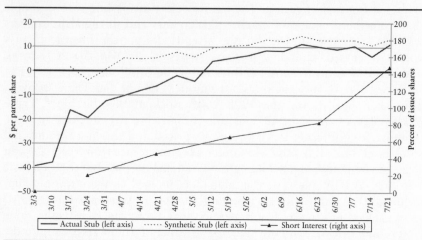

weak measure of shorting demand. Overpricing falls over time, while the level of short interest rises. Thus short interest can be negatively correlated with shorting demand and overpricing.

Outrageous Options Pricing

For pessimists, an alternative to shorting Palm would have been to buy puts (and write calls) on Palm. Exchange-traded options were introduced about two weeks after the IPO. Would this have been a good way to profit from the overpricing? The answer requires a careful examination of option prices, specifically a relationship called *put-call parity*.

Put-call parity only holds exactly for European options with no transactions costs; with American options in the presence of transactions costs, put-call parity is a set of bounds on prices rather than an exact relationship. One can speak loosely of put-call parity holding for American options, meaning that the relationship between securities prices approximates the exact situation with European options. One way of expressing put-call parity for Palm is to say that synthetic shares of Palm (constructed using options and borrowing and lending) should have the same price as actual shares of Palm.

A weaker condition than put-call parity, which should always hold for nondividend paying American options, is the following inequality: $C - P > S - X$, where C is the price of a call, X is the strike price, P is the price of put, and S is the price of the underlying security. For options that are at-the-money (so that S is equal to X), this inequality says that call prices should be greater than put prices. Since Palm does not pay dividends, this inequality should hold for Palm options.

Most empirical studies of options prices have found that the inequality is almost always satisfied, with small violations due perhaps to transactions costs. Options on Palm proved to be a dramatic exception to this pattern. Exhibit 7.1 shows options prices for Palm for March 16, on the first day that exchange options traded. Options on Palm display massive violations of put-call parity, and violate the weaker inequality as well. Instead of observing at-the-money call prices that are greater than put prices, we find puts were about twice as expensive as calls.

We also calculate the implied price of synthetic securities. For example, on March 17 one can create a synthetic short position in Palm by buying a November put (at the ask price), writing a November call (at the bid price), and borrowing dollars. Both the synthetic short and the actual short position, if held until November, give the same payoff of the negative of the price of Palm in November. These calculations are done using the assumption that one can borrow from March to November at 6-month LIBOR. On March 16 the price of the synthetic short was about $39.12, far below the actual trading price of Palm of $55.25. May and August options also showed substantial, though smaller violations of put-call parity.

The synthetic shorts at different horizons in Exhibit 7.4 can be used to calculate the implied holding cost of borrowing Palm's shares. For an investor who is indifferent to shorting actual Palm shares from March until May, and creating a synthetic short, the holding costs must be 14% over two months or about 119% at an annual rate. For an investor planning to short for 8 months, until November, the holding costs must be 29% or 147% at an annual rate. Thus the options prices suggest that shorting Palm was either incredibly expensive, or that there was a large excess demand for borrowing Palm shares, a demand that the market could not meet for some institutional reasons. Since the evidence from D'Avolio indicates a much lower 35% shorting cost for Palm during this period, it is clear that there must be other risks and costs associated with shorting Palm.

One can use the synthetic short price of Palm to create a synthetic stub value. On March 17, 2000, the actual stub value for Palm was −$16.26 per share. The synthetic stub for Palm, constructed using the synthetic short price implied in 6-month at-the-money options, was positive at $1.56. Although this value seems low (i.e., less than the cash 3Com held), it is at least positive and thus no longer so close to a pure arbitrage opportunity. Exhibit 7.3 displays the time series of the actual stubs along with the synthetic stubs for the time period up to the distribution date (constructing synthetic stubs using options that are closest to six months

EXHIBIT 7.4   Palm Options on 3/17/00

LIBOR

3-month	6.21
6-month	6.41

Stock Prices

Palm	55.25
3Com	68

Options Prices

	Call		Put		Synthetic Short	Percent Deviation	Synthetic Long	Percent Deviation
	Bid	Ask	Bid	Ask				
May 55	5.75	7.25	10.625	12.625	47.55	−14	51.05	−8
August 55	9.25	10.75	17.25	19.25	43.57	−21	47.07	−15
November 55	10	11.5	21.625	23.625	39.12	−29	42.62	−23

Note: May options expire 5/20/00. August options expire 08/19/00, November options expire 11/18/00. A synthetic short position buys a put (at the ask price), sells a call (at the bid price), and borrows the present value of the strike price. A synthetic long position sells a put (at the bid price), buys a call (at the ask price), and lends the present value of the strike price. We discount May cash flows by 3-month LIBOR and August and November cash flows by 6-month LIBOR. Source of options price data: CBOE. Source of LIBOR: Datastream.

and at-the-money). The solid line, the actual stub, goes from strongly negative at the beginning to positive $10 a share. The dotted line, the synthetic stub, is positive in all but one week. By the distribution date, the difference between the two lines is close to zero, roughly consistent with put-call parity. The pattern shows that options prices adjust to virtually eliminate profitable trading opportunities. Put differently, the implied cost of shorting falls as the desirability of shorting falls.

Thus we have three ways of inferring Palm's true value: the embedded value reflected in 3Com's share price, the value reflected in options prices, and the actual price. The market for November options and the shareholders in 3Com seemed to agree: Palm was worth far less than its market price. The direction of the deviation from put call parity is consistent with the difficulty of shorting Palm. To profit from the difference between the synthetic security and the underlying security, one would need to short Palm and buy the synthetic long. If shorting is costly, then the deviation can be interpreted as the cost of borrowing (shorting) Palm shares.

Again, although the prices here are consistent with very high shorting costs, one can turn the inequality around and ask why anyone would ever buy Palm (without lending it). On March 17 one can create a synthetic long Palm by buying a call and selling a put, and this synthetic long is 23% cheaper than buying an actual share of Palm and holding until November.

Arguments that the planned spin-off may not occur are irrelevant to the synthetic long constructed using options. Why are investors who buy Palm shares directly willing to pay much more than they could pay using the options market? One plausible explanation is that the type of investor buying Palm is ignorant about the options market and unaware of the cheaper alternative.

It is worth noting that the 3Com/Palm case is very unusual. In most cases, put-call parity holds. Ofek, Richardson, and Whitelaw study options prices during the tech stock mania period (a period where we would expect to find the most extreme cases of mispricing, such as 3Com/Palm). They find the average deviation between actual prices and synthetic prices to be very small. For a handful of firms, though, there are extreme violations. Confirming the 3Com/Pam results, for this handful of firms, Ofek, Richardson, and Whitelaw (forthcoming) find abnormal returns of about –2% per month for the period 1999–2002.

The 3Com/Palm case reflect several elements of the Harrison and Kreps story. First, Lamont and Thaler find that volume on the overpriced subsidiaries (such as Palm) to be far higher than volume on the underpriced parents (such as 3Com). Volume is key part of the story. Second, the story predicts that otherwise identical securities which cannot be traded at date 1 should have lower prices. Puts and calls are illiquid assets (especially compared to the highly traded Palm) with high bid/ask spreads. Thus, the difference between the price of Palm and the synthetic shares of Palm constructed from November options can be interpreted as a measure of the "speculative premium" of Harrison and Kreps. Third, Palm was a young company with a short operating history, and great uncertainty about its future. Thus it is easier to disagree about the true value of Palm than about 3Com, a mature company with less uncertainty.

The case of 3Com and Palm, while special, is interesting because it is a situation in which it is particularly easy for the market to get things right. To price Palm correctly versus 3Com requires investors to merely multiply by 1.5. If the market is flunking these no-brainers, what else is it getting wrong?

TECH STOCK MANIA AND SHORT SALE CONSTRAINTS

Can short sale constraints explain the amazing gyrations of stock prices in recent years? Prices seemed absurdly high in the period 1999–2000, especially for technology-related stocks. The Palm example shows that for some specific stocks, short sale constraints relating to mechanical problems in stock lending are surely the answer. More generally though, difficulty in borrowing stock cannot be the answer. Although Ofek and Richardson report that Internet stocks had higher average short interest and were more expensive to short than non-Internet stocks in this period, the average difference in cost was only 1% per year.[18] And one can always easily short NASDAQ or the S&P using futures or exchange-traded funds.

So if short sale constraints do play a wider role, it is not because of the stock lending difficulties, but because of more generic short sale constraints. It must be that investors are *unwilling* to establish short positions because of risk (such as fundamental risk or noise trader risk) or institutional constraints (such as the fact that mutual funds are mostly long only). Perhaps many investors thought that Internet stocks were overpriced during the mania, but only a small minority were willing to take a short position, and these short sellers were not enough to drive prices down to rational valuations.

Looking now at the aggregate market instead of individual stocks, there is a variety of evidence that is consistent with the short sale constraints story. Many of the factors leading to differences of opinion and thus to overpricing were present in this period. Reading Miller, it is hard not be impressed with the eerie similarities between his descriptions and the events of 1998–2000. The first factor that creates differences of opinion is that the firm has a short track record, or has intangible prospects: "The divergence of opinion about a new issue are greatest when the stock is issued. Frequently the company has not started operations, or these is uncertainty about the success of new products or the profitability of a major business expansion."[19]

The second is that the company has high visibility, so that there are many optimists: "Some companies are naturally well known because their products are widely advertised and widely consumed...Of course, the awareness of a security may be increased if the issuing company receives much publicity. For instance, new products and technological breakthroughs are news so that companies producing such products receive more publicity."[20]

---

[18] Eli Ofek and Matthew Richardson, "DotCom Mania: The Rise and Fall of Internet Stock Prices," *Journal of Finance* (June 2003), pp. 1113–1138.

[19] Miller, "Risk, Uncertainty, and Divergence of Opinion," p. 1156.

[20] Miller, "Risk, Uncertainty, and Divergence of Opinion," p. 1165.

Tech stocks certainly fit both of these criteria. Stocks like Amazon or AOL were familiar to the investing classes who used them, but unlike other familiar products (such as Coca-Cola) had a short operating history, so that optimists could construct castles in the sky without fear of contradiction by fact. Vissing-Jorgensen reports survey data on Internet use that seems to fit in with this story.[21] Investors who had actually used the Internet thought Internet stocks had higher expected returns than other stocks, and were more likely to include Internet stocks in their portfolio.

Recall in the Harrison and Kreps model, overpricing is associated with high volume, high dispersion of opinion, and widespread agreement that the market is overpriced in the long run but is unlikely to decline in the short run. Each one of these predictions is borne out in the data. First, volume on NASDAQ more than doubled between January 1999 and its peak in January 2001. Second, Vissing-Jorgensen finds that measures of investor disagreement with each other peaked in early 2000 around when stock prices peaked. Third, Exhibit 7.5, from a con-

EXHIBIT 7.5   Yale School of Management Stock Market Confidence Indexes™
The Percent of the Population Who Think that the Market Is Not Too High.

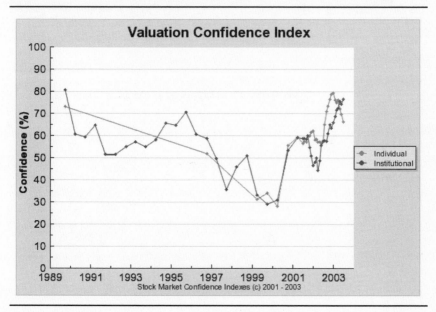

[21] Annette Vissing-Jorgensen, "Perspectives on Behavioral Finance: Does Irrationality Disappear with Wealth? Evidence from Expectations and Actions," in Mark Gertler and Kenneth Rogoff (eds.), *NBER Macroeconomics Annual 2003* (Cambridge, MA: MIT Press, 2004).

tinuing survey conducted by the Yale School of Management, shows that about 70% of those surveyed thought the market was overvalued in early 2000. Remarkably, Exhibit 7.6 shows that simultaneously, 70% of those surveyed also thought market would continue to go up. If everyone agrees the market is overvalued, but expects it to continue to go up amid high volume—this is the essence of the greater fool theory, and in particular the Harrison and Kreps version.

Another fact explained by the overpricing hypothesis is the very high level of stock issuance that occurred from 1998 to 2000. One interpretation is that issuers and underwriters knew that stocks were overpriced and so rushed to issue. Evidence arising out of subsequent legal action against underwriters (such as emails sent by investment bank employees) is certainly consistent with the hypothesis that the underwriters thought the market was putting too high a value on new issues. One way to think about issuance is as a mechanism for overcoming short sale constraints. Both short selling and issuance have the effect of increasing the amount of stock that the optimists can buy; both are examples of supply increasing in response to high prices. Suppose you think Lamont.com is overpriced in 1999. One way to take advantage of this fact is to short the stock. In doing this, you are selling overpriced

EXHIBIT 7.6   The Percent of the Population Expecting an increase in the Dow in the Coming Year.

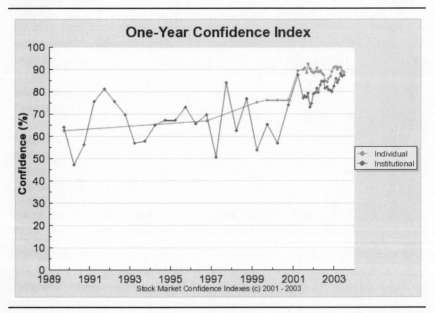

shares to optimists. This action is very risky, however, as Lamont.com might well double in price. A safer alternative action is for you to start a new company that competes with Lamont.com, call it Lamont2.com, and issue stock. This IPO is another way to sell overpriced shares to optimists.

SUMMARY

The overpricing hypothesis says stocks can be overpriced when something constrains pessimists from shorting. In addition to short sale constraints, there also needs to be either irrational investors, or investors with differences of opinion. This chapter has shown a variety of evidence consistent with the overpricing hypothesis. First, I have discussed three studies of extreme overpricing leading to extremely low subsequent returns. Second, I have discussed some suggestive evidence that the tech stock mania period that peaked in March 2000 may also have been overpricing due to the reluctance of pessimists to go short.

CHAPTER 8

How Short Selling Expands the Investment Opportunity Set and Improves Upon Potential Portfolio Efficiency

Steven L. Jones, Ph.D.
Associate Professor of Finance
Indiana University, Kelley School of Business–Indianapolis

Glen Larsen, Ph.D., CFA
Professor of Finance
Indiana University, Kelley School of Business–Indianapolis

Harry Markowitz's seminal work on mean-variance portfolio optimization did not allow for short sales of risky securities.[1] Professional money managers who use portfolio analysis have traditionally ignored this opportunity as well, due either to institutional constraints or the difficulties involved with short selling.[2] Yet, short selling clearly repre-

---

[1] Harry M. Markowitz, "Portfolio Selection," *Journal of Finance* (March 1952), pp. 77–91; and Harry M. Markowitz, *Portfolio Selection: Efficient Diversification of Investments* (Somerset, NJ: John Wiley and Sons, 1959).

[2] Harry M. Markowitz, "Nonnegative or Not Nonnegative: A Question about CAPMs," *Journal of Finance* (May 1983), pp. 283–295. Markowitz notes that his assumption of no short selling is generally consistent with institutional practice. He is particularly critical of portfolio optimization models that allow short sales but ignore escrow and margin requirements and thus tend to give solutions with extreme positive and negative weights that cannot be implemented in practice.

sents an opportunity to expand upon the long-only investment set, and there are several reasons to believe that this offers the potential to improve upon realized (*ex post*) mean-variance portfolio efficiency.

First, as several of this book's chapters point out, there is considerable evidence of transitory overpricing in stocks that are expensive to short sell as well as in stocks with high short interest. Thus, short selling such stocks, when they are thought to overpriced, has the potential to improve upon mean portfolio returns. Second, the opportunity to short sell effectively doubles the number of assets, from N to $2N$. This clearly offers the potential to reduce portfolio variance since the covariances of the second set of N stocks (potentially held short) have the opposite sign from the respective covariances in the first set of N stocks (potentially held long).

It is important to recognize, however, that while short selling offers the potential to improve realized portfolio efficiency, there is no guarantee without perfect foresight (ex ante). That is, if one can be certain of the forecasted means and covariances, then short selling improves mean-variance efficiency as a simple matter of portfolio mathematics. Recent empirical research, however, suggests that covariance forecasts are so fraught with error that realized portfolio efficiency might actually be improved by restricting or even prohibiting short positions. In addition, very little work has been done on how best to reflect the margin requirements of short selling in the portfolio optimization model. For example, the so-called "full-investment constraint" is usually defined such that the portfolio weights are constrained only in that they must sum to one, with negative weights assigned to short positions, and without any constraint on the magnitudes of the weights. This assumes there are no escrow and margin requirements, which implies that all of the proceeds from short selling are available to finance additional investment in long positions.

We begin the next section by explaining the predictions of mean-variance portfolio theory and its logical extension, the *Capital Asset Pricing Model* (CAPM). In theory, short selling is not needed to optimize portfolio efficiency as long as market prices reflect equilibrium required returns. But despite this result, we do not dismiss short selling as unnecessary; instead, the result serves to emphasize the importance of distinguishing between investors based on their information set. We assume that active investors trade based on some informational advantage, while investors lacking any such advantages are logically passive. Thus, indexing, rather than short selling, is probably the best way for passive investors to optimize their potential portfolio efficiency. Other practical implications emerge from considering the theoretical predictions in light of the actual requirements of short selling. Although we focus on the effects of margin requirements and escrowed short sale proceeds, we also point out that the risk of recall and the transitory nature of overpricing means that short positions must be actively managed. We then consider the evidence on whether short selling improves realized portfolio efficiency, which is mixed, as was mentioned above. We close by summarizing the practical implications of the theory and evidence.

SHORT SELLING IN EFFICIENT PORTFOLIOS: THE THEORY AND ITS PRACTICAL IMPLICATIONS

We first consider the role of short selling in mean-variance portfolio theory and the CAPM. While the theory predicts a minimal role for short selling in a passive investor's portfolio, the analysis provides a useful framework for thinking about the conditions necessary for short positions to appear in efficient portfolios. This framework provides the basis for later consideration of (1) how active investors can improve expected portfolio efficiency, ex ante, by short selling, and (2) how margin requirements and the escrowing of short sales proceeds affect the feasible asset allocation.

Short Holdings in a Passive Investor's Efficient Portfolio

Passive management has become almost synonymous with *indexing*, but this definition omits any description of *passive* or *active investors*. Active investors believe they can identify and profit from mispriced securities, either through their own analysis or by paying for active management. *Active management* is usually associated with a goal of improving mean returns by trading on transitory advantages. Passive investors remain so because they lack the time or the skill to identify mispriced securities, and they do not believe active management is worth the higher fees, so their goal is adequate diversification. Although both types of investors may short sell, the important distinction is that only active investors can short sell with the expectation of improving mean returns; passive investors will short sell only for the purpose of diversification.

Mean-Variance Portfolio Theory and the CAPM

Markowitz's mean-variance portfolio theory is a prescription for how to choose and construct efficient portfolios. The resulting frontier shown in Exhibit 8.1, in terms of expected mean returns (Er) and standard deviations (σ, the square root of the variance), represents the minimum variance attainable at every level of return based on estimates of the expected returns for individual securities and the return covariances for pairs of securities. The positively sloped portion of this *minimum-variance frontier*, above the unique *minimum-variance portfolio* (MV), is referred to as the *efficient frontier* of risky assets. Note that it would be

EXHIBIT 8.1 Minimum-Variance Frontier

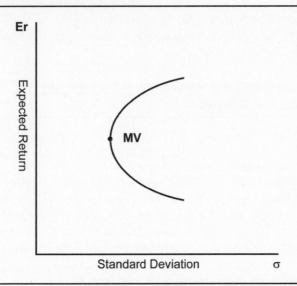

suboptimal to hold any portfolio on the negatively sloped portion of the frontier when there is a portfolio with the same standard deviation but a higher expected mean return on the positively sloped portion. While the ex post minimum-variance frontier can be computed from historical returns, the portfolio analyst is primarily concerned with forecasting the frontier of the future, ex ante. Thus, the analyst is focused on predicting the expected return and covariance inputs, and this is usually done through a combination of statistical analysis and judgment.

The CAPM is based on Markowitz's portfolio theory in that it describes how equilibrium (i.e., market clearing) expected returns are determined when investors care only about expected return and variance and thus hold mean-variance efficient portfolios. Although the standard Sharpe-Lintner CAPM[3] allows for short selling, the assumptions of homogeneous expectations and borrowing and lending at a risk-free rate imply that no investor will hold a short position in equilibrium. This is illustrated in Exhibit 8.2, where the opportunity to borrow or lend at a risk-free rate (r_f) results in a unique mean-variance efficient

---

[3] William F. Sharpe, "Capital Asset Prices: A Theory of Market Equilibrium Under Conditions of Risk," *Journal of Finance* (September 1964), pp. 425–442. John Lintner, "The Valuation of Risk Assets and the Selection of Risky Investments in Stock Portfolios and Capital Budgets," *Review of Economics and Statistics* (February 1965), pp. 13–37.

EXHIBIT 8.2   Standard CAPM with Risk-Free Lending and Borrowing

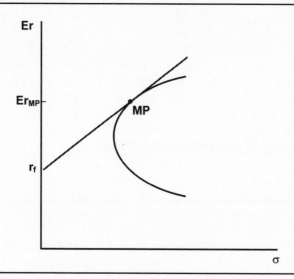

portfolio of risky assets that is also the *market portfolio* (MP), by definition, given that all risky assets must be held in equilibrium. Homogenous expectations mean that all investors share common beliefs about the joint probability distributions of future returns (i.e., means and covariances); thus, the market portfolio comprises the risky portion of their individual portfolios. More risk averse investors move down the line, toward r_f, by holding MP and lending at the risk-free rate, while more aggressive investors move up the line, above MP, by holding MP and borrowing at the risk-free rate.

The fundamental pricing relation predicted by the standard CAPM is that an asset's expected return (Er) equals the risk-free rate (r_f) plus the product of its beta (β), and the risk premium on MP over the risk-free rate $(Er_{MP} - r_f)$. An asset's beta represents its return volatility relative to MP (i.e., the covariance risk the asset contributes to the risky market portfolio). This pricing relation will hold for individual assets as long as investors view the unique mean-variance efficient portfolio as optimal; in which case, it is the market portfolio, where the quantity of shares supplied for each stock equals the quantity demanded. This implies that MP represents all investors' consensus expectation as to the mean-variance, efficient-risky portfolio of the future.

Lintner shows, in later work, that dropping the assumption of homogeneous expectations does not alter the pricing implications of the CAPM since the demands of heterogeneous investors still aggregate to the mean-variance efficient market portfolio.[4] That is, MP still represents the prevailing expectation, across all investors, as to the optimal risky portfolio. Thus, while dropping homogeneous expectations at least introduces the possibility of short selling by individual investors based on their own expectations, the CAPM still predicts that investors without special insights would do well to follow a passive strategy of holding MP and then either borrow or lend as their risk aversion dictates. The uniqueness of MP, however, depends on the ability of investors to borrow or lend at the same risk-free rate, which by definition must have a variance of zero.

The CAPM Without Risk-Free Lending and Borrowing

While it is obvious that no one can borrow at a risk-free rate, it is arguably impossible to lend at a risk-free rate, as well, given that even U.S. Treasury bills are subject to the risk of unexpected inflation. Granted, *Treasury inflation-protected securities* (TIPS) are available as U.S. Treasury notes and bonds, but these are also risky to the extent that interest rates fluctuate for reasons other than the Consumer Price Index. Dropping the assumption that investors can borrow or lend at a risk-free rate means the CAPM survives in the form of Fischer Black's so-called zero-beta CAPM,[5] in which short selling plays a critical role.

The zero-beta CAPM makes use of the *two-fund separation theorem*, which states that any point on the minimum-variance frontier can be achieved by holding some combination of any two portfolios on the frontier. Thus, as illustrated in Exhibit 8.3, more risk-averse investors can create the minimum-variance portfolio of risky assets (MV), or some other relatively low risk portfolio, from long positions in MP and Z, where portfolio Z is unique in that it is the minimum-variance portfolio that is uncorrelated with MP (i.e., portfolio Z has a beta of zero.)[6] To move above MP, however, more aggressive investors must short sell Z to raise the additional funds necessary to invest more than 100% of their wealth in MP. Thus, in the zero-beta CAPM, short sales provide a method of financing for aggressive investors in the absence of risk-free borrowing.[7]

---

[4] John Lintner, "The Aggregation of Investors' Diverse Judgments and Preferences in Perfectly Competitive Markets," *Journal of Financial and Quantitative Analysis* (December 1969), pp. 347–400.

[5] Fischer Black, "Capital Market Equilibrium With Restricted Borrowing," *Journal of Business* (July 1972), pp.444–455.

[6] Black proves that a unique zero-beta portfolio (Z) lies below the minimum-variance portfolio (MV), on the inefficient portion of the minimum variance frontier.

[7] The pricing relation of zero-beta CAPM is the same as the standard CAPM, except the expected return on the zero-beta portfolio (Z) replaces the risk-free rate, and Black shows, by proof, that the expected return on portfolio Z is higher than the risk-free rate.

EXHIBIT 8.3 Zero-Beta CAPM

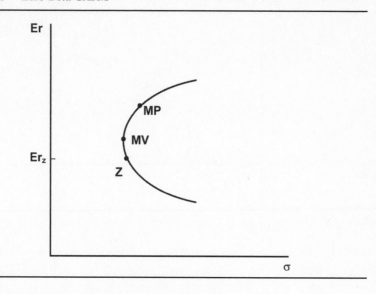

The CAPM with Differential Risk-Free Rates on Lending and Borrowing

Rather than simply ignore opportunities to borrow or lend at fixed rates, it is probably more realistic to just recognize that borrowing costs more (r_B) than lending yields (r_L) and to assume that these differential rates are effectively risk free. In this case, as is illustrated in Exhibit 8.4, a series of efficient risky portfolios lie on the efficient frontier between portfolios L and B. More risk-averse investors hold the risky portfolio L, which is effectively a combination of long positions in MP and Z, and they may move down the solid line, toward r_L, by investing in Treasury bills or TIPS. More aggressive investors hold the risky portfolio B, which can be created by going-long portfolio MP and short-selling Z. They can move up the solid line from B by borrowing at the broker's call rate and thus increasing their investment in B. The dashed line is meant only to demonstrate that the intercept of the higher solid line, anchored at B, is r_B, the broker's call rate.

Thus, in this arguably realistic scenario, short selling may be optimal for aggressive investors, although beyond B, it makes sense for more aggressive investors to begin to margin their long positions, rather than continue to sell short. This outcome is more realistic than that of the above zero-beta model, which assumed unlimited short selling such that the sellers had full use of the sale proceeds. Note that unlimited

EXHIBIT 8.4   CAPM with Differential Lending and Borrowing Rates

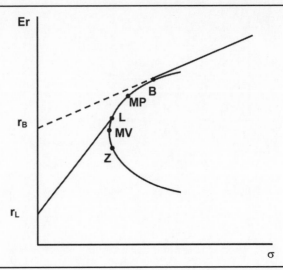

short selling is implied when the full-investment constraint is specified such that the weights of the portfolio holdings sum to one, with negative weights assigned to short positions. This specification, however, ignores that in practice the full amount of the proceeds from a short sale are placed in escrow with the broker and the short seller is required to put up margin of at least 50% of the proceeds, as well.[8] Under these restrictions, only limited short selling is possible. Fortunately, limited short selling is more than adequate to span (i.e., move along) the frontier from portfolio L to B.

To see this, consider the top panel in Exhibit 8.5. We assume an investor initially has $15,000 long in portfolio MP, $5,000 long in portfolio Z, and long margin is 100% (= equity/assets or $20,000/$20,000). The combined positions will locate three-quarters of the distance from Z toward MP on the minimum-variance frontier in Exhibit 8.4. This is slightly above portfolio L, which lies about equal distance between Z and MP. Now assume the investor sells the $5,000 long position in portfolio Z and uses the funds as margin to short sell $10,000 of portfolio Z. The middle panel

---

[8] Some long-short hedge funds effectively get around the 50% margin requirement of the Federal Reserve Board's Regulation T, as well as the escrowing of short sale proceeds, by borrowing additional funds from their brokerage firm. Thus, every $1 short finances another $1 long. This is sometimes called 3-for-1 investing, where $3 are invested ($2 long and $1 short) for every $1 of capital. In some cases, it may be possible to use even more margin than this example implies.

EXHIBIT 8.5   Limited Short Sales with 50% Margins

Initial Long Positions in Portfolios MP and Z (Combined position locates slightly above Portfolio L on the Minimum-Variance Frontier in Exhibit 8.4.)

Assets		Liabilities	
Portfolio MP	$15,000	Margin Loan	0
Portfolio Z	$5,000	Equity	$20,000
Long margin = Equity/Assets = $20,000/$20,000 = 100%			

Sell $5,000 of Portfolio Z—use funds as Margin to Short Sell Portfolio Z

Assets		Liabilities	
Short Sale Proceeds	$10,000	Portfolio Z	$10,000
Margin Requirement	$5,000	Equity	$5,000
Short margin = Equity/Liabilities = $5,000/$10,000 = 50%			

Final Long Position in Portfolio MP

Assets		Liabilities	
Portfolio MP	$30,000	Margin Loan	$15,000
		Equity	$15,000
Long margin = Equity/Assets = $15,000/$30,000 = 50%			

Final Weights in the Portfolio of Risky Assets: W_{MP}^{R} = $30,000/$20,000 = 1.5 and W_{Z}^{R} = –$10,000/$20,000 = –0.5 (Combined position locates at Portfolio *B* on the Minimum-Variance Frontier in Exhibit 8.4, or just below *B* if borrowing rate > lending rate.)

Total equity from Long + Short positions = $20,000; Net lending, borrowing = 0 as Escrowed short sale proceeds + Short margin requirement = Long margin loan.

of Exhibit 8.5 shows the short position in portfolio *Z* as a liability, the escrowed proceeds and margin as assets, and the $5,000 in equity necessary to satisfy the 50% margin requirement of the Federal Reserve Board's Regulation T (short margin = equity/liabilities = $5,000/$10,000). Next, in the bottom panel, the investor buys $15,000 more of portfolio MP and finances this purchase with a $15,000 margin loan. Thus, with the final long and short margins both at the 50% minimum, the ending portfolio weights are W_{MP} = 1.5 and W_Z = –0.5, which locates (approximately) at portfolio *B* in Exhibit 8.4 since B lies above MP by about one-half of the distance from *Z* to MP on the minimum-variance frontier.

Thus, in this example, the investor can use combinations of portfolios MP and Z to span from *L* to *B* without violating margin requirements. Note that the dollar amounts of lending (the assets of the short position) and borrowing (the liabilities of the long position) must offset if the resulting combination is to lie on the minimum-variance frontier. The costs, however, will not offset given that we allow for differential rates, here in Exhibit 8.4, and the broker's call rate on a margin loan is certain to be higher than both the rebate rate on the escrowed short sale proceeds, as well as the rate of return on the $5,000 short margin requirement.[9] This means that the final portfolio weights in Exhibit 8.5 will actually locate just below portfolio B, rather than right on it, indicating a slightly lower expected return. Still, Exhibit 8.4 is a reasonable approximation of a passive investor's opportunity set.

Investors may hold portfolio L and move down the solid line toward r_L by purchasing U.S. Treasury bills or TIPS; they can move up the minimum-variance frontier from L by increasing the weight in the market portfolio (MP), and they can move above MP, toward portfolio B, by short selling portfolio Z. If, however, an investor constructs portfolio B such that $W_{MP} = 1.5$ and $W_Z = -0.5$, as in Exhibit 8.5, then it is impossible to borrow and move up the solid line from B without violating the 50% margin requirements.[10] However, it may still be possible to borrow and move up the solid line, from portfolio B, given that B can be constructed from long-only positions under conditions established by Richard Green.[11]

Short Positions on the Minimum-Variance Frontier   Green shows that all the positions on the minimum-variance frontier, and thus the efficient frontier, can be achieved with portfolios of long-only positions, unless there remains an asset with an expected return of zero, or less, that is positively correlated with all other assets. The existence of such an asset represents a short selling opportunity that will improve the efficiency of any portfolio made up of long positions only. To see this, recall that a short position's expected return and correlations have the opposite sign as that of a long

---

[9] If the borrowing and lending rates are equal, then the model reduces to the standard CAPM with a unique optimal risky portfolio. In fact, Lintner assumed equal rates when he concluded that margin requirements on short sales do not alter the CAPM or its prediction of a unique optimal risky portfolio. John Lintner, "The Effects of Short Selling and Margin Requirements in Perfect Capital Markets," *Journal of Financial and Quantitative Analysis* (December 1971), pp. 1173–1195.

[10] Later, in this chapter, we discuss in detail the limitations that margin requirements place on active short sellers in their attempts to achieve enhanced portfolio efficiency. These limitations are irrelevant to passive investors since they may construct portfolio B from long positions, as explained immediately hereafter.

[11] Richard C. Green, "Positively Weighted Portfolios on the Minimum-Variance Frontier," *Journal of Finance* (December 1986), pp. 1051–1068.

position in the same asset. Thus, short selling an asset with an expected return of zero and positive correlations (with all other assets) will not change the expected return, but it will reduce the variance of any long-only portfolio (as a result of the short position's negative correlation with all other assets). If the asset had a negative expected return, then it would represent an even better hedging opportunity since short selling it would actually increase the expected return and reduce the variance of any long-only portfolio.

Green points out that the existence of such an opportunity is inconsistent with the CAPM's equilibrium pricing relation, as well as with equilibrium as defined in most other recognized asset-pricing models. This is because pricing models logically predict that assets that have positive return correlations with most other assets must offer positive expected returns to compensate investors for exposing their wealth to covariance risk. Although pricing inefficiencies and disequilibrium may result in transitory short selling opportunities, attempting to identify and exploit such opportunities is for active, not passive, investors. Passive investors lack the time or the skill to identify overpriced securities, and they do not believe active management is worth the higher fees.

In theory, limited short selling will span the efficient frontier, but passive investors can optimize their potential efficiency with a long-only portfolio, and indexing offers a low-cost solution. Individual securities could be used to adjust the index for an investor's risk aversion. Those whose risk aversion lies well above or below average should use either a margin loan or very low-risk lending, respectively, as in Exhibit 8.4, rather than let their risky portfolio deviate too far from the target index.

Short Holdings in an Active Investor's Efficient Portfolio

We have seen that short selling has little to offer passive investors. The question is how should active investors, who have some prospects of identifying overpriced stocks, go about short selling so as to improve potential portfolio efficiency. We analyze the theoretical justifications for three specific strategies: (1) enhanced indexing with short selling, (2) long-plus-short portfolios, and (3) integrated long-short portfolios. Risk-neutral and dollar-neutral long-short portfolios are not addressed here because they represent arbitrage strategies that are not primarily concerned with portfolio optimization.[12] Later, we consider how margin requirements and the escrowing of short sales proceeds affect the feasible asset allocation.

---

[12] Risk or dollar neutral portfolios may offer arbitrage profits, but these portfolios, alone, are unlikely to maximize an investor's utility. See Bruce I. Jacobs, Kenneth N. Levy, and David Starer, "On the Optimality of Long-Short Strategies," *Financial Analysts Journal* (March/April 1998), pp. 40–51.

Enhanced Indexing with Short Selling

As several other chapters in this book point out, a considerable amount of evidence indicates that individual stocks may occasionally become over-priced, and short interest or the costs of short selling may offer some clues for identifying these stocks. This suggests a strategy of enhanced index-ing, where long positions reflect a passive index and short positions are held in a separate active portfolio.[13] This active portfolio is comprised of positions that represent a conscious attempt to "beat the market." Long positions could be included in this active portfolio, but short positions have a distinct advantage in that they offer the opportunity to hedge against the long-only index. That is, return correlations between the short positions and the long-only index tend to be negative since the opposite is true for the long positions. Thus, we will assume that our active portfolio is made up only of short positions. Part of the logic for separate portfolios is that the short positions in the active portfolio are speculative, by nature, and at risk of recall; therefore, they have shorter durations and require more attention than the positions in the long-only index.

Enhanced indexing with short selling offers a clear advantage over long-only enhanced indexing in that the latter limits active investors from fully utilizing negative information about a security. Richard Grinold and Ronald Kahn point out that the opportunity costs of long-only indexing are especially high in small-capitalization stocks.[14] To see this, consider an example in which a stock comprises only 0.1% of the benchmark index, long-only investors can materially overweight this stock, in their enhanced index, but only a 0.1% underweight can be established. That is, if long-only investors believe the stock will significantly underperform, there is not much they can do other than sell their long position in the stock.

To see graphically how an active short-only portfolio can improve effi-ciency, we consider an opportunity, like the one described by Richard Green, with returns that are positively correlated with those of most other assets and an expected return that is negative. The returns to a short posi-tion in this hypothetical asset are negatively correlated with most other assets and the expected return is positive. Exhibit 8.6 plots a short position (S^H) that meets these conditions and shows that the position acts like a hedging asset when introduced to a preexisting minimum-variance frontier. The newly feasible tangency portfolio, P^*, now replaces MP as the optimal

---

[13] The idea of holding a passive portfolio supplemented by a separate actively man-aged portfolio comes from Jack L. Treynor and Fischer Black, "How to Use Security Analysis to Improve Portfolio Selection," *Journal of Business* (January 1973), pp. 66–86.

[14] Richard C. Grinold and Robert C. Kahn, "The Efficiency Gains of Long-Short In-vesting," *Financial Analysts Journal* (November/December, 2000), pp. 40–53.

risky portfolio, despite the fact that P^* has a lower expected return than MP. This is because P^* has the higher *Sharpe ratio* (i.e., a higher ratio of excess return to standard deviation). Sharpe ratios are represented in Exhibit 8.6 as the slopes of the lines, SR_{P^*} and SR_{MP}, anchored at r_f and tangent to the respective minimum-variance frontiers.[15] The portfolio with the highest Sharpe ratio is considered more efficient since holding portfolio P^* and either borrowing or lending at the risk-free rate, so as to move up or down the line from P^*, offers opportunities that dominate those that can be generated from MP.[16] Note that, in this example, the primary reason for the improved portfolio efficiency is the negative return correlation between this short position (S^H) and the market portfolio (MP), which results in the more exaggerated convexity of the new minimum-variance portfolio (relative to the expected return axis) in Exhibit 8.6.

EXHIBIT 8.6   Enhanced Indexing by Hedging with Short Sales

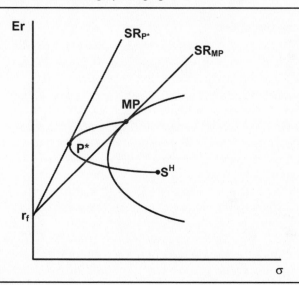

---

[15] The square root of the increase in the Sharpe ratio is equivalent to the *Information ratio*. This ratio is popular for measuring the performance improvement attributable to actively managed strategies. It is defined as the ratio of excess return (or *alpha*) over residual risk, where alpha and residual risk are usually estimated with the empirical CAPM. The empirical CAPM is simply a CAPM-based regression model.

[16] Note that we have gone back to the assumption of lending and borrowing at a single risk-free rate in Exhibit 8.6 only to simplify the graph. The larger point, that such a short position improves portfolio efficiency, still holds even with differential lending and borrowing rates. We will soon reintroduce the effect of differential rates and that margin requirements severely limit borrowing when short selling.

Interpreting Exhibit 8.6 in terms of enhanced indexing implies that the market portfolio (MP) is the desired long-only index, while the short position (S^H) can be thought of as a short-only portfolio in one or more stocks. Since the long-only index is passive, the line between passive and active has been somewhat blurred. One can imagine that an otherwise passive investor might short sell one or few securities to hedge against a specific source of risk. As mentioned earlier, the distinction gets back to whether the goal is return enhancement or risk reduction. In this example, the nature of the short position (S^H) indicates that the goal is risk reduction, but with a different short position, the goal could have been return enhancement, just as easily. An alternative to enhanced indexing involves taking an active strategy in both the short-only portfolio and the long-only portfolio. We refer to this as an active long-plus-short strategy, where the long and short positions are held in separate portfolios, just as with enhanced indexing.

Long-Plus-Short Portfolios

There are two reasons why long-plus-short portfolios might beat enhanced indexing with short selling. First, the investor may be adept at picking underpriced stocks, as well as overpriced stocks. In which case, short selling provides what is *expected* to be a low-cost method of leveraging knowledge of underpricing, but this works only if the price of the short-sold asset behaves as expected. If the price increases or if the short position is recalled before the price has time to decline, then short selling can be disastrously expensive. Thus, as a means of leveraging long positions, short sales present much more risk than long margin.

Second, if an investor believes the market portfolio (or index) is less than mean-variance efficient, ex ante, then the investor may be better off constructing their own long portfolio. For example, if the capital markets place a relatively high value on liquidity, such that the CAPM is misspecified, then holding the market portfolio long amounts to paying for liquidity, and an investor who is more buy-and-hold oriented on the long side may have little need for this liquidity. Consequently, constructing a long-only portfolio that is mean-variance efficient based on relatively passive inputs may be preferred to the market portfolio (or a similar index). In this case, the long-plus-short strategy is meant to provide better passive long-side efficiency than enhanced indexing with short sales.

Clearly, the long-only portfolios account for the difference between enhanced indexing with short sales and long-plus-short; thus, the strategies appear much the same graphically. Exhibit 8.7 illustrates how an active long-plus-short strategy can enhance efficiency. The actively managed long-only portfolio (L) results from optimizing on an investor's mean-variance inputs. Portfolio S^O represents an actively managed short-only portfolio. The location of S^O, on the mean-variance plane, is intended to reflect a strategy of identifying and short selling overpriced stocks; thus, the higher expected return and the less exaggerated convexity, when compared to that of portfolio S^H, which served to illustrate a hedging motive in Exhibit 8.6.[17] Note that this alternative short position, S^O, is introduced as a way of generalizing the illustrations and is not meant to imply any inherent difference between the short positions used in enhanced indexing versus those used in active long-plus-short portfolios.

The resulting optimal risky portfolio P^*, in Exhibit 8.7, has a higher expected return and about the same standard deviation as the active long-only portfolio (L); thus, P^* is clearly more efficient since its Sharp ratio, SR_{P^*}, is higher than SR_L. As mentioned above, the only advantage of a long-plus-short strategy over enhanced indexing with short selling is, of course, the potential for the actively managed long-only portfolio (L) to achieve greater efficiency than the market portfolio (MP). But even in that case, if the return correlation with the active short-only portfolio is lower for MP than for L, then enhanced indexing could still achieve greater overall efficiency.

EXHIBIT 8.7   Enhanced Efficiency with Long-plus-Short Portfolios

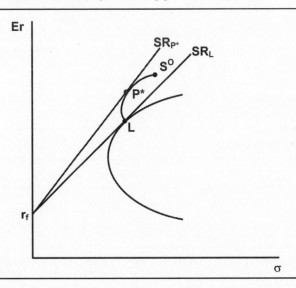

[17] The less exaggerated convexity of the frontier between portfolios S^O and L in Exhibit 8.7, when compared to that between portfolios S^H and MP in Exhibit 8.6, indicates that the return correlation between portfolios S^O and L is higher (less negative) than that between portfolios S^H and MP.

Effects of Margin Requirements and Escrowing Proceeds on Asset Allocation   In using Sharpe ratios to evaluate portfolio efficiency, we have effectively assumed unlimited borrowing and lending at the same risk-free rate. But the rate on borrowing is certainly higher than the rate on lending. In addition, when the optimal risky portfolio involves short positions, as with portfolio P^* in Exhibit 8.7, margin requirements severely restrict the amount of net borrowing possible. To see this, consider an investor with $10,000 in equity and assume that mean-variance optimization identifies the weights of the portfolios L and S^O in the optimal risky portfolio, P^*, of Exhibit 8.7, as $W_L^R = 1.5$ and $W_{S^O}^R = -0.5$. Exhibit 8.8 shows that these weights can be achieved while satisfying the margin requirements by going short $5,000 in portfolio S^O and long $15,000 in portfolio L. Just as in the previous example, in Exhibit 8.5, this set of weights results in offsetting dollar amounts of lending and borrowing. Short sale proceeds and short margin total $7,500, while the final long margin, in the bottom panel, is $7,500.

Recall, however, that the short positions in Exhibits 8.6 and 8.7 are plotted as if they were long positions. Thus, the portfolio weights need to be adjusted to reflect the perspective of these exhibits. This is done by taking the absolute value of the unadjusted weights, above, as a propor-

EXHIBIT 8.8   Asset Allocation in the Optimal Risky Portfolio (P^*)
Short Position in Portfolio S^O

Assets		Liabilities	
Short Sale Proceeds	$5,000	Portfolio S^O	$5,000
Margin Requirement	$2,500	Equity	$2,500
Short margin = Equity/Liabilities = $2,500/$5,000 = 50%			

Long Position in Portfolio L

Assets		Liabilities	
Portfolio L	$15,000	Margin Loan	$7,500
		Equity	$7,500
Long margin = Equity/Assets = $7,500/$15,000 = 50%			

Unadjusted Weights in P*, *the Optimal Risky Portfolio:* $W_L^R = \$15,000/\$10,000 =$ 1.5 and $W_{S^O}^R = -\$5,000/\$10,000 = -0.5$

Adjusted Weights in P*, *the Optimal Risky Portfolio:* $W_{|L|}^R = \$15,000/\$20,000 =$ 0.75 and $W_{|S^O|}^R = \$5,000/\$20,000 = 0.25$

Total equity from long + Short positions = $10,000; Net lending, borrowing = 0 as Escrowed short sale proceeds + Short margin requirement = Long margin loan.

tion of the sum of these absolute values. This yields adjusted weights for L and S^O, in the optimal risky portfolio P^*, of

$$W^R_{|L|} = 1.5/2.0 = 0.75 \text{ and } W^R_{|S^O|} = 0.5/2.0 = 0.25$$

where the absolute value signs in the subscripts indicate that the weights have been computed so that a positive weight in S^O represents a short position in that portfolio. Note that when assigning the dollar amounts invested, these adjusted weights should be applied to the total dollar amount available for investment, whereas the unadjusted weights are applied to the total equity amount. The total dollar amount available for investment is $20,000, the product of total equity and the sum of the absolute values of the unadjusted weights, where 2.0 indicates that both the long and short margin have been pushed to 50%.[18]

This procedure for calculating adjusted weights is basically the same as for the so-called "Lintnerian" definition of short sales (named for the short-sale constraint as formulated in John Lintner's version of the CAPM). Under the Lintnerian definition, however, the dollar amounts invested are assigned by multiplying the adjusted weights by the total equity. Thus, given the Lintnerian definition of short sales, the adjusted weights,

$$W^R_{|L|} = 0.75 \text{ and } W^R_{|S^O|} = 0.25$$

would dictate that $10,000 in equity be invested as a $7,500 long position in portfolio L and a $2,500 short position in portfolio S^O. This, of course, implies 100% long and short margin. We suggest that a more realistic dollar allocation can be computed, as above, by multiplying the amount available for investment (given the desired level of margin) by the adjusted weights. This is what we did in Exhibit 8.8, except there we targeted the optimal risky portfolio. (That particular combination of weights resulted in no net borrowing or lending at 50% long and short margin.) Next, we consider how risk-averse investors can lend or borrow to achieve their own optimal complete portfolio (over the risk-free and risky assets).

---

[18] We consider the margin requirements in a manner similar to Gordon J. Alexander, "Short Selling and Efficient Sets," *Journal of Finance* (September, 1993), pp. 1497–1506. In addition to addressing portfolio optimization with short selling and fractional margin requirements, Alexander specifies that the expected return on a short position equals the negative of the expected return on the respective long position plus rebate interest on escrowed short sale proceeds and interest on the short margin requirement.

Let us first consider an investor with greater than average risk-aversion, implying that utility is maximized by holding the optimal risky portfolio, P^*, in combination with lending. Assume, for example, that the investor's optimal complete portfolio is $W_L^C = 0.6$, $W_{S^O}^C = -0.2$, and $W_{Lending}^C = 0.6$ in terms of unadjusted weights. (Note that the weights for portfolios L and S^O remain in the same relative proportions as in the optimal risky portfolio, P^*, in Exhibit 8.8.) Exhibit 8.9 shows that these weights can be achieved while satisfying the margin requirements by going short \$2,000 in portfolio S^O and long \$6,000 in portfolio L. There is also \$6,000 in lending, \$3,000 of which is required in the form of short margin and escrowed short sale proceeds.

From the perspective of Exhibit 8.7, this complete portfolio lies on the line, below portfolio P^*, with a slope (i.e., Sharpe ratio) of SR_{P^*}. The adjusted weights for this complete portfolio are computed, as before, by taking the absolute value of these unadjusted weights as a proportion of the sum of these absolute values.

$$W_{|L|}^C = 0.6/1.4 = 0.43, \quad W_{|S^O|}^C = 0.2/1.4 = 0.14, \quad \text{and} \quad W_{|Lending|}^C = 0.6/1.4 = 0.43$$

EXHIBIT 8.9 Optimal Asset Allocation with Lending

Short Position in Portfolio S^O

Assets		Liabilities	
Short Sale Proceeds	\$2,000	Portfolio S^O	\$2,000
Margin Requirement	\$1,000	Equity	\$1,000
Short margin = Equity/Liabilities = \$1,000/\$2,000 = 50%			

Long Position in Portfolio L

Assets		Liabilities	
Portfolio L	\$6,000	Margin Loan	
Lending at r_f	\$3,000	Equity	\$9,000
Long margin = Equity/Assets = \$9,000/\$9,000 = 100%			

Unadjusted Weights in the Complete Portfolio: $W_L^C = \$6,000/\$10,000 = 0.6$, $W_{S^O}^C = -\$2,000/\$10,000 = -0.2$, and $W_{Lending}^C = \$6,000/\$10,000 = 0.6$

Adjusted Weights in the Complete Portfolio: $W_{|L|}^C = \$6,000/\$14,000 = 0.43$, $W_{|S^O|}^C = \$2,000/\$14,000 = 0.14$, and $W_{|Lending|}^C = \$6,000/\$14,000 = 0.43$

Total Equity from long + Short positions = \$10,000; Total lending = \$6,000 = Escrowed short sale proceeds + Short margin requirement + Lending at r_f.

The denominator of 1.4 indicates that \$14,000 is available for investment here, in Exhibit 8.9, whereas \$20,000 was available for the example in Exhibit 8.8. The difference arises because long margin is not utilized in the example of Exhibit 8.9. Thus, \$9,000 is available for investment long, while the use of 50% short margin generates a \$2,000 for investment in portfolio S^O, and this in turn, requires an additional \$3,000 in lending, in the form of escrowed proceeds and margin requirement.

Of course, the short margin requirement and the escrowed proceeds qualify as lending only if they yield interest, and individual investors are rarely in a position to demand this interest from their broker. Thus, the complete portfolio of an individual investor, with this allocation, will actually locate below the line, SR_{P*}, as a result of the forgone interest. Even the portfolios of institutional investors, with this allocation, will locate slightly below the line, SR_{P*}, because the rebate rate they earn on escrowed proceeds is less than the risk-free rate.

Next, we consider an investor with less than average risk aversion, so that utility is maximized if it is possible to lever the optimal risky portfolio, P^*, up the line, SR_{P*}, by borrowing. We have assumed, to this point, however, that the optimal risky portfolio, P^*, is made up of the particular combination of portfolio weights,

$$W_L^R = 1.5 \text{ and } W_{S^O}^R = -0.5 \text{ (i.e., } W_{|L|}^R = 0.75 \text{ and } W_{|S^O|}^R = 0.25,$$

adjusted) that happens to utilize all available margin, as was demonstrated in Exhibit 8.8.[19] Thus, it is impossible to move up the line, from P^*, by borrowing. If, however, the optimal risky portfolio, P^*, is made up of some less extreme combination of portfolio weights, such as

$$W_L^R = 1.4 \text{ and } W_{S^O}^R = -0.4 \text{ (} W_{|L|}^R = 0.78 \text{ and } W_{|S^O|}^R = 0.22)$$

then the long margin would not be fully utilized, and it would be possible to move up the line from this new P^*. Exhibit 8.10 considers this combination of weights, first with no net lending or borrowing (in the top two panels) and then with net lending (in the bottom two panels).

---

[19] Recall that the particular combination of unadjusted weights, $W_L^R = 1.5$ and $W_{S^O}^R = -0.5$ is the most extreme combination of long and short weights (i.e., the maximum difference in the absolute values of the weights) possible given that the 50% margin requirements are satisfied and no net lending or borrowing. Thus, this is the most extreme combination of long and short weights possible in the optimal risky portfolio, P^*, since there can, by definition, be no net lending or borrowing in the optimal risky portfolio, P^*.

EXHIBIT 8.10 Optimal Asset Allocation with Borrowing

Short Position in Portfolio S^O in the Optimal Risky Portfolio, P^*

Assets		Liabilities	
Short Sale Proceeds	$4,000	Portfolio S^O	$4,000
Margin Requirement	$2,000	Equity	$2,000

Short margin = Equity/Liabilities = $2,000/$4,000 = 50%

Long Position in Portfolio L in the Optimal Risky Portfolio, P^*

Assets		Liabilities	
Portfolio L	$14,000	Margin loan	$6,000
		Equity	$8,000

Long margin = Equity/Assets = $8,000/$14,000 = 57%

Unadjusted Weights in P*, *the Optimal Risky Portfolio:* W_L^R = $14,000/$10,000 = 1.4 and $W_{S^O}^R$ = –$4,000/$10,000 = –0.4

Adjusted Weights in P*, *the Optimal Risky Portfolio:* $W_{|L|}^R$ = $14,000/$18,000 = 0.78 and $W_{|S^O|}^R$ = $4,000/$18,000 = 0.22 (*Note:* Lending and borrowing amounts offset.)

Short Position in Portfolio S^O in an Levered Optimal Complete Portfolio

Assets		Liabilities	
Short Sale Proceeds	$4,400	Portfolio S^O	$4,400
Margin Requirement	$2,200	Equity	$2,200

Long Margin = Equity/Assets = $2,200/$4,400 = 50%

Long Position in Portfolio L in a Levered Optimal Complete Portfolio

Assets		Liabilities	
Portfolio L	$15,400	Margin Loan	$7,600
		Equity	$7,800

Long Margin = Equity/Assets = $7,800/$15,400 = 51%

Note: The weights (unadjusted and adjusted) in P^*, the Optimal Risky Portfolio are unchanged from above, although net borrowing of $1,000 increases the dollar amounts of the long and short positions by $1,400 and $400, respectively.

Unadjusted Weights in the Complete Portfolio: W_L^C = $15,400/$10,000 = 1.54, $W_{S^O}^C$ = –$4,400/$10,000 = –0.44, and $W_{\text{Net Borrowing}}^C$ = –$1,000/$10,000 = –0.1

Adjusted Weights in the Complete Portfolio: $W_{|L|}^C$ = $15,400/$18,800 = 0.82, $W_{|S^O|}^C$ = $4,400/$18,800 = 0.23, and $W_{|\text{Net Borrowing}|}^C$ = –$1,000/$18,800 = –0.05

The top two panels show that with $10,000 in equity, an allocation of $14,000 long in portfolio L and $4,000 short in portfolio S^O results in no net lending or borrowing, but additional borrowing capacity remains (as long margin = 57%). The bottom two panels show that the less risk-averse investor can move up the line SR_{P*}, from P^*, by increasing the long margin loan by $1,600, buying $1,400 more of portfolio L, and putting up another $200 short margin, which allows for the short sale of an additional $400 of portfolio S^O. The relative proportions of the risky assets remain the same as before, but now net borrowing equals $1,000 (= long margin loan − short sale proceeds − short margin requirement). The weights in this investor's optimal complete portfolio are

$$W_L^C = 1.54, \ W_{S^O}^C = -0.44, \text{ and } W_{\text{Borrowing}}^C = -0.1$$

$$(W_{|L|}^C = 0.82, \ W_{|S^O|}^C = 0.23, \text{ and } W_{|\text{Borrowing}|}^C = -0.05).$$

These adjusted weights are computed as before, and the amount available for investment equals the $15,400 held long, plus the $4,400 short position, less the $1,000 in net borrowing. Net borrowing is a liability that reduces the amount available for investment (the denominator of this allocation ratio), which, in turn, increases the weights for portfolios L and S^O in the optimal complete portfolio. Likewise, net lending increases the amount available for investment, as we saw in Exhibit 8.9. (Although short selling also creates a liability, it is treated as a long position in the calculation of these adjusted weights.) What if the investor wishes to move further up the line SR_{P*}? It cannot be done in any material amount given this definition of P^*.

$$(W_L^R = 1.4 \text{ and } W_{S^O}^R = -0.4)$$

because the ending asset allocation results in 51% long margin, which is just a few dollars short of using up all remaining borrowing capacity.

Any further increase in net borrowing results in moving the risky asset allocation away from P^*, where

$$W_L^R = 1.4 \text{ and } W_{S^O}^R = -0.4 \ (W_{|L|}^R = 0.78 \text{ and } W_{|S^O|}^R = 0.22)$$

Specifically, the short position in portfolio S^O cannot make up as large a proportion of the resulting complete portfolio. This is because the escrowed proceeds and margin requirement associated with short selling effectively represent lending, which forces the location of a complete portfolio down the line, SR_{P*}. To see this, consider Exhibit 8.11, where the dollar amount of portfolio S^O sold short is the same as in Exhibit 8.9. The difference is that here, in Exhibit 8.11, we fully utilize the long margin, whereas before we had not borrowed against the $9,000 of equity in the long position. The asset weights in the resulting complete portfolio are

$$W_L^C = 1.8, \ W_{S^O}^C = -0.2, \text{ and } W_{\text{Borrowing}}^C = -0.6$$

$$(W_{|L|}^C = 1.29, \ W_{|S^O|}^C = 0.14, \text{ and } W_{|\text{Borrowing}|}^C = -0.43)$$

EXHIBIT 8.11 Suboptimal Asset Allocation with Net Borrowing

Short Position in Portfolio S^O

Assets		Liabilities	
Short Sale Proceeds	$2,000	Portfolio S^O	$2,000
Margin Requirement	$1,000	Equity	$1,000
Short margin = Equity/Liabilities = $1,000/$2,000 = 50%			

Long Position in Portfolio L

Assets		Liabilities	
Portfolio L	$18,000	Margin loan	$9,000
		Equity	$9,000
Long margin = Equity/Assets = $9,000/$18,000 = 50%			

Unadjusted Weights in the Complete Portfolio: $W_L^C = \$18,000/\$10,000 = 1.8$, $W_{S^O}^C = -\$2,000/\$10,000 = -0.2$, and $W_{\text{Net Borrowing}}^C = -\$6,000/\$10,000 = -0.6$

Adjusted Weights in the Complete Portfolio: $W_{|L|}^C = \$18,000/\$14,000 = 1.29$, $W_{|S^O|}^C = \$2,000/\$14,000 = 0.14$, and $W_{|\text{Net Borrowing}|}^C = -\$6,000/\$14,000 = -0.43$

Unadjusted Weights in the Risky Portfolio: $W_L^R = \$18,000/\$16,000 = 1.12$ and $W_{|S^O|}^R = -\$2,000/\$16,000 = -0.12$

Adjusted Weights in the Risky Portfolio: $W_{|L|}^R = \$18,000/\$20,000 = 0.9$ and $W_{|S^O|}^R = \$2,000/\$20,000 = 0.1$

Total equity from Long + Short positions = $10,000; Net borrowing = $6,000 = Long margin loan − (Escrowed short sale proceeds + Short margin requirement)

This allocation for the complete portfolio results in a portfolio of risky assets with the weights

$$W_L^R = 1.12 \text{ and } W_{S^O}^R = -0.12 \ (W_{|L|}^R = 0.9 \text{ and } W_{|S^O|}^R = 0.1)$$

Thus, any attempt to further leverage the optimal risky portfolio, P^*, would reduce the proportional amount of short selling allowed, so that the highly levered investor would actually move up a line closer to the original line, SR_L, in Exhibit 8.7, rather than SR_{P*}.

It is apparent from this analysis that portfolio optimization with realistic asset allocation constraints, reflecting margin requirements and escrowed proceeds, results in a three-step solution procedure. First, determine the weights for portfolios L and S^O in the optimal risky portfolio, P^*. Second, based an investor's risk aversion, determine their preferred mean-variance location on the lending-and-borrowing line, SR_{P*}, along with the associated dollar allocation. Third, determine whether this allocation satisfies the margin requirements. If not, then search for the closest complete portfolio in terms of mean and variance that still satisfies the margin requirements. Although our discussion of the effects of margin requirements has focused on the long-plus-short strategy illustrated in Exhibit 8.7, everything mentioned here also applies to enhanced indexing with short selling, illustrated in Exhibit 8.6, as well as for integrated long-short portfolios, the third and final strategy we consider.

Integrated Long-Short Portfolios

Managing an active long-only portfolio requires much more analysis and monitoring than holding an index long. In which case, if all positions, long and short, require active monitoring, this calls into question the reason for separating the short positions from the long positions. The portfolio manager would do better to consider all possible positions together in one integrated long-short portfolio. The advantage of this integrated approach is that all the possible pairwise return correlations are considered at once so the optimization results in an allocation with improved portfolio efficiency, ex ante.[20] This is illustrated in Exhibit 8.12, where everything is as in Exhibit 8.7, except now we optimize over all possible long and short positions, at once, to generate a newly efficient frontier spanning portfolios S^O to X. Clearly, the new optimal risky portfolio,

---

[20] The advantages of integrated long-short portfolios are extolled in Bruce I. Jacobs, Kenneth N. Levy, and David Starer, "Long-Short Portfolio Management: An Integrated Approach," *Journal of Portfolio Management* (Winter 1999), pp. 23–32.

EXHIBIT 8.12   Enhanced Efficiency with an Integrated Long-Short Portfolio

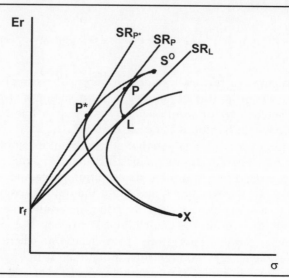

P^*, has a higher Sharpe ratio than the previous optimal risky portfolio (now labeled as P), which was based a long-plus-short strategy.

It is important to emphasize, however, that the clear advantage of integrated long-short portfolios represents only potential, ex ante. This level of efficiency will not necessarily be realized, ex post, unless we have perfect foresight regarding the portfolio optimization inputs (i.e., the means and covariances). In reality, these inputs are very difficult to forecast. In fact, the difficulty and importance of minimizing forecast error justify the restrictions of the first two strategies we have discussed. The restrictions on choices reflect investors' limitations. Enhanced indexing is better suited for investors who focus their active efforts exclusively on the short side. A long-plus-short portfolio strategy makes more sense for investors who would rather not to rely on a long index but lack the time or expertise to monitor their long positions as actively as their short positions, as an integrated long-short portfolio requires.

The point is, depending on the difficulty involved in forecasting the optimization inputs, an investor may be better off sticking with what he or she does best, rather than attempting to exploit the potential advantages of integrated long-short portfolios. Thus, what is optimal in practice varies for investors depending on their individual skills, or the skills of the managers they may hire. In the next section, we consider the empirical evidence on the difficulty of reducing forecast error in portfolio optimization when short selling is allowed.

THE EMPIRICAL EVIDENCE ON SHORT POSITIONS IN EX POST EFFICIENT PORTFOLIOS

A great deal of empirical work investigates the extent to which short positions enter ex post efficient portfolios. For example, Haim Levy constructs the ex post efficient frontier for portfolios of 15 stocks and finds that 7 to 8 stocks, or about half, are held as short positions.[21] Richard Green and Burton Hollifield compute the ex post global minimum-variance portfolio for 90 different sets, of 10 stocks each, and find that 89 of the resulting minimum-variance portfolios include short positions.[22] They also find that while most stocks are held in small proportions in these minimum-variance portfolios, a few stocks take on extremely large investment weights (both long and short) of up to 24%. More recently, Moshe Levy and Yaacov Ritov investigate the composition of mean-variance efficient portfolios when the number of stocks varies up to 200.[23] They find that the percentage of stocks held short increases from 30% in portfolios of 25 stocks, to 50% in portfolios of 200 stocks.

The motivation for much of this empirical work is both practical and theoretical. The practical goal of primary interest here is to determine whether disallowing short selling (i.e., the nonnegativity constraint) in portfolios represents a costly restriction. A related goal, that is also practical but not of primary interest here, is to determine the statistical techniques that produce the best mean and covariance estimates, in terms of forecasting high performance investment weights (i.e., efficient portfolios). The theoretical goal is to test the CAPM's prediction that the long-only market portfolio is the ex ante optimal efficient portfolio. But finding short positions in the ex post efficient portfolios does not disprove the CAPM because there are at least two other explanations, and considering these alternatives allows us to pursue our practical interests.

First, measurement error in the estimated means and covariances could produce the extreme empirical solutions mentioned. For example, Peter Frost and James Savarino point out that the stocks with highest estimated covariances tend to enter the optimal solution with large neg-

---

[21] Haim Levy, "The Capital Asset Pricing Model: Theory and Empiricism," *Economic Journal* (June 1983), pp. 145–165.

[22] Richard C. Green and Burton Hollifield, "When Will Mean-Variance Efficient Portfolios be Well Diversified?" *Journal of Finance* (December 1992), pp. 1785–1809.

[23] Moshe Levy and Yaacov Ritov, "Portfolio Optimization With Many Assets: The Importance of Short Selling," working paper 7-01, Anderson Graduate School of Management, UCLA, 2001.

ative weights;[24] yet this solution will be wrong to the extent the high covariance estimates represent upward bias.[25] More recent empirical work by Ravi Jagannathan and Tongshu Ma indicates that the nonnegativity constraint bounds this measurement error so that the constraint actually improves out-of-sample performance (i.e., realized portfolio efficiency).[26] They point out, however, that the desirability of the nonnegativity constraint depends on the tradeoff between specification error introduced by the nonnegativity constraint (a benefit lost) versus the magnitude of the estimation error (a potential cost avoided). While their empirical work favors the constraint, in this tradeoff, the implications of their simulation results are less clear.

Green and Hollifield acknowledge the possibility of measurement error, but they suggest a second explanation for the prevalence and magnitude of short positions in ex post efficient portfolios. They show that a dominant single factor underlying the determinants of the variance-covariance matrix will result in extreme investment weights (positive and negative) in the global minimum-variance portfolio. This implies that the short positions in the optimal solution represent stocks that have incurred systematic negative returns, either due to news or corrected overpricing. In which case, the cost of the non-negativity constraint may outweigh the benefit. More recently, Levy and Ritov emphasize that the difference in performance with and without the constraint (i.e., the specification error) increases with the number of assets in the optimization. Simulations with portfolios of 100 stocks yield Sharpe ratios for the unconstrained case that average more than twice those with the nonnegativity constraint in place. But still, as measurement error increases, the cost of the nonnegativity constraint declines.

Since the evidence is mixed, it is probably inappropriate to draw anything more than conditional conclusions in qualitative form. We can say that if measurement error is low (or not too high), then short positions in optimal portfolio solutions may represent opportunities to improve realized portfolio efficiency. We use the word "may" because

---

[24] Peter A. Frost and James E. Savarino, "An Empirical Bayes Approach to Efficient Portfolio Selection," *Journal of Financial and Quantitative Analysis* (September 1986), pp. 293–306.

[25] Mean and covariance estimates based on sample (historical) returns have been shown to be poor predictors of future means and covariances because higher (lower) than normal estimates tend to include positive (negative) bias. Thus, a great deal of work has gone into developing statistical techniques to improve covariance estimators. The means are too unstable from the in-sample to the out-of-sample forecasts.

[26] Ravi Jagannathan and Tongshu Ma, "Risk Reduction in Large Portfolios: Why Imposing the Wrong Constraints Helps," *Journal of Finance* (August 2003), pp. 1651–1683.

there is, of course, no certainty without perfect foresight. If short positions make up only a small portion of the optimal portfolio solution, then investors may feel comfortable ignoring short-sale opportunities. But this "comfort" would only be in regards to portfolio optimization unconditional on any superior knowledge an active investor may have about future returns. Note that the evidence presented here focuses on whether short selling improves portfolio efficiency through risk reduction. It does not consider whether active investors can identify overpriced stocks, but for those who can with reasonably low measurement error, improved portfolio efficiency is highly likely.

CONCLUDING REMARKS AND PRACTICAL IMPLICATIONS FOR INVESTORS

Indexing, rather than short selling, is probably the best way for passive investors to optimize their potential portfolio efficiency since, in theory, short selling is not needed to optimize portfolio efficiency as long as market prices reflect equilibrium required returns. But market prices do not always reflect equilibrium required returns. In which case, active investors (who trade based on what they perceive to be some informational advantage) may short sell as a means of improving potential portfolio efficiency. In addition, the rather mixed evidence on whether short selling improves realized portfolio efficiency focuses on risk reduction, so it does not diminish the fact that active investors can improve realized portfolio efficiency, *ex post*, if they successfully identify and short sell overpriced securities. Of course, this may be more difficult in the future given the growing number of hedge fund managers constructing portfolios with both long and short strategies. Other practical implications follow:

- The risk of recall and the transitory nature of overpricing result in unpredictable durations that require active management of short positions.
- *Enhanced indexing with short selling* offers active investors the option of focusing on the sell-side of the market. Passive investors may use this strategy to hedge by short selling one or a few stocks, or possibly an index.
- *Long-plus-short portfolios* allow active investors to manage each side of the market as a separate task. This can be helpful given the unpredictable duration of short positions. Passive investors may use this strategy to hedge their passively constructed long-only portfolio.

- *Integrated long-short portfolios* are similar to long-plus-short portfolios, except they consider all possible positions together in one integrated optimization. This integrated approach has the potential for improved portfolio efficiency; however, it may be impractical given the unpredictable duration of short positions, especially if the long positions tend to be more passive.

- The magnitude of the short positions in an investor's portfolio are limited by margin requirements as well as the requirement to escrow short-sale proceeds.

- Adding more leverage to an otherwise fully levered efficient portfolio (i.e., a portfolio in which the margin has been fully utilized given the risky asset allocation) will reduce the proportional amount of short selling allowed, so that the efficiency of the resulting more highly levered portfolio will be reduced.

- Thus, portfolio optimization with realistic asset allocation constraints, that reflect margin requirements and escrowed short-sale proceeds, results in a three-step solution procedure. First, determine the investment weights for long and short positions in the optimal risky portfolio. Second, based an investor's risk aversion, determine their preferred mean-variance location on the lending-and-borrowing line, along with the associated dollar allocation. Third, determine whether this allocation satisfies the margin requirements. If not, then search for the closest complete portfolio in terms of mean and variance that still satisfies the margin requirements.

- While these short margin requirements apply to individual investors, some long-short hedge funds are effectively able to get around the Federal Reserve Board's Regulation T short margin requirement of 50% by borrowing additional funds from their brokerage firms.

CHAPTER 9

The Information Content of Short Sales

Steven L. Jones, Ph.D.
Associate Professor of Finance
Indiana University, Kelley School of Business—Indianapolis

Glen Larsen, Ph.D., CFA
Professor of Finance
Indiana University, Kelley School of Business—Indianapolis

Transactions data on short sales are not publicly available in the United States. However, the New York Stock Exchange (NYSE), American Stock Exchange (AMEX), and NASDAQ report *short interest* figures for individual stocks on a monthly basis. The short interest in a stock is the aggregate number of shares that have been sold short and not yet covered. Whether these short interest figures contain valuable information about future performance has been a long-running controversy. Wall Street technicians, on the one hand, have traditionally viewed high short interest as a bullish technical indicator. On the other hand, most academic studies find that high short interest predicts negative future returns and therefore signals bearish sentiment.

At first glance, it may seem surprising to suggest that short interest can reliably predict anything about future performance because competitive trading should erode the information content of a technical indicator. Trading is what impounds information into prices and competitive trading should result in an "efficient capital market." Even in a weak-form efficient market, by Fama's definition, it is not possible to reliably predict future performance from technical indicators or trading rules that are based on public market data.[1] Fama recognizes, however, that traders will impound information into prices only to within the cost of attaining and trading on the information. It follows that the high cost of short selling, relative to regular sell or buy orders, constrains the trading necessary to fully impound bad news into security prices, and as a result some academic studies hypothesize that overpricing may exist in stocks that are costly to short sell.

Academic studies also suggest that the high costs of short selling imply that those who are willing to short sell, despite these costs, are likely to be trading based on superior information. In which case, increases in short interest may signal that informed traders have become more bearish about a stock; hence, the price should drop. On the other hand, the technician's view of short interest, as a bullish indicator, is based on the idea that short interest represents latent demand because short positions must eventually be covered by repurchasing the stock; thus, the price should increase in the future. Implicit in the technician's view is the risk of a so-called "short squeeze," in which prices move up very quickly as short sellers are forced to cover.

In this chapter, we analyze the theory and evidence on the information content of short interest in individual stocks. The very limited evidence on short-sale transactions is also considered. We start with brief explanations of how short interest is reported and the constraints on short selling. We then consider the theoretical academic work on short-sale constraints and contrast its predictions for short interest to the traditional technical analyst's view of short interest. Most of the remainder of the chapter synthesizes the empirical evidence. This begins with a review of the early work on predicting short-term returns with short interest and proceeds to the motives for short selling, as well as the use of options and their implications for the information content of short

---

[1] Eugene F. Fama, "Efficient Capital Markets: II," *Journal of Finance* (December 1991), pp. 1575–1617. In a weak-form efficient market, prices reflect the information in all public market data, including the history of past prices, trading volume, odd-lot trades, put/call ratios, short interest, etc. In a semistrong efficient market, prices reflect all publicly available information, including the public market data (in weak form) as well as the content of financial reports, forecasts, company announcements, and the like. In strong form, the highest level of market efficiency, prices reflect all public and private information. All three forms require traders to act quickly on their information out of fear of losing their advantage. The effective difference in these forms is the speed with which information is impounded into prices. This *speed* is sometimes described in more general terms as simply the *informational efficiency* of a market.

interest. We also investigate whether long-term returns are predictable from short interest and identify the determinants of short interest. Then the costs of short selling are considered as limits to arbitrage. Finally, we conclude and offer some implications for investors.

SHORT SALES: REPORTING, FREQUENCY, AND CONSTRAINTS

The Securities and Exchange Commission (SEC) requires that a short-sale order be marked as such, while a regular sell order, in which the person placing the order owns the shares, is marked as long sale. The NYSE, AMEX, and NASDAQ compile the short interest in individual stocks from member firms' reports as of settlement on the 15th of each month, or the prior business day if the 15th is not a business day. The NYSE and AMEX release the data within four business days, while the NASDAQ takes eight business days.

A popular indicator for the intensity of short interest is the *short interest ratio* (SIR). This is the aggregate short interest in a stock as a percent of its average daily trading volume over some preceding period, usually four weeks. The denominator is sometimes modified to account for seasonality in volume, or measured over longer intervals to smooth out the effects of unanticipated changes in trading activity. In addition, many academic studies focus on the *relative SIR* (RSI), the aggregate short interest in a stock as a percent of the firm's total shares outstanding.

Although short selling is fairly common, most stocks have relatively little short interest. Tom Arnold, Alexander Butler, Tim Crack, and Yan Zhang report that about 5,000 NASDAQ and about 3,000 NYSE stocks had short interest at sometime between 1995 and 1999, but the RSI was less than 0.5% for the typical stock, and 3 to 4% was average for the quintile of stocks with the highest RSI.[2]

Constraints on short sales include: (1) the direct monetary costs of borrowing shares, (2) the difficulty (or impossibility) of establishing a short position, (3) the risk that the short position cannot be maintained, and (4) the legal and institutional restrictions on short selling. Items 1, 2, and 3 are normally referred to as the costs of short selling.[3] The most widely known constraints are the "uptick" and "zero-plus-tick" rules, which prohibit short selling in a stock except at a price higher than the

---

[2] Tom Arnold, Alexander Butler, Timothy Crack, and Yan Zhang, "The Information Content of Short Interest: A Natural Experiment," working paper, August 2003. Forthcoming in the *Journal of Business*.

[3] While the nouns, *constraint* and *restriction* have subtly different meanings in this context, we will use their verb forms interchangeably.

price of the last trade, or at a price equal to that of the last trade if the previous price change was positive.[4]

While these rules restrict short selling in the near term, there are several other constraints that make short selling much more costly or may prevent it all together. For example, short sellers must: (1) maintain a margin requirement of 50% (per the Federal Reserve Board's Regulation T); (2) locate the shares to borrow; (3) leave the proceeds of the sale as collateral with the lender of the borrowed shares; and (4) pay the amount of any dividend to the lender and possibly interest (i.e., incur a negative rebate rate) if the borrowed shares are in high demand. The borrowed shares are usually located with the assistance of a broker, but this may be difficult if the shares are in high demand. In addition, to have any reasonable expectation of success, short sellers must be able to maintain the position (i.e., avoid having the shares recalled by the lender) long enough to give their contrary view a chance of being realized in the market price. Finally, many institutions are restricted from short selling all together.

ACADEMIC THEORY VERSUS THE TECHNICAL ANALYST'S VIEW

Edward Miller was one of the first to recognize the implications of costly short-sale constraints for capital market efficiency.[5] Miller argues that stocks with a wide divergence of opinion, as to intrinsic value, are likely to become overpriced if the more optimistic investors can absorb the shares and short sales are constrained such that the less optimistic investors cannot fully participate in setting the price. We refer to this as *Miller's overpricing hypothesis*. Miller does not, however, offer suggestions for how one might take advantage of this potential overpricing. Should one short the stocks that are already under the most intense pressure from short sellers, or might high short interest indicate that the price has already bottomed out?

Douglas Diamond and Robert Verrecchia assume that investors glean information from trading activity with the knowledge that short-selling is costly. In other words, investors form expectations rationally (as efficient markets theory assumes).[6] For example, higher costs pre-

---

[4] As of November 2003, the SEC was considering a proposal to no longer apply the uptick and zero-plus-tick rules to widely traded stocks. The motivation is to reduce the incentive to use put options.

[5] Edward M. Miller, "Risk, Uncertainty, and Divergence of Opinion," *Journal of Finance* (September 1977), pp. 1,151–1,168.

[6] Douglas W. Diamond and Robert E. Verrecchia, "Constraints on Short-Selling and Asset Price Adjustment to Private Information," *Journal of Financial Economics* (June 1987), pp. 277–311.

vent short sellers from trading as frequently on private information; thus, a prolonged period of trading inactivity portends that the next trade is likely to reflect bad news, rather than good news. The overpricing predicted by Miller cannot survive the assumption of rational expectations; however, two relevant pricing effects still result from short-sale constraints. First, for stocks under heavy short-selling pressure, the distribution of returns is skewed heavily to the left (i.e., toward negative returns), such that incremental price changes are likely to be larger on the down side. Rational market makers will respond to this by widening their bid-ask spreads. Second, the reduction in informed trading lowers the speed of price adjustment, especially to bad news.

Diamond and Verrecchia recognize that the high costs may drive out uninformed liquidity-based short sellers, and they consider whether this might actually improve informational efficiency, as an unintended consequence. They dismiss this, however, as highly unlikely on the grounds that few short sales are motivated by liquidity. Regardless, as long as the high costs of short selling are more likely to prevent uninformed trades, as opposed to driving out informed traders, the resulting pool of short sales will reflect proportionally more informed trades than the combined pool of all short sell and long sell orders. In which case, their model predicts that an unexpected increase in short interest is bad news. It indicates that a higher proportion of past sales than previously realized came from short sellers who should be more informed than long sellers.

It is worth emphasizing that Diamond and Verrecchia do not require the systematic overpricing of Miller to generate information content from unexpected changes in short interest. In fact, their argument relies on unexpected changes, not absolute short interest; thus, it is consistent with weak-form market efficiency. They do, however, predict slower price adjustment to bad news, and this suggests that the opportunity to profit from unexpected changes in short interest (or any other signal of bad news) may persist for longer than we might otherwise expect.[7]

Diamond and Verrecchia also consider the traditional technical analysts' view that increased short interest in a stock foreshadows positive returns due to latent buying pressure from short sellers as they cover. They dismiss this view, however, on the grounds that it necessitates rela-

---

[7] In an efficient capital market, stock prices fully reflect available information in equilibrium. Once information is released, prices adjust to new equilibrium levels. As the market searches for a new equilibrium, it is said to be in "disequilibrium." The faster is this adjustment process, the greater the informational efficiency of the market. Hence, Diamond, and Verrecchia imply that short-sale constraints reduce the general informational efficiency of the market; however, the weak-form version of market efficiency is not violated because it is a description of prices in equilibrium.

tively uninformed short sellers. Technical analysts, on the other hand, do not think so highly of short sellers.

The traditional technical analysts' view is that relatively high short interest indicates a buy signal.[8] This view is based largely on two points: (1) that short sales represent latent future demand to cover and (2) the proposition that high short interest results from speculative excess in the form of increased short selling into lengthy price declines that tend to eventually reverse. The first point reflects not only the fact that all short positions must eventually be covered, but also the risk that a short seller may be forced to cover early. This can happen when a short seller's broker recalls the borrowed shares at the request of the lender, with no other shares available to lend, or if the price of the shorted asset increases until the short seller receives a margin call.

The risk of being forced to cover may be at its highest during a so-called *short squeeze*, where one or more buyers intentionally drive the price of an asset up until the shorts are forced to cover at a loss.[9] Hence, high short interest can attract buyers and make a short position extremely risky. The second point, that short selling tends to increase after sustained price declines, reflects the possibility of short sellers creating downward price pressure in which the last short sellers are more likely to be the least informed, especially if short interest was high to begin with. Thus, the price may have been pushed too low and a rebound is inevitable. This, of course, is simply the analogue of the view that the least informed investors usually wait and jump on the bandwagon just before the market peaks.

It is apparent that the traditional technical analysts' view of short interest is not nearly so naïve as Diamond and Verrecchia suggest. In fact, although less impressive in terms of formal rigor, one could argue that its logic is at least as compelling. It does ignore the higher costs of short selling that are the key in Diamond and Verrecchia, but then they fail to recognize that a short seller's information may depend on whether he or she short sold early on or late, as short interest was accumulating.

---

[8] Norman G. Fosback, *Stock Market Logic: A Sophisticated Approach to Profits on Wall Street* (Fort Lauderdale, FL: The Institute for Econometric Research, 1976).

[9] Possibly the most famous short squeeze of recent memory is the attempt of the Hunt Brothers, Nelson Bunker, and William Herbert, to corner the silver market. By mid-summer 1979, they had control of half the world's deliverable supply, and the price of silver had reached $50 per ounce, a ten-fold increase. To corner a market is to be in a position to force the shorts to cover with you and to keep raising the price as they do so. By March 1980, the price of silver was back down to $10 per ounce. The Hunt Brothers were eventually forced into bankruptcy.

THE EMPIRICAL EVIDENCE

In this section, we synthesize the evidence on the information content of short interest in individual stocks and relate it back to the theories. The theories serve as a useful framework for following the progression of the investigation and for understanding why at least some information content appears to survive. We start with a review of the early work on predicting short-term returns and proceed to the motives for short selling as well as the use of options and their implications for the information content in short interest. We also investigate whether long-term returns are predictable from short interest and identify the determinants of short interest. Then the costs of short selling are considered as possible limits to arbitrage. Finally, we consider the information content of transaction level short-sales data and whether it should be made publicly available on a timely basis.

Predicting Short-Term Returns With Short Interest: The Early Evidence

In 1978, Luis Hurtado-Sanchez set out to test the technical analyst's traditional view of high short interest as a bullish indicator, but his results apply to the academic models as well.[10] He wondered if the inclusion of hedging and arbitrage-motivated trades in short interest data obscures the information content of speculative short sales. Rather than test directly for the prevalence of these trades, he considers whether short interest predicts future returns using a sample of stocks from the Standard & Poor's 425 Industrials of 1966 and 1967. He fails to detect any evidence that levels or changes in absolute short interest, the SIR, or RSI, can predict future performance in individual stocks. He does find, however, that stocks with high (low) return performance experience increases (decreases) in short interest in the following month. His conclusion is that short interest data contain no information about future returns, but short sales help stabilize the market by adding to selling pressure after prices have risen.

Stephen Figlewski was one of the first to consider the implications of Miller's overpricing hypothesis.[11] Figlewski assumes that observed levels of short interest proxy for the amount of unfavorable information

---

[10] Luis Hurtado-Sanchez, "Short Interest: Its Influence as a Stabilizer of Stock Returns," *Journal of Financial and Quantitative Analysis* (December 1978), pp. 965–985.

[11] Stephen Figlewski, "The Informational Effects of Restrictions on Short Sales: Some Empirical Evidence," *Journal of Financial and Quantitative Analysis* (November 1981), pp. 463–476.

excluded from market prices as a result of the constraints on short sales. In other words, a relatively high level of short interest in a stock indicates that short interest would have been even higher yet, if unconstrained. He also refines Miller's overpricing hypothesis by pointing out that rational investors, with knowledge of the effects of short-sales constraints, would not overprice some stocks without underpricing others. Thus, he hypothesizes that high (low) levels of short interest predict overpricing (underpricing) in individual stocks.[12]

He finds mixed support for this hypothesis in a sample of Standard & Poor's 500 Index stocks from the years 1973 to 1979. Specifically, a short position in the stocks ranking the highest on RSI outperforms a long position in the lowest RSI stocks by a statistically significant amount, but only if the short seller captures the interest on the proceeds from the short sale. Of course, most small traders receive no interest on short-sale proceeds, and even large traders must pay a loan free as compensation to the lender. Excluding the interest on proceeds, the mean return to stocks ranking highest in terms of RSI is actually positive in the post-ranking month, although insignificant.

The inability of both Hurtado-Sanchez and Figlewski to detect compelling evidence of return predictability from short interest suggests that hedging and arbitrage-motivated trades may be obscuring any information content in the data. Examples of such trades include the arbitrage of going long convertibles or warrants and short the converting common stock, the arbitrage of mergers (i.e., going long the targets stock while shorting the acquirer's stock), and general "pairs trading."[13] The need to understand the motivations of short sellers took on added importance with the introduction of Diamond and Verrecchia's previously mentioned work. They, of course, indicate that large unexpected increases in short interest predict negative future returns because short sellers are better informed. They also claim that the information content in short interest is obscured for stocks that have traded options.

---

[12] Figlewski's appeal to rational expectations is somewhat of a precursor to Diamond and Verrecchia, "Constraints on Short-Selling and Asset Price Adjustment to Private Information," except Figlewski allows for informational inefficiency at the firm level. That is, in his model investors have yet to learn that short interest proxies for the amount of unfavorable information excluded from market prices. Diamond and Verrecchia get around the assumption of firm-level inefficiency by focusing on the information content of unexpected changes in short interest.

[13] *Pairs trading* is a general term used to describe strategies that involve buying a stock that is thought to be underpriced, for any of a number of reasons, and shorting a statistically paired stock to neutralize risk and possibly to further enhance return.

Predicting Short-Term Returns with and Without Hedging and Traded Options

In a study published in 1990, Averil Brent, Dale Morse, and E. Kay Stice considered the motivations of short sellers using random samples of 200 NYSE stocks from the years 1981 to 1984.[14] Their tests confirm the results of Hurtado-Sanchez in that changes in RSI fail to predict future returns, but stocks with high returns subsequently experience large increases in RSI. The latter finding is in direct opposition to one of the key assumptions behind the technical analysts' bullish view of short interest: that short selling supposedly increases in down markets. Thus, it appears that short sellers are attempting to anticipate mean reversion in returns. They also observe that stocks with high short interest tend to have high betas, traded options, and listed convertible securities. They therefore conclude that hedging and arbitrage, as opposed to speculation, motivates a material amount of short selling.

Another hedging strategy that may obscure information in short interest is "shorting against the box" (i.e., selling short a stock already held long) at the end of the year to delay capital gains to the following year. Using NYSE and NASDAQ short interest data from 1995 to 1999, Tom Arnold, Alexander Butler, Tim Crack, and Yan Zhang demonstrate the popularity of this strategy prior to the Tax Payer Relief Act of 1997. The Act disallowed this practice as a means to delaying taxes, and they find that year-end short interest declined significantly with the introduction of the Act. They also show that the Act had the effect of strengthening the negative relation between changes in a stock's RSI and its return in the following month. This clearly indicates that short interest announcements contain information about subsequent returns, in the manner of Diamond and Verrecchia, as long as information-motivated trades make up an adequate proportion of the short interest.

In a study published in 1993, A.J. Senchack and Laura Starks test the predictive power of short interest with an event study on a sample 2,419 stocks selected so as to be less susceptible to the problem of obscured information content.[15] They begin with all NYSE and AMEX stocks whose short interest was published in the *Wall Street Journal* from 1980 through 1986. The sample is then purged of stocks reported to be the subject of arbitrage activities, although this does not account for pairs trading and shorting against the box. They also eliminate all

---

[14] Averil Brent, Dale Morse, and E. Kay Stice, "Short Interest: Explanations and Tests," *Journal of Financial and Quantitative Analysis* (June 1990), pp. 273–288.
[15] A.J. Senchack, Jr. and Laura T. Starks, "Short-Sale Restrictions and Market Reaction to Short-Interest Announcements," *Journal of Financial and Quantitative Analysis* (June 1993), pp. 177–194.

observations in which the reported increase in short interest, from the previous month, is less than 100%. This is done to better reflect the model of Diamond and Verrecchia, which applies only to large, unexpected increases in short interest. Finally, the sample differentiates between stocks that have traded options and those that do not.

Senchack and Starks point out that buying puts and writing calls is a low-cost alternative to short selling, and this means that any unfavorable private information about a stock may be observable from option premiums and volumes, well before the short interest announcement. Note that the short interest figures may be relatively unaffected if put writers hedge by selling short. They find that stocks without traded options have a small but statistically significant negative price reaction to the announcement of large percent increases in short interest. The cumulative negative returns over both 5- and 9-day event windows are slightly less than one-half of one percent. In addition, the larger the percent increase in short interest, the more negative is the price reaction to the announcement. Stocks with traded options, on the other hand, display no significant reaction to announcements of large percent increases in short interest. These results support both Diamond and Verrecchia's prediction that large, unexpected increases in short interest are bearish signals, as well as the claim that traded options obscure the information content in short interest announcements.

Stephen Figlewski and Gwendolyn Webb take a somewhat different approach in their study of the effect of options on short sale constraints.[16] They recognize that options decrease the costs of effectively going short and suspect that this improves informational efficiency by making constraints on short sales irrelevant. Note that the combination of reduced trading costs and increased informational efficiency should weaken, if not eliminate, the ability of short interest to predict future returns.

Using samples of Standard & Poor's 500 stocks from the 1970s and 1980s, they establish that the options market is actively used as a complement to short selling. Stocks with traded options have significantly higher RSI levels than stocks without traded options, and the introduction of traded options in a stock tends to increase the stock's RSI. They also find that option premiums tend to be higher in puts than in calls for stocks with high levels of RSI. These results suggest that option trading enables more negative information to enter the market, and impact stock prices, than would have otherwise. The impact on stock prices occurs as a result of put writers selling short to hedge, as well as from the arbitrage when the puts become expensive relative to the calls. This arbitrage involves writing the put, buying the call, and shorting the stock.

---

[16] Stephen Figlewski and Gwendolyn P. Webb, "Options, Short Sales, and Market Completeness," *Journal of Finance* (June 1993), pp. 761–777.

For stocks with high levels of RSI, Figlewski and Webb find that those without traded options earn negative returns in the month after the announcement, but these negative returns are not significantly less than the returns to the stocks with traded options. Senchack and Starks, of course, find this difference to be significant, as is expected if options actually improve informational efficiency. The discrepancy is likely due to the cleaner sample used by Senchack and Stark, as well as the concentrated focus of their 5- and 9-day event windows. In addition, Senchack and Starks analyze only large percent changes in short interest, while Figlewski and Webb analyze levels of RSI.

A study published in 1994 by two money managers, Kenneth Choie and James Hwang, supports the view that large percent changes in short interest signal more about short-term returns than do high levels or large increases in short interest.[17] They find that a short position in the stocks with the largest percent increases in short interest, as reported by the *Wall Street Journal* in the years 1988 to 1991, earned a mean return of more than 1% in excess of the S&P 500 Index in the month following publication. This is about double the excess return from shorting the stocks with the highest short interest levels or the largest SIRs. In addition, the stocks with the largest simple increases in short interest actually outperformed the S&P 500 Index, on average, in the month following publication. This suggests that percent changes are more difficult to predict and therefore are unexpected in the manner of Diamond and Verrecchia.

Most of the work we have reviewed, up until now, finds that large changes and, to a lesser extent, high levels of short interest predict small negative returns in the month or days after the announcement. However, these returns are statistically significant in only a few cases, and their economic significance is even less certain. Probably the most compelling evidence comes from Senchack and Starks, who focus on large percent increases in short interest and find support for the predictions of Diamond and Verrecchia.

Focusing on the short-term price reaction to large percent increases in short interest is an appropriate test of Diamond and Verrecchia, but it is not clear that any of the above work provides a fair test of Miller's overpricing hypothesis because it results from short sale constraints. Thus, it will not be eliminated by a short-interest announcement, whether the focus is on short interest levels or changes. The price adjustment process may be much slower, and therefore, detectable only over longer horizons. This implies that short interest may need to accumulate for some unspecified time before any correction occurs.

---

[17] Kenneth S. Choie and S. Huang, "Profitability of Short-Selling and Exploitability of Short Information," *Journal of Portfolio Management* (Winter 1994), pp. 33–38.

Predicting Long-Term Returns With Short Interest

Paul Asquith and Lisa Meulbroek investigate the long-term returns to NYSE and AMEX stocks with very high RSI at some point from 1976 to 1993.[18] While the previously mentioned work relies on short interest data reported in the financial press, Asquith and Meulbrook construct their own comprehensive data set. This is done because the financial press reports this data only for stocks with high levels or large changes in short interest. In August 1995, for example, the *Wall Street Journal* reported short interest only for those stocks with positions larger than 300,000 shares or changes of more than 50,000 shares from the previous month. Asquith and Meulbrook, on the other hand, wish to analyze RSI, not large levels or changes in short interest. This is because RSI reflects the supply of shares outstanding in the denominator, and they believe that supply together with demand (the numerator in RSI) will dictate the longer-term return. (Note that relying on the *Wall Street Journal* might preclude some stocks with high RSI if they do not also satisfy the reporting cutoffs.)

Asquith and Meulbrook focus on the excess returns to stocks that attain relatively high levels of RSI for as long as the high levels persist and for up to two years afterwards. In this way, they avoid the timing problem of earlier studies that requires precise alignment of the price reaction with the short interest announcement. They also point out several reasons why traded options may not obscure the information content in short interest. First, interviews with practitioners, including hedge fund managers, reveal that establishing large short positions with put options on hard-to-borrow stocks is more expensive and offers less liquidity than direct short selling. In addition, although one may be forced to cover a short sale early, there is no definite expiration date as with options, and this can be a serious disadvantage when speculating on a possible downturn in a stock. Finally, very few stocks under heavy selling pressure have listed put options. For stocks with RSI at or above the 95th percentile, less than 2% have listed put options traded.

Slightly under 24% of the stocks in the sample reach the 95th percentile of RSI at some point from 1976 to 1993; the RSI at this percentile is roughly 2.5%, on average, over the period. Stocks that attain this 95th percentile, or above, earned mean size-adjusted returns of –18% while remaining at or above this level, plus an additional –23% in the two years subsequent to falling below this level. The excess returns to stocks at the 99th percentile of RSI are even more stunning, but only

---

[18] Paul Asquith and Lisa K. Meulbroek, "An Empirical Investigation of Short Interest," working paper, Harvard University, September 1995.

about 7.5% of the stocks ever reached this level, and it is probably safe to assume that it is almost impossible to borrow these stocks. Note also that these returns do not include the rebate interest that institutional short sellers may receive. The statistically significant negative excess returns persist over the entire 18-year period, and they are even more negative for firms that are heavily shorted for more than one month.

Although it may be difficult to borrow stocks with RSI at or above the 95th percentile, these returns would still appear to be of economic significance. Even if these stocks cannot be sold short, a high RSI should still serve as a sell signal to those who are long the stock, and at a minimum, these results would seem to relegate to myth status the traditional technical analysts' view that high short interest is a bullish indicator. In addition, the slow reaction of stock prices, that takes months if not years, is strong support for the overpricing hypothesized by Miller, as well as Figlewski.

A recent study by Hemang Desai, K. Ramesh, Ramu Thiagarajan, and Bala Balachandran extend the work of Asquith and Meulbrook to NASDAQ market stocks with comprehensive monthly short interest data obtained directly from the NASDAQ for the years 1988 to 1994.[19] Based on improved methods from the performance measurement literature, they measure long-term excess returns by controlling for market-to-book ratios and momentum, as well as size and beta. Their results suggest that short sellers target highly liquid stocks whose prices have recently improved relative to fundamentals.

Stocks with RSI of 2.5% or more earn mean excess returns of – 6.6% within one year and –8.8% within two years of attaining this level. Upon falling back below this 2.5% level, they continue to earn negative excess returns, on average, of –7.3% within one year and – 11.2% within two years. These negative returns increase with higher RSI levels. They also find that the heavily shorted stocks are liquidated or forced to delist with a higher frequency than their size, book-to-market, and momentum-matched control firms. Joseph A. Farinella, J. Edward Graham, and Cynthia G. McDonald, in a study published in 2001, verify these results independently.[20] Thus, Asquith and Meulbrook's conclusion that high short interest signals bearish sentiment

---

[19] Hemang Desai, K. Ramesh, S. Ramu Thiagarajan, and Bala V. Balachandran, "An Investigation of the Informational Role of Short Interest in the NASDAQ Market," *Journal of Finance* (October 2002), pp. 2,263–2,287.
[20] Joseph A. Farinella, J. Edward Graham, and Cynthia G. McDonald, "Does High Short Interest Lead Underperformance?" *Journal of Investing* (Summer 2001), pp. 45–52.

about future returns applies to the NASDAQ market as well as the NYSE and AMEX.

Although these studies detect highly negative long-term returns without removing the stocks with traded options, it would be a mistake to assume that traded options have little or no effect on overpricing. Bartley Danielson and Sortin Sorescu's study of options introductions between 1981 and 1995 clearly shows that options improve informational efficiency by reducing the cost of short selling.[21] They find that prices decline and short interest increases for stocks just after their options are first listed. The increase in short interest appears to be due to the purchase of puts by previously constrained short sellers whose intent is then transferred into short sales by the hedging activities of the put writers. As long as the marginal put writer is a market professional, with transactions cost advantages at short selling, the put contracts will represent a reduction in the cost of constructing an effective short position.

Diamond and Verrecchia predict that the lower costs of options will obscure the information content of short interest, but Danielson and Sorescu's price declines are unique to the overpricing hypothesized by Figlewski and Miller. Also consistent with the overpricing hypothesis, Danielson and Sorescu find that the price declines are larger in stocks with higher betas and greater dispersion of investor opinions, as proxied for by volume, return volatility, and analysts' forecasts. They suggest, however, that these predictable price declines are not exploitable because of the high cost of short selling these stocks prior to the listing of their options.

The magnitude of these negative returns, reported by Asquith and Meulbroek as well as Desai, et al., raises an important question. That is, beyond the point that high short interest predicts negative future returns, what factors determine the level of short interest in a stock? The fact that excess returns remain negative for up to two years suggests that accumulated short selling does, eventually, move prices in the direction of fundamentals. Understanding the determinants of short interest may offer some insights into identifying short sale candidates early, before short interest increases until costs are prohibitive or borrowing becomes impossible. Of course, acting early is less costly, but there is also the added risk of acting too soon. The negative returns may take longer, or they may not materialize at all.

---

[21] Bartley R. Danielson and Sorin M. Sorescu, "Why Do Option Introductions Depress Stock Prices? A Study of Diminishing Short-sale Constraints," *Journal of Financial and Quantitative Analysis* (December 2001), pp. 451–484.

Determinants of Short Interest: Strategies, Profitability, and Information Content

It is well known that stocks with relatively low fundamental-to-price ratios experience systematically lower returns in the future. Using data on NYSE and AMEX stocks from 1976 to 1993, Patricia Dechow, Amy Hutton, and Lisa Meulbroek in a study published in 2001 document that short sellers target stocks that rank low based on ratios of cash-flow-to-price, earnings-to-price, book-to-market, and value-to-market.[22] A stock is considered "targeted" if its RSI is 0.5% or higher. Short positions in these stocks earn positive excess returns in the year after they are targeted, as prices fall, and the ratios mean-revert. Furthermore, short sellers refine this strategy in three ways by avoiding stocks: (1) that are expensive to short, such as small stocks with low institutional ownership and high dividends; (2) with low book-to-market ratios that appear justifiable due to high growth potential; and (3) with justifiably low fundamentals. These motives are confirmed by a telephone survey of major global hedge fund managers whose responses indicate that they short sell to profit from overpriced stocks.

Andreas Gintschel investigated the determinants of short interest in all the NASDAQ stocks eligible for margin trading between 1995 and 1998.[23] Proxies for the float (i.e., the supply of shares available to borrow), such as market capitalization and turnover, explain almost 60% of the cross-sectional variation in RSI. The significant time-series determinants of short interest are firm size, turnover, put option volume, as well as variables relating to technical and fundamental strategies, including future operating performance. He finds that short interest is equally sensitive to both positive and negative innovations in value and operating performance, suggesting it is motivated by hedging, while the short interest attributable to past returns is motivated by overpricing.

From an expectations model based on these findings, Gintschel computes unexpected changes in RSI and finds a significantly negative mean return of about 0.5% in the 15 days after the announcement of unexpectedly high RSI. He also detected a negative mean return of about 1% from the time short interest data are collected until the actual announcement, which indicates considerable leakage. In addition, he suggests that the negative long-term returns reported by Asquith and Meulbroek and Desai, et al. may be due to very high market capitalizations and low book-to-market ratios, rather than overpricing.

---

[22] Patricia Dechow, Amy Hutton, Lisa Meulbroek, and Richard Sloan, "Short-Sellers, Fundamental Analysis, and Stock Returns," *Journal of Financial Economics* (July 2001), pp. 77–106.

[23] Andreas Gintschel, "Short Interest on NASDAQ," working paper, Emory University, November 2001.

Rodney Boehme, Bartley Danielson, and Sorin Sorescu argue that tests of overpricing should use a two-dimensional framework based on Miller's 1977 article.[24] Recall that Miller indicates that binding short-sale constraints and high dispersion of investor beliefs are both necessary conditions for overpricing. Using RSI as a proxy for short-sale constraints, and return variance as well as share turnover as proxies for dispersion of beliefs, Boehme, Danielson, and Sorescu find that controlling for both yields low returns in constrained, high-dispersion NASDAQ and NYSE stocks between 1988 and 1999. Specifically, these stocks have a mean raw return of zero and a mean excess return of –20% over a one-year horizon, although this underperformance is less severe in stocks with traded options. (Considering either short interest or dispersion of beliefs separately does not yield significant excess returns.) Boehme, Danielson, and Sorescu suspect, however, that much of this underperformance cannot be arbitraged due to the high costs of short selling and the difficulty in borrowing these shares.

Grace Pownall and Paul Simko examine the fundamentals of stocks that are targeted by short sellers in "short spikes" (i.e., abnormally large increases in short interest), as announced in the *Wall Street Journal* during the years 1989 through 1998.[25] They also consider the price response to the announcement of a spike in short interest as well as whether the short sellers are profitable. The stocks targeted by short sellers are not materially different, in terms of fundamentals, from the population of NYSE firms during the period immediately prior to the spike. However, in the year subsequent to the short spike, the targeted stocks experience significant declines in key earnings-based fundamentals, such as earnings-to-price and earnings growth.

Their sample-wide mean excess return over the five-day intervals beginning with the announcement of the short spike is negative but small. For individual stocks, excess returns are more negative the larger the price run-up in the months prior to the spike. The profitability of short selling is measured by computing excess returns from the date the spike is announced until short interest returns to normal levels. The mean return for stocks that revert to normal levels of short interest within four months is –1% and significant, with all of this return coming in the month the reversion occurs. The sample-wide mean cumulative excess return is –5% and significant; however, most of this profit is attributable to the one-third of the sample that takes more than nine

[24] Rodney D. Boehme, Bartley R. Danielson, and Sorin M. Sorescu, "Short-Sale Constraints and Overvaluation," working paper, Texas A&M University, July 2002.
[25] Grace Pownall and Paul Simko, "The Information Intermediary Role of Short Sellers," working paper, Emory University, January 2003.

months to revert to normal levels of short interest. (Over 75% of the sample stocks revert to normal levels within less than a year.)

These cumulative excess returns are significantly larger for stocks without traded options, for stocks with RSI greater than 2.5%, and for spikes that occur prior to 1994 (when hedge fund trading began in earnest). This last finding is of particular importance since the large post-announcement returns reported by Asquith and Muelbroek and Desai, et al. were observed from samples that end in 1993 and 1994, respectively. The implication is that hedge fund managers are either exploiting (through speculation) or obscuring (through hedging) the information content of short interest such that it no longer persists for long periods, post announcement.

Pownall and Simko conclude that the profits to trading on short spikes are small, except in extended positions, which may be difficult to maintain and thus are more risky. This is similar to Boehme, Danielson, and Sorescu's conclusion, as well as that of Gintschel. Although it would appear that the emergence of hedge funds has eroded much of the highly negative pre-1994 returns, it may be slightly premature to dismiss the post-1994 returns as unexploitable. Instead, it would be better to more carefully consider the various costs of short selling.

The Costs of Short Selling as Limits to Arbitrage

In an earlier section, we briefly described the constraints on short sales: (1) the direct monetary costs of borrowing shares; (2) the difficulty (or impossibility) of establishing a short position; (3) the risk that the short position cannot be maintained; and (4) the legal and institutional restrictions on short selling. Now we wish to more carefully consider items 1, 2, and 3 since these are costs that limit the arbitrage of information contained in short interest data.[26]

The direct monetary cost of short selling is reflected in the rebate rate the lender of the stock pays to the borrower. Recall that the borrower sells the stock and the lender then has the use of the short-sale proceeds. Thus, the rebate rate represents the stock lender's cost of accessing funds less a compensating loan fee for lending the stock. Although rebate rates are usually positive, they can be negative if a stock is in such high demand (to borrow) that the loan fee is greater than the cost of funds. Rebate rates apply almost exclusively to institutional investors. Individual investors usually receive no interest on the proceeds from their short sales.

---

[26] The legal and institutional restrictions, in item 4, constrain short selling, but they do not represent a cost that an individual short seller actually faces.

There is no centralized market for lending shares in the United States, and rebate rates are not publicly available. However, the activities of a large institutional lending intermediary during 2000 and 2001 are revealed in a study by Gene D'Avolio published in 2002.[27] He finds that fewer than 10% of the stocks that this institution had available to loan are so-called *specials*, which have loan fees above 1%. The value-weighted loan fee across the entire available supply of shares is 0.25%. The average loan fee for specials is 4.3%, but fewer than 10% of these specials (less than 1% of all available stocks) are in such high demand that their rebate rates are negative.

For the stocks in the highest decile of short interest, D'Avolio reports an average loan fee of just under 1.8%, while about 33% of these stocks are specials. Stocks in the second highest short interest decile have an average loan fee of 0.8% and about 15% of these stocks are specials. Unfortunately, we do not know if the specials with high short interest experienced lower future returns than the general population of high-short-interest stocks. We do know, however, from Charles Jones and Owen Lamont published in 2001 that stocks with low or negative rebate rates have high market-to-book ratios and low subsequent returns, consistent with overpricing.[28] Their results are based on a centralized market for lending stocks that was operated on the floor of the NYSE from 1919 to 1933. When stocks were newly listed on this lending market, they were overpriced by more than can be explained by the direct monetary costs of short selling. Jones and Lamont suggest that some other constraint on short selling must be limiting the arbitrage of this apparent opportunity.

The most obvious candidate is difficulty in borrowing the shares. However, Christopher C. Geczy, David K. Musto, and Adam V. Reed in a study published in 2002 find that at least some of the profits to a number of popular shorting strategies are available to a hypothetical small investor who cannot short specials nor receive rebate interest. Their data are from a major institutional equity lender for 1998 and 1999. Unfortunately, they do not consider strategies based on short interest.[29] In a study also published in 2002, Joseph Chen, Harrison Hong, and Jeremy Stein suggest that overpricing survives because most institutional investors are restricted from short selling, and the rest of the market simply cannot

---

[27] Gene D'Avolio, "The Market for Borrowing Stock," *Journal of Financial Economics* (November/December 2002), pp. 271–306.

[28] Charles M. Jones and Owen A. Lamont, "Short-Sale Constraints and Stock Returns," *Journal of Financial Economics* (November/December 2002), pp. 207–239.

[29] Christorpher C. Geczy, David K. Musto, and Adam V. Reed, "Stocks are Special Too: An Analysis of the Equity Lending Market," *Journal of Financial Economics* (May 2003), pp. 241–269.

absorb the opportunities.[30] If this is true, it may bode well for the exploitation of carefully constructed short interest strategies that consider the accumulation of short interest over time. However, D'Avolio points out that loan fees are sticky in these decentralized lending markets; if so, stocks under increasing demand may be rationed prior to becoming specials, and this too could explain the Geczy, Musto, and Reed's results.

If short sellers worry that the risks of an early recall are high, or about being caught in a short squeeze, then they will require a premium for risky arbitrage. D'Avolio reports that the unconditional probability of a recall is low, with only 2% of the stocks on loan recalled in a typical month of his sample, but he also notes that recalls often occur when lenders receive negative information about a stock, which causes them to recall the shares, either to sell them or to reprice the loan. The possibility that negative information, possibly in the form of a rumor, could result in a recall is potentially unnerving for a short seller, and this introduces noise-trader-risk as an additional limitation to risky arbitrage.[31] That is, a lender may rationally recall shares based on how less-than-fully-rational investors may react to news, rather than based on fundamentals. Some short sellers request the identity of a potential lender to minimize the possibility of such a recall.

It is clear that constraints on short selling result in overpricing. It is also apparent from the studies by Gintschel, Boehme, Danielson, and Sorescu, and Pownall and Simko that even the post-1994 short interest data contain some information about future returns. Although there is no direct evidence, it would appear from D'Avolio as well as Geczy, Musto, and Reed that the monetary costs of short selling are probably not large enough to render short interest data unexploitable, at least not totally. It may, however, be difficult to borrow shares with high short interest, and possibly even more difficult to maintain the short position for long enough to realize a profit. In addition, D'Avolio points out that there is considerable risk associated with the early recall of a short position. It follows that these results may be viewed as consistent with market efficiency, at least to the extent that arbitrage opportunities are pursued to the limits of the costs and risks.[32]

---

[30] Joseph Chen, Harrison Hong and Jeremy C. Stein, "Breadth of Ownership and Stock Returns," *Journal of Financial Economics* (November/December 2002), pp. 171–205.

[31] J. Bradford DeLong, Andrei Shleifer, Lawrence H. Summers, and Robert Waldmann, "Noise Trader Risk in Financial Markets," *Journal of Political Economy* (1990), pp. 703–738.

[32] Andrei Shleifer and Robert Vishny, "The Limits to Arbitrage," *Journal of Finance* (1997), pp. 35–55.

It is worth emphasizing that the existence of overpricing does not necessarily imply that short interest data contain information. Persistent overpricing relies on Miller's claim that the high costs of short selling constrain the less optimistic investors from trading based on their information, so that the market clearing price is determined by the overly optimistic investors. High short interest is a proxy for high costs only to the extent that short interest would have been proportionally that much higher, if unconstrained. Clearly, some stocks have low short interest precisely because short selling them is relatively costly.

The other academic justification for analyzing short interest comes from Diamond and Verrecchia's rational expectations model, which relies on short sellers with superior information. In their model, overpricing occurs only when the current level of short selling is higher than anticipated, and the entire correction comes with the short interest announcement that follows. It follows from Diamond and Verrecchia that higher frequency reporting of short interest, or transparency in short-sales transactions, should improve the informational efficiency of the U.S. stock markets. Next, we consider whether improvements are likely to actually result from any such changes.

Short Sales Transactions and the Implications of More Frequent Reporting

Michael Aitken, Alex Frino, Michael McCorry, and Peter Swan were the first to provide evidence of the information content in short-sales transactions.[33] Their data are from the Australian Stock Exchange for the years 1994 to 1996. This exchange reports transactions-level data, including short sales information, to brokers and institutions online in real time. They report that short sales cause a rapid reassessment of price, with a mean of −0.2% within 15 minutes or 20 trades. There is less of a reaction to short sales associated with hedging activities, just as Diamond and Verrecchia would predict.

Aitken, Frino, McCorry, and Swan interpret their results as evidence that transparent short sales convey information as suggested by Diamond and Verrecchia. Note that this is claiming more than just short sellers have superior information. This is claiming that the execution of a short sale in this transparent market must immediately be recognized as an informed trade by other market observers who then, in turn, quickly sell long (or possibly short), and the price then moves accordingly. In other

---

[33] Michael J. Aitken, Alex Frino, Michael S. McCorry, and Peter L. Swan, "Short Sales Are Almost Instantaneously Bad News: Evidence from the Australian Stock Exchange," *Journal of Finance* (December 1998), pp. 2,205–2,223.

words, the price moves directly as a result of other traders reacting to the short seller's perceived information, rather than as a result of the short seller's actual information. Of course, the short seller does have to be informed if market efficiency is to improve as a result of transparency.

James Angel, Stephen Christophe, and Michael Ferri use daily transactions data from late 2000 to show that short sellers in NASDAQ-listed stocks have the ability to predict the direction of future earnings surprises as well as stock returns.[34] But does this mean that the U.S. stock markets should become more transparent and issue more frequent and detailed reports about short sales?

The problem is that the very price adjustment process that should make a transparent market more efficient, that of Diamond and Verrecchia, is also a process that is ripe for manipulation and abuse. For example, almost daily we hear of short sellers being accused of "ganging up" on some stock in the hopes up driving its price down and then exiting at the opportune moment. Imagine how much easier this type of manipulation would be in a market with transparent short sales. This might result in the marginal short seller being a noise trader rather than an informed trader. In which case, the market would be less efficient than before. Finally, greater transparency can only address temporary mispricing that is consistent with rational expectations, as in Diamond and Verrecchia's model. Greater transparency does not reduce the costly constraints on short selling that drive the persistent overpricing Miller's model predicts. Thus, transparency may be of little benefit given that there is considerable support for Miller's overpricing hypothesis.

CONCLUSIONS AND IMPLICATIONS FOR INVESTORS

Large percent increases in short interest predict negative future returns over short horizons, of a month or several days, although the relation is weak. It is clear, however, that short sellers tend to target stocks that have recently increased in price, or that have historically optimistic fundamentals, such as low book-to-market ratios. This indicates that short sellers attempt to profit from mean reversion, and since it is well known that mean reversion in stock prices is a long-horizon process, it should not be surprising that we observe that short sellers earn larger profits

---

[34] See, Stephen E. Christophe, Michael G. Ferri, and James J. Angel, "Short-Selling Prior to Earnings Announcements," Working paper, George Mason University (November 2002); and James J. Angel, Stephen E. Christophe, and Michael G. Ferri, "A Close Look at Short Selling on NASDAQ," *Financial Analysts Journal* (November/December 2003), pp. 66–74.

over long horizons, of up to two years. This, however, implies that short interest must accumulate, over time, before it contains any material information about future returns. Considering this accumulative process in their tests was thus the key insight of Asquith and Muelbroek who detect a very strong negative relation between accumulating RSI and long-term future returns.

More recent (post-1994) evidence, however, suggests that the emergence of hedge funds has weakened this signal, either as a result of their speculation on short interest or their hedging activities, both of which would obscure the information content of short interest. The post-1994 returns, to trading on short interest, appear large enough to survive the direct monetary costs of short selling. Whether they represent excessive compensation, however, is not so clear given the potential difficulties in borrowing shares and the risks of an early recall or a short squeeze. Thus, on the one hand, these results may be interpreted as consistent with Fama who defines an efficient capital market as one in which traders reflect information in prices only to within the cost of attaining and trading on the information. On the other hand, if noise traders impact the risks of a recall or a short squeeze, and they certainly may, then market efficiency exists only in the sense of the limits to arbitrage argument of Andrea Shleifer and Robert Vishny.

Most of the evidence presented here is consistent with the academic theories of either Miller or Diamond and Verrecchia. Short-sale constraints clearly result in overpricing, and there definitely is information content in short interest data, although it may be difficult to exploit. Short sellers' profits come from taking advantage of the reversion of prices back, down, to the mean. There is no evidence to support the traditional technical analysts' bullish view of high short interest, which actually relies on a reversion in prices back, up, to the mean. This bullish view of short interest appears to be rooted more in a fear of recalls and short squeezes than anything else. Some practical implications are listed below.

- Large percent increases in short interest are a weak signal of negative short-term returns. Other measures of short interest are weaker yet.
- Accumulating and sustaining levels of RSI are strong signals of negative returns in the long-term, although this relation is somewhat weaker post-1994. In addition, optimal entry and exit may be tricky with the accumulating short interest strategy. "Short spikes," especially those that have been sustained, represent an attractive point of entry.
- Traded put options in a stock may obscure the information content of the stock's short interest figure.

- Arbitrage and hedging activities in a stock may obscure the information content of the stock's short interest figure.
- The short interest data reported in the print media are incomplete and includes only stocks with very large levels or changes in aggregate short interest.
- Rebate rates are usually not available to individual investors.
- For stocks in high demand to borrow, rebate rates may be negative: meaning that the short seller must pay interest to the equity lender because the loan fee exceeds the cost of funds.
- It may be difficult to borrow stocks in high demand, especially if their loan fee is "sticky" low, and the risk of recall is higher in this situation.
- Identifying stocks before they are in high demand to borrow insures the ability to borrow at a modest loan fee. This may be done by studying the determinants of short interest. Recall that stocks with high valuations attract short sellers. Unfortunately, an early recall is more likely if the stock later becomes popular to borrow but your loan fee is low.
- Watch out for short squeezes! Avoiding them, as well as recalls, appears to be the logic behind the traditional technical analysts' view of high short interest. An example of a possible short squeeze set off by high short interest is that of Martha Stewart Living Omnimedia stock in January 2004. Investors scorned the stock through much of 2003 because in June 2002, Stewart had been tied to an insider-trading scandal at ImClone Systems. She was also charged with illegally trying to prop up the stock of her own company and deceive its shareholders. Although Stewart stepped down as CEO and chairwoman of the company after being indicted, Martha Stewart Living continued to struggle with slumping sales and earnings. But from mid-December 2003 to the end of January 2004, shares of Martha Stewart Living climbed from just over $9 to $13.39—its highest level in 19 months. Those bullish on the stock stated that the rally was a result of investors believing that closure would soon come with the end of the case and that, regardless of the outcome, the company would thrive once its executives got back to focusing on the business, rather than the trial. Technician's, however, claimed the rise was due in part to a short squeeze resulting from high short interest and the associated increase in demand to cover. More than 50% of the shares available for trading had been shorted during the December 2003 through January 2004 period.
- The only reason to buy or hold a stock with high short interest is if you have reason to believe that a short squeeze may soon come into play.
- Higher frequency reporting of short interest or greater transparency of short-sale transactions may actually reduce the informational efficiency of a market.

Short Selling Strategies

CHAPTER 10

Spotting Clues in Qs

Ron Gutfleish, Ph.D.
Elm Ridge Capital

Lee Atzil
Elm Ridge Capital

Shorting stocks is both difficult and frightening. The upside is limited while the downside is not. One competes against the market's long-term positive slope, other investors, and the companies' management teams, all trying to make shorts lose money. A short strategy needs to take into account these factors as well as the psychological limits of those implementing it. One needs to decide: (1) What kinds of targets to pursue; (2) how to screen for potential candidates; (3) how to vet them; and—most importantly—(4) how to live with them. In this chapter, we'll discuss how we deal with these issues, as well as providing a few examples (with the company names withheld in order to protect the innocent/guilty) along the way. We want to note at the outset that there are many approaches to shorting stocks. The following is our crack at it. But before reviewing our strategy, we would like to insert a quick caveat.

We are not dedicated short-sellers, but instead run a somewhat balanced long-short portfolio. Hence, we are sometimes willing to accept losses on the short side, if they can be balanced by gains on the long one. In practice, that means that we can take aim at short targets that could be bailed out by some macro development, provided that we have longs we think would benefit as well. A dedicated short seller does not have this luxury.

LOOKING FOR THE EASIER FIGHT

Our basic strategy on both the long and short sides is rather simple: Why fight the good fight if you can pick on the weak link instead? Everyone would love to own those companies that are easy to figure out, that have great growth prospects, and that give good earnings guidance. And if you are among the first to get in, out of thousands trying that route and, more importantly, the first to get out when the party ends, you will be well rewarded. But we're too slow to compete there. We buy stress and short comfort.

This approach runs against the grain of most investment organizations, whose industry-focused research staffs are designed to out-gather the information that all agree is key. In this system, analysts funnel information and ideas to portfolio managers who make the final investment decisions. The portfolio managers often take credit for the good ideas while those that don't work out become the fault of the analyst (for not anticipating the new data point). This produces an incentive structure that has most analysts more focused on avoiding mistakes than on trying to sensibly maximize expected returns. They tend to run with the crowd after "stories" that look like they're working at the moment, while avoiding more murky but potentially lucrative opportunities. They take comfort in the fact that there are lots of people who agree with them. The more facts they get (which are almost always interpreted as supporting their thesis), the more confident they become.[1] A rising stock price is likely to confirm their brilliance, build their confidence and—most importantly for our purposes—diminish their sense of vigilance.

But we think we operate in a business of odds making and inference, where conviction can become a double-edged sword. Most companies do not provide as much disclosure as we might want (and if all did, we would not have the time nor patience to pore through it all), making the link between analysis and results tenuous at best. Our strategy keys off the tendency of perpetual optimists, cheerleaders (including analysts, portfolio managers, and salespeople), and speculators to ignore the telltale signs that some of their expectations are not being confirmed in the business (as opposed to Wall Street) marketplace. We look for evidence that companies are beginning to compromise their future in order to continue to produce the growth trajectory that their supporters expect. They may be able to continue this trade-off for a few more quarters to keep Wall Street happy, but the divergence between their reported num-

---

[1] For more on this point see David Dreman, *Contrarian Investment Strategies: The Next Generation* (New York: Simon & Schuster, 1998).

bers and underlying business trends will only grow. While we may get beat up in the interim if we short these stocks—after all the direction of least resistance is usually up for these kind of issues—our eventual pay-off should only grow along with the size of the gap (that is, as long as we keep scaling into the position).

In fact, it can be rather simple to uncover problems in these "stories"—although we note that the evidence is rarely overwhelming. You don't find the latest/greatest/safest/most dependable by scrutinizing balance sheets, cash flow statements, and footnotes (nor does such an effort help you get much in the way of television exposure), so that's where we look to find the holes that the ever-confident believers ignore. Buried here might be the red flags hinting that a company may already be running up against some obstacles—but in a manner practically invisible to most of their shareholders. In many cases, it seems, even the largest of them neglect to thoroughly scrutinize financial documents. As the Vice Chairman of one of Enron's largest institutional investors noted, "nobody except very smart short sellers dug into all the footnotes that might have been there."[2]

PUTTING ON THE GREEN EYESHADES[3]

So we focus on accounting tricks to uncover our short targets. Until January 2001, our two cents on accounting was probably two cents above the bid. But, as we continue to see evidence that the late nineties' profit boom was driven more by bookkeepers than cash registers, the world paid a little more attention, that is for a short time.[4] In fact, we would venture to say that accounting abuse is pervasive. While current practices may technically adhere to the standards, they are not true to their spirit.

We do not want to become the accounting police. We do not short those companies exhibiting aggressive accounting because we're going to turn them in, or even because we think they'll eventually get caught at their games. We need to look to motivation. If we think management teams are pulling a few fast ones to mask some underlying problems in their business (or they are just not performing as well as their supporters believe), then we might short them, because eventually their bag of

---

[2] Mitchell Pacelle and Cossell Byran-Low, "Belfer Family is Big Loser in Collapse of Enron Stock," *Wall Street Journal*, January 5, 2001.
[3] Most of this section was first hashed out in our April 2002 quarterly letter. We returned to the subject in our July 2003 missive, "Give 'em a Mulligan."
[4] Our second quarter 2003 letter dwelt on this argument.

tricks will run out. We note here that a key part of our job is learning how to survive until that reality becomes evident. And, as will be discussed later, this effort can make one quite uncomfortable. In any case, here are just a just a few gimmicks used to mask a weaker business than is trumpeted by an earnings release; some that we see practiced over and over.

Earnings Before Bad Stuff

As owners of a private business, we would probably measure our business's success by how much cash we were able to pull out over the long haul. But the "earnings" found in public company releases are a very different animal. At best, they are "earnings" according to *generally accepted accounting practices* (GAAP), a scorecard which can be rather easily gamed (with often real cash costs) to enable one to report steady "earnings" gains, while more and more of the green stuff seems to fall through the cracks. At worst they are of the pro forma variety, where the company itself sets the rules, where managers try to shine as positive a light as possible on their results. Here they exclude costs relating to unsold inventory, product flops, bad purchases, and excess overhead, reporting the results of all their good decisions while excluding those of their bad ones, calling the latter "nonrecurring."[5] For quite a few companies, these nonrecurring events tend to recur with regularity. In fact, we think that many of these charges are accounting-related reversals of income that was never really generated in the first place. A heavy reliance on "earnings before bad stuff" (EBBS) serves as a red flag to us that consensus earnings and revenue numbers do not tell the whole story. This one has a number of variants.

- A company can "sell" product to customers who probably cannot afford it. The associated profits are considered "recurring," while taking a nonrecurring charge two quarters later to write off the receivables.
- One favorite in high fixed-cost businesses is to run factories full when there are only orders for half that level. This move allows them to book lower unit costs and inflate gross margins, as fixed costs are allocated to units held in the warehouse. Later, they can write off the inventory, moving the real cost of producing goods into a nonrecurring charge while the inflated profit stays in the operating line. Some firms go one step further and resell the inventory at a premium to its written down value, thus booking the same profit twice.

---

[5] The golfers among you might say that they have a penchant for taking "Mulligans."

■ A company can decide to close down the ventures that don't perform well and exclude those results form its EBBS headline. Off course, for many of these companies, start-up losses are a regular part of their business.

EBBS accounting has a very real cost. For instance, if we know we're going to get a "do-over" for an errant golf shot, then we're much more of an incentive to give that golf ball our leg-lifting full, wind-up whack, more than likely sending it off at a nearly 90 degree angle right through a neighbor's picture window. The corporate equivalent would have us devoting substantial resources without proper risk-reward calculations toward ventures with big potential payoffs, yet little likelihood of success (e.g., lottery tickets). In practice, this means that companies run plants full without the corresponding orders, extend credit to shaky customers, throw too much money at new ventures, and overpay for senseless acquisitions. Hence, it is no coincidence that in the three years through 2002, we saw write-offs of "nonrecurring" charges totaling $50 per S&P share—more than the entire amount reported during the previous 30 years.[6]

Hiding Debt

Enron may have set a Joe DiMaggio-like mark in this category, but many companies have tried a more subtle version.

■ Some get third-party financing for their customers, backed by their own guarantees. The related debt (or inventory, if the company would have been forced to hold it closer to the point of end-customer need) stays off the books. This trick can have an EBBS benefit too, as revenues and profits from these customers stay in recurring income while any associated credit losses may get classified as nonrecurring.
■ A company can finance its dealers' floor plans through a *joint-venture* (JV) finance arm. It can then book a gain on moving receivables and inventory into the JV. The company may even agree to take back product at something approaching guaranteed prices and may not be allowed to withdraw capital until the financier makes an adequate profit. Debt and receivables stay off the balance sheet and are not readily disclosed.
■ A company can sell facilities to a JV while retaining a minority interest. This interest is subordinated to other investors, again waiting for them to earn an adequate return. Assets and debt leave the balance sheet but

---

[6] Our calculations were taken from statistics from Sanford C. Bernstein & Co. research, 2003.

the company gets to record a gain on sale as well, included, of course, in recurring earnings (sometimes as an undisclosed reduction in general expenses).

Buying Profits

Serial acquirers have lots of tools at their disposal to create reported profits (and even cash flow in some cases) from the accounting treatment of their transactions. These usually involve moving what normally would be considered ongoing expenses into acquisition costs, thereby minimizing their impact on the income statement.

For one, a company can slice the reported compensation of its target's management by boosting the purchase price in return for them signing long-term employment contracts at below-market rates. This tactic also works well for financial services firms coming public where the employees/owners accept dramatic hits in reported annual compensation while they wait for the right to sell their shares.

Some technology and healthcare companies like to keep *research and development* (R&D) off their books by waiting to buy a target until its product is commercially feasible. They can then write-off the entire purchase price as "in process R&D" and then run acquired sales through the EBBS income statement, without the associated development costs. In fact, they can be even more proactive, by creating the R&D house themselves. They can move their employees and associated expenses to the new venture while retaining less than a 20% interest— that is as long as it is losing money. Meanwhile, they structure the necessary "loans" so that they have the option of buying the venture back later if it becomes (and as it becomes) profitable.

Finally, a company can write down purchased inventory and equipment, allowing them to sell some artificially low-cost inventory to make a quarter's earnings guidance. And reduced depreciation can help reported EBBS right away.

Running the Business to "Make the Number"

Finally, if the bookkeepers are having a hard time making earnings numbers, management can always tinker with how they run the business. They can ship boatloads of product at the end of the quarter to distributors ("stuffing the channel"), giving them price protection, lenient payment terms, and return provisions. If the product doesn't sell, they can always take a nonrecurring charge later on. They can start using rebate vouchers, booking the entire purchase price up front and later record the cost of the vouchers as they come in. If too many do so, they can eliminate the problem with a nonrecurring charge.

Some software firms get customers to make large cash license payments by giving them very long-term deals that allow for lots of future users. This will accelerate cash inflows, albeit at significant discounts that may require a hit to revenue somewhere in the future (maybe after senior managers have cashed in their options).

Workers for Nothing and Your Options for Free

We think that options expensing, or lack thereof, is the big megillah, an area where investors may actually be asking for their blinders. As Cliff Asness has noted: "You might think that nobody could argue that earnings should be looked at gross of giving away free, valuable and easily valued stock as compensation. You would be wrong."[7] The technology industry, politicians, and large institutional investors leading the charge to keep the *Financial Accounting Standards Board* (FASB) from requiring their expensing, argue that to do so would seriously constrain their use.[8] In fact, their arguments actually support a key premise of our short strategy—most investors don't read the footnotes. Options create an incentive structure favoring risky moves, as corporate executives see only the upside and not the downside of their actions. (Note that an option's value increases with volatility of the underlying stock.) Accordingly, many corporate managers have taken a risk-all approach (availing themselves of all the tools above) to "goose" their stock prices, selling shares when stocks are high, and retiring rich thereafter.

SO WHAT? IT'S ONLY ACCOUNTING

All of the tricks described in the previous section require real cash outlays. It costs money to produce, ship, and pay commissions on a product that a customer can't pay for. There is a real cost to having too much inventory in the distribution system no matter where the financing is hidden. R&D schemes prop up prices paid for acquisitions. And, since they don't have to expense them, companies are giving options away like water, diluting the stakes held by outside investors.

These are not isolated instances. The offenders are often multibillion dollar companies and, in some cases, entire industries. In fact, most of these practices conform to the letter of the relevant accounting stan-

---

[7] AQR Capital Management, Letter to Investors, 7/22/03.

[8] In fact, Senator Barbara Boxer argued that "we can't stand by and let accountants wearing green eyeshades decide who is going to get the American dream." Marilyn Geewax, "Senator Vows to Protect Use of Stock Options," *Atlanta-Journal Constitution*, March 6, 2003, p. F3.

dards. Most auditor reports, however, end with a statement that the "financial statements present fairly, in all material respects, the financial position" of the company reporting. If you believe that our list above complies with the last statement, then you too have a future as a television market tout.

While there is a demonstrated link between the level of expenses excluded from earnings and future stock market returns, we are not so naïve as to think that the world will suddenly crave more illuminating accounting.[9] We put on the green eyeshades because creative bookkeeping often portends upcoming earnings disappointments and egregious options grants ought to raise serious questions about the quality both of a company's corporate governance and the vigilance of its board of directors. More importantly, it signals, to us at least, that its investors have taken a less critical approach in conducting their own due diligence on its stock.

In fact, we believe that accounting gimmickry is like heroin. As economic earnings and the reported kind diverge, companies require more and more of the stuff to work its magic. Their investors would rather turn their heads the other way in the hope that the firms somehow turn themselves around, but this need becomes overwhelming. Eventually the company overdoses and is forced to get clean. We can afford to let the cycle play out. The longer companies wait, the more the self-inflicted damage.

HOW DO YOU FIND THESE CASES?

Given our charming personalities and the fact that we fit so well into the mainstream, have we been able to develop a network of people that feed these ideas to us? No, we set up simple screens that look for companies that are maybe playing some of these games. This is just the first step in the research process, to tell us where to look for our shorts. There are many data services that allow you to analyze financial statements automatically and even search for key words within the text of SEC filings. Our screens basically look at seasonally adjusted quarterly financials trying to identify red flags. A few are noted below.

1. We rank companies according to the extent to which there is a growing difference between net income and *cash flow from operations* (CFFO). Management may have less flexibility in shaping cash flow statements

---

[9] Jeffrey T. Doyle, Russell J. Lundholm, and Mark T. Soliman, "The Predictive Value of Expenses Excluded from 'Pro Forma' Earnings," *Review of Accounting Studies* (June 2003), pp. 145–174

than in reporting earnings, as the latter involve a number of rather subjective estimates (including, for instance, allowance for bad debts, product returns, pension returns, etc.). Furthermore, the cash flow statement rarely receives the same level of investor attention. For example, a growing divergence between net income and cash flow may indicate more aggressive cost capitalization or non-operating gains buried in income.

2. We search for situations where accounts receivable are growing faster than revenue, also known as increases in *days sales outstanding* (DSO). Here one should remember that very few companies sell products directly to end users, so that they may frequently offer customers incentives to hold more of their inventory (having booked revenue upon "transfer of title"). As noted above, a company falling behind its quarterly sales plan has several tools at its disposal to boost short-term sales. Management may give out discounts to customers at the end of the period or it may entice customers to accelerate purchases by extending payment terms. Both of these measures will boost DSO.

3. We scan for inventories rising at a greater rate than sales, or growing *days sales of inventory* (DSI). This may indicate that a company is falling behind its internal sales plan, as it was not able to sell all that it produced. It may also indicate that a company is trying to boost margins by allocating fixed costs across the units added to inventory rather than to cost of goods. Unfortunately, we learned about this trick the hard way. We remember buying the stock of a supplier to the steel industry, initially awed by its ability to cut costs. That is until one quarter when unit costs unexpectedly shot through the roof. It was only then that we bothered to check the inventory and realized that the "cost cuts" were sitting there. We believe this practice has been used periodically by a number of players in the high fixed cost semiconductor industry. Retailers, on the other hand, may try to boost margins by ordering more inventory than necessary in order to enjoy volume discounts from suppliers. As we said before, EBBS can always address the aftermath when the gamble doesn't pay.

4. We look for increases in *other current assets* relative to revenue. These may indicate growing cost capitalization, thus boosting earnings. This line item often serves as a home for various expenses. Management teams that are aware that their investors actually focus on receivables and inventories sometimes abuse this catchall line item in order to manage earnings. An extreme example is the software developer that changed the wording of its sales force's employment contracts (the company added a clause that allowed it, under rare circumstances, to require the salesperson to return the commission) and was able to capi-

talize and defer booking their commissions, even though it continued to pay out the cash.

5. We screen for declines in depreciation relative to *gross property plant and equipment* (PP&E). A company coming up a penny short need only change its estimate of the useful life of its equipment to boost earnings. It can also take an EBBS write-off here, which accomplishes the same thing. Again, this one has its fans in the semiconductor industry. We have found several companies that write off facilities even though they continue to utilize them.

6. We focus on declines in various allowances. These may include allowance for doubtful accounts relative to gross accounts receivable, sales return allowance relative to revenue, and inventory obsolescence reserve relative to inventory. Declines in any of these may boost earnings at management's discretion.

7. We search for key words such as: (a) "reversals," as often one-time boosts are considered part of EBBS, but one-time hits to earnings are not; (b) "off-balance sheet" or "special purpose entity," which, as we mentioned previously, can finance customer purchases, dealers' inventory, keep R&D off the books, and so on; (c) "related party," where a company may be funding a joint-venture that in turn purchases its products; and (d) words like "previously" or "change" near "recognized," which often foretell of a change in the company's accounting policy.

8. We also look for declining shares short relative to the company's float (publicly traded shares) over the last three months. Let's step back for a second here. The term "Short Squeeze" originally referred to a situation where many holders of a company's stock simultaneously ask for their shares back from their broker so that they could no longer be borrowed by those selling them short. This forces short sellers to buy shares in the open market so they can return them to their original owners. When this happens to many shorts at once, the stock rises due to the increased demand. While this form of a short squeeze happens now and again, the term has evolved to a simpler form. When a stock price increases, shorts sellers' losses mount and the resulting scare causes more and more of them to cover. If there are many shares short of a given stock, the stock price boost can be material. In fact, long holders and the companies themselves can trigger these squeezes with determined efforts to bid up a stock. The more shares that are borrowed short, the higher the likelihood that the stock price will rise based on a short squeeze. Thus a declining ratio implies that it is less likely that this will happen.

If the above screens reveal promising candidates, the next step is to confirm the presence and validity of these symptoms in the financial filings. Some of the additional things that catch our eye include:

- *Gains buried in the income statement as an offset to selling, general, and administrative (SG&A) expense.* These can sometimes be gleaned from the cash flow statement or from the footnotes. They can be the result of one-time asset sales, legal settlements, and the like, and can explain sudden drops in operating expenses.
- *Significant recurring charges.* We look at charges as percent of revenue over the last few years. We then evaluate components of the charge and impact on earnings that followed. Here you can find the write-offs of inventory built to help earnings or the consequences of extending credit to dubious customers.
- *Unexplained changes in goodwill.* These may help buy profits through acquisitions. According to GAAP, a company may change an acquired company's asset and liability accounts up to a year following an acquisition. Increases here may indicate payments to workers formerly employed by the acquired company that did not flow through the income statement. Other changes may include asset write-downs in order to lower future expense or reserve increases that can later boost earnings if reversed. Changes to these assets and liabilities are usually offset by increased goodwill.
- *Large options expense.* We noted earlier how the existence of large options grants hints that neither a company's board of directors nor its shareholders may be keeping a watchful eye on management. Using this trick can boost profits by cutting cash compensation and replacing it with un-expensed options.
- *Significant insider sales.* After all, insiders know best what is going on in their business.

There are a number of additional things we look for. We evaluate whether a company is making loans to customers or investing in them. We try to determine whether management is compensated based on EPS or whether management's options vesting accelerates based on achieving operating margin goals or the stock price exceeding a certain threshold. We look for poor corporate governance, such as a small board of directors without truly independent members. We try to identify related party transactions. We are always interested in disagreements with auditors. These can all serve as red flags.

DIAGNOSIS

After our initial screens and reading financial statements, we look to determine what is the "bull case" and what is wrong with it. This is critical because we are trying to find companies that are going to fail to meet Wall Street's expectations. We need to know what these are. If the investment case rides on a company having a better widget several years out or a particular FDA approval, then our perusal of financial analysis should prove fruitless. We need to make sure that people will care about the deterioration we uncovered and its impact on the company's financials. We might talk to the company, its competitors, customers, Wall Street analysts, and other industry participants, as we seek to understand what has produced these symptoms. Maybe receivables are only growing because a problem with the company's billing system led to delays in invoicing. Perhaps one key customer paid its bill right after quarter's end. If we cannot find such benign explanations, then we try to identify what spurred the red flags. Are there real barriers to entry? Is there a new competitor entering the market? Are the company's products obsolete? Has the business just received a short-term boost from some nonrecurring source? Is the market saturated?

Once we determine that there are real financial symptoms of distress, and identified some potential reasons them, we have to estimate the financial implications of what we've found. We want to see how our forecasts differ from those banking on a better outcome.

Finally, we determine reasonable upside/downside scenarios. We consider the magnitude of a potential earnings miss versus possible earnings upside (if product X does better than expected for example). It is also important here to try to assess likely multiples in best case and worst case scenarios based on the level of expectations compared to actual results. After answering all of the above, we can decide whether we have found a good short or not. However, not all shorts are created equal. Thus, sizing a short properly is critical as discussed below.

KEEPING YOUR SHORTS ON

So far, so good. Look for holes and then the story crumbles. If life were only so easy. Remember, the world is not on our side. Go try and bring up accounting issues to a large institutional shareholder. More often than not you'll get the following: "I've known so-and-so for ten years [and my fund is loaded to the gills on its stock] and so-and-so is one of the most honest people I've met [and so-and-so has always made his or her earnings guidance]. You're grasping. Wait till you see the consumer take-up on newfangled gizmo, then all this will be irrelevant." We live in fear that they will then get off the phone with us and dial one of their favorite brokers. "Go buy 5,000 shares of XYZ Co. I hear there's a big short that we can squeeze." The stock could be up 5% in an instant. In fact, even if existing shareholders see our point, they often own too much of the stock (exceeding 20% of the company in some cases), or have pumped it too often in marketing meetings and the media to change course. And once they know there are shorts on the case, then they also know that they can make them scurry. As noted earlier, short squeezes can be quite vicious.

So we size our investments with the recognition that the market is continually going to find reasons supporting the contention that the herd is right and that we are off base. We understand that we will rarely be able to call absolute tops or bottoms and that most positions are likely to move against us at first. And if they do so, then we have two choices: (1) unwind them if something fundamental has changed; or (2) increase their size—if the stock is overreacting to some news or rumors—right at the time the market is telling us that we are wrong. In fact, a key piece of our modus operandi stems from our willingness and ability to "take a licking and keep on ticking." We need to make sure that positions do not cause so much pain as to provoke extreme irrationality and panic. We do believe value and a semblance of reality does win out in the end, we just want to be around to watch it unfold. As a result, we have a diversified short portfolio, with up to 120 positions sized according to their risk, meaning that a volatile technology short, where we think we can make 50% or more, will be smaller than an established player in consumer staples, where we think the upside (and our downside) is more limited. We also leave room to increase position sizes and respond to "next quarter's beating" because we know one is often likely to come. We are willing to take these punches, because if the underlying problems continue, we'll just get paid more in the end. Finally, we always try to keep in mind that we are human; we make mistakes (sometimes too often) and sometimes we may just be unlucky. This is another reason a diversified short portfolio makes sense—to us at least.

TALES FROM THE FRONT LINES: THREE EXAMPLES

Having discussed our strategy and implementation in the abstract, we thought we would give you a few real world examples to see how it can play out in practice. We chose the first two cases to illustrate how Wall

Street can ignore a large number of what were, to us, fairly obvious red flags. The third can then serve as an illustration of how the existence of, what we think are, red flags need not spell trouble (for the owners of the stock that is).

Before moving on, we offer a short apology. Although it might make for more interesting reading, we have withheld the names of the stocks in question for our own protection. The management teams of companies that we short have lots of weapons at their disposal (if they choose to use them) to fight short sellers, including initiating short squeezes or forcing us to spend large amounts of time and money fighting legal battles. We would rather focus our time on research.

Example 1: The Information Technology (IT) Outsourcer

This IT Outsourcer showed up on our screens at first because it was reporting strong net income and EPS growth while cash flow was actually declining. This was particularly interesting because the company signed multiyear outsourcing contracts with its customers and recognized revenue on these under the *percentage-of-completion* (POC) method. Under POC accounting, a company recognizes revenue during a given period equal to the total revenue for the contract's duration multiplied by the ratio of costs incurred during the period to total estimated costs for the entire contract life. (That is, the company estimates a total profit margin for the contract and recognizes it as costs are incurred.) The POC method is a perfectly reasonable and generally appropriate for long-term contracts. Under POC, a company can overestimate contract profitability if it underestimates total costs. It can thus report higher levels of profitability in the early parts of a contract, and announce massive losses near completion.[10] For the outsourcer, however, cash flow is reflective of the underlying economics of the business, and is thus not subject to estimation. While cash flow may fluctuate during any given quarter, if there is a recurring disconnect between it and earnings, one should ask why. We saw a number of red flags here.

For one, the company's cash flow and EPS were moving in different directions. For its then most recently reported quarter, EPS had climbed by 14% from a year earlier while CFFO fell 6%. This drop in CFFO stemmed in part from rising DSOs, which had risen steadily over the pervious three quarters. Quarterly *depreciation and amortization expense* (D&A) as percent of PPE and intangibles fell to 4.6% during the quarter compared to 6.2% the previous one and 6.7% a year earlier.

---

[10] In fact, some defense companies with a conservative bias tend to have much lower profits at the beginning of a long-term complex contract and higher ones at the end, as some of their worst-case fears fail to pan out.

The ratio had not been below 6.2% over the last two years and had been as high as 8.5%. We thought that the company might have been stretching useful life assumptions or writing off assets to lower D&A. If the company had continued to report this expense at the same rate as it had in the previous quarter, it would have knocked $0.09 off the reported pro forma EPS of $0.69 (a figure a penny better than consensus expectations).

Meanwhile, SG&A expenses had dropped relative to revenue, giving one the impression that the company was doing an excellent job of controlling costs. Yet, as this was accompanied by significant growth in intangible assets, it occurred to us that costs might have been capitalized as part of some recent acquisitions. Contract signings, indicating future revenue trends, were increasing, but the rate of growth was declining. More importantly, after adjusting for renewals, new signings declined 35% over the previous year. Furthermore, deferred revenue, representing customers' prepayments for future services and thus a good indicator of future sales, eased to 9.5% of revenue, from 10.8% in the preceding quarter and 10.6% a year earlier.

Looking further back, we found that in the prior 10 years, the company generated *cumulative free cash flow* (CFFO less capital spending and related items) of just 2% of its current enterprise value (equal to market capitalization plus net debt). These weak cash flows helped lead to a $5 billion increase in the company's total commitments (debt, preferred stock, leases, minimum software subscription commitments, and other contingencies) in just three years, while the company posted profits of less than $3 billion over that time. Meanwhile, the company had spent $2 billion over the previous six months on four acquisitions that seemed only loosely related to its core business. Finally, several key executives had left or were leaving the company and a number of the remaining insiders had been selling shares.

Wall Street, however, saw a different picture. The charismatic CEO told a credible, conceptual, growth story based on long-term outsourcing trends. More importantly, the company almost always beat EPS expectations. The CEO really did deliver, saving many investors and sell-side analysts a lot of anxiety. Signings were strong, as was revenue. Margins were expanding and EPS was steadily marching upward. What more could one ask for?

However, we thought that the cheerleaders might have been missing something. The company was operating in an intensely competitive industry, signing contracts that may have had very poor underlying economics. The business model had the company acquiring equipment and personnel from its customers while paying them cash upfront. It then hoped to recoup those investments over time. In order to entice customers to sign these contracts, it had to promise them savings by agreeing to receive fixed payments lower than the customer's cost of running IT in-house. The company seemed to lack any clear competitive advantage over its peers, so that winning customer contracts may have been simply driven by price. All in all, we thought that this was probably a risky, low return business.

To make things worse, the IT industry was slowing down, yet the company seemed bent on reporting strong signing and EPS growth. If aggressive pricing could drive new business, then the earnings trajectory could have easily been maintained under POC accounting by bidding low for new contracts as long as the company "estimated" that the new business was profitable. Furthermore, management could have been seeking to acquire their way out of trouble by using a high stock price as currency.

We decided to "stress-test" our findings and set up a meeting with a sell-side analyst, who was one of the company's leading champions on Wall Street. We presented our concerns and listened as he explained each away. We concluded that his explanations were indeed plausible, and frankly even better than ours for every single one. However, he could not address the fact that we had found so many of them at the same time. The probability that all were unrelated seemed low to us. The analyst didn't see our point.

We saw enough here to think that we may have been onto something since there were no reasonable explanations we could uncover for the existence of so many warning signs. Meanwhile, the company's stock was trading at 20 times forward EPS estimates that we thought were unattainable. We figured that this was a bet worth putting on.

Three quarters after putting on the position, the company's shares came under pressure. Following several articles in the press questioning its accounting (which also might have provoked some additional questions from the analyst community), the company made a series of announcements regarding problem contracts and delays. And it terminated negotiations with a few potential customers as well. Another two quarters went by and the company finally caved in and announced that EPS would be *one fifth* of original guidance. It is possible that the increased scrutiny limited its ability to manage earnings, or perhaps it ran out of levers to pull. Or just maybe the business deteriorated so much that it could not hide it anymore. In any case, the stock lost over 50% of its value following the EPS miss and over 70% compared to our entry point. We have to admit that we were not lucky enough to enjoy the entire ride. We did, however, reap a handsome reward.

It wasn't that we were smarter than anyone on this one (we rarely are). We just have a hard time falling in love with a company and, hence, we let ourselves get bothered with the details.

Example 2: The Book Publisher

The Book Publisher initially showed up on our screens when it reported extremely strong earnings growth in its latest reported quarter while CFFO was actually declining. Furthermore, bad debt expense was down significantly over the past year. We decided to take a closer look.

First, while pro forma EPS had more than tripled from a year earlier, CFFO had actually dropped 35%. In addition, bad debt expense had fallen to 2.5% of revenue in the quarter from 4.6%, which could have boosted earnings by $0.10 per share (a material change as the company reported $0.31 per share in the quarter, just meeting analysts' expectations). Furthermore, the company took a massive charge three quarters earlier, leading to a significant drop in the amortization of pre-publication costs (advances, art, prepress, and other costs incurred in the creation of a master copy of a book). This deferral of some very real costs could have helped earnings by $0.07 per share. Furthermore, accrued liabilities, which may have contained reserves and other allowances, dropped. This may have been related to management under-reserving for bad debts or reversing reserves.

We figured that the publisher was operating in a no-to-low growth segment of the industry. However, it was fortunate enough to have one hot author under contract. She had released her first book in the previous year, a blockbuster selling significantly more than expected. Her widely anticipated next book was due to come out about 12 months later and management established very high expectations for this release. In the interim, in an apparent effort to maintain earnings momentum, the company promised to cut costs.

However, it appeared to us that there was no real meat in the cost cuts. Of the $35 million supposedly achieved at that point, $6 million came from cutting allowances for doubtful accounts, $10 million was due to the fact that goodwill no longer needed to be amortized (as accounting standards had changed), and $17 million was due to lower prepublication cost amortization following the write-offs. Out of $35 million, $33 million could have been generated by a few strokes of the calculator.

While taking encouragement from the company's cost-cutting efforts, Wall Street focused on the next promised bestseller. While we were not experts in this field, it appeared to us that analysts had already baked a very successful book into their estimates. Furthermore, we doubted whether the author, who was due to sign a new deal for the upcoming book, would settle for terms similar to those of the previous deal inked before she became such a runaway success. Management claimed otherwise, and asserted that the new deal would have similar terms to the previous one. All told, we figured that most of the upside of the upcoming book was already incorporated into earnings estimates.

Finally, management was also promising organic revenue growth, even without the new bestseller. After looking at industry data, showing little to no growth over time, as well as spending a considerable amount of time trying to estimate the contribution of acquisitions, we came away feeling that the company was not really growing organically and could have a tough time doing so in the future.

We uncovered other disturbing trends. While earnings were strong over the previous few years, CFFO was lagging and free cash flow was basically nonexistent. Moreover, the company may have been over-reporting profits as capitalized prepublication costs had grown. These significant cash costs did not show up in the income statement, but rather found their way to the investing section of the cash flow statement below the CFFO line.[11]

We decided we had enough evidence to put on a small position. The following three quarters seemed to indicate that things were getting worse. Other current assets began to build as did inventory, accounts receivable, and long term assets. The tax rate was declining, along with the inventory obsolescence reserve. Several lines of business showed signs of weakness, and the company began making contingent earn-out payments (to people who might still have been employed by the company) The stock price, however, continued to climb. Earnings were growing, and the hot author signed a new deal, although the terms were not disclosed. All was well as far as Wall Street was concerned. Throughout this period, we traded around the position but steadily increased it.

And then, almost a year after we began looking at the company, we got paid. The first sign of trouble was a slight EPS miss and lowered guidance that led to a nearly 10% drop in the stock during the day following the announcement. The company blamed the miss on weak performance in a couple of product lines, and its lower guidance on delays in the new book release. The company did, however, guide for increased cost cutting to offset some of the EPS shortfall. The following quarter, the company preannounced, stating that it would report a loss in the upcoming quarter rather than the expected $0.31 profit, and guided down the next quarter as well. The stock tumbled 24% the following day. We covered our last share approximately 50% lower than where we initiated the position.

---

[11] By the way, we believe this is akin to how Tyco booked the costs incurred in signing up new home security customers. Since, the company was buying the contracts from technically independent contractors it could book the associated installation costs under acquisitions.

Example 3: Failure—The Consumer Electronics Component Maker

The Consumer Electronics Component Maker showed up on our screens for cutting allowances for doubtful accounts, and building other current assets. In this case, the company actually reported pro forma EPS (aka EBBS) that were $0.07 better than expected in the most recent quarter. The good numbers, combined with 10% of shares being short, led to a 20% move in the stock price following that release.

But the financial reports revealed that the "blow-out" quarter just reported might not have been so impressive. One could argue that lower allowances for doubtful accounts had boosted earnings by $0.04 per share. Other current assets had increased dramatically from the quarter before, hitting 9.5% of quarterly revenue from 5.5%. If the company were to keep other current assets as percent of sales flat on a sequential basis, EPS might have been $0.04 lower. In addition, the company sold some previously written down inventory that could have helped EPS by $0.03. So the company might have had a total of $0.11 in what could be considered one-time EPS boosts.

Wall Street loved the company. Analysts and investors alike were infatuated with its strong unit growth. This was one of those "everyone will have one" stories as the company's products found their way into many more consumer electronics goods. Already, they were selling into fast growing digital camera markets where there were reports of component shortages. Our research, however, uncovered significant supply additions planned within the next few quarters, as several competitors focused on gaining share. In addition, insider sales were significant and option costs were material.

We put on only a small position. We were still worried about the large short interest and also about our inability to accurately forecast the timing of supply additions in the face of very strong demand. Yes this was risky, but the rewards could have been huge. Wall Street tends to miss the inflection point when supply shortages (which force customers to double order further exacerbating imbalances) turn into gluts (as increasing availability leads them to cut back on double ordering and draw down existing stocks) and the resulting EPS disappointments can be spectacular. We thought we might have had one here. The stock proceeded to more than double over the next two months as the stock market ran. We slowly added to our position as we found more evidence that lots of supply was soon going to come online.

When the company reported the following quarter, it again blew by estimates as revenue soared. More concerning, to us, was the fact that the quarter seemed clean. We could not find any material indicators of EPS management in the financials. The stock, however, eased back to a level only slightly higher than where we initially put on our position, indicating some rather lofty investor expectations had not been met. While we trimmed our position slightly, we still anticipated more downside.

When the annual report arrived on our desks (as that last reported quarter ended the fiscal year), we saw more EPS management signs, but we could not conclude how much they helped the latest quarter. We should have recognized that many of the symptoms that we saw previously had disappeared and that it was time to realize a small loss. The combination of a high short interest and significant unit demand growth was a potent one. Yet we decided to stick around and wait for another quarter. That was a mistake.

The following quarter the company beat EPS by an even greater margin. Revenues were much better, and while we took issue with some of the line items, we had to agree that this was a strong quarter. The following day the stock opened up over 20% and it never looked back.

We eventually admitted defeat after the stock had almost tripled from our entry. While prices for the company's products were declining, unit growth was explosive and supply additions were coming on slowly. Our main mistake was waiting to see another quarter after the company reported a clean one in which it handily beat estimates. We paid a dear price.

SUMMARY

So much for our tales from the front. Sometimes you win and sometimes you lose. The key for us is to keep an even keel and not allow hubris to boost our levels of conviction and bet sizes during winning streaks; nor should we allow obstinance to keep us from realizing losses when we get some wrong. We could go on and on—we're lots of fun at dinner parties—but though the topic fascinates us, we doubt that we'd keep your attention.

In short, we try to pick our fights, and do so in a consistent manner in order that we might live to talk about them.[12] We want to emphasize that this is only one strategy for short selling, and there are many viable and successful alternatives. Your approach should reflect both your analytical and emotional strengths and weaknesses. The first three years of the new millennium gave too many people the impression that shorting was easy. This past year (2003) has shown that it can be rather hazardous to your financial and emotional well-being. Vigilance is key.

---

[12] Given our record on the short side in 2003, that "might" is still open to question. Again, we remind the reader that since we run a somewhat balanced book, we may have a higher threshold for pain than some, as our longs might be benefiting from some of the same phenomena that have boosted our shorts.

CHAPTER 11

The Economic Profit Approach to Short Selling

James A. Abate, CPA, CFA
Investment Director
GAM USA Inc.

James L. Grant, Ph.D.
President
JLG Research

While short selling based on poor or deteriorating fundamentals is a time-tested investing strategy, the application of the technique has all too often been implemented using accounting earnings and relative valuation indicators (such as price-to-earnings and price-to-book value) that have little direct relation with wealth creation—or more aptly, wealth destruction in the case of shorting. That said, we set out in this chapter to provide a foundation on how short selling arises in an active investing strategy that is driven by *net present value* (NPV) and economic profit or *economic value-added* (EVA) considerations.[1]

We begin by examining how short selling arises in the theory of finance. This allows us to depart from a traditional accounting/relative value approach to a more deliberate focus on the fundamentals of wealth creation—or the fundamentals of wealth destruction as a primary motive for shorting a company's stock. Along the way, we examine the financial characteristics of wealth creators and wealth destroyers, among other company profiles between the extremes. We also provide practical insights,

---

[1] EVA® is a registered trademark of Stern Stewart & Co.

based on quantitative and qualitative considerations, from the portfolio manager's perspective in the identification of short selling candidates. In the development of a short selling process, we emphasize the discovery of growth companies that are facing economic profit challenges and the discovery of troubled companies through their problematic NPV and EVA events.[2]

SHORT SELLING IN THE THEORY OF FINANCE

In theory, short selling arises when a portfolio manager identifies a negative turn in a company's economic or financial outlook relative to that which is already embedded in stock price. But this begs the question of how a manager determines whether a company is actually pointing in the right or wrong direction. That is, before shorting a company's stock, an investor must have a robust framework for determining when a company is in fact overvalued. Fortunately, we can turn to financial theory to obtain a foundation on what constitutes a "good" company versus a "bad" company in the discovery of short selling candidates.

Specifically, we will show how the theory of finance—with its focus on positive and negative NPV companies—can be used to identify good companies that might represent a buy opportunity compared with risky troubled companies that represent a sell or short sell opportunity.[3] We will begin with a look at the financial characteristics of wealth creators (namely, positive NPV and EVA companies) followed by a look at the financial characteristics of wealth destroyers (negative NPV and EVA companies). With a solid foundation on the financial characteristics of wealth creators and destroyers (among other company profiles), we will see that shorting naturally arises in the context of companies that are pointing in the direction of negative economic profit generation and, therefore, wealth destruction.

TENETS OF GOOD AND BAD COMPANIES

The question of whether a company is a "bad" company (sell or short sell opportunity) presumes that a portfolio manager knows why the com-

---

[2] In this chapter we draw from general EVA investing material presented in James L. Grant, *Foundations of Economic Value Added Second Edition* (New York: John Wiley & Sons, 2003) and James L Grant and James A. Abate, *Focus on Value: A Corporate and Investor Guide to Wealth Creation* (New York: John Wiley & Sons, 2001).

[3] We emphasize intrinsic value that has not been "priced" in the capital market.

pany is not a "good" company (buy opportunity). In the next section, we will use a two-period wealth model to illustrate the financial tenets of companies that are pointing in the direction of wealth creation (good companies). Following that, we will use the two-period NPV (or EVA) model to obtain insight on companies that are pointing in the direction of wealth destruction (bad companies). Given capital market inefficiencies, it follows naturally that wealth creators are potential buy opportunities, while the wealth destroyers are sell or short sell opportunities.

POSITIVE NPV: DISCOVERY OF GOOD COMPANIES

Since a bad company can be viewed as a deviation from what one would normally consider as a starting point for investment action, we need a foundation on what constitutes a good company. To facilitate this background, assume a two-period world where an investment (C) of, say, C = $100 million (or 100% of any initial capital amount) leads to an after-tax cash flow of $125 million in the future.[4] For our purpose, we will denote this *one-time* expected cash flow as "NOPAT."[5] Further suppose that the firm's *cost of capital* (COC) is 10%. Based on these assumptions, the *gross present value* (GPV) of the firm's investment decision is the present value of the one-time expected cash flow:

$$
\begin{aligned}
\text{GPV} &= \text{Present value of expected cash flow} \\
&= \text{NOPAT}/(1 + \text{COC}) \\
&= \$125/(1 + 0.1) = \$113.64 \text{ million}
\end{aligned}
$$

In turn, the NPV or market value added[6] of the firm's investment opportunity is given by

---

[4] The after tax cash flow is *before* financing charges. This is important because the cost of debt and equity capital shows up in the dollar cost of capital.

[5] In practice, NOPAT refers to a firm's *net operating profit after tax*. Because we are using a two-period model to show the link between NPV and EVA, the NOPAT figure (at $125 million) shown in the text includes the initial investment (at $100 million) and the dollar return on invested capital (at $25 million). In equation form, this can be expressed as $C \times (1 + \text{ROC})$, where C is the capital investment and ROC is the after-tax operating return on invested capital. This two-period interpretation of NOPAT is different from the conventional view of NOPAT as after-tax operating profit or the dollar return earned on an "on-going" firm's existing assets, namely $C \times \text{ROC}$.

[6] In practice, Stern Stewart & Co. (among others) use MVA to denote NPV.

$$NPV = MVA$$
$$= GPV - C$$
$$= NOPAT/(1 + COC) - C$$
$$= \$113.64 - \$100 = \$13.64 \text{ million}$$

Due to the wealth-creating investment, the firm's managers have added $13.64 million (or 13.64%) to the initial capital employed. In this instance, the representative firm is a "good" company (potential buy opportunity) because it is pointing in the direction of wealth creation.

Exhibit 11.1 provides a graphical look at the financial characteristics of a wealth creator. Assume that the firm's ability to transform current resources into future resources can be represented by a Production Possibilities Curve (PPC). Further suppose that the firm has *no* internal start up funds such that the invested capital, C = $100 million, is raised entirely from external capital market sources. With these assumptions, the length "C = $100" in Exhibit 11.1 represents the amount borrowed to finance the capital investment. As before, we assume that the investment generates an after-tax cash flow of $125 million in the future period—which, in a multiperiod context can be viewed as the after-tax cash flow generated next period *plus* the present value of all future cash flows thereafter.

With NOPAT of $125 million, the after-tax cash flow from the firm's production decision is represented by the vertical distance in Exhibit 11.1

EXHIBIT 11.1 Wealth Creation with Positive NPV

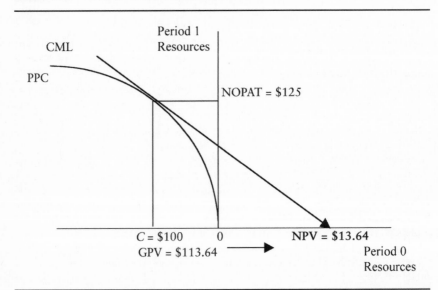

from length C up to the PPC. At $113.64 million, the present value of the anticipated NOPAT is the firm's gross present value. The horizontal length noted as GPV in the exhibit represents this distance. The firm's positive NPV, at $13.64 million, is measured along the horizontal axis by the difference between the *gross present value* (GPV), at $113.64 million, and the initial capital of $100 million. Moreover, with positive NPV, this company type provides a benchmark for deciding what constitutes the converse—a risky troubled company (sell or short sell opportunity).

Role of EVA

We can recast the above findings in the context of an economic profit measure called *economic value added* (EVA). Unlike accounting earnings, EVA is consistent with NPV because it looks at profit over-and-above the dollar cost of capital (including the pivotal cost of equity). Based on the figures supplied in the wealth model, it is a simple matter to show that the firm's expected future EVA is $15 million (or 15% of the initial capital). This economic profit figure results from subtracting the expected financing payments—including "interest" (at $10 million) and the return of "loan principal" (at $100 million) to external suppliers of capital—from the expected cash flow denoted previously as NOPAT:[7]

$$EVA = NOPAT - \$Capital\ charge$$
$$= \$125 - \$100 \times (1 + 0.1) = \$15\ million$$

With positive EVA, at $15 million, the firm's cash operating profit after tax (NOPAT) is more than sufficient to cover the anticipated financing cost—including the "rental charge" and return of borrowed principal, C × (1 + COC) = $110 million, of the capital employed in the business.

Exhibit 11.2 shows how the firm derives its NPV in an economic profit context. Note that EVA is simply the difference between the firm's estimated NOPAT and the dollar capital charge. At $15 million, this economic profit amount is labeled EVA in Exhibit 11.2. Upon discounting the firm's economic profit back to the current period by the cost of capital, at 10%, we again obtain the firm's NPV, at $13.64 million. Hence, the firm's net present value is equal to the present value of the anticipated future EVA.

From an investing perspective, this company represents a buy opportunity if the positive NPV and EVA are not fully reflected in stock price. Moreover, we now see that both NPV and EVA can be used to make a distinction between good companies (buy opportunities) that are point-

---

[7] For an ongoing concern, EVA is the difference between the unlevered NOPAT and a dollar charge for capital employed in the business—measured by the amount of capital *times* the weighted average cost of capital, C × COC.

EXHIBIT 11.2   Wealth Creation with Positive EVA

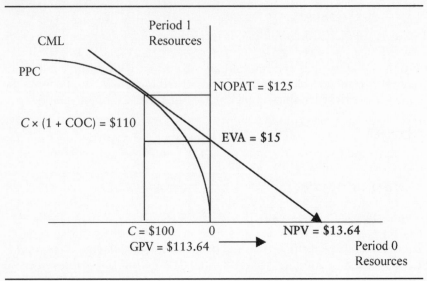

ing in the direction of economic profit and wealth creation versus bad companies that are pointing in the direction of wealth destruction. With this background, we will now focus on the financial characteristics of risky troubled companies (short sell opportunities).

NEGATIVE NPV: DISCOVERY OF BAD COMPANIES

Now that we have provided a conceptual foundation on the financial characteristics of wealth creators, we can use the wealth model to gain insight into the financial characteristics of wealth destroyers. Not surprisingly, this latter company type represents a potential sell or short sell opportunity. To see this, suppose that the firm's managers anticipate that the $100 million investment will generate an after-tax cash flow of, say, $107.50 million in the future period. The NPV consequence of the firm's 7.5% ($107.50/$100) investment opportunity is shown in Exhibit 11.3.

Exhibit 11.3 shows that the firm's initial capital is $100 million. The exhibit also shows that the firm's expected cash operating profit is $107.50 million. Upon subtracting the company's expected financing costs, at $110 million, from the anticipated cash operating profit, NOPAT at $107.25 million, the manager or investor (in our case) sees that the firm is left with negative residual income of –$2.5 million. This

EXHIBIT 11.3   Wealth Destruction with Negative EVA

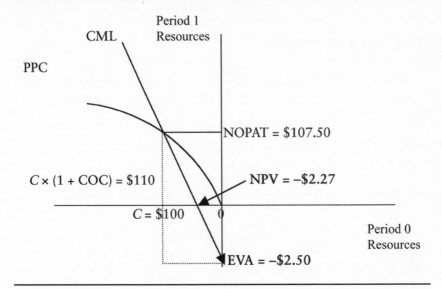

residual income is the firm's expected EVA in the reduced operating (that is, return on capital now at 7.5%) environment.

Note that if a company is a wealth destroyer in the future (due to the negative-anticipated EVA), then it must also be a wealth waster in the present. By discounting the negative EVA by the 10% cost of capital we obtain the adverse NPV result:

$$NPV = MVA = EVA/(1 + COC)$$
$$= -\$2.50/(1.1) = -\$2.27 \text{ million}$$

As a wealth destroyer, it is apparent that the firm's NPV is negative because the after-tax return on capital (ROC) at 7.5% falls short of the cost of capital at 10%. Equivalently, the NPV of –$2.27 million can be obtained by multiplying the firm's residual return on capital, at –2.5%, by the initial capital, $100 million, and then discounting the EVA result:

$$NPV = MVA = C \times (ROC - COC)/(1 + COC)$$
$$= \$100 \times (0.075 - 0.1)/(1.1) = -\$2.27 \text{ million}$$

In this case, the firm's negative NPV is due to the poor economic profit outlook. The adverse EVA outlook is in turn caused by the negative residual return on capital (ROC – COC), at –2.5%. As noted before, this company profile represents a sell or short sell opportunity to the degree that the negative NPV and EVA happenings are not fully reflected in share price.[8]

A Closer Look at the EVA Spread

We can use the two-period wealth model to further explain the *residual return on capital* (RROC) or the *EVA spread*. The EVA spread can be used as a convenient measure in the discovery of good companies and bad companies because this measure is adjusted for firm size.[9] Specifically, the EVA spread refers to the difference between the return on capital and the cost of capital. To show this, we will begin by unfolding NOPAT (again, in terms of a two-period model) into the firm's initial capital and the rate of return on that capital according to

$$NOPAT = C \times (1 + ROC)$$

In this expression, ROC is the firm's "operating cash flow return on investment" and C is the initial capital investment. We can now express the firm's NPV directly in terms of dollar EVA and the residual return on capital (ROC – COC) according to

$$
\begin{aligned}
NPV &= NOPAT/(1 + COC) - C \\
&= C \times (1 + ROC)/(1 + COC) - C \\
&= C \times (ROC - COC)/(1 + COC) \\
&= EVA/(1 + COC)
\end{aligned}
$$

In these expressions, we see that the firm's NPV derives its sign from the difference between the operating cash flow *return on investment* (ROC) and the weighted average *cost of capital* (COC). The spread between ROC and COC is variably referred to in the economic profit literature as (1) the "residual return on capital," (2) the "surplus return on capital," (3) the "excess operating return on invested capital," and, of course, (4) the "EVA spread." Upon substituting the numerical values into the two-period wealth model, we obtain

$$
\begin{aligned}
NPV &= MVA \\
&= \$107.5/(1.1) - \$100 \\
&= \$100 \times (0.075 - 0.10)/(1.1) \\
&= -\$2.5/(1.1) = -\$2.27 \text{ million}
\end{aligned}
$$

---

[8] In practice, this short selling argument should be qualified by the fact that NPV may reach a "floor" for reasons of cyclicality or perceived takeover (especially).

[9] The EVA spread, ROC – COC, can also be expressed as EVA/Capital.

As before, the firm's anticipated ROC is 7.5%, the assessed residual return on capital is –2.5% (RROC, or the EVA spread), and the firm's assessed economic profit is equal to –$2.27 million. We can now say that the wealth-destroying firm shown in Exhibit 11.3 represents a sell or short sell opportunity to the degree that the negative EVA spread is not fully impounded in stock price.

ZERO NPV: WEALTH NEUTRAL COMPANIES

Before moving forward, it is helpful to note that the wealth model can be used to explain the investment consequences of zero EVA, among other EVA-based company profiles. With zero expected EVA, a company is in equilibrium and represents neither a buy nor sell opportunity. Based on our previous illustration, if the firm's assessed return on capital is 10%, then its expected EVA is zero. This results because the expected cash operating profit from the firm's investment opportunity is the same as the anticipated financing costs, at $110 million. In this instance, the company's NPV would be zero.

Practically speaking, if a company has unused capital resources, then its shareholders would be just as well off if managers were to pay out the unused funds as a dividend payment on the firm's stock. In the event of capital market imperfections—such as differential tax treatment of dividends and capital gains—the shareholders might be better off if the firm's managers were to repurchase the firm's outstanding common stock. In principle though, the stock repurchase program is a wealth-neutral (or zero expected EVA) investment activity and does not in and of itself imply a directional impact on stock price.

CASE STUDIES

Armed with an EVA background for wealth creators and destroyers, we will look at two representative companies to distinguish between good and bad company characteristics. From an investing perspective, the "good" company can be interpreted as a potential buy opportunity while the "bad" company represents a sell or short sell opportunity. However, this trading distinction is *not* meant to imply that there were no times during the sample period when the good company should have been sold or that the bad company should have been bought. That being said, the EVA cases shown below are meant to profile the fundamental characteristics of companies that would normally present buy or short sell opportunities.

Case A: Microsoft Corporation—Good Company (Positive EVA)

Consider the positive EVA experiences of Microsoft Corporation in the 1990s. We will examine this behavior in the context of the residual return on capital or the EVA spread. Exhibit 11.4 shows the after-tax return on capital (ROC) versus the cost of capital (COC) for the computer software company during the 1990 to 2000 period. During this period, Microsoft had a large positive NPV (MVA not shown) because its EVA was positive and growing at a rapid rate over time.[10] In Exhibit 11.4, we see that the firm's positive EVA was due to its strongly positive residual return on capital—where the after-tax return on invested capital is greater than the cost of capital (equity capital in Microsoft's case) by a wide margin.

A closer look at Exhibit 11.4 shows that Microsoft's after-tax capital return varied from 44.16% in 1990, to a high of 54.75% in 1997, and then settled at 39.06% by year-end 2000 (mainly due to growth in capital via retained cash). For the 11-year reporting period, the computer software company had an outstanding average return on capital of 45.54%. Meanwhile, Microsoft's cost of capital ranged from a high of 16.90% in 1991 (up slightly from 1990), to a low of 10.74% in 1996, and then settled at 14.29% by year-end 2000. The firm's average cost of (equity) capital was 14.20% for the 11-year reporting period shown in the exhibit.

EXHIBIT 11.4   Microsoft Corporation: Return on Capital, Cost of Capital, and Residual Return on Capital: 1990–2000

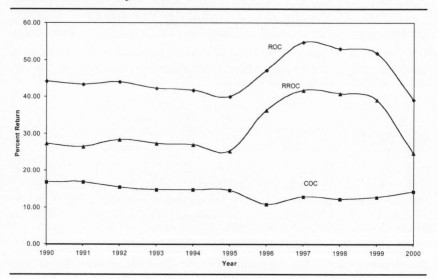

---

[10] Microsoft's EVA and MVA growth rates over the years 1990 to 2000 were about 40%.

Taken together, the capital return and capital cost findings for Microsoft indicate that the EVA spread was substantially positive during the reporting period. Exhibit 11.4 shows that the residual return on capital ranged from 27.32% in 1990, up to a high of 41.82% in 1997, and then settled at 24.77% by year-end 2000. The exhibit also reveals that volatility in this software firm's residual return was due primarily to variations in the after-tax return on capital. In contrast, the cost of capital for Microsoft was relatively stable during the 11-year reporting period.

Overall, the EVA findings for Microsoft are quite remarkable:[11] The company not only generated positive residual returns on capital—due to its highly desirable computer products—but it also exhibited substantial "staying power" in the presence of severe legal challenges from competitors and the U.S. Justice Department in the late 1990s. Not surprisingly, Microsoft's financial characteristics are representative of those that should be associated with a buy opportunity.

Case B: WorldCom Inc.—Bad Company (Negative EVA)

Now consider the negative EVA experiences of WorldCom. Before proceeding, it is important to note that in July 2002, the telecommunications giant filed for Chapter 11 bankruptcy protection. At that time, this was the largest corporate bankruptcy in U.S. history. However, as we will now see, WorldCom's financial problems were larger than those caused by the accounting gimmickry that mostly occurred during 2001 and the first quarter of 2002. Indeed, the telecom giant had consistently *negative* EVA in the 8-year reporting period spanning 1993 to 2000. This was due to the incredible growth in capital driven by serial acquisitions without ample time to absorb and exploit returns on the acquired assets. Exhibit 11.5 provides a visual look at the EVA happenings for WorldCom by showing the firm's after-tax return on capital versus the cost of capital for the 1990 to 2000 period. Interestingly, the exhibit shows that WorldCom's post-tax return on capital was consistently below the cost of capital after 1992.

A closer look at Exhibit 11.5 shows that from 1990 to 1992, WorldCom's after-tax return on capital was about the same as its cost of capital, at 12%. In 1993, a notable EVA event occurred when the telecommunication giant's capital return fell below 10%. At that time, WorldCom's return on capital was 8.51%, while its cost of capital was 12.37%. The exhibit also shows that from 1993 to 2000, the telecom giant's return on

---

[11] We are, of course, aware of the dramatic downturn in Microsoft's MVA (and that of other tech companies) during 2000. Again, our goal here is to profile the financial characteristics of a company that is *largely* pointing in the direction of wealth creation (buy opportunity).

EXHIBIT 11.5   WorldCom: Return on Capital, Cost of Capital, and Residual
Return on Capital: 1990–2000

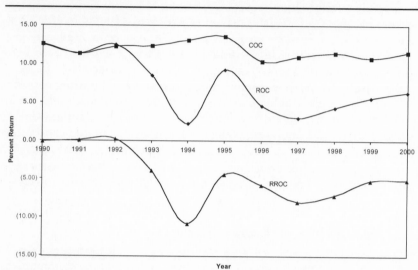

capital ranged from lows of 2.23% and 2.95% in 1994 and 1997, respectively, to a high of *only* 9.21% in 1995. Meanwhile, WorldCom's cost of
capital was consistently above the 10% watershed mark during the 11-
year reporting period.

The average return on capital for WorldCom during the 1990 to 2000
period was 7.26%, while the firm's average capital cost was 11.82%.
Taken together, the capital return and capital cost experiences for the telecommunications giant produced a sharply negative residual return on
capital during the eight years spanning 1993 to 2000. Equivalently, the
average residual return on capital for WorldCom was negative, at –4.56%,
over the reporting decade. These negative EVA findings for WorldCom
can be seen in Exhibit 11.5 by focusing on either (1) the negative gap
between the ROC and COC series or (2) the mostly negative residual
return on capital (RROC) series during 1990 to 2000.

The empirical findings for WorldCom are indicative of the financial
dangers that ensue when a company's after-tax capital returns fall short
of the capital costs. With a positive after-tax return on capital for each
year during 1990 to 2000, it would seem that the telecommunications
giant was actually making money—albeit, a generally smaller amount
when measured relative to capital as the years progressed. However, the
EVA evidence reveals that WorldCom was in fact a large wealth
destroyer for most of the 1990s. The persistently negative EVA spread—

that began in the post-1992 years—was the economic source of the collapse in the telecom giant's *market value-added* (MVA) that occurred at the century's turn. Indeed, WorldCom's filing for Chapter 11 bankruptcy protection in July 2002 was just the "nail in the coffin" for a company that was already busted from an economic profit perspective. For obvious reasons, this company type represents a strong sell or short sell opportunity to the degree that the negative EVA consequences (among other serious problems) could be anticipated.

ROLE OF THE VALUE/CAPITAL RATIO

Wall Street analysts often speak in terms of the "price-to-earnings" and "price-to-book value" ratios. By themselves, these ratios say little if anything about wealth creation, which is the primary focus of our good-versus-bad-company distinction in the discovery of short selling candidates. Along this latter line, one of the key benefits of the economic profit approach to measuring financial success is that we can see why a company has a price-to-book ratio above or below unity.

We can show this NPV and EVA relation by simply dividing the firm's *enterprise value* (V) by *invested capital* (C) according to:

$$V/C = C/C + NPV/C$$
$$= 1 + NPV/C$$

With this, we see that a firm's enterprise value-to-capital ratio, V/C, exceeds *one* if and only if—in a well-functioning capital market—the firm has positive NPV. In contrast, the V/C ratio falls below unity when the firm invests in wealth destroying or negative NPV projects, such that the NPV-to-capital ratio turns negative. In the former case, the company is a "good" company and represents a potential buy opportunity, while in the latter case the firm is a sell or short sell opportunity.[12] Further, upon substituting EVA into the enterprise value-to-capital ratio produces:[13]

$$V/C = 1 + [EVA/(1 + COC)]/C$$
$$= 1 + [(C \times (ROC - COC))/(1 + COC)]/C$$
$$= 1 + [ROC - COC]/(1 + COC)$$

---

[12] Recall that in practice, we must temper the short selling argument by a possible premium valuation due to perceived takeover.

[13] For convenience, we continue with NPV-EVA aspects of the two-period model.

We now see that wealth-creating firms have an enterprise value-to-capital ratio that exceeds unity because they have positive NPV (good company characteristics). The source of the positive NPV is due to the discounted positive economic profit. In turn, EVA is positive because the firm's after-tax cash return on investment (ROC) exceeds the weighted average cost of capital (COC). From this value-to-capital formulation, we also see that wealth-destroying companies have negative EVA, a negative EVA spread, and a value-to-capital ratio that falls below unity (bad company characteristics).

Upon substituting the values from the wealth destroyer illustration into the value-to-capital ratio yields:

$$V/C = 1 + [-\$2.5/(1.1)]/\$100 = 0.977$$

Thus, while Wall Street considers a company having a value-to-capital ratio that falls below unity to be a "value stock," it is hardly a real value opportunity—unless of course a reversal is made by the existing managers or a "new" and more profit conscious management is anticipated. Fortunately, with economic profit there is little uncertainty as to (1) why a wealth-creating firm has a value-to-capital ratio (or "price-to-book" ratio in popular jargon) that exceeds one; and (2) why a wealth waster has a value-to-capital ratio that lies below unity. Unlike accounting profit measures, economic profit metrics give investors the necessary financial tools to see the *direct* relationship between corporate investment decisions and their expected impact on shareholder value. Furthermore, with a solid foundation on the principles of wealth creation (and destruction), investors can utilize the value-to-capital ratio in a transparent way to distinguish between buying and selling opportunities.

INVESTED CAPITAL GROWTH

While our focus thus far on EVA is instructive—because it allowed us to use financial principles to distinguish between good and bad companies—the analysis is incomplete because it does not address how EVA is changing. In this section, we explain the role of invested capital growth in the discovery of companies that are pointing in the direction of positive and negative economic profit change (potential buy and sell opportunities, respectively).

We begin the focus on capital formation by demonstrating the relationship between changes in economic profit and the level of capital investment. In the model development, we take capital additions to mean those required beyond maintaining the NOPAT earnings stream from existing assets. To focus directly on the strategic role of invested capital growth, we express the change in economic profit for any given year as a function of the presumed constant residual return on capital[14] multiplied by the change in (net) invested capital according to

$$\Delta EP = \Delta C \times [ROC - COC]$$

In the above expression, we see that *change* in economic profit for any company is determined by (1) the sign and magnitude of the residual return on capital and (2) the sign and dollar magnitude of the change in invested capital. When ΔC is positive, the firm is making an internal/external (acquisitions) growth decision, while when ΔC is negative, the firm is making an internal decision by presumably restructuring business units and/or processes. In either case—corporate expansion or corporate contraction—managers and investors must make a correct assessment of the expected EVA spread when making strategic investment decisions (active buy or sell decisions in the case of investors).

Since we have previously shown that NPV and economic profit are linked via present value, it is a simple matter to show that changes in wealth are related to changes in invested capital. We will now use a simple EVA perpetuity model to show this NPV result.[15] In order to emphasize the importance of capital formation, we will once again assume that the residual return on capital is constant in the model development. The resulting constancy in the economic profit spread implies that changes in economic profit and NPV are directly related to changes in the level of invested capital. This allows active investors to focus on companies that are pointing in the direction of wealth creation (or destruction) based on their capital spending activities for a given EVA spread.

With these assumptions, we express the change in NPV for any given company as

---

[14] We take the EVA spread constant in the model so that we can focus directly on the strategic role of invested capital growth on economic profit and wealth creation. In practice, we realize that a firm's marginal return on capital and its cost of capital may vary due to changes in the level of capital investment. For example, ROC may fall and COC may rise in the presence of capital expansion.

[15] We do not have to assume that economic profit is constant each year as in a perpetuity model. For example, we could view EVA as the annualized equivalent of the *variable* economic profit figures that produce the original NPV. Then, a similar interpretation of annualized EVA change could be applied to induce a change in NPV.

$$\Delta NPV = \Delta EP / COC$$
$$= \Delta C \times [ROC - COC] / COC$$
$$= \Delta C \times [RROC] / COC$$

In this simple valuation model, we see that capital expansion or capital contraction can have a meaningful impact on wealth creation. Also, just like with changes in economic profit, changes in NPV are dependent on both the sign and magnitude of change in invested capital and the residual return on capital—where RROC is the economic profit spread.

MANAGERIAL AND INVESTOR IMPLICATIONS

Exhibit 11.6 summarizes the general relationship between the sign of the economic profit spread and predicted changes in economic profit and NPV for a presumed invested capital growth rate—that is, ΔC is assumed greater than zero, or ΔC is less than zero. The EVA-capital growth relationships are interesting in several managerial and investor respects. First, the exhibit shows that economic profit and NPV *rise* when the level of capital investment is expanded in a company having a positive expected EVA spread (that is, $\Delta C > 0$ and RROC > 0). This, after all, is the essence of real company growth as opposed to illusory company growth that merely expands the revenue and/or corporate asset base. From the investor's perspective, this company type is a potential buy opportunity to the extent that the sustainable economic profit change is not fully reflected in stock price.

Exhibit 11.6 also implies that economic profit and wealth decline when a company expands a growth-oriented business with a (now) neg-

EXHIBIT 11.6   Wealth Creation, Changes in Invested Capital

Capital Expansion ($\Delta C > 0$)			Active Trading Decision
RROC > 0	$\Delta EP > 0$	$\Delta NPV > 0$	Buy
RROC $= 0$	$\Delta EP = 0$	$\Delta NPV = 0$	Avoid
RROC < 0	$\Delta EP < 0$	$\Delta NPV < 0$	Sell/Short sell

Capital Contraction ($\Delta C < 0$)			Active Trading Decision
RROC > 0	$\Delta EP < 0$	$\Delta NPV < 0$	Sell/Short sell
RROC $= 0$	$\Delta EP = 0$	$\Delta NPV = 0$	Avoid
RROC < 0	$\Delta EP > 0$	$\Delta NPV > 0$	Buy

ative residual return on capital ($\Delta C > 0$ and RROC < 0). Capital expansion beyond the optimal point—as reflected in maximum NPV—can arise in a firm that is focused more on maximizing some financial or nonpecuniary variable that is inconsistent with the principles of economic profit and shareholder value maximization. Such misguided business expansion includes a revenue or asset-maximizing manager replete with an agenda of corporate acquisitions. Moreover, misguided investment decisions also arise in corporate organizations that expand a heretofore growth company at the peak of its competitive cycle. Herein lays an EVA perspective on a "overzealous" growth company that now represents a strong sell or short sell opportunity.

Corporate Contraction

Exhibit 11.6 presents some interesting facets of capital contraction. Specifically, the exhibit shows that economic profit and shareholder value decline when a manager contracts a company with a positive EVA spread ($\Delta C < 0$ and RROC > 0). In this case, the decline in economic profit is caused by the negative change in invested capital in the presence of a positive residual capital return. This is a company that—other things being the same—should be expanded rather than contracted. As with the NPV consequences of the overzealous growth company (but for different reasons), the manager that misguidedly contracts a positive-EVA-spread business is pointing the firm in a direction of wealth destruction for the shareholders. Not surprisingly, this company profile represents a potential sell or short sell opportunity.

In contrast, Exhibit 11.6 illustrates the positive side of capital contraction. Indeed, a manager in a risky troubled company that is *seriously* concerned about wealth recapture must shed those business assets or processes that are plagued by negative economic profit. Corporate managers (and investors) must realize that turn-around value—or recaptured shareholder value—can be realized by contracting a stale business with a negative expected economic profit spread. In formal terms, when $\Delta C < 0$ and RROC < 0, then ΔNPV > 0. Alas, the positively restructured company represents a real value opportunity (buy)!

MATRIX OF GOOD AND BAD COMPANIES

Exhibit 11.7 presents a matrix of company growth and value regions to help investors identify the EVA spread/capital formation combinations that lead to wealth creation (or destruction). In the two quadrants with positive capital growth, Quadrants II and III, we see a good company

EXHIBIT 11.7   Company Growth and Value Matrix

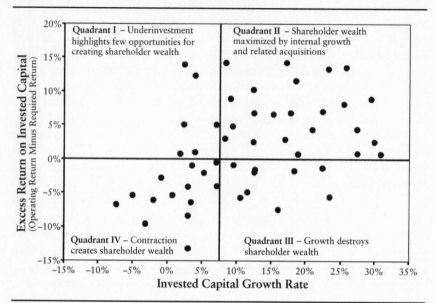

growth region (Quadrant II) and a bad or overzealous company growth region (Quadrant III). In the two quadrants with negative capital growth, Quadrants IV and I, we see a good company value region where capital contraction creates shareholder value (Quadrant IV) and a bad company value region where underinvestment highlights few opportunities for creating shareholder wealth (Quadrant I).[16]

From an investment perspective, Quadrants II and IV represent potential buy opportunities while Quadrants III and I represent (short) sell-to-avoid regions, respectively. In practice, we interpret Quadrant I as a region to avoid because it is typically populated by the currently positive EVA spread businesses of mature growth companies—such as food and tobacco companies—that have limited future growth opportunities. This underinvestment or poor utilization of capital region is different from Quadrant IV where companies are restructuring for positive economic profit change and thereby wealth creation.

In Quadrant II, we see that growth-oriented companies that are expanding their capital base with a positive EVA spread are poised for

---

[16] We interpret "growth"—whether good or bad—in terms of companies that are still expanding their capital base, while "value" refers to companies in the EVA schematic that are—by default—contracting their capital base.

continued—albeit substantial--improvement in shareholder value. Investing in positive economic profit and (therefore) positive NPV projects—both now and in the anticipated future—is the essence of real company growth. On the other hand, Exhibit 11.7 suggests that growth-oriented companies that are moving toward the overzealous company growth quadrant (Quadrant III) are heading in a direction that can lead to substantial compression in stock price and shareholder value.

The movement into the "growth for growth sake" region is most unfortunate for investors in companies with managers who naively believe that revenue and/or asset growth will automatically transfer into economic profit and wealth creation. Worse yet, the movement into Quadrant III is troublesome for investors who are wedded to companies having overzealous growth managers—with inordinate preoccupation with revenue and/or asset growth—that fail to heed the principles of wealth creation. Not surprisingly, growth companies that now face a misguided growth profile are strong sell or shorting candidates.

Revisiting Capital Contraction

As mentioned above, Exhibit 11.7 identifies two regions of capital contraction, Quadrants IV and I. There are several company types that might fall into these regions of the company growth-and-value matrix. For instance, we could be talking about a slow-to-negative growth company in the automotive, food, mining, steel, or railroad industries that are viewed as "Old Economy" companies. These companies are different from the high growth companies usually found in technology, health care or consumer segments. They are also companies that have currently negative economic profit (Quadrant IV companies) or limited EVA growth potential (Quadrant I companies) due to the commodity-oriented nature of their businesses. Moreover, because these slow growth companies can either restructure for positive change or hardly change at all, we take Quadrants IV and I as regions of good company value and bad company value, respectively. Consequently, companies in Quadrant IV are viewed as potential buy opportunities (due to the positive restructuring) while the mature-to-stale companies in Quadrant I should be avoided (due to the lack of profitable reinvestment opportunities or poor utilization of capital).

Strictly speaking, Quadrant I is represented by firms that are downsizing a positive EVA spread business. If this deinvestment activity persists, it can only lead to decreases in economic profit and shareholder value. In practice, we interpreted this quadrant as a capital formation region that is reflective of managers that cannot expand their mature businesses without significantly lowering returns on capital. In contrast, Quadrant IV is viewed as a region of constructive deinvestment in the company growth-and-value matrix. With capital contraction, we see that companies in this region are downsizing or restructuring negative EVA spread businesses—since the expected residual return on capital is less than zero. Based on the financial math of this region, one can say that a negative change in invested capital *times* a negative EVA spread (business) leads to a *positive* expected improvement in economic profit and shareholder value. Again, because of efficient restructuring, Quadrant IV companies represent potential buy opportunities.

On balance, Exhibit 11.7 shows that Quadrants II and IV have the greatest potential for improvement in stock price and shareholder value. While companies and industries in these regions can be radically different—we would expect that high barrier-to-entry growth companies would show up in Quadrant II, while forward looking "Old Economy" companies would show up in Quadrant IV—we get to the same economic profit conclusion. That is, companies in Quadrant II are expanding positive EVA spread businesses that stand to create substantial shareholder value. Companies in Quadrant IV are efficiently restructuring stale or troubled businesses and should also see noticeable improvement in economic profit and stock price. Consequently, we view these EVA-based regions as the good company growth and good company value regions, respectively. Moreover, from the active investors perspective, companies in Quadrants II and IV represent potential buy opportunities while, as we explained before, the bad company growth and bad company value firms in Quadrants III and I represent (short) sell-to-avoid opportunities, respectively.

RECONCILING MARKET IMPLIED GROWTH

Up to this point we have been careful to emphasize the word "potential" when referring to buy or sell opportunities. This qualification is necessary because market implied expectations of economic profit growth (even if positive) might already be reflected in share price. For example, we recognize that "good" companies that show up in Quadrants II and IV of the company growth and value matrix (Exhibit 11.7) can have good *or* bad stock characteristics. To illustrate this, Exhibit 11.8 shows the "Excess Return on Invested Capital" versus the "Market Value of Invested Capital to Replacement Cost of Invested Capital"[17] for a sample of companies that we track at GAM USA.

---

[17] Note that the "excess return on invested capital" is equivalent to the EVA-to-capital ratio as well as the EVA spread. Also, the use of market value-to-replacement cost of invested capital is really just a scaling on our previous usage of the NPV-to-capital ratio.

EXHIBIT 11.8   Excess Returns Relative to Valuation

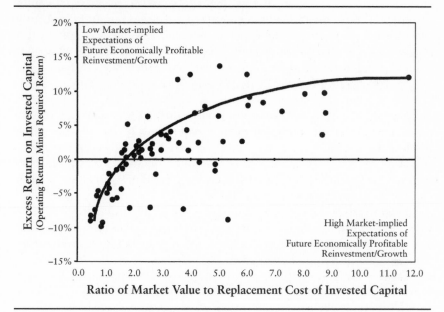

In this exhibit, the excess return on invested capital is simply the after-tax return on invested capital less the cost of capital. This is just the EVA spread that we defined before. Also, we report the market value of invested capital (or enterprise value) relative to replacement cost of capital for consistency with the traditional way of evaluating companies in profitability versus "price-to book" context. There is *no* slippage of economic profit focus because the market value of invested capital-to-replacement cost of invested capital ratio is *directly* related to the NPV-to-invested capital ratio that we explained before.[18]

Exhibit 11.8 shows a scatter plot of "good" companies (culled from an Exhibit 11.7 analysis) measured relative to a curve through the data points. Points in the exhibit that lie above the curve are considered to be buy opportunities, while data points that fall below the curve represent

---

[18] Recall that the enterprise value-to-capital ratio can be written as:

$$V/C = 1 + NPV/C$$

In this expression, V is enterprise value (or market value of invested capital) and C is a measure of invested capital. Hence, V/C is greater than one when NPV is positive, while V/C is less than unity when NPV is negative. The market value of invested capital-to-replacement cost of invested capital is also a measure of "Tobin's Q."

sell or short sell opportunities.[19] For companies that plot above the curve, Exhibit 11.8 shows that at such excess return on invested capital positions, the companies should command a higher valuation. If correct, this upward revaluation is reflected in a rise in the Value-to-Capital ratio. In this case, internal or warranted expectation of economic profit growth is higher than market implied EVA growth imbedded in stock price.

Specifically, while the capital market expects compression in future economic profit down to the curve (Exhibit 11.8) for any given market value-to-replacement cost of capital ratio, internal expectations of economically profitable reinvestment for combinations above the curve imply a higher valuation for a company's stock. Astute investors can therefore expect to earn risk-adjusted returns on stocks that plot above the curve because of the fortuitously positive (and presumed consistent) economic profit position of these companies.

In contrast, companies that plot below the curve represent sell or short sell opportunities. Exhibit 11.8 suggests that these firms should command a lower relative valuation. In this case, internal expectation of economic profit growth is lower than market implied growth imbedded in current stock price. Here, the capital market incorrectly expects an upward revision in economic profit to the curve for any given market value of invested capital-to-replacement cost of capital ratio. However, consistently low expectations of economically profitable reinvestment for companies that fall below the curve imply a lower valuation. Active-minded investors should look elsewhere if they are restricted to a "long only" strategy, while they should consider a "long-short" strategy if shorting is permissible.

Hence, the stocks of companies that plot above the curve (Exhibit 11.8) are viewed as buy opportunities, while stocks that plot below the curve are viewed as sell or short sell opportunities. In practice, the quantitative insight should be tempered by qualitative considerations that impact the actual trading decision. This additional research is necessary because the data points in Exhibit 11.8 are constantly changing over time. Moreover, we now see that the economic profit approach to investing—on both the long *and* short side—emphasizes three key elements: expected EVA spread, capital formation, and the reconciliation of actual-versus-market-implied expectations of economic profit growth.

---

[19] The buy or sell recommendations in Exhibit 11.8 presume that we are focusing on "good" companies that show up in Quadrants II and IV of Exhibit 7. This joining of exhibits recognizes that there are good companies with "good" or "bad" stock characteristics (buy or sell opportunities). Note that companies in Quadrants III and I of the company growth and value matrix (Exhibit 11.7) were previously identified as (short) sell-to-avoid opportunities, respectively—although in practice, even these sell considerations can be tempered by finer distinctions regarding fundamentals versus valuation in the event of anticipated management change or takeover.

SUMMARY

We argue in this chapter that the discovery of good companies and bad companies—buying and selling opportunities—should be grounded in the fundamentals of wealth creation. Good companies are pointing in the direction of economic profit creation while bad companies are pointing in the direction of economic profit deterioration. Along the way, we argue that the decision to buy or short sell securities should be based on (at least) three economic profit criteria: namely, the expected EVA spread, capital formation (positive or negative), and the reconciliation of actual versus market implied expectations of economic profit growth imbedded in share price. We believe that with an EVA research platform, investors will have a robust framework for buying and selling securities that is consistent with economic profit and NPV principles espoused in the theory of finance.

CHAPTER 12

Long-Short Equity Portfolios

Bruce I. Jacobs, Ph.D.
Principal
Jacobs Levy Equity Management

Kenneth N. Levy, CFA
Principal
Jacobs Levy Equity Management

To create a long-short equity portfolio, the investor buys "winners"—securities that are expected to do well over the investment horizon—and sells short "losers"—securities that are expected to perform poorly. Unlike traditional, long-only equity investing, long-short investing takes full advantage of the investor's insights. Whereas the traditional investor would act on and potentially benefit only from insights about winning securities, the long-short investor can potentially benefit from insights about winners and losers.

As we will see, by combining long and short positions in a single portfolio, the investor increases flexibility in pursuit of return and in control of risk. This increased flexibility reflects the greater freedom afforded the investor to act on negative insights, and also the freedom from traditional index constraints afforded by the ability to reduce risk by offsetting long and short positions. The potential result is improved performance vis-à-vis a traditional long-only portfolio.

A long-short portfolio also offers increased flexibility in asset management. For example, the investor can choose to construct a market-neutral long-short portfolio, which eliminates systematic (market) risk while providing the risks and returns of security selection. Alternatively, the investor can combine a market-neutral long-short portfolio with derivatives that perform in line with a desired market benchmark to create a position that offers the security selection performance of the long-short portfolio on top of the chosen asset's performance. That asset may be the market from which the securities were selected or a totally different market. In this way, any skill in security selection can be "transported" to any desired asset class.

CONSTRUCTING A MARKET-NEUTRAL PORTFOLIO

In a market-neutral portfolio, the investor holds approximately equal dollar amounts of long and short positions. Of course, careful attention must be paid to the securities' systematic risks: The long positions' price sensitivities to broad market movements should virtually offset the short positions' sensitivities, leaving the overall portfolio with negligible systematic risk. This means that the portfolio's value will not rise or fall just because the broad market rises or falls. The portfolio may thus be said to have a beta of zero. The portfolio is not risk-free, however; it retains the risks associated with the selection of the stocks held long and sold short. The value-added provided by insightful security selection, however, should more than compensate for the risk incurred.[1]

Exhibit 12.1 illustrates the operations needed to establish a market-neutral equity strategy, assuming a $10 million initial investment. Keep in mind that these operations are undertaken virtually simultaneously, although they will be discussed in steps.

The Federal Reserve Board requires that short positions be housed in a margin account at a brokerage firm. The first step in setting up a long-short portfolio, then, is to find a "prime broker" to administer the account. This prime broker clears all trades and arranges to borrow the shares to be sold short.

Exhibit 12.1 shows that, of the initial $10 million investment, $9 million is used to purchase the desired long positions. These are held at the prime broker, where they serve as the collateral necessary, under Federal Reserve Board margin requirements, to establish the desired short positions. The prime broker arranges to borrow the securities to be sold short. Their sale results in cash proceeds, which are delivered to the stock lenders as collateral for the borrowed shares.[2]

---

[1] Bruce I. Jacobs and Kenneth N. Levy, "Long/Short Equity Investing," *Journal of Portfolio Management*, Fall 1993, pp. 52–63. Bruce I. Jacobs, "Controlled Risk Strategies," in ICFA *Continuing Education: Alternative Investing* (Charlottesville, VA: Association for Investment Management and Research, 1998), pp. 70–81.

[2] In practice, lenders of stock will usually demand that collateral equal something over 100% of the value of the securities lent (usually 105%).

EXHIBIT 12.1 Market-Neutral Deployment of Capital (millions of dollars)

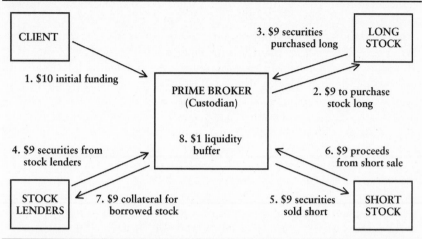

Source: Bruce I. Jacobs and Kenneth N. Levy, "The Long and Short on Long-Short," *Journal of Investing* (Spring 1997).

Federal Reserve Board Regulation T requires that a margined equity account be at least 50% collateralized to initiate short sales.[3] This means that the investor could buy $10 million of securities and sell short another $10 million, resulting in $20 million in equity positions, long and short. As Exhibit 12.1 shows, however, the investor has bought only $9 million of securities, and sold short an equal amount. The account retains $1 million of the initial investment in cash.

This "liquidity buffer" serves as a pool to meet cash demands on the account. For instance, the account's short positions are marked to market daily. If the prices of the shorted stocks increase, the account must post additional capital with the stock lenders to maintain full collateralization; conversely, if the shorted positions fall in price, the (now overcollateralized) lenders release funds to the long-short account. The liquidity buffer may also be used to reimburse the stock lenders for div-

---

[3] "Reg T" does not cover U.S. Treasury or municipal bonds or bond funds. Furthermore, Reg T can be circumvented by various means. Hedge funds, for example, often set up offshore accounts, which are not subject to Reg T. Broker-dealers are subject to much less stringent requirements than Reg T, and hedge funds and other investors may organize as their own broker-dealer or arrange to trade as the proprietary account of a broker-dealer in order to attain much more leverage than Reg T would allow. See Bruce I. Jacobs, Kenneth N. Levy, and Harry M. Markowitz, "Portfolio Optimization with Factors, Scenarios and Realistic Short Positions," Jacobs Levy Equity Management, 2004.

idends owed on the shares sold short, although dividends received on stocks held long may be able to meet this cash need. In general, a liquidity buffer equal to 10% of the initial investment is sufficient.

The liquidity buffer will earn interest for the market-neutral account. We assume the interest earned approximates the Treasury bill rate. The $9 million in cash proceeds from the short sales, posted as collateral with the stock lenders, also earns interest. The interest earned is typically allocated among the lenders, the prime broker, and the market-neutral account; the lenders retain a small portion as a lending fee, the prime broker retains a portion to cover expenses and provide some profit, and the long-short account receives the rest. The exact distribution is a matter for negotiation, but we assume the amount rebated to the investor (the "short rebate") approximates the Treasury-bill rate.[4]

The overall return to the market-neutral equity portfolio thus has two components—an interest component and an equity component. The performances of the stocks held long and sold short will determine the equity component. As we will see below, this component will be independent of the performance of the equity market from which the stocks have been selected.

Market Neutrality Illustrated

The top half of Exhibit 12.2 illustrates the performance of a market-neutral equity portfolio. It assumes the market rises by 30%, while the long positions rise by 33% and the short positions by 27%. The 33% return increases the value of the $9 million in long positions to $11.97 million, for a $2.97 million gain. The 27% return on the shares sold short increases their value from $9 million to $11.43 million; as the shares are sold short, this translates into a $2.43 million loss for the portfolio.

The net gain from equity positions equals $540,000, or $2.97 million minus $2.43 million. This represents a 6.0% return on the initial equity investment of $9 million, equal to the spread between the returns on the long and short positions (33% minus 27%). As the initial equity investment represented only 90% of the invested capital, however, the equity component's performance translates into a 5.4% return on the initial investment (90% of 6.0%). (Of course, if the shorts had outperformed the longs, the return from the equity portion of the portfolio would be negative.)

We assume the short rebate (the interest received on the cash proceeds from the short sales) equals 5%. This amounts to $450,000 (5.0% of $9 million). The interest earned on the liquidity buffer adds another

---

[4] As we have noted, the short rebate is arrived at by negotiation. The investor may incur a larger or a smaller haircut than we have assumed here. Retail investors who sell short rarely receive any of the interest on the proceeds.

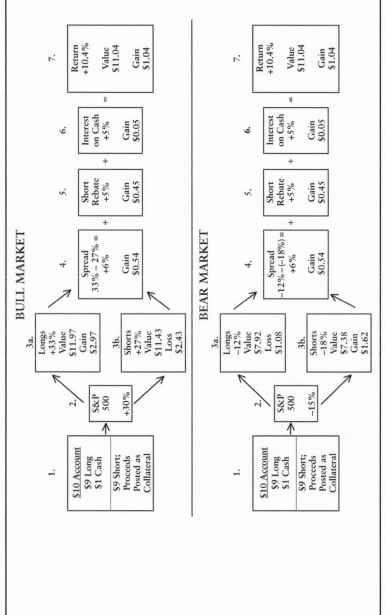

Source: Bruce I. Jacobs and Kenneth N. Levy, "The Long and Short on Long-Short," *Journal of Investing* (Spring 1997).

$50,000 (5.0% of $1 million). (A lower rate would result, of course, in a lower return.) Thus, at the end of the period, the $10 million initial investment has grown to $11.04 million. The long-short portfolio return of 10.4% comprises a 5% return from interest earnings and a 5.4% return from the equity positions, long and short.

The bottom half of Exhibit 12.2 illustrates the portfolio's performance assuming the market declines by 15%. The long and short positions exhibit the same market-relative performances as above, with the longs falling by 12% and the shorts falling by 18%. In this case, the decline in the prices of the securities held long results in an ending value of $7.92 million, for a loss of $1.08 million. The shares sold short, however, decline in value to $7.38 million, so the portfolio gains $1.62 million from the short positions. The equity positions thus post a gain of $540,000—exactly the same as the net equity result experienced in the up-market case. The interest earnings from the short rebate and the liquidity buffer are the same as when the market rose, so the overall portfolio again grows from $10 million to $11.04 million, for a return of 10.4%. (Obviously, if the shorts had fallen less than the longs, or interest rates had declined, the return would be lower.)

A market-neutral equity portfolio is designed to return the same amount whether the equity market rises or falls. A properly constructed market-neutral portfolio, if it performs as expected, will incur virtually no systematic, or market, risk; its return will equal its interest earnings plus the net return on (or the spread between) the long and short positions. The equity return spread is purely active, reflecting the investor's stock selection skills; this return spread is not diluted (or augmented) by the underlying market's return.

THE IMPORTANCE OF INTEGRATED OPTIMIZATION

The ability to sell short constitutes a material advantage for a market-neutral investor compared with a long-only investor. Consider, for example, a long-only investor who has an extremely negative view about a typical stock. The investor's ability to benefit from this insight is very limited. The most the investor can do is exclude the stock from the portfolio, in which case the portfolio will have about a 0.01% underweight in the stock, relative to the underlying market (as the median-capitalization stock in the Russell 3000 universe has a weighting of 0.01%). Those who do not consider this to be a material constraint should consider what its effect would be on the investor's ability to overweight a typical stock. It would mean the investor could hold no more than a 0.02% long position in the stock—a 0.01% overweight—no matter how attractive its expected return.

The ability to short, by increasing the investor's leeway to act on his or her insights, has the potential to enhance returns from active security selection. The scope of the improvement, however, depends critically on the way in which the portfolio is constructed. In particular, an integrated optimization that considers both long and short positions simultaneously not only frees the investor from the nonnegativity constraint imposed on long-only portfolios, but also frees the portfolio from the restrictions imposed by securities' benchmark weights. To see this, it is useful to examine in some detail the ways in which market-neutral portfolios can be constructed, and their implications for portfolio performance.

For instance, many investors construct market-neutral portfolios by combining a long-only portfolio, perhaps a preexisting one, with a short-only portfolio. This results in a long-plus-short portfolio. The long side of the portfolio is identical to a long-only portfolio, hence it offers no benefits in terms of incremental return or reduced risk. Furthermore, the short side of the portfolio is statistically equivalent to the long side, hence to the long-only portfolio. In effect,

$$\alpha_L = \alpha_S = \alpha_{LO}$$

$$\omega_L = \omega_S = \omega_{LO}$$

The excess return or alpha, α_L, of the long side of the long-plus-short portfolio will equal the alpha of the short side, α_S, which will equal the alpha of the long-only portfolio, α_{LO}. Furthermore, the residual risk of the long side of the long-plus-short portfolio, ω_L, will equal the residual risk of the short side, ω_S, which will equal the residual risk of the long-only portfolio, ω_{LO}.

These equivalencies reflect the fact that all the portfolios, the long-only portfolio and the long and short components of the long-plus-short portfolio, are constructed relative to a benchmark index. Each portfolio is active in pursuing excess return relative to the underlying benchmark only insofar as it holds securities in weights that depart from their benchmark weights. However, departures from benchmark weights introduce residual risk. Controlling portfolio risk thus involves balancing expected excess (to benchmark) returns against the added risk they introduce. In this balancing act, the investor faces the probability of having to forgo some increment of expected return in order to reduce portfolio residual risk. Portfolio construction is benchmark-constrained.[5]

---

[5] Bruce I. Jacobs and Kenneth N. Levy, "More on Long-Short Strategies," *Financial Analysts Journal* (March/April 1995), pp. 88–90.

Consider, for example, an investor who does not have the ability to discriminate between good and bad oil stocks, or who believes that no oil stock will significantly out- or underperform the underlying benchmark in the near future. In long-plus-short, this investor may have to hold some oil stocks in the long portfolio and short some oil stocks in the short portfolio, if only to control each portfolio's residual risk relative to the benchmark.

In long-plus-short, the advantage offered by the flexibility to short is also curtailed by the need to control risk by holding or shorting securities in benchmarklike weights. The ratio of the performance of the long-plus-short portfolio to that of the long-only portfolio can be expressed as follows:

$$\frac{IR_{L+S}}{IR_{LO}} = \sqrt{\frac{2}{1 + \rho_{L+S}}}$$

where IR is the information ratio, or the ratio of excess return to residual risk, α/ω, and ρ_{L+S} is the correlation between the alphas of the long and short sides of the long-plus-short portfolio. If this correlation is less than one, the long-plus-short portfolio will enjoy greater diversification and reduced risk relative to a long-only portfolio, for an improvement in IR. However, a long-only portfolio can derive a similar benefit by adding a less than fully correlated asset with comparable risk and return, so this is not a benefit unique to long-short.[6]

The Real Benefits of Long-Short

The real benefits of long-short portfolio construction emerge only when the portfolio is conceived of and constructed as a single, integrated portfolio of long and short positions.[7] In an integrated optimization, selection of the

---

[6] The long-only portfolio can also engage in leverage, just like the long-plus-short portfolio. (However, a long-only portfolio would have to borrow funds to achieve leverage, and this can have tax consequences for otherwise tax-exempt investors; borrowing shares to sell short does not result in unrelated business taxable income.) Furthermore, derivatives such as index futures contracts can be used to make the long-only portfolio market neutral—just like the long-short portfolio. Thus neither market neutrality, nor leverage, nor even shorting constitutes an inherent advantage over long-only portfolio construction. See Bruce I. Jacobs and Kenneth N. Levy, "20 Myths About Long-Short," *Financial Analysts Journal* (September/October 1996), pp. 81–85; and Bruce I. Jacobs and Kenneth N. Levy, "The Long and Short on Long-Short," *The Journal of Investing* (Spring 1997), pp. 73–86.

[7] Bruce I. Jacobs, Kenneth N. Levy, and David Starer, "On the Optimality of Long-Short Strategies," *Financial Analysts Journal* (March/April 1998), pp. 26–30; and Bruce I. Jacobs, Kenneth N. Levy, and David Starer, "Long-Short Portfolio Management: An Integrated Approach," *Journal of Portfolio Management* (Winter 1999), pp. 23–32.

securities to be held long is determined simultaneously with the selection of the securities to be sold short, taking into account the expected returns of the individual securities, the standard deviations of those returns, and the correlations between them, as well as the investor's tolerance for risk. The result is a single portfolio, not one long portfolio and one short portfolio.

With integrated optimization, a long-short portfolio is not constrained by benchmark weights. Once an underlying benchmark has been used to determine the systematic risks of the candidate securities, its role in portfolio construction is effectively over. The offsetting market sensitivities of the aggregate long and aggregate short positions control risk. The investor is not constrained to moving away from or toward benchmark weights. To establish a 1% overweight or a 1% underweight, the investor merely has to allocate 1% of capital long or allocate 1% of capital short.

Suppose, for example, that an investor's strongest insights are about oil stocks, some of which are expected to do especially well and some especially poorly. The investor does not have to restrict the portfolio's holdings of oil stocks to benchmarklike weights in order to control the portfolio's exposure to oil sector risk. The investor can allocate much of the portfolio to oil stocks, held long and sold short. The offsetting long and short positions control the portfolio's exposure to the oil factor.

Conversely, suppose the investor has no insights into oil stock behavior. Unlike the long-only and long-plus-short investors discussed above, the integrated market-neutral investor can totally exclude oil stocks from the portfolio. The exclusion of oil stocks does not increase portfolio risk, because the integrated market-neutral portfolio's risk is independent of any security's benchmark weight. At the same time, freed of the need to hold deadweight in the form of securities that offer no abnormal expected returns, the investor can allocate more capital to securities that do offer expected abnormal returns.

Just as one cannot attribute the qualities of water, its wetness say, to its hydrogen or oxygen components separately, one cannot reasonably dissect the performance of an integrated market-neutral portfolio into one element attributable to long positions alone and another attributable to short positions alone. Only jointly do the long and short positions define the portfolio. Rather than being measurable as long and short performances in excess of an underlying benchmark, the performance of an integrated long-short portfolio is measurable as the overall return on the long and short positions—or the spread between the long and short returns—relative to their risk. Compared with the excess return/residual risk of long-only management, this performance should be enhanced by the elimination of benchmark constraints, which allows the market-neutral portfolio increased flexibility to implement investment insights, both long and short.

ADDING BACK A MARKET RETURN

A market-neutral portfolio offers an active return from the specific securities the investor selects to hold long or sell short, plus a return representing an interest rate. The neutral strategy does not reflect either the return or the risk of the underlying equity market. As Exhibit 12.2 illustrated, the value added from stock selection skill, represented by the long-short spread, is independent of the performance of the equity asset class from which the securities were selected.

That value-added can be transported to other asset classes through the use of derivatives overlays. An investor can, for example, add back the risk and return of the equity market by purchasing stock index futures equal in amount to the investment in the market-neutral strategy. The resulting "equitized" long-short portfolio captures the performance of the underlying market while allowing the investor to benefit from the enhanced flexibility in stock selection afforded by long-short management.

Exhibit 12.3 illustrates the deployment of capital for equitized long-short portfolio construction. Note that the major difference between Exhibit 12.3 and Exhibit 12.1, other than the addition of the $10 million of stock index futures, is the size of the liquidity buffer. As noted, the liquidity buffer is used, among other things, to meet marks to market on the short

EXHIBIT 12.3 Equitized Deployment of Capital (millions of dollars)

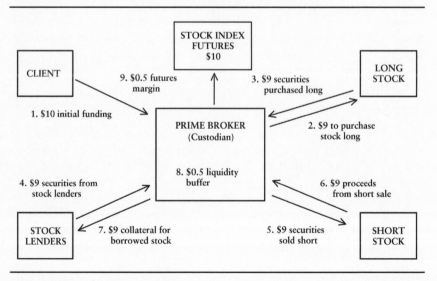

Source: Bruce I. Jacobs and Kenneth N. Levy, "The Long and Short on Long-Short," *Journal of Investing* (Spring 1997).

positions. With an equitized strategy, an increase in the price of short positions induced by a market rise is generally accompanied by an increase in the price of the futures contract held long; the marks to market on the futures can be used to meet the marks to market on the short positions. The capital freed up from the liquidity buffer is used to margin the futures positions.[8] Thus, in Exhibit 12.3 as in Exhibit 12.1, $9 million of the initial $10 million investment is assumed available for purchase of securities.

Exhibit 12.4 illustrates the performance of the equitized long-short portfolio in bull and bear market scenarios, using the same assumptions as Exhibit 12.2. Returns to the long-short portfolio are the same as in Exhibit 12.2. Cash returns are also the same, as the reduced interest from the smaller liquidity buffer is combined with the interest earned on the futures margin.

Total returns on the portfolios in Exhibits 12.2 and 12.4 differ markedly, however. The entire difference is due to the performance of the overall market, which is reflected in the equitized but not the market-neutral portfolio. Unlike the market-neutral portfolio, the equitized portfolio does not behave the same in both bull and bear market scenarios. Its overall return is sensitive to market movements. At the same time, it benefits fully from the return spread of the long-short portfolio, which (insofar as it is positive) serves to augment the increase from an up market and to cushion the decline from a down market.

Return Transportability

In essence, the return on a market-neutral portfolio represents a return to security selection alone, independent of the overall return to the market from which the securities are selected. This return, and all the benefits of long-short construction that it reflects, can be transported to other asset classes through the use of derivatives.[9] The equitized long-short portfolio transports the return to the equity market class, adding the security selection return (and its associated risk) to the equity market return (and its risk). Other derivatives overlays may be used to establish exposures to fixed income, foreign equity, and so forth.

The "transportability" of the long-short spread has at least two implications for investment management. First, it implies that the identity of a long-short portfolio is flexible. A market-neutral long-short

---

[8] We assume futures can be purchased on margin of about 5% of the face value of the contracts purchased.
[9] Bruce I. Jacobs and Kenneth N. Levy, "Alpha Transport with Derivatives," *Journal of Portfolio Management* (May 1999), pp. 55–60; and James Rutter, "How to Make Volatility Pay—The Next Step Forward Could Be Portable Alpha," *Global Investor*, June 2003.

EXHIBIT 12.4 Equitized Hypothetical Performance in Bull and Bear Markets (millions of dollars)

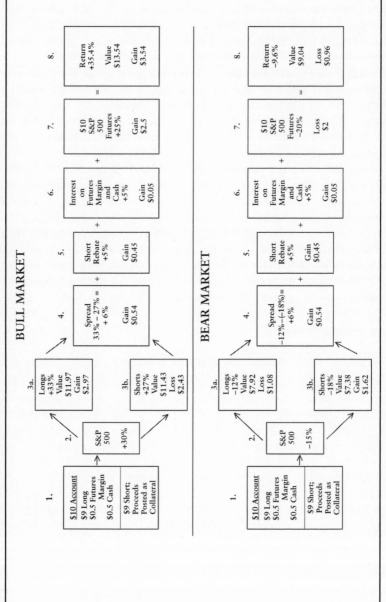

Source: Bruce I. Jacobs and Kenneth N. Levy, "The Long and Short on Long-Short," *Journal of Investing* (Spring 1997).

portfolio offers a return (and risk) from security selection on top of a cash return. An equitized long-short portfolio offers the security selection return on top of the equity asset class return. Long-short portfolios do not constitute a separate asset class; the existing asset class to which they belong will depend upon the choice of derivatives overlay.

Second, and of perhaps more practical importance, transportability allows the investor to separate security selection skills from asset allocation decisions. This is not an inconsiderable benefit. The task of combining asset allocation with security selection often involves a tradeoff. The investor may be able to find active managers who have demonstrated an ability to add value, but the universes exploited by these managers may not encompass the asset class desired by the investor. More often than not, it is the return from security selection that is sacrificed.

Consider the case of an investor who has both large-cap and small-cap equity managers. On the one hand, to the extent that small-cap stocks are less efficiently priced than their large-cap counterparts, the potential of the small-cap manager to add value relative to an underlying small-cap universe may be greater than the potential of the large-cap manager to add value relative to an underlying large-cap universe. The investor may thus want to allocate more to the small-cap than the large-cap manager.

On the other hand, small-cap stocks may be considered too risky in general, or may be expected to underperform larger-cap stocks. In the interest of optimizing overall fund return and risk, the investor may wish to limit the allocation to the small-cap manager and allocate significantly more to the large-cap manager. In that case, however, the investor sacrifices the potential alpha from small-cap security selection in exchange for overall asset class return and risk. The investor's asset allocation decision comes down to a choice between sacrificing security selection return in favor of asset class performance and sacrificing asset class performance in favor of security selection return.

With alpha transport, investors need no longer face such Solomonic decisions. Market-neutral portfolio construction techniques and derivatives can be used to liberate managers, and manager performance, from their underlying asset classes. Investors, or managers, can deploy derivatives to transport the skill of any manager to any asset class. Alpha transport enables the overall fund to add value from both asset and manager allocation.

A More Aggressive Stance

The investor can choose to take a more aggressive stance toward benchmark positions. For example, the investor can choose to reduce (increase) derivatives positions if the underlying market is expected to decline (rise). This would incorporate an element of market timing (and additional risk) into the market-neutral-plus-derivatives construct.

In Jacobs, Levy and Starer, we explain how to optimize the utility of a portfolio that combines a position in a desired benchmark with long and short positions in benchmark securities.[10] As with the market-neutral equity portfolio, the answer lies in integration: Portfolio construction considers explicitly the risks and returns of the individual securities and the benchmark holding, as well as their correlations.

SOME CONCERNS ADDRESSED

Long-short construction maximizes the benefit obtained from potentially valuable investment insights by eliminating long-only's constraint on short selling and the need to converge to securities' benchmark weights in order to control portfolio risk. While long-short offers advantages over long-only, however, it also involves complications not encountered in long-only management.

Many of the complications are related to the use of short selling. For example, shares the investor desires to sell short may not be available for borrowing, or shares that have been sold short may be called back by their lenders.[11] Short selling is also subject to various exchange trading rules (uptick rules), which may exact trading opportunity costs by preventing or delaying desired executions.[12]

---

[10] Jacobs, Levy, and Starer, "Long-Short Portfolio Management: An Integrated Approach."

[11] Shares sold short are subject to recall by the lender at any time. In most cases, the prime broker will be able to find alternative lenders for the securities subject to recall, but if these are not available, the market-neutral investor will be subject to "buy-ins" and have to cover the short positions. One also occasionally hears about a "short squeeze," in which speculators buy up lendable stock to force a buy-in at elevated prices. This will be more of a problem for dedicated short sellers who take concentrated positions in illiquid stocks than for a market-neutral investor holding small positions diversified across many stocks.

[12] Securities and Exchange Commission (SEC) Rule 10a-1, for example, states that exchange-traded shares can be shorted only at a price that is higher than the last trade price ("uptick") or the same as the last trade price if that price was higher than the previous price ("zero-plus-tick"). Uptick rules vary across the different exchanges and proprietary trading systems. The SEC is currently considering lifting uptick rules for most common stock for an experimental period. Furthermore, futures on single stocks have recently begun trading and, if they develop sufficient liquidity (a problem so far in European single-stock futures markets), they may offer an alternative to short selling.

The cost associated with securing and administering lendable stocks averages 25 to 30 basis points.[13] This cost is incurred as a "haircut" on the short rebate the investor receives from the interest earned on the short sale proceeds.

A more serious impediment to long-short strategies may be the discomfort many investors feel with the idea of shorting. While it is true that the risk of a short position is theoretically unlimited because there is no bound on a rise in the price of the shorted security, this source of risk is considerably mitigated in practice. It is unlikely, for example, that the prices of all the securities sold short in a market-neutral portfolio will rise dramatically at the same time, with no offsetting increases in the prices of the securities held long. Also, the trading imperatives of market neutral, which call for keeping dollar amounts of longs and shorts roughly equalized on an ongoing basis, will tend to limit short-side losses, because shorts are covered as their prices rise. And if a gap-up in the price of an individual security does not afford the opportunity to cover, the overall portfolio will still be protected provided it is well diversified.

Other perceived impediments to long-short investing are just as illusory. Take, for example, the issue of trading costs. A long-short portfolio that takes full advantage of the allowed leverage will engage in about twice as much trading activity as a comparable unleveraged long-only strategy. The additional trading costs, however, must be weighed against the expanded potential for return. Most investors will be willing to pay the additional trading costs in exchange for the expected incremental return. Nevertheless, leverage is not an inherent part of long-short. Given capital of $10 million, for example, an investor could choose to invest $5 million long and sell $5 million short; trading activity for the resulting long-short portfolio would be roughly equivalent to that for a $10 million long-only portfolio.

The differential between management fees for a long-short versus a long-only portfolio is also largely a reflection of the leverage involved. If one considers the management fee per dollar of securities positions, rather than per dollar of invested capital, there should not be much difference between long-short and long-only. And if one considers the amount of active management provided per fee dollar, long-short may be revealed as substantially less costly than long-only! As we've noted, long-only portfolios contain a sizeable "hidden passive" element; only overweights and underweights relative to the benchmark are truly active. By contrast, virtually the entire long-short portfolio is active.

---

[13] Harder-to-borrow names will require a higher haircut and may even entail negative interest (i.e., the short seller pays, rather than receives, interest).

Because it does not have to converge to securities' benchmark weights in order to control risk, a long-short strategy can take larger positions in securities with higher (and lower) expected returns compared with a long-only portfolio whose ability to take active positions is limited by benchmark weights. It does not necessarily follow, however, that a long-short portfolio is riskier than a long-only portfolio. The long-short portfolio will incur more risk only to the extent that it takes more active positions and/or engages in more leverage. Both the portfolio's "activeness" and its degree of leverage are within the explicit control of the investor. Furthermore, proper portfolio construction should ensure that any incremental risks and costs are compensated by expected incremental returns.

EVALUATING LONG-SHORT

Besides analyzing the operational considerations involved in long-short portfolio construction and management, investors need to evaluate carefully the value-added potential of the security selection approach underpinning it. Any active equity management approach can be adapted to a long-short mode. In the past, investors (including hedge funds) that engaged in short selling tended to focus on in-depth fundamental analyses of specific companies, as they attempted to exploit given situations such as perceived fraud or expected bankruptcy. As short selling began to be incorporated into structured long-short portfolios, however, a more quantitative approach took hold. Today, most market-neutral managers use a quantitative rather than a traditional judgmental approach.

Traditional judgmental approaches, because of their in-depth nature, are usually limited in the number of stocks they can cover. This in turn limits the range of opportunities that can be exploited by the portfolio. Traditional analyses also generally result in subjective buy, hold, and sell recommendations that are difficult to translate into directions for building portfolios.

By contrast, quantitative approaches can be applied to a large universe of stocks, which tends to increase the number of potential investment opportunities detected. A quantitative process also generally results in numerical estimates of risk and return for the whole range of securities in the universe. Short sale candidates fall out naturally as the lowest-ranking members of the universe. Furthermore, the numerical estimates are eminently suitable inputs for portfolio optimization, allowing for the construction of portfolios that take explicit account of risk in their pursuit of return.

Of course, the performance of a market-neutral portfolio ultimately depends on the goodness of the insights going into it, whether those insights come from a judgmental or a quantitative approach. We believe that the best insights into security behavior come out of a quantitative approach that grapples with the complexity of the stock market.[14] The market is subject to myriad influences. Mispricing arises from investors' cognitive errors, such as herding or overreaction, and from companies' differing abilities to adapt to changing economic fundamentals. Furthermore, the nature of mispricings changes over time. The market's complexity demands quantitative modeling guided by human insight and ongoing research.

The return to any one stock may demonstrate an exploitable (i.e., predictable) response to a number of variables. It is important to examine all these variables simultaneously, so as to isolate the effect of each one. For example, does a consistent abnormal return to small-cap stocks reflect their relatively low P/E levels? A lack of coverage by institutional investors? Tax-related buying and selling? Or some combination of factors? Only by "disentangling" effects can one uncover real profit opportunities.[15]

Good insights also demand breadth of inquiry combined with depth of analysis. Breadth of inquiry maximizes the number of insightful profit opportunities that can be incorporated into a portfolio and provides for greater consistency of return. Depth of analysis, achieved by taking into account the intricacies of stock price behavior, maximizes the "goodness" of such insights, or the potential of each one to add value.[16] Breadth and depth together help to ensure consistent value-added, whether in long-short or long-only portfolio management. market-neutral portfolio construction, with the flexibility it affords in pursuing returns and controlling risk, enhances the ability to implement, and profit from, these insights.

---

[14] See James A. White, "How Jacobs and Levy Crunch Stocks for Buying—and Selling," *Wall Street Journal* (March 20, 1991), p. C1.
[15] See Bruce I. Jacobs and Kenneth N. Levy, "Disentangling Equity Return Regularities: New Insights and Investment Opportunities," *Financial Analysts Journal* (May/June 1988), pp. 18–43. See also, Bruce I. Jacobs and Kenneth N. Levy, *Equity Management: Quantitative Analysis for Stock Selection* (New York: McGraw-Hill, 2000).
[16] Bruce I. Jacobs and Kenneth N. Levy, "Investment Analysis: Profiting from a Complex Equity Market," in Frank J. Fabozzi (ed.), *Active Equity Portfolio Management* (New Hope, PA: Frank J. Fabozzi Associates, 1998).

Short Selling and Market Efficiency

Short Sales in Global Perspective

Arturo Bris, Ph.D.
Robert B. & Candice J. Haas Associate Professor of Corporate Finance
Yale School of Management

William N. Goetzmann, Ph.D.
Edwin J. Beinecke Professor of Finance and Management Studies &
Director of the International Center for Finance
Yale School of Management

Ning Zhu, Ph.D.
Assistant Professor of Finance
University of California, Davis

Over the last three decades, world investors have participated in a dramatic rebirth of the global equity markets. From a low point in the immediate post-World War II era, the number and capitalization of global stock markets has grown dramatically—punctuated, of course, by occasional financial crises. We are now quite nearly back to the point the world equity markets had reached about a century ago, but with a fundamentally different financial architecture. The former world equity markets were dominated by exchanges in a few capitals of colonial empires:

We thank Frank Fabozzi for considerable help in obtaining the data used in this chapter, Gustavo Rodríguez from the NYSE for providing us with the ADR data, and Carolina Velosa for excellent research assistance.

London, Brussels, and Paris. Now, considerable trading takes place in local exchanges according to local laws, regulations and practice.

In this chapter, we collect information on short sales regulation and practice about more than 80 markets around the world. Our survey of world markets suggests that, while as much as 93% of the world's equity market capitalization is potentially shortable, there are particular regions of the world where it is difficult to take a short position. These include several countries in Southeast Asia and South America. When dual listings in markets allowing short sales are considered, the potentially shortable capitalization increases to 96%. These numbers, however, mask important constraints to the global investor due to the inability to short particular sectors of the equity universe. In this chapter, we examine what factors in the global equity universe are not shortable and consider the implications for long-short strategies tied to global indices and futures instruments. We find important periods when an index of nonshortable securities is a major determinant of the global equity portfolio. We ask whether short sales constraints are binding on global index arbitrage.

The issue of short sales is important from the broad perspective of global equity market development. Our previous research has shown that markets that prevent or do not practice short sales are characterized by poor information diffusion and price discovery.[1] While stocks in these markets might be slightly less prone to extreme price drops, they are also less efficiently priced. Investors who rely upon the fundamental efficiency of a market price are likely to prefer these trading environments—all things being equal, liquidity and a level playing field are preferred by international investors. Evidence in this chapter strongly supports this trend. For a large sample of countries in which short sales are not allowed or not practiced in the local market, we find a migration of capital over the last decade towards the *American Depository Receipt* (ADR) or *Global Depository Receipt* (GDR) market. Simply put, markets with regulations facilitating efficiency are winning the battle for international capital flows.

Aside from these broad issues of global exchange competition and efficiency, however, the issue of whether a security is easily shortable is an important one for many sophisticated institutional investors and investment managers who hedge equity and index positions on a regular basis. These activities include everything from hedging spreads in

---

[1] See, for example, the following: Charles Jones and Owen Lamont, "Short Sale Constraints and Stock Returns," *Journal of Financial Economics* 66 (2002), pp. 207–240; Arturo Bris, William N. Goetzmann, and Ning Zhu, "Efficiency and the Bear: Short Sales and Markets Around the World," working paper, Yale International Center for Finance, 2004; and Chapter 7.

exchange-traded funds (ETFs) such as MSI EAFE iShares traded on the American Stock Exchange (AMEX), to establishing offsetting exposures for a global equity portfolio tracking a world investment benchmark. With respect to this hedging activity, the question we pose in this chapter is whether the short sales constraints in markets around the world have any material effect on the capacity of an investor to hedge an international equity index.

The chapter is structured as follows. In the next section, we describe regulation and practice of short sales in global equity markets. In the third section of the chapter, we explore the time trends in the shortable versus nonshortable components of world equity markets. The focus of the fourth section is on the degree to which the dynamics of the world equity index can be captured by shortable securities, and by the same token, how important the effects of having to exclude nonshortable securities from a hedge position are. In the last section we provide the five conclusions of our study—the main result being that there are key episodes in global financial markets during which the nonshortable component of the world equity portfolio is important. To the extent that a global hedging strategy is designed to protect the investor against occasional, risky events, the nonshortable component of the world portfolio might represent a binding constraint on the ability to bound investor value-at-risk. While the growth in the ADR listings over the past decade has helped to some extent, we find that a portfolio of ADR/GDR stocks are not a good proxy for those that continue to list solely in markets for which short sales are restricted.

SHORT SALES RESTRICTIONS AROUND THE WORLD

We draw our data on international short sales practices from several sources, including investment banks, regulators, specialized publications, and standard finance databases. Two investment banks generously provided information about current practice. The Morgan Stanley Dean Witter Global Network Management Division (GNM) gave us a summary of information for 59 countries about short sales regulation and practice, compiled by their global network of subcustodian banks. The International Securities Lending Division at Goldman Sachs (ISL) gave us similar data. The ISL also contained information about the tax implications of securities lending and short sales for 46 countries. Both datasets indicated that there are several countries around the world in which short-selling is allowed. These sources were sometimes at odds with a widely used guide, the *Worldwide Directory of Securities Lend-*

ing and Repo (WDSLP). We resolved this ambiguity by requesting further information from institutions listed in the WDSLP as facilitating short sales in countries that apparently prohibit short sales. In most cases the banks were accurate in characterizing these markets as lacking short sales capabilities. Singapore is the only country in the dataset where short selling is practiced but not formally allowed. Short sales in Singapore are typically executed off-exchange between depository agents. Our published resources also included the *International Securities Services Association* (ISSA) *Handbook*.

For 59 countries we augmented the bank and published information with data collected from direct inquiries to the exchanges and regulatory bodies governing the markets. This information allowed us to document changes in regulation and practice through time. Not only are we interested in current practice, but the shifts in short sales restrictions through time are particularly important for understanding the development of the global investing environment in the recent era, and also allowed us to perform relatively powerful tests of the effects of short sales on markets and investment flows.

In the course of contacting regulators and market participants in various countries around the world, we were able to develop some understanding of the major factors governing their views on short sales restrictions. We circulated a formal survey to all market regulators in countries with stock markets, and in this survey, we asked specific questions about the perceived need for the regulation of short sales.[2] We found that regulators were largely concerned with market efficiency and the probability of market crashes. The representative of the Estonian market regulatory body, for instance, discussing the effects of using the proceeds of short sales to then purchase other securities, mentioned to us that "as the Estonian market is rather small, any type of financial leverage can create a bubble effect on the market very quickly, and therefore it makes markets risky." The representative of the Hellenic Capital Market Commission in Greece reported to us that "[the availability of short sales]...is expected to present multiple advantages as regards the liquidity and reliability of the market. More specifically, it is expected to help in the rationalization of prices of shares and the restriction of their extreme fluctuations." These and many other comments helped us formulate a series of research questions we hoped would be of use to regulators in their future consideration of short sales rules and

---

[2] In particular, we asked (1) whether your country has a "short-selling" regulation; (2) if there has been a change in "short-selling" regulation; (3) the major restrictions (if any) that exist in the country; and (4) the expert opinion on the impact of changes in regulation on the stock market.

practices. In our previous work cited above, we tested the proposition that short sales restrictions made markets less informationally efficient, and we also tested whether markets with short sales restrictions were less prone to precipitous price declines. We found positive evidence on both of these questions. In this chapter, we turn to broader questions about the effects of short sales restrictions on global investing and international capital flows.

Exhibit 13.1 summarizes our information about short sales regulations and practice. Out of the 59 countries in the GNM dataset, we exclude the countries for which we could not find individual firm stock price data. This leaves a sample of 47 countries. In 35 of these, short selling was allowed as of December 2001, the final date of our sample period. In 12 of these 47, short sales were prohibited for the entire sample period of January 1990 to December 2001. In 12 of the 35 countries where short sales are currently allowed, restrictions existed in 1990 but were lifted at some point within the sample period. These countries are Chile, Hong Kong, Hungary, Malaysia, New Zealand, Norway, Philippines, Poland, Spain, Sweden, Thailand, and Turkey. In three cases— Malaysia, Hong Kong, and Thailand—restrictions on short selling were removed and later re-enacted gradually.[3]

---

[3] In Malaysia, the Securities Commission issued in December 1995 the Guidelines on Securities Borrowing and Lending; and the Securities Industry Act of 1993 was amended to allow short sales. The regulatory changes came into force on March 7, 1996, and allowed the local exchange—the Kuala Lumpur Stock Exchange—to enact short selling rules. With that, regulated short selling commenced on September 30, 1996. However, in August 28, 1997, and in the onset of the Asian financial crises, these activities were suspended as interim measures to prevent excessive volatility in the markets. In February 2001 the Securities Commission launched a plan— the Capital Market Masterplan—that recommended the reintroduction of short selling and securities lending activities.

In Hong Kong, short selling was prohibited before January 3, 1994. The SEHK then allowed 17 out of the 33 constituent stocks of the Hang Seng Index (HSI) to be sold short subject to several restrictions. These restrictions were lifted on March 25, 1996 at the same time that 113 of the firms listed on the exchange, including all the constituent stocks of the index, were allowed to be sold short.

In Thailand, the Securities Exchange Commission first enforced short sales regulations on July, 1997, suspending them because of the currency crises. Beginning on January 1, 1998, short sales were allowed again in the Thai capital market, through financial institutions licensed to operate securities borrowing and lending (SBL) business. The practice of short selling has increased gradually: in 1999 there were only three securities companies licensed to operate SBL. Although ISL and GNM characterize Thailand as a country where short sales are a common practice, market regulators were aware of only one transaction since 1997, apart from "mistaken" transactions done by brokers.

EXHIBIT 13.1 Short Selling Restrictions Around the World

Country	When Was Short Selling Allowed	When Was Securities Lending Allowed	Whether Short Selling Is Practiced
Argentina	1999	1991	No
Australia	Before 1990	Before 1990	Yes
Austria	Before 1990	Before 1990	Yes
Belgium	Before 1990	Before 1990	Yes
Brazil	Before 1990	Before 1990	No
Canada	Before 1990	Before 1990	Yes
Chile	Allowed in 1999	Allowed in 1999	No
Colombia	Not allowed	Not allowed	No
Czech Republic	Before 1990	Before 1990	Yes
Denmark	Before 1990	Before 1990	Yes
Finland	Allowed in 1998	Before 1990	No
France	Before 1990	Before 1990	Yes
Germany	Before 1990	Before 1990	Yes
Greece	Not allowed	Not allowed	No
Hong Kong	Allowed in 1996	Before 1990	Yes
India	Before 1990	Before 1990	No
Indonesia	Not allowed	Allowed in 1996	No
Ireland	Before 1990	Before 1990	Yes
Israel	Before 1990	Before 1990	No
Italy	Before 1990	Before 1990	Yes
Japan	Before 1990	Before 1990	Yes
Jordan	Not allowed	Not allowed	No
Luxembourg	Before 1990	Before 1990	Yes
Malaysia	Allowed in 1995; prohibited again in 1997	Allowed in 1995; prohibited again in 1997	Yes
Mexico	Before 1990	Before 1990	Yes
Netherlands	Before 1990	Before 1990	Yes
New Zealand	Allowed in 1992	Not allowed	No
Norway	Allowed in 1992	Allowed in 1996	Yes
Pakistan	Not allowed	Not allowed	No
Peru	Not allowed	Not allowed	No
Philippines	Allowed in 1998	Allowed in 1998	No
Poland	Allowed in 2000	Before 1990	No
Portugal	Before 1990	Before 1990	Yes

EXHIBIT 13.1 (Continued)

Country	When Was Short Selling Allowed	When Was Securities Lending Allowed	Whether Short Selling Is Practiced
Singapore	Not allowed	Before 1990	Yes
Slovak Republic	Not allowed	Not allowed	No
South Africa	Before 1990	Before 1990	Yes
South Korea	Not allowed	Before 1990	No
Spain	Allowed in 1992	Allowed in 1992	No
Sweden	Allowed in 1991	Allowed in 1991	Yes
Switzerland	Before 1990	Before 1990	Yes
Taiwan	Not allowed	Not allowed	No
Thailand	Allowed in 1997	Allowed in 1999	Yes
Turkey	Before 1990	Allowed in 1996	No
United Kingdom	Before 1990	Before 1990	Yes
United States	Before 1990	Before 1990	Yes
Venezuela	Not allowed	Not allowed	No
Zimbabwe	Not allowed	Not allowed	No

Note: For each country in the sample, the table describes the date when short selling was allowed if this happened on or after 1990. Otherwise countries are classified as "Allowed Before 1990," or "Not Allowed." "Securities Lending" refers to the ability of an investor to borrow securities from another party. "Short Selling" refers to the ability of an investor to sell a borrowed security to a third party. Short selling is practiced when there are indications from market participants, market regulators, or institutions within a country, that short selling is a common practice. Data is obtained from the Global Network Management Division at Morgan Stanley Dean Witter, the International Securities Lending at Goldman Sachs, the corresponding market regulators, the *International Securities Services Association Handbook*, and practitioners listed in the *Worldwide Directory of Securities Lending and Repo*.

There is clearly a difference between what the law allows and what is common practice. Although short selling is currently legal in most countries, it is only practiced in 28. In some countries, tax rules significantly inhibit short sales. In Chile for instance, although short selling and securities lending have been possible since 1999, they are rarely used because lending is considered an immediate, taxable sale. Given that there is no sale price, the relevant price is the highest price of the stock on the day it is lent; if it is higher than the purchase price, capital gains tax will apply. In Turkey, stock lending is treated as a normal transaction by the tax authorities, and as such it is liable to capital gains tax. In Finland, transfer laws also place a serious burden on this activity. In the Philippines and Turkey short selling is allowed but the rules are not clearly defined. In Thailand, evidence of the practice of shorting is murky. Regulators in that country believe that short selling is not practiced because the market for borrowing stock is very narrow, especially on the supply side, due to the absence of a futures market.

There are some other features of short selling practices throughout the world that are relevant for our purposes. In some markets only the largest and most liquid stocks may be shorted. Until 1996, Hong Kong only allowed short sales in securities specifically designated by the Hong Kong Exchanges and Clearing Ltd. A similar rule currently operates in Greece. More objective criteria are found in Poland, where any security with a market capitalization of at least 250 million zloties qualifies. We adopt the convention of classifying Hong Kong as a country where short selling is allowed only after 1996, even though it was allowed for a subset of stocks beginning in 1994.[4] For Poland and Greece, GNM reports that short selling is not practiced.

We also regard short selling as allowed and practiced in a country even if some investors are prohibited from entering into such transactions. In Sweden, for example, traders take short positions without borrowing the shares in advance, while individual investors must borrow the shares before they go short.[5] In Greece prior to 2001, short selling was only available to the members of the Athens Derivatives Exchange. Some countries only impose short sales restrictions on foreign investors. In Brazil, for instance, a short seller must have a domestic legal representative. In India, foreign investors are prohibited from short selling. In fact, every country in the sample has its own law, custom, and environment that determine the capacity and costs of short sales.

We classify countries into four groups, depending on whether short selling is legal and practiced. In the first group we have the countries where short selling became legal some time before 1990, and where short selling is currently practiced. This group includes the United States, the United Kingdom, Australia, Austria, Belgium, Canada, the Czech Republic,[6] Denmark, France, Germany, Ireland, Italy, Japan, Luxembourg, Mexico, the Netherlands, Portugal, South Africa, and Switzerland. The second group consists of the countries in which short sales were prohibited as of December 2001. These are Colombia, Greece, Indonesia, Jordan, Paki-

---

[4] See footnote 3.

[5] They must borrow the stock before the end of the day, however.

[6] The Prague Stock Exchange was established on November 1992, and the automated trading system started operations in January 1993. We include the Czech Republic in the group of countries where short selling is allowed and practiced, although we only have data on Czech firms since 1993.

stan, Peru, Singapore, the Slovak Republic, South Korea, Taiwan, Venezuela, and Zimbabwe. The third group is comprised of countries in which short selling is allowed but rarely practiced: Argentina, Brazil, Chile, Finland, India, Israel, New Zealand, the Philippines, Poland, Spain, and Turkey.[7] Finally, the remaining five countries—Hong Kong, Norway, Sweden, Malaysia, and Thailand—comprise a group for which short sales regulation and practice changed sometime between January 1990 and December 2001.

The classification above ignores firm specific information, as well as gradations within country of cost and difficulty of taking and maintaining a short position. Even within the United States, these are known to have pricing effects. For instance, the feasibility of short sales may depend in some cases on the existence of a futures instrument. In some countries, futures are traded only for a subset of stocks, usually the most liquid or largest. We ignore such within-country differences to simplify our analysis, but these can be of paramount consideration to market participants. Where short sales are restricted or prohibitively expensive, however, another mechanism for shorting sometimes exists: dual-listed shares.

FOREIGN LISTING AND SHORT SELLING

Over the last two decades, one of the most significant institutional changes in international investing has been the growth of the *depository receipt market* in the United States and Europe. Once restricted to a very few bellwether securities from a handful of non-U.S.exchanges, ADRs now allow domestic investors to achieve considerable exposure to the world equity markets without leaving the comfort of the U.S. regulatory environment. A major factor in this domestic environment, of course, is the ability to short a stock. A good example is Nokia, which represents about 2/3 of the total market capitalization of the Helsinki Stock Exchange (HEX). As per our own data, Finland is a country where short sales are not practiced. However, Nokia has been listed on the New York Stock Exchange since July 1, 1994. These Nokia depository receipts can be shorted, although only in the United States. Thus, taking into account shares that list abroad, the percentage of the Finnish market that is shortable is 66.13 percent at the end of 2002 (see Exhibit 13.2). Hence, these shortable components of national exchanges must be considered when examining the effects of short sales restrictions on markets.

---

[7] Chile made short selling legal only in 2000, but there is no current practice. Spain legalized short selling in 1992, but only securities lending facilities are common among institutions as a way of facilitating hedging strategies.

EXHIBIT 13.2 Indexes of Total Return for Three Capital-Weighted Portfolios

Note: A portfolio of nonshortable world equities, labeled "NONSHORTABLE-ALL" A portfolio of shortable world equities labeled "SHORTABLE-ALL" and a portfolio of non-U.S. shortable equities labeled "SHORTABLE-NON US."

We compiled data on non-U.S. companies that list in NYSE, NASDAQ, and the London Stock Exchange (LSE). We obtained data on U.S. listings directly from the NYSE.[8] Data for the LSE came from that exchange's Web site. We obtained the date of the first listing of each foreign firm in these markets through direct listing (IPO), ADRs (in the United States), and GDRs (in the United Kingdom). We also obtained from Datastream stock market information about all firms listed in the 59 countries in our database. In particular, we obtained stock price and capitalization data. For the countries and years where short sales are not allowed/not practiced, we decomposed the market capitalization into domestic market capitalization of stocks with a foreign listing, and otherwise. The first group corresponds to stocks that could be shorted elsewhere, and we called those the "shortable portfolio." We then constructed value-weighted indices corresponding to the shortable portfolio and the nonshortable portfolio. In countries where short sales are allowed and practiced, the shortable portfolio is obviously the total market. Exhibit 13.3 shows the performance of these two indices over the period 1989 through 2002. Also included is a shortable index of only non-U.S. stocks. The exhibit suggests some meaningful differences between the shortable and nonshortable indices. The nonshortable index is more volatile than both of the shortable indices. The annual standard deviation of the nonshortable index is 24%, while the non-U.S. shortable index has an annual standard deviation of 19%. Including U.S. stocks drops the volatility to 16% over the time period.

---

[8] We thank Gustavo Rodríguez from the NYSE for providing us with the data.

EXHIBIT 13.3 World Market Capitalization and Short Sales Restrictions

	World Market Capitalization in Countries Where:			World Market Capitalization			World Market Capitalization (Excluding the U.S.)		
Year	Short Sales Are Allowed and Practiced	Short Sales Are Not Allowed/ Not Practiced	Ratio	Shortable	Nonshortable	Ratio	Shortable	Nonshortable	Ratio
1990	$81,163,692	$5,827,897	93.30%	$81,553,367	$5,438,222	93.75%	$56,865,489	$5,438,222	91.27%
1991	$85,274,817	$5,578,387	93.86%	$85,715,565	$5,137,639	94.35%	$56,835,668	$5,137,639	91.71%
1992	$87,417,000	$6,781,783	92.80%	$87,900,639	$6,298,144	93.31%	$53,974,960	$6,298,144	89.55%
1993	$101,620,765	$8,627,665	92.17%	$102,206,024	$8,042,406	92.71%	$64,002,465	$8,042,406	88.84%
1994	$117,619,058	$14,023,882	89.35%	$119,007,014	$12,635,926	90.40%	$78,746,862	$12,635,926	86.17%
1995	$129,496,520	$13,732,840	90.41%	$131,265,871	$11,963,489	91.65%	$82,970,840	$11,963,489	87.40%
1996	$159,746,807	$12,226,042	92.89%	$161,709,752	$10,263,097	94.03%	$98,492,806	$10,263,097	90.56%
1997	$190,287,927	$14,968,125	92.71%	$192,744,804	$12,511,248	93.90%	$108,143,224	$12,511,248	89.63%
1998	$228,150,782	$14,201,662	94.14%	$231,067,238	$11,285,206	95.34%	$118,961,927	$11,285,206	91.34%
1999	$289,400,736	$17,971,174	94.15%	$294,573,817	$12,798,093	95.84%	$148,475,055	$12,798,093	92.06%
2000	$341,861,145	$23,188,939	93.65%	$350,966,615	$14,083,469	96.14%	$180,748,296	$14,083,469	92.77%
2001	$286,069,825	$17,845,533	94.13%	$292,645,485	$11,269,873	96.29%	$145,440,441	$11,269,873	92.81%
2002	$246,785,645	$17,596,158	93.34%	$252,772,035	$11,609,768	95.61%	$125,930,823	$11,609,768	91.56%

Note: This table classifies the World Market capitalization into countries where short sales are allowed and practiced and otherwise. The interpretation of the third column is that, from year 1990 to year 2000, short sales were allowed in markets representing from 93.30% to 93.34%. The next three columns show the actual amount of the world market capitalization that is either shortable or not. To calculate the numbers in these columns, we have taken into account firms in countries where short sales are not allowed/not practiced that list in markets where short sales are allowed and practiced, in particular the United States (NYSE and NASDAQ) and the United Kingdom (LSE). The table shows that, after accounting for ADRS, the percentage of the world market capitalization that is shortable has increased from 93.31% in 1990, to 95.61% in 2002. Finally, the last two columns in the table display the market capitalization that is shortable via ADRs in countries where short sales are not allowed/not practiced. The percentage of shortable capitalization in these countries has increased from 7.13% in 1990, to 34.02 in 2002. Data are in $Million.

Exhibit 13.2 shows that, without taking foreign listings into consideration, the percentage of the world market capitalization that is shortable varies between 89.35% in 1994 and 94.15% in 1999. When foreign listings are included, we find that up to 96.29% of the world market is shortable as of 2001. The numbers are very similar, even if we exclude the U.S. markets from the calculations.

In Exhibit 13.4 we specifically consider the countries where short sales are not allowed or not practiced, but where there are firms that list in a U.S. or U.K. market. The exhibit illustrates the changing importance of cross-listings through time. The aggregate percentage of shortable capitalization via depository receipts for all short sales-restricted countries shows a moderate but significant increase from 29% in 1990 to 33% in 2002. However in some countries the shortable capitalization is considerable: in Brazil, Finland, and South Korea, more than 50% of the market is shortable via cross-border listings. In Norway more than 30% of the market was shortable even before short sales restrictions were removed in the country in 1996. While clearly the ability to short securities off-exchange will matter to asset pricing on the domestic exchange, our interest in this chapter is on the hedging capabilities of the global investor.

Exhibit 13.5 shows the effectiveness of a global equity hedge portfolio over the period 1991 through 2002. It is constructed by regressing a 12-month rolling window of MSCI world equity index returns on our capital-weighted shortable portfolio and alternatively on our shortable and our nonshortable indices. The two lines track the explanatory power of this regression over time. While the model performed pretty well on average—explaining between 85% and 95% of market moves, there were also clear interruptions in the ability of the cap-weighted portfolios to hedge the MSCI World Index. The fraction of variance associated with tracking error, represented by 1 minus the R-square, was as high as 20% of monthly returns at certain times. Late 1993, summer 1996, and most of 1999 represented notable periods of deviation. Exhibit 13.5 suggests that during these periods, the basic linear model an investor might use to hedge the MSCI world index with a cap-weighted index of monthly returns—either shortable alone or including nonshortable securities—left occasional, significant exposures to tracking error.

The second Y axis in Exhibit 13.5 records the implied portfolio weight accorded to the nonshortable portfolio. These weights are estimated via a technique pioneered by William Sharpe, which works by constraining the coefficients in the regression to be positive and sum to one—thus effectively representing an achievable long-only composite benchmark.[9] Note that there are four periods when the implied weight

---

[9] The estimation procedure is performed with the Ibbotson Associates Encorr Attribution Model.

EXHIBIT 13.4   World Market Capitalization and Short Sales Restrictions: Countries Where Short Sales Are Not Allowed/Not Practiced

		1990–1993	1994–1998	1999–2002
All Countries	Shortable	$1,897,433	$10,288,018	$26,192,296
	Nonshortable	$4,816,782	$32,949,937	$49,355,463
	Ratio	39.39%	31.22%	53.07%
Argentina	Shortable	$8,102	$1,024,311	$666,285
	Nonshortable	$229,947	$1,546,307	$689,511
	Ratio	3.52%	66.24%	96.63%
Brazil	Shortable		$23,855	$500,140
	Nonshortable		$1,686,104	$7,171,007
	Ratio	1.41%	6.97%	
Colombia	Shortable		$142,199	$8,749
	Nonshortable		$682,718	$277,786
	Ratio	20.83%	3.15%	
Chile	Shortable	$31,812	$364,135	$387,336
	Nonshortable	$261,107	$2,509,766	$1,835,409
	Ratio	12.18%	14.51%	21.10%
Cayman Islands	Shortable	$6,534	$30,362	
	Nonshortable	$37,854	$42,318	
	Ratio	17.26%	71.75%	
Spain	Shortable	$1,455,740	$3,756,426	$7,316,242
	Nonshortable	$2,917,323	$6,652,798	$8,689,613
	Ratio	49.90%	56.46%	84.20%
Finland	Shortable	$2,531	$822,144	$6,879,939
	Nonshortable	$535,100	$2,245,906	$3,012,711
	Ratio	0.47%	36.61%	228.36%
Greece	Shortable		$13,615	$642,146
	Nonshortable		$489,461	$2,949,436
	Ratio	2.78%	21.77%	
Hungary	Shortable		$22,955	$30,599
	Nonshortable		$265,816	$561,289
	Ratio	8.64%	5.45%	
India	Shortable		$437,688	$313,740
	Nonshortable		$1,904,905	$940,594
	Ratio	22.98%	33.36%	

EXHIBIT 13.4 (Continued)

		1990–1993	1994–1998	1999–2002
Indonesia	Shortable			$873,110
	Nonshortable			$4,071,179
	Ratio	21.45%		
Israel	Shortable	$21,097	$247,327	$471,415
	Nonshortable	$189,225	$915,396	$1,315,841
	Ratio	11.15%	27.02%	35.83%
South Korea	Shortable		$2,093,501	$4,553,557
	Nonshortable		$3,130,015	$4,062,195
	Ratio	66.88%	112.10%	
Norway	Shortable	$269,854	$203,628	
	Nonshortable	$441,251	$399,236	
	Ratio	61.16%	51.00%	
New Zealand	Shortable	$101,763	$468,082	$267,386
	Nonshortable	$204,975	$1,125,216	$794,001
	Ratio	49.65%	41.60%	33.68%
Peru	Shortable		$41,134	$32,006
	Nonshortable		$297,433	$284,246
	Ratio	13.83%	11.26%	
Philippines	Shortable		$188,073	$112,636
	Nonshortable		$2,307,005	$1,050,876
	Ratio	8.15%	10.72%	
Poland	Shortable		$9,845	$412,332
	Nonshortable		$86,116	$744,895
	Ratio	11.43%	55.35%	
Taiwan	Shortable		$390,150	$2,708,204
	Nonshortable		$6,003,072	$8,630,181
	Ratio	6.50%	31.38%	
Turkey	Shortable		$8,590	$16,472
	Nonshortable		$660,347	$2,274,695
	Ratio	1.30%	0.72%	

Note: This table classifies the world market capitalization into shortable and non-shortable for countries where short sales are not allowed/not practiced. To calculate the numbers in these columns we have taken into account firms in countries where short sales are not allowed/not practiced, that list in markets where short sales are allowed and practiced, in particular the United States (NYS E and NASDAQ) and the United Kingdom (LSE). The table shows that, after accounting for ADRS, the percentage of the market capitalization that is shortable has increased from 29% in 1990, to 33% in 2002. Data are in $Million.

EXHIBIT 13.5   Explanatory Power of the Nonshortable and Shortable Portfolios

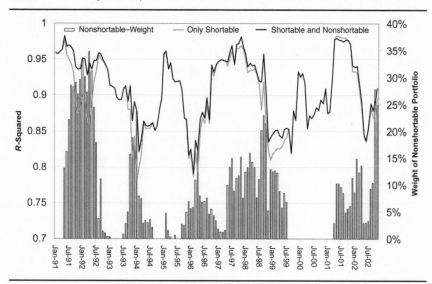

Note: The figure reports the R-square from a rolling 12-month regression of the MSCI World Index returns on the shortable and nonshortable portfolio returns. The figure also includes the implied long-only portfolio weight from the regression, for which the coefficients are constrained to sum to one.

on the nonshortable index exceeds 20%. These correspond roughly to periods when the explanatory power of the hedging model declines, and when there are significant advantages to the inclusion of the nonshortable index. Note also that there are long stretches of time during which the implied weight on the nonshortable portfolio is zero—indeed half the time, the weight on this factor is less than 5%. The clear implication of Exhibit 13.5 is that the nonshortable index captures some factor in world equity returns that manifests itself only occasionally, and is associated with significant tracking error in a global hedging model.

The characteristics and respective significance of the shortable and nonshortable portfolios is evident when we isolate effects at the country level. Exhibit 13.6 reports the estimated portfolio weights for a regression of MSCI world index returns on the MSCI U.S. total return index, and the shortable and nonshortable portions of Argentina's stock market. In effect, we are explaining the world index with the U.S. and the two parts of the Argentinean market. Exhibit 13.6 shows the time-varying estimated positive portfolio weights for the U.S., shortable and nonshortable Argentinean market. Notice that the U.S. market dominates, however there are periods in which the nonshortable index is relevant.

EXHIBIT 13.6 Foreign Direct Investment

	Total Sample				Countries with Regulatory Change			
	Outflows		Inflows		Outflows		Inflows	
Short Sales Dummy	-9,457.3***	-3.51	-4,508.1	-1.44	-5,285.9*	-1.88	-2,569.7	-0.82
GDP – Total	2E-08***	3.15	4E-08***	3.54	2E-08	0.22	2E-08	0.23
GDP per capita	0.934	1.38	0.890*	1.77	0.253	0.34	0.022	0.02
Financial Risk Rating	-1,349.4***	-4.90	-848.0***	-3.34	-488.5	-1.23	-914.3*	-1.75
Economic Risk Rating	592.9**	2.52	346.2	1.62	838.8**	2.43	1,246.8	1.68
Political Risk Rating	583.9***	2.92	593.8***	3.29	141.2	0.77	300.2	1.12
Intercept	-12,653.7	-0.85	-44,867.9***	-3.72	-24,393.6	-1.32	-31,740.8	-1.11
Number of Observations	459		462		39		39	
Adjusted R-squared	0.6595		0.6916		0.6228		0.382	
Year – Fixed Effects	YES		YES		YES		YES	
Country – Fixed Effects	YES		YES		YES		YES	

*, **, *** denotes significant at the 10%, 5%, 1% levels or better, respectively.

Regression of outflows and inflows of Foreign Direct Investment on Short Sales Dummy. Data on FDI is obtain from the United Nations Conference on Trade and Development, Division on Investment, Technology and Enterprise Development. GDP data is from the World Bank Development Indicators. FDI and GDP are in $ million. The financial risk variable is a composite index of several macroeconomic ratios: the percentage of foreign debt to GDP; foreign debt service as a percentage of exports of goods and services; current account as a percentage of exports of goods and services; net liquidity as months of import cover; and exchange rate stability. Financial risk ratings range from a high of 50 (least risk) to a low of 0 (highest risk). The political risk variable is an average of the following indicators: government stability; socioeconomic conditions; investment profile; internal conflict; external conflict; corruption; military in politics; religion in politics; law and order; ethnic tensions; democratic accountability; and bureaucracy quality. Risk ratings range from a high of 100 (least risk) to a low of 0 (highest risk). The economic risk index is the average of the component factors of GDP per head of population, real annual GDP growth, annual inflation rate, budget balance as a percentage of GDP, and current account balance as a percentage of GDP. Risk ratings range from a high of 50 (least risk) to a low of 0 (highest risk). The first set of regressions include all 56 countries in our sample. The second set of regressions include only countries with regulatory changes (Malaysia, Honk Kong, Thailand, Norway, and Sweden). We calculate robust standard errors.

While this figure does not represent an explicit hypothesis test about the value of the nonshortable component of a country as a factor in market returns, it is certainly suggestive of this possibility.

Although the nonshortable component of the world index is small by capitalization, we find strong evidence that it is not irrelevant as a factor in the world equity markets. Even the recent growth of the depository receipt market has not eliminated the need to hold some portion of the nonshortable portfolio as a hedge against variations in the world equity index. One key reason for this might be the fact that dual listing of shares is driven by regulatory feasibility. Only firms that meet international accounting standards have the potential for dual listing. There is in fact considerable theoretical and empirical literature on the value of dual listing—in simplest terms it signals to investors that the company is strong enough and honest enough to abide by tougher standards than those imposed by its domicile exchange. However, as a result of this certification process, our analysis suggests that the money center exchanges screen out a significant factor in the world equity markets that occasionally explains market dynamics. Depository receipts appear to allow investors to buy and short the higher quality stocks around the world on the major exchanges, but sometimes the movement of lower quality securities is an important trend.

SHORT SELLING CONSTRAINTS AND INTERNATIONAL CAPITAL FLOWS

A central concern of regulators is what factors explain shifts in international capital flows into and out of their domestic markets. Ever since the Asian currency crisis of 1997, economists and policy makers have been concerned with the question of whether accommodating the needs of international investors actually exposes markets to financial crises brought on by, or at least exacerbated by, volatile international capital flows. One of the interesting questions our data allow us to answer is whether short sales constraints have a positive or a negative effect on international capital flows to and from a market. There are reasonable arguments to be made on both sides of this question. short sales constraints, for example, might make a market more attractive to international investors because they may reduce the demand to sell stocks and thus reduce the risk of a crash. Thus, an investor may be attracted to markets with lower downside risk, all else equal. By the same token, short sales constraints might be viewed as protection against the manipulation of share prices through "Bear Raids" that were blamed in the early 20th century U.S. market crashes. For these reasons, a market that forbids short sales might attract a disproportionate share of global capital. On the other hand, short sales constraints may be associated with limitations on the ability of an investor to hedge out long positions. Short sales are a frequently-used risk control tool by U.S. investment managers. Any constraints on the ability to hedge positions might cause a manager to be wary of taking those positions in the first place. In addition, empirical evidence suggests that short sales constraints make markets less informationally efficient. All else equal, an efficient market will be more attractive to investors without a comparative informational advantage. Thus, markets that allow short sales might attract passive investment.

We explore this issue by examining the international inflows and outflows of investment capital as a function of short sales constraints. Given that we have a number of countries in our sample which have changed their short sales policies during our sample period, we are able to test the effects of these policy decisions, while controlling for a host of other effects.

Our measure of capital inflows and outflows is based upon national income accounts. We obtain Foreign Direct Investment flows from the United Nations Conference on Trade and Development (UNCTAD) Division on Investment, Technology and Enterprise Development.[10] We model inflows and outflow separately, and include in the regression an indicator variable for the country-year if short sales are not legal or not practiced. For those countries that actually changed policy in the sample period, the indicator equals one in the year following the change only.

---

[10] Foreign direct investment (FDI) is defined as an investment involving a long-term relationship and reflecting a lasting interest and control by a resident entity in one economy (foreign direct investor or parent enterprise) in an enterprise resident in an economy other than that of the foreign direct investor. FDI implies that the investor exerts a significant degree of influence on the management of the enterprise resident in the other economy. Such investment involves both the initial transaction between the two entities and all subsequent transactions between them and among foreign affiliates, both incorporated and unincorporated. FDI has three components: equity capital, reinvested earnings and intracompany loans. FDI flows are recorded on a net basis (capital account credits less debits between direct investors and their foreign affiliates) in a particular year.

Inflows of FDI in the reporting economy comprise capital provided (either directly or through other related enterprises) by a foreign direct investor to an enterprise resident in the economy (called FDI enterprise). Outflows of FDI in the reporting economy comprise capital provided (either directly or through other related enterprises) by a company resident in the economy (foreign direct investor) to an enterprise resident in another country (FDI enterprise). Source: UNCTAD.

This panel regression has 459 observations of country-years, and the standard errors are adjusted by the usual techniques for serial correlation, and robustness to outliers. Since so many different factors could conceivably affect the attractiveness of cross-border investing, we control for three types of broad risks, consistent with the current literature: financial risk, political risk, and economic risk. All risk indices are obtained from the *International Country Risk Guide*, and they are time-varying for each country.[11] The specification also controls for year- and country-fixed effects so that the power of the results is based fundamentally on the countries that changed their policy during the sample period. Finally, we use the GDP of the county as a regressor, as well as GDP per capita, in order to control for differences in market scale and development. In any case, we also specify a regression with only those countries that change the regulatory regime in the sample period.

The regression output is reported in Exhibit 13.6. The outflow regression has a negative coefficient on the short sales variable indicating that the relaxation of short sales constraints tended to reduce capital outflows, or conversely, the imposition of short sales constraints tended to reduce inflows. The magnitude of the coefficient is such that a one standard deviation increase in the short selling variable reduces outflows by 0.17 standard deviations (significantly different from zero at the 1 percent level).[12] In economic terms, the second set of regressions show that allowing short sales in a country reduces investment outflows by $5.2 billion per year, relative to an average of $10.53 billion per year throughout the sample period (the coefficient is significantly different from zero at the 10% level). Moreover, outflows are larger when (1) both political and economic risks are lower; and (2) financial risks are

---

[11] The financial risk variable is a composite index of several macroeconomic ratios: the percentage of foreign debt to GDP, foreign debt service as a percentage of exports of goods and services, current account as a percentage of exports of goods and services, net liquidity as months of import cover, and exchange rate stability. Financial risk ratings range from a high of 50 (least risk) to a low of 0 (highest risk). The political risk variable is an average of the following indicators: government stability, socioeconomic conditions, investment profile, internal conflict, external conflict, corruption, military in politics, religion in politics, law and order, ethnic tensions, democratic accountability, and bureaucracy quality. Risk ratings range from a high of 100 (least risk) to a low of 0 (highest risk). The economic risk index is the average of the component factors of GDP per head of population, real annual GDP growth, annual inflation rate, budget balance as a percentage of GDP, and current account balance as a percentage of GDP. Risk ratings range from a high of 50 (least risk) to a low of 0 (highest risk).

[12] The standard deviations of the short sales dummy and the outflows variable is 0.50 and $26.358 billion.

higher. While the regression tells us something about the determinants of outflows in this period, we learn little from the inflow regression. Although the sign on inflows in negative, it is not significantly different from zero at conventional statistical levels.[13] Thus, while many things may influence cross-border capital flows—particularly over an interval that includes the Asian currency crisis, our basic test of the effects of short sales constraints provides some evidence in favor of the proposition that international investors are attracted to markets that facilitate the capacity of hedging and the efficient diffusion of information.

CONCLUSION

An equilibrium theory of short sales restrictions would posit that the distribution of short sales restricted markets around the world is far from random. In a rational world in which a country could chose to allow of forbid short selling, some countries may have reasons for choosing one policy over the other—these reasons should logically have to do with fundamental differences between markets, whether due to the volatility of assets, the information structure of the industry, or even the political or macroeconomic landscape. Whatever these differences, however, they must be such that the short sales regulatory policy somehow is optimal for that market. A case in point is Malaysia. During our sample period, Malaysia switched from allowing to disallowing to partly allowing short sales. These policy choices were based upon the perceived advantages they provided for the stability and recovery of the domestic market.

Our empirical analysis of hedging and tracking error is largely consistent with this equilibrium view that the short sales choice for countries—as well as for stocks—is potentially due to value-relevant cross-sectional economic differences. We see that nonshortable markets (or market components) behave differently are certain times, and that ignoring them, in effect, ignores a relevant dimension of risk in the world capital markets. Thus, the results reported in this chapter suggest that there is something different about nonshortable stocks and countries other than that they are nonshortable, and even the continued development of depository receipt markets has not allowed global investors to capture or hedge these latent factors.

---

[13] We have reestimated the model using the net flows (inflows minus outflows) as the dependent variable, but the short selling dummy is not significant.

Although it is fascinating to provide even a little evidence on these lofty issues, the basic conclusions of our study are fairly straightforward. First, we find there are times in global market history when tracking error was significantly higher due to the exclusion of nonshortable securities from the portfolio. In practical terms that means hedging a long position in the world equity index will involve some level of risk, regardless of access to country factors via depository receipts. This first finding should be of interest to institutional investors and active long-short equity managers, and if nothing else, spur additional quantitative investigation. Our second finding is more likely to interest policy makers who are concerned with attracting international investment flows. Allowing short sales seems to reduce global capital outflows. Although we perform only one test of this proposition, it suggests that market efficiency and the ability to hedge investments are attractive factors to sophisticated global investors.

Short Selling and Financial Puzzles

Edward M. Miller, Ph.D.
Research Professor of Economics and Finance
University of New Orleans

In Chapter 5, it was explained how restrictions on short selling coupled with divergence of opinion led to a model where prices were increased by both greater divergence of opinion and stronger restrictions on short selling. In such a world, the level of short selling and the amount of divergence of opinion can help predict stock returns, with higher returns found for stocks with lower levels of short selling and lower divergence of opinion.

There are several other long-standing puzzles in finance that can be explained with the aid of divergence of opinion in the presence of restrictions on short selling. These include:

1. Why nonsystematic risk is sometimes rewarded.
2. Why, in other cases, incurring risk brings little or no reward.
3. In particular, the theory can explain the low returns to beta that are found in empirical studies.
4. The discounts found on closed-end funds.
5. The often low prices for conglomerates.
6. The tendency for firm's to sell money-losing divisions even though the buying firm will operate them no differently
7. That value additivity does not hold.

Another was mentioned in Chapter 5. This is the low long-term returns to initial public offerings. In spite of the high risk of initial public offerings, which investors should be willing to accept only in exchange for higher returns, initial public offerings have yielded less than other stocks. As shown in Chapter 6, the explanation is that the divergence of opinion declines over time as a company acquires a track record. The result is a decline in price relative to other stocks that more than offsets the risk premium.

DIVERGENCE OF OPINION AND RISK

In the discussion in Chapter 6 there appeared evidence that divergence of opinion could be interpreted as a risk measure or was correlated with a risk measure. Let's look at why divergence of opinion may be a surrogate for risk, and what evidence there is that divergence of opinion and risk are correlated. The Qu et al. model has already been discussed, in which volatility (an element of risk) results from investors trading as they observe prices that imply that others have information they lack.[1]

People usually disagree most when there is little solid information, and they are most uncertain. Disagreements about the true value of a security increase with the uncertainty about its value. Risk is, in turn, correlated with uncertainty. Consider different types of securities. Most observers would say there was the least uncertainty about the value of a bond issued by a company with a high credit rating. Next would be a utility stock with highly predictable earnings. Then there would be a typical industrial company whose earnings could fluctuate widely. Finally, there would be a developmental stage company with only a new product idea. There is considerable risk to investment in such a company, and considerable uncertainty about its future. In general, it is the companies about whose future there is the greatest uncertainty that are considered the riskiest and about whose value there is the greatest divergence of opinion. Thus, it is to be expected that there will be a positive correlation between risk and divergence of opinion.

Such a relationship has been found by Daley et al.[2] They showed that the disperdion of analysts' beliefs (as measured by coefficient of variation)

---

[1] Shiseng Qu, Laura Starks, and Hong Yan, "Risk, Dispersion of Analysts Forecasts and Stock Returns," working paper, University of Texas, September 30, 2003. Presented at the FMA meeting in 2003.

[2] Lane A. Daley, David W. Senkow, and Robert L Vigeland, "Analysts' Forecasts, Earnings Variability, and Option Pricing: Empirical Evidence," *Accounting Review* (October 1988), pp. 563–585.

was correlated with the magnitude of the unexpected earnings when next reported. The correlation was 0.347 with the absolute value of the unexpected earnings and 0.201 with the square of the expected earnings (both were statistically significant). Unexpected earnings are the difference between the mean analysts' forecasts of earnings and the earnings actually reported. Prices usually respond when company earnings are other than expected. Thus unexpected earnings can be considered a measure of risk.

It is not hard to come up with reasons to explain why the dispersion of analysts' predictions and unexpected earnings should be correlated. Imagine that a company's earnings depend on a factor that varies (such as the state of the economy) and analysts have different predictions for this factor. If the company's earnings are only a little affected by this factor, the analysts' estimates of its impact on earnings will be similar, and if the factor proves to be different than estimated by the typical analyst, there will be little impact on earnings. However, if the company's earnings are very sensitive to this factor, the same analysts' divergence of opinions about this factor will lead to a wider dispersion in earnings estimates. Also, whenever the factor is different from what typical analysts expected (say, there is an unexpected decline in the economy), earnings will differ from the mean of the estimates. Thus, one would expect the companies for which there was considerable divergence of opinion among the analysts to also be the ones most likely to produce disappointing earnings (or unexpectedly good earnings).

There is another reason for a positive correlation between divergence of opinion and earnings variability. There are usually a large number of factors and potential events that could affect a company significantly. Due to limitations of time and human brain-processing capacity, no analyst or investor can take into account all of these. Much of the divergence of opinion among analysts and investors probably arises from differences in which factors they explicitly consider. For instance one may consider new competition in a particular product, but not the state of the business cycle in different markets, while another considers the business cycles, but not competition in that product. If a company is exposed to a large number of such factors, they can produce large variations in earnings, as well as large variations in analysts' forecasts.

Ajinkya, Atiase, and Gift also found a strong correlation between the divergence of opinion as measured by analysts' earnings forecasts (standardized by the mean forecast earnings per share) and the month to month changes in the mean of analysts' estimates.[3] The Spearman correlations

---

[3] Bipin B. Ajinkya, Rowland K. Atiase, and Michael J. Gift, "Volume of Trading and the Dispersion in Financial Analysts' Earnings Forecasts," *Accounting Review* (April 1991), pp. 389–401.

ranged from 0.467 (for 1978) to 0.519 (for 1981) and the Pearson correlations from 0.550 (for 1979) to 0.605 (for 1981). Since the standardization for size in the analysts' forecast was achieved by dividing by the mean forecast, and the standardization of the change in analysts' mean forecast was achieved by dividing by price, the correlation was not merely because price was used in calculating both variables, which would happen if the standardization of divergence of earnings forecasts was done by the alternative procedure of dividing by price, as is sometimes done.[4] Since most researchers would agree that revisions in earnings estimates were correlated with risk, this finding shows that the divergence of analysts' opinions is both a measure of risk and of pure divergence of opinion.

If stocks with high divergence of opinion among analysts frequently report earnings different than expected, their stocks will also be more volatile. Ajinkya, Atiase, and Gift[5] and Ajinkya and Gift[6] also documented a risk and divergence of opinion correlation. They measured investors' divergence of opinion by the divergence in analysts' opinions and risk by the variability in returns as measured by the standard deviation of returns implied by option prices. This correlation between the dispersion of analysts' forecasts and the volatility held—whether the volatility was measured historically, or whether it was with the expected volatility calculated from option prices.

Daley et al. found a correlation of 0.554 between the variance of analysts' forecasts and the variance of return (calculated over 30 days).[7] They also used option data to calculate the implied volatility. For implied volatilities calculated for options expiring after the next earnings reporting date, the correlation was positive and statistically signifi-

---

[4] Since not all analysts' forecasts are reported at the same time, some of the correlation may be due to this. Imagine there was no divergence of opinion among analysts. This would mean that at any one time they were in agreement. However, if only some reported this month, and in the database for this month some analysts were represented by their estimates as of last month, there would be a positive correlation between the dispersion in analysts' forecasts and the change in the mean of analysts' forecasts. This artificial correlation could be reduced if the change in mean forecasts was calculated for a pair of months that did not include the month over which the dispersion in analysts forecasts was calculated.

[5] Ajinkya, Atiase, and Gift, "Volume of Trading and the Dispersion in Financial Analysts' Earnings Forecasts."

[6] Bipin B. Ajinkya and Michael J. Gift, "Dispersion of Financial Analysts' Earnings Forecasts and the (Option Model) Implied Standard Deviations of Stock Returns," *Journal of Finance* (December 1985), pp. 1353–1365.

[7] Lane A. Daley, David W. Senkow, and Robert L Vigeland, "Analysts' Forecasts, Earnings Variability, and Option Pricing: Empirical Evidence," *Accounting Review* (October 1988), pp. 563–585.

cant. For options expiring before the next earnings announcement, the correlation was positive, but nonsignificant. The latter result was what they predicted from a simple model in which a new earnings announcement affected stock prices upon announcement, but not before. However, given that much information relevant to earnings appears before the earnings announcement (industry sales, macro-economic data, product introductions, other firms' earnings reports, etc.) and that both divergence of analysts' estimates and volatility are serially correlated, I would have expected a positive correlation also before the earnings were announced. I suspect a larger sample over a longer period would have shown significance.

A more recent study of analysts' estimates of earnings is by Anderson, Ghysels, and Juergens.[8] They find for 1991–1997 that not only does the divergence in analysts' estimates of earnings (unstandardized) forecast variance in return for the next year, but that a model using it alone provides better forecasts of variance than other models tested.

Malkiel concluded "the best single risk proxy is not the traditional beta calculation but rather the dispersion of analysts' forecasts."[9]

Barry and Gultekin show that betas increase with their measure of analysts' dispersion of opinion.[10] The beta increases from 0.770 for the lowest coefficient of variation groups to 1.136 for the groups with the highest coefficient of variation. Barron and Stuerke also found a positive correlation between beta and the log of the dispersion in analysts' forecasts and between beta and the log of analysts forecasts updated within 30 days of the release of earnings.[11] They also showed that these measures correlated with the variance of daily returns over the year preceding the earnings announcement and with the absolute value of the cumulative abnormal return around the next earnings announcement. Not surprisingly, beta also correlated with the variance of daily returns over the year preceding the announcement.

---

[8] Evan W. Anderson, Eric Ghysels and Jennifer L. Juergens, "Do Heterogenous Beliefs and Model Uncertainty Matter for Asset Pricing?" working paper, June 13, 2003.

[9] Burton Malkiel, "Risk and Return: A New Look," in Benjamin M. Friedman (ed.), *The Changing Role of Debt and Equity in Financing U.S. Capital Formation* (Chicago, IL: University of Chicago Press, 1982), pp. 27–45.

[10] Christopher B. Barry and Mustafa N. Gultekin, "Differences of Opinion and Neglect: Additional Effects on Risk and Return," Table 4 in John B. Guerard and Mustafa N. Gultekin (eds.), *Handbook of Security Analyst Forecasting and Asset Allocation* (Greenwich, CT, JAI Press Inc., 1992).

[11] Orie E. Barron and Pamela S. Stuerke, "Dispersion in Analysts' Earnings Forecasts as a Measure of Uncertainty," *Journal of Accounting, Auditing, & Finance* (Summer 1998), pp. 245–269.

Thus divergence of opinion appears useful as an indicator of risk. Variances of return estimates are useful for investors. Even if this risk is non-systematic risk, active investors may take large enough positions in a stock they believe will outperform the market for that stock's variance to make an appreciable contribution to their portfolio's variance.

This correlation between risk and divergence of opinion creates econometric problems for any one trying to test the effects of divergence of opinion on asset prices or on returns because the pure divergence of opinion effect is to reduce returns while the risk effect is to increase them.

There appear to be several reasons for investors to avoid stocks with high divergence of opinion. One is the "winner's curse" effect.[12] The opinions the "winner" invests in may be the wrong set of opinions (and winner's curse theory suggests that if he (or she) chooses to invest in them, he has an above average chance of acting on a wrong set of opinions). Then he will be disappointed. A second factor is that such stocks tend to be riskier, and most investors should wish to avoid risky stocks.

A third factor applies to those investing other people's money (and perhaps a few individual investors who are worried about their spouse's opinions or their own self-esteem). Investing in high divergence of opinion firms is risky for a manager's career. There are likely to be analysts' reports implying, or even stating, that the investment should not have been made. In the event the investment loses money, his superiors and those who hire managers will have something to point to implying he was imprudent or even stupid. If the reports were actually recommendations to sell or to hold (i.e., not to buy), you need to explain why you acted contrary to them. If the most pessimistic reports merely indicated that earnings were likely to be much lower than others expected, it can be argued that you should have believed analyst X and anticipated the disappointing earnings and the price decline that followed the earning announcement. It is safer to fail conventionally, that is, to buy a stock in a company that did worse than anyone predicted.

In theory, if some investors are avoiding a stock for any of these reasons, the price should be lower and the expected return higher. The winner's curse effect has had relatively little discussion anywhere (it appears in no textbook or popular investment book for instance). Thus, it is implausible that prices adjust for it.

Modern financial theory divides risk into that which can be easily diversified away and that which cannot (systematic risk). It will be argued here that divergence of opinion is correlated with both. This, in

---

[12] Edward M. Miller (Principal investigator and author of most), *Study of Energy Fuel Resources*, vol. 1 (Cambridge, MA: Abt Associates, 1969).

the presence of restrictions on short selling, has interesting implications for the security markets and for investment policy.

Price and Diversifiable Risk

Most investors are aware of reasons for avoiding risky stocks in their portfolios. They understand that higher risk should only be accepted if there is also higher return. All things being equal, this implies a risk-return trade-off among securities. Emphasis is put on "all things being equal" condition, because the divergence of opinion effect is excluded in most discussions. Conventional wisdom is that prices have adjusted so that there is such a tradeoff between risk and return. The textbook version of this wisdom is that returns should only be related to systematic risk because investors can and have diversified away all nonsystematic risk.

The most popular model among academics of portfolio building is Markowitz optimization. This results in a fully diversified portfolio (the textbook market portfolio) only if the returns put into the models are those predicted by the capital asset pricing model. In this case, some of every asset is held and there are no short positions. If one puts in expected returns that differ appreciably from those predicted by the capital asset pricing model, the portfolios no longer resemble the market portfolio. If short sales are permitted, typically there will be a position in virtually all stocks, but many of these will be short positions. However, the typical investor constrains weights to be nonnegative, because he is either legally unable to go short, or unwilling to go short (or believes the obstacles to short selling make such positions undesirable). For such investors, Markowitz optimization (with noncapital asset-pricing-model-predicted rates of return) will typically produce zero holdings for most stocks.

If the investor has a reasonably high acceptance of risk (variability in final value of portfolio) and believes some stocks will have much higher risk-adjusted returns than others, the optimization process will produce a nondiversified portfolio. Such an optimized portfolio reflects a tradeoff between risk and return such that putting any more money into the stocks expected to have the highest returns will increase risk to an unacceptable degree. The relevant measure of risk for each investor is a form of "systematic risk" since it reflects the correlation of each stock with the optimized portfolio.

In Markowitz optimization, which seems a reasonable model for many investors, the limit to the stock's weight is set by a risk-return trade-off. At the optimum weight for the stock, the loss of utility from increased risk caused by further increases in the weight will exceed the gain in utility from a higher portfolio return. All things equal, the higher a stock's standard deviation in returns, the lower the optimal weight for any given estimated expected return. The optimal weight also decreases as the covariance of the stock with the rest of the portfolio increases. In turn, this covariance increases with the stock's standard deviation. With the high divergence of opinion stocks also having high return variances (standard deviation squared), the limit to holdings of a stock is reached at a lower weight in a particular portfolio. This means that the stock has to be priced lower in order to be included in more portfolios (a requirement for markets to clear). This somewhat reduces the price raising effect of high divergence of opinion in the absence of a correlation with return variance or volatility.

For instance, if an investor believes Yahoo will have high returns, the optimization program will cause him to buy Yahoo. It will stop adding Yahoo only when adding any more Yahoo to the portfolio produces less utility than adding another, lower return stock whose return is less correlated with this portfolio. Since the optimized portfolio heavily weights Yahoo, the alternative stock will typically be one that whose return has a low correlation with Yahoo. The optimization model rejects additional holdings of Yahoo because the return on Yahoo has a high correlation with the returns of this portfolio, which is one that overweights Yahoo.

The higher the variance of the return to Yahoo, the less of Yahoo the computer buys. Thus, the optimal purchases of a stock depend not only on the beta (calculated relative to the portfolio as a whole) of the stock, but also on the nonsystematic or diversifiable risk of the stock. In a stock market where there is high diversity of opinion and investors are risk averse, it follows that "nonsystematic risk" could be priced. Since the typical investor will be less than fully diversified, they should rationally require higher returns from stocks with high "diversifiable risk." Thus, each investor will purchase less of stocks with a high diversifiable risk (for a given forecast return). When the market aggregates the demand curves of all investors, these lower purchases imply a higher average return for stocks with high diversifiable risks (all things equal). This effect could produce a tendency for nondiversifiable risk to be priced. This is in addition to the recognized tendency for "systematic" risk to be priced. Since high divergence of opinion stocks tend also to be high diversifiable risk stocks, this is an effect opposite in direction to the pure divergence of opinion effect.

This is a way that recognition of divergence of opinion (along with restricted short selling) changes financial theory. When investors disagree about the merits of securities, investors will concentrate their portfolios on the securities they value highly. This will lead to diversifiable risk being priced, while it is not priced in models with rational investors and unrestricted short selling.

Xu and Malkiel document that there is a strong tendency for the stocks in the S&P 500 with a high idiosyncratic risk (diversifiable risk) to have high annual returns for the period 1963–1994.[13] Idiosyncratic risk was calculated as the standard deviation of the residuals from estimating the betas. The average annual returns increase fairly steadily from about 12% for the lowest idiosyncratic risk stocks to 19% for the highest idiosyncratic risk stocks. They document that this idiosyncratic risk (a measure of volatility) is correlated strongly with firm size (small capitalization firms being more volatile), leaving open the possibility that much of the effect found should be attributed instead to size.

Since diversity of opinion can increase risk while lowering return through its price increasing effect, there is an issue as to the net effect. It should be noticed that whichever effect dominates, it does not eliminate the logical case for the other effect.

Implications for the Market Risk Return Trade-Off

This raises an interesting possibility. There is general agreement that investors dislike risk and will only take on increased risk if promised a higher return. As stated, this rule applies only to individuals. However, it is usually generalized to a statement that there is an inverse relationship between risk and return in the market. This involves a "fallacy of composition." The result is assumed to apply for the market, an aggregation of individuals, merely because it applies at the individual level.

With heterogeneous expectations, it does not follow automatically that there must be a corresponding aggregate relationship between risk and return. As shown above, with divergence of opinion and every investor basing his estimates on unbiased estimates of value, there will be a shortfall between the return an investor anticipates in earnings and the average amount he actually earns. Furthermore, this shortfall increases with the divergence of opinion and with the risk. Exhibit 14.1 shows a possible effect of this. The straight line shows the risk-return trade-off for the typical individual. Subtracted from the anticipated return for each level of risk is the expected shortfall due to the winner's curse effect. As can be seen, it is quite possible for the market return/ risk line to slope downwards over some values for risk. This might explain the Haugen and Heins'[14] finding of a slightly negative correlation between portfolio risk (standard deviation of return) and return for 1926–1971, and the finding by Soldofsky and Miller that the lowest

---

[13] Yexiao Xu and Burton G. Malkiel, "Risk and Return Revisited," *Journal of Portfolio Management* (1997), pp. 9–14.

[14] Robert A. Haugen and A. James Heins, "Risk and the Rate of Return of Financial Assets: Some Old Wine in New Bottles," *Journal of Financial and Quantitative Analysis* (December 1975), pp. 775–784.

EXHIBIT 14.1   Market versus Individual Return/Risk Trade-Off

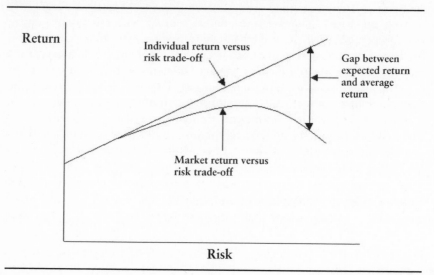

returns on stocks were actually earned on those that were considered by the rating agencies to have the greatest risk.[15]

To understand the effect, consider the riskiest class of stocks, those for development stage companies with no history. These are generally agreed to be very risky. They are also the companies about which there is the greatest divergence of opinion. For each of them, the price is set by the most optimistic investors, those who have persuaded themselves (perhaps using correct logic) that these companies have a bright future. If these investors are sufficiently optimistic (which need not imply that on average that their estimates exhibit any bias), the return will be far below that which they anticipated earning, possibly even negative.

The argument as expressed above also applies to risk when measured by beta. Beta is correlated with divergence of opinion, partially because beta is correlated with total risk. As beta goes up the difference between the anticipated return and the return actually experienced will increase. As a practical matter, the observed betas will likely be positive. If the measure of risk is beta and the market return versus risk relationship has a slope lower than that for a single representative individual, the line of best fit will have an intercept on the return axis above the

---

[15] Robert M. Soldofsky and Roger L. Miller, "Risk-Premium Curves for Different Classes of Long-Term Securities, 1950-1966," *Journal of Finance* (June 1969), pp. 429–445.

intercept for the individual. If the investor is using Markowitz optimization, theory suggests the intercept would be the risk-free rate. Even if every individual is engaged in Markowitz optimization, the intercept of the fitted risk-return relationship for the market may be above the risk-free rate. As is well known, observed tests of the capital asset pricing model have shown that the intercept is above the risk-free rate.

The above theory predicts that the greater the divergence of opinion, the higher the price will be (all things equal). A higher price implies a lower long run return given the same future set of dividends. Thus, the above predicts that the greater the divergence of opinion, the lower the returns will be.

Again note that stocks with high divergence of opinion need not have below-average returns because the divergence of opinion is highly correlated with traditional risk measures, which are believed to lead to higher returns. The effect of divergence of opinion may be just to neutralize some of the effects of risk.

RETURNS TO BETA

The evidence is that the predictions of the CAPM regarding the returns to beta do not hold. If beta is correlated with risk and uncertainty, and these are correlated with divergence of opinion as they seem to be, the effect will be to reduce the returns to high-beta stocks more than to low-beta stocks. Intellectually, this can explain why the returns to beta are so low. Practically, the effect is to make it possible to create low-beta portfolios that hold up well in market declines without sacrificing much, if any return.

If the standard deviation of returns on the investment is correlated with the standard deviation of estimates of return among investors, the beta of a stock should be correlated with the divergence of opinion about the stock. The reason is that beta is

$$\frac{r_{i,m} s_i s_m}{s_m^2}$$

where s_m is the standard deviation of the market, s_i is the standard deviation of the return on the stock in question, and $r_{i,m}$ is the correlation coefficient between s_m and s_i. This simplifies to

$$\frac{r_{i,m}s_i}{s_m}$$

Thus, beta increases proportionately with the stock's standard deviation. With the simplifying assumptions being used here, the uncertainty-induced bias can then be shown to be proportional to the stock's beta.

There is other evidence that beta increases with divergence of opinion. It was argued in Chapter 6 that short interest should measure divergence of opinion. Brent, et al. using a separate equation to predict relative short interest (after a transformation to make it closer to normal) for each year from 1981–1984 found that in each year's equation that the beta had a statistically significant (at the 99% confidence level) effect.[16] The equations controlled for the existence of options (which were likely to be more common on high-beta stocks), the disagreement among analysts in forecasts of earnings, the existence of convertible securities, stock residual variance, firm size, and prior-year-average monthly return. Interestingly, two other surrogates for divergence of opinion, stock residual variance and the analysts' forecasts standard deviation, failed to be consistently related to the short interest measure used. The exception was that for one year only during which the analysts' forecast variance did have a statistically significant effect at the 1% level.

To facilitate the argument, let d be a constant of proportionality between the standard deviation of the divergence of opinion, denoted as S, and the standard deviation of returns, denoted as s.[17] Thus, $S = ds$. Also assume that the gap between the average of the returns expected by all investors, and the return of the marginal investor was pS_i. Hence the bias is pds_i. These equations imply that $s_i = \beta_i (s_m/r)$. Substituting this into the equation for the shortfall, pds_i, the reduction in the return due to the uncertainty induced bias is $pd\beta_i (pds_{im}/r)$. The bias is proportional to the beta (β_i).

This brings us to Exhibit 14.2. The upper line on the exhibit describes the relationship between a typical investor's expected return and the betas of his or her stocks. However, due to uncertainty induced bias, the marginal investor (who is more optimistic than the average

---

[16] Averil Brent, Dale Morese, and E. Kay Stice, "Short Interest: Explanation and Tests," *Journal of Financial and Quantitative Analysis* (June 1990), pp. 273–289.

[17] The standard deviation of returns is an estimate, and each investor may have a different estimate. However, for the purposes of the current discussion it was assumed the investors agreed on the risk parameters for the securities, and this would include the standard deviation. Generalizing the argument of this chapter to where investors disagree about the risk parameters is possible.

EXHIBIT 14.2 Relationship Between Beta and Return

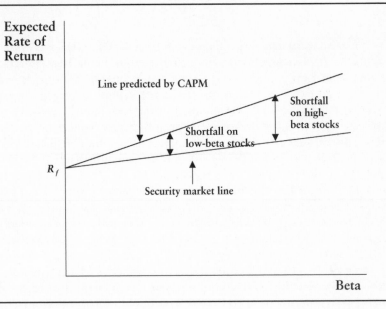

investor) has bid the price of the stocks up. Thus, on average there is a gap between the returns the typical investor expects and the returns the stocks actually earned. This return shortfall is subtracted from the upper line's return. This gives the return that will actually be earned by the typical stock with a beta of β. Because there is no disagreement about the returns for the risk-free asset, this gap is zero there. However, as beta increases, the gap between the return predicted by the model and the typical investor's anticipated expected return increases. Since the gap increases linearly with beta, the line showing the observed return versus beta has the same intercept as each individual's risk-free line, but has a lower slope (which could even be negative).

The Security Market Line

Intuitively, when the uncertainty-induced bias is deducted from the typical investor's line relating systematic risk and return (see Exhibit 14.2), the result is a slope that is much flatter.

Earlier it was argued that the uncertainty-induced bias would be $pd\beta_i s_m/r$.

We can subtract this from the expected return, $E(R_i) = R_f + \beta_i(R_m - R_f)$, to get the actual return that will be earned in the market. Thus, for the market as a whole,

$$E(R) = R_f + \beta(R_m - R_f) - \frac{p\,d\beta_i s_m}{r} = R_f + \beta\left(\frac{R_m - R_f - p\,d s_m}{r}\right)$$

This equation describes the security market line. It is a straight line starting at R_f, but with a lower slope than in the standard capital asset pricing model (and could even have a negative slope). A stock's return still depends on beta. Unlike the standard capital asset pricing model, the security market line is different from the line describing the relationship between a typical investor's expected return from a stock, and its beta. This difference creates an opportunity for the manager to craft a portfolio that provides a better risk-return trade off than the market, or an index representing it.

In Exhibit 14.2, the lower line represents the security market line that will actually be observed (averaged over many conditions). This is why the relationship between beta and observed returns is so small, and negative in many studies. It is not because investors do not require higher returns for the riskier stocks; they do. However, because of a winner's curse type effect called uncertainty-induced bias, they are typically disappointed. This disappointment is greatest for the riskiest stocks, which are those with the greatest divergence of opinion.

The evidence is that the predictions of the CAPM regarding the returns to beta do not hold. Earlier studies tended to show that the returns to beta were positive, but less than CAPM theory suggested. Even the earliest tests found the returns to low-beta stocks to be higher than predicted.[18] In an update, Black found low-beta stocks outperformed high-beta stocks for every decade since the 1930s.[19] Lakonishok and Shapiro also found a much weaker beta effect than theory predicts.[20]

Later researchers discovered an interesting peculiarity. Tinic and West found that the positive relationship between beta and return is observed only in the month of January.[21] In others months the relationship was nonsignificant, confirming an earlier observation of Rozeff and

---

[18] Fischer Black, Michael C. Jensen, and Myron Scholes, "The Capital Asset Pricing Model: Some Empirical Tests," in Michael C. Jensen, (ed.), *Studies in the Theory of Capital Markets* (New York: Praeger, 1972).

[19] Fischer Black, "Return and Beta," *Journal of Portfolio Management* (Fall 1993), pp. 8–18.

[20] Josef Lakonishok and Alan C. Shapiro, "Systematic Risk, Total Risk and Size as Determinants of Stock Market Returns," *Journal of Banking and Finance* (March 1986), pp. 115-132.

[21] Seha M. Tinic and Richard R. West, "Risk and Return: January and the Rest of the Year," *Journal of Financial Economics* (December 1984), pp. 561–574.

Kinney.[22] Even the January effect may not be a true return to risk, but a result of stocks bouncing back from tax-loss selling. The most volatile stocks are likely to be overrepresented among those with losses near the end of the year (as they will be overrepresented among those with gains). This volatility will make them high-beta stocks. The bounce back from tax loss selling probably causes the high-beta stocks to have the highest returns, an effect that is quite different from investors being rewarded for assuming beta risk.

For the United Kingdom, Corhay, Hawawini, and Michel found that the beta versus return relationship was statistically significant only for April, also a month of unusually high returns.[23] The British tax year ends in March, so the April effect may be explained by the same mechanism as explains the American high-January return to beta. The authors found that in France, Belgium, and the United Kingdom, the beta versus return relationship was significantly negative when the month of January was excluded.

Fama and French state of the Sharp, Lintner, and Black (SLB) model that, "In short, our tests do not support the most basic prediction of the SLB model that average stock returns are positively related to market βs."[24] Fama is the founder of the efficient market theory.

Haugen plots out the Fama and French results for return versus beta (for 1963–1990) for each of ten size deciles, noting they are all negative.[25] The higher the beta, the lower the monthly return. This result is quite opposite to the prediction of the theory.

Haugen makes the very important point that the relevant investment horizon is much longer than the month used by Fama and French, as well as other researchers. Because the geometric average (relevant to compounding) is always lower than the arithmetic average, a flat relationship between monthly return and risk (standard deviation) would correspond to a strongly negative relationship between five-year returns and risk. Thus, Fama and French (and the work of many other researchers), by using monthly returns, understate the penalty in return from accepting high systematic risk.

---

[22] Michael S. Rozeff and William R. Kinney, "Capital Market Seasonality: The Case of Stock Returns," *Journal of Financial Economics* (October 1976), pp. 379–402.

[23] Albert Corhay, Gabriel Hawawini, and Pierre Michel, "Seasonality in the Risk-Return Relationship: Some International Evidence," *Journal of Finance* (March 1987), pp. 49–68.

[24] Eugene F. Fama and Kenneth R. French, "The Cross-Section of Expected Stock Returns," *Journal of Finance* (June 1992), p. 428.

[25] Robert A. Haugen, *The New Finance: A Case Against Efficient Markets*, 2nd edition (Upper Saddle River, NJ: Prentice Hall, 1999).

Haugen has done other things to point out how low the return is to assuming beta risk.[26] He demonstrated that a portfolio designed (with optimization) to minimize risk actually had higher returns than the Standard and Poor's index for 1928 to 1992, while portfolios designed to maximize risk actually had lower returns. Similar results were found for small-value stocks, large-value stocks, and small-growth stocks, and for large-growth stocks. The same pattern is found in 5-year rolling averages for 1972–1992 using the Standard & Poor's 500 stocks. A striking result is that the low volatility portfolio always had higher returns than the S&P index, and the high volatility portfolio always had lower returns than the S&P index.

Haugen and Baker demonstrated for France, Germany, the United Kingdom, and Japan the same tendency for an optimally designed low volatility portfolio to have higher returns than a country index, and higher returns than a high volatility portfolio.[27] This was also true for a combination of the portfolios of these countries (plus the United States). Winston has also demonstrated that from 1975 to 1992, the higher return on optimally designed low volatility portfolios holds for a wide range of methods for constructing such portfolios.[28] Haugen and Heins in 1975 had shown that beta and return were uncorrelated.[29]

Xu and Malkiel using data for 1963–1994 using a methodology somewhat similar to Fama and French (but a somewhat longer period) found that there was essentially no relationship between beta and annual returns after controlling for size.[30]

Even rejecting the extreme assumptions of the capital asset pricing model, it is still amazing to see that systematic risk appears to be rewarded. One might have expected that there were enough investors trying to purchase stocks that would hold up well in the next bear market to have bid these stocks to at least a slight premium (implying lower returns).

Of course, for certain periods the returns to beta may be much higher. The late 1990s was such a period. Merrill Lynch's comparison of the highest beta 50 companies from the S&P 500 to an equally weighted index showed a relative performance that was at about 100 in mid-1996, but had risen to 230 by the beginning of 2000.[31]

---

[26] Haugen, *The New Finance: A Case Against Efficient Markets.*

[27] Robert A. Haugen and Nardin L. Baker, "Commonality in the Determinants of Expected Stock Returns," *Journal of Financial Economics* (July 1996), pp. 401–439.

[28] Kenneth Winston, "The "Efficient Index" and Prediction of Portfolio Variance," *Journal of Portfolio Management* (Spring 1993), pp. 27–35.

[29] Haugen and Heins, "Risk and the Rate of Return of Financial Assets: Some Old Wine in New Bottles."

[30] Xu and Malkiel, "Risk and Return Revisited."

[31] Richard Bernstein, *Quantitative Profiles: Monthly Insights for Equity Management, May* (New York: Merrill Lynch, Pierce, Fenner & Smith Inc., 2000), p. 31.

Because growth stocks (especially story stocks) tend to have high betas, periods when growth stocks greatly outperform value are likely to be periods when the returns to beta are positive. Haugen tries to explain the low returns to beta by a very plausible theory in which investors extrapolate growth too far into the future.[32] As noted above, one need not claim investors as a group make these errors (or that the typical investor makes them), but merely that a substantial minority, constituting the more optimistic investors makes these mistakes.

Empirically, there appear to be waves of optimism and pessimism in the market. When optimism is strong, people will pay more for equity securities than for debt, and within equity securities will pay more for those with the prospects of future growth, especially for story stocks. Thus as the risk premium goes up and down, growth stocks fluctuate more than value stocks and hence come to have higher betas. If, on average, their return is less than that of value stocks, because the more optimistic investors who set their price are too optimistic, the return to beta can actually be negative. Notice this effect is quite consistent with investors as a class having unbiased expectations, every investor avoiding high-beta stocks (if he believes them to have equal returns to other stocks), and even with every investor having unbiased expectations when averaged over all stocks. However, his expectation will be biased on average for the stocks in which he chooses to take a long position.

The Usefulness of Beta and the Possibility of Risk Reduction

The conclusion for investors is not that "beta is dead." Indeed the opposite is true. In the classic version of the CAPM, beta is not useful for stock portfolio managers because they merely have to hold the "market portfolio." This is usually interpreted as an index (such as the S&P 500). While certain stocks have lower betas than others, buying the lower beta stocks would reduce returns. Furthermore, it happens that the disadvantage to the investor from the lower returns just equals the utility gain from lowering the portfolio beta (remember the slope of the security market line is the price of risk). Even worse, concentrating a portfolio on lower beta stocks reduces diversification, making it utility reducing.

However, if the return to beta is either negative or very low, a strategy of reducing the risk of the portfolio by emphasizing low-beta stocks becomes desirable for most investors. Actually, the capital asset pricing model is not needed to make the case for beta being useful. It appears large number of investors would be willing to sacrifice some return in

---

[32] Haugen, *The New Finance: A Case Against Efficient Markets* and *The Inefficient Stock Market: What Pays Off and Why*, 2nd ed. (Upper Saddle Rier, NJ: Prentice Hall, 2001).

up markets for greater protection from down market losses. This would be true of anyone who has the bulk of their wealth in stocks, a category that probably includes many retirees, widows, endowments, pension funds, and those with inherited money. The decreasing utility of wealth is enough to make this true.

Without the aid of the CAPM, we can define a historical beta as the slope of a regression line of the stocks' returns to the return on a market return index. Except in rare cases, such a number can always be calculated (and with modern computers at a low cost). It has now been documented that historical betas have a useful degree of consistency over time (although regression to the mean cause extreme values do move towards one). Thus we can make useful projections of future betas. It then follows, that by emphasizing low-beta stocks, portfolios can be designed that should decline less in bear markets. Exploitation might be by explicit use of optimization programs with reasonable estimates of returns as inputs (perhaps derived from a multifactor model). Beta estimates can be used to construct a covariance matrix if the correlation between any two stocks is assumed to be due only to their common covariance with the market, or to their covariance with the market along with other factors, including industry factors. Even simpler, investments might be selected from lists of low-beta securities and/or value stocks.

Markowitz optimization provides one way of selecting portfolios once one has estimates of future returns and reasonable estimates of a covariance matrix. Although the CAPM is usually derived by assuming everyone uses Markowitz optimization, if the CAPM holds, optimization is not needed. All that is required is to hold the index. An explicit optimization can be expected to emphasize low-beta stocks if good estimates of future returns are put in (such as estimates that might come from a model such as Haugen or others used).

In considering whether Markowitz optimization would be a reasonable tool, it must be remembered that one of the key assumptions is that the investor's utility involves only the return and the variance of the portfolio value at some future date. Whether variance or some other measure of the width of the distribution of future wealth is used is not critical since most well diversified stock portfolios are likely to have returns that are approximated by a normal distribution (which is described by merely the mean and standard deviation). Among other things, the assumption that investors care only about the return and standard deviation of their portfolios implies that they are indifferent to the state of nature in which low returns are realized. While investors that have all of their wealth in the U.S. stock market may care primarily about means and deviation of their portfolios, others may care about other things.

Many investors receive most of their income from other than the stock market. This is true of most working people. These people are frequently saving for emergencies, or planning to sell their investments if they lose their jobs or if their businesses have a bad year. Naturally, they care about how valuable their investments will be when they need their money. In practice, this is disproportionately likely to be when the economy is in a recession. Such investors rationally should prefer investments that are less exposed to the risk of a recession (i.e., noncyclical investments). For these people cyclicality is another measure of risk.[33] Fortunately, Haugen's results show that lowering exposure to most *arbitrage-pricing-theory* (APT)-type factors does not reduce returns.[34] In particular, he included the monthly change in industrial production as a measure of the business cycle.

Investors who were planning to spend their savings in the distant future (say, retirees) might prefer that their portfolios have higher values if they were spending the money when prices were higher. This would suggest preferring securities whose returns were correlated with the rates of inflation. Haugen's APT model included the monthly change in the consumer price index. Investors who had liabilities in the distant future (such as life insurance companies and pension funds) might prefer stocks that rose in value when interest rates fell. Again, the Haugen APT evidence suggests protection could be purchased at a low price in terms of return sacrificed. Thus, there would appear to be scope for active management, not only in seeking higher returns, but in protecting investors from the various risks that in theory they might be concerned about.

Long-Run Prospect for High Returns from Low-Beta Stocks

If the higher returns to low-beta stocks is a result of uncertainty-induced bias being greater for high-beta stocks, the effect may continue for a while. There is very little recognition of this bias. It is not discussed in textbooks. While if recognized it might disappear, it seems likely to remain unrecognized for a while. Thus, it appears the excessive flatness of the security market line is an effect that is likely to remain exploitable into the future.

There are two other reasons that may have led to overinvestment in high-beta stocks, which may continue to depress returns on such stocks. Black suggests that the low return to beta may be due to borrowing restrictions.[35] In theory, one can achieve a high-return/high-beta portfolio by levering a lower risk portfolio. The optimal strategy with the CAPM model

---

[33] I developed this idea in Edward M. Miller, "Portfolio Selection in a Fluctuating Economy," *Financial Analysts Journal* (May/June 1978), pp. 77–83.
[34] Haugen, *The Inefficient Stock Market: What Pays Off and Why.*
[35] Fischer Black, "Capital Market Equilibrium with Restricted Borrowing," *Journal of Business* (1972), pp. 444–455.

assumptions is to use margin to invest more than your wealth in the market portfolio. This is superior to focusing investments on high-beta stocks, because investing in them reduces diversification, leading to more risk for any level of return than use of a leveraged strategy. However, most institutions are not allowed to use leverage and many individual investors are reluctant to borrow. Given a borrowing constraint, these investors may seek higher returns through high-beta growth stocks. This is done even though higher returns for the same risk could be obtained by leveraging a lower beta portfolio. This causes the high-beta risky stocks to be bid up too high, creating investment opportunities in low-beta stocks (which investors willing to accept the risks of leverage can exploit by using margin). It is interesting that Black drew attention to the investment merits of low-beta stocks back in 1972, indicating how persistent this effect has been.

Another problem is that many institutional investors are evaluated by their performance relative to a benchmark, typically the S&P 500. Adopting a low-beta strategy increases their risks of deviating from the benchmark in the downward direction (in particular, in strong bull markets they are likely to underperform the benchmark and the market). Thus, even if aware of the low-beta investment opportunity, it may not be in their interest to design a portfolio that exploits it. This would sacrifice diversification, leaving them overexposed to certain industries that might underperform. In theory, they could come closer to the benchmark by using borrowed funds to bring the beta back to that of the benchmark, but as Black noted, managers are usually not allowed to borrow. Futures or call options could also be used to raise the beta (reducing the chance of underperforming the benchmark in a bull market), but again these derivative instruments are frequently not allowed. Thus, investment managers' incentive structures may discourage many from buying a low-beta portfolio, or using strategies likely to result in holding low-beta stocks (such as value investing).

Implications are obvious. Those hiring investment managers should think about what their goals are. If, as is likely, they want portfolios that do well in bear markets (and are willing to sacrifice some return in bull markets for this), they should write agreements that provide for this. Custom benchmarks can easily be devised, or they might adopt a published value index as a benchmark. Likewise, managers who think their investment strategies will result in a low-beta portfolio should seek to write compensation agreements that reflect this. They should also warn their clients that there will be certain times when overvaluation of growth and story stocks increases. Underperformance should be expected in these years.

Most pension funds, endowments, etc. seem to have positions in bonds and stocks (as well as other asset classes). Separate managers are often hired to manage each portfolio. Part of the rationale seems to come from the CAPM tradition where risk is managed by adjusting the proportion of the assets in the market portfolio (or the optimal portfolio of risky assets), and then the risk level is optimized by changing the proportion of risky assets and risk-free (or low-risk) assets. Stocks are often viewed as the risky portfolio and bonds as the low risk. If the stock portfolio is to have a systematic risk similar to the S&P 500, it makes sense to give that manager a fixed percentage of the funds to manage (perhaps with some rebalancing every so often), and a bond manager the remainder.

Once it is realized that low beta can be obtained at only a small sacrifice of return, this logically should result in placing more of the funds in the stock portfolio, which is normally expected to have higher long-run returns. Ideally the allocation between bonds and stocks (and the logic applies to other assets) should depend not on how risky and profitable stocks as a class will be, but on how risky and profitable your own stock portfolio is expected to be. Suppose your stock manager can reduce the total pension fund's risk by designing a low-beta portfolio at less sacrifice of expected return than the sponsor would incur though increasing the allocation to the fixed income manager. Then the stock manager should seek a lower beta portfolio, and the loss of the expected returns made up by shifting funds from bonds to stocks.

The stock manager should be given an incentive structure that encourages him or her to lower beta. Once the model of a perfectly efficient market is given up, it seems likely that the opportunities to reduce systematic risk by buying low-beta securities may vary over time. If traditionally low-beta stocks (usually value ones) appear unusually underpriced, the allocation to stocks might be increased and funds removed from bonds. If these sectors appear overpriced, perhaps the weight of them in the stock portfolio should be reduced and then the systematic risk reduced by raising the allocation to bonds. Here is an implication for plan sponsors.

Sponsors might adopt an explicit policy of shifting more funds to equities if the equity manager achieves a lower beta. If the equity manager knows he (or she) will get to manage more assets if he lowers the beta, he may be able to do so. With modern computers he could be given a low-beta portfolio as a benchmark, lowering his concern about underperformance in a bull market. He might be given an incentive increase in fee if his portfolio has a lower beta (the sponsor could more than make up the cost of this fee by lowering the allocation to bonds).

However, both the above theory and the empirical evidence (discussed above) shows that one does not have to sacrifice much, if any, return to achieve a low-beta portfolio. The optimal equity portfolio would have a lower beta than the universe from which the stocks were selected. This would permit a higher percentage of the portfolio to be invested in stocks without increasing the losses during the next crash, and without increasing the volatility. The nice separation of risk management from security selection in modern financial theory disappears.

Fallacy of Composition

The low returns on high-beta stocks reflect a "fallacy of composition." Samuelson in his introductory economics textbook publicized the idea of a fallacy of composition.[36] A *fallacy of composition* arises when what is true for a single individual is presumed to be true for the economy as a whole.[37]

In theoretical finance, we assume that all investors are basically identical (except perhaps for risk preference). Once the equilibrium conditions for an individual investor are derived, it is casually assumed that these also apply to the market. Equilibrium for an individual means that given his beliefs, there is no way to increase his utility. Equilibrium for the market means that no one wishes to trade at the prevailing prices. It is necessary to avoid the fallacy of composition.

It is a basic result from portfolio theory (not the CAPM) that if the assumptions required for Markowitz optimization are met (notably that the portfolio utility is determined only by expected return and the standard deviation of return) and there is a risk-free asset, that the optimal solution lies on a line between the risk-free asset and an optimized portfolio of risk assets. This is a mathematical result and would hold even if there was only one investor in the economy who used Markowitz optimization. In fact, the optimization might be most useful in those circumstances. It could be very useful if there was one advisor who could compute an optimal portfolio of risky assets and then by mixing this with the risk-free asset deliver a suitable portfolio to each of his clients. He need run the optimization only once.

The textbooks typically at this point then assume homogeneous expectations (that everyone has the same expectations about risk and return) and that everyone uses Markowitz optimization (perhaps defended by calling it rationality). Because they are all using in effect the same computer programs (a Markowitz optimization) with the same inputs, it follows they must all calculate the same set of optimal portfolio weights. If these weights are different from the weights in the "market portfolio," everyone's computer programs will be giving off orders to buy or sell the same stocks. These orders will quickly force prices up or down to a level where no one wants to trade, which is equilibrium in the security markets. It then follows that everyone will hold the "market portfolio" for their risky

---

[36] Paul Samuelson, *Economics* (New York: McGraw-Hill, 1964), p. 11.
[37] The definition Samuelson gives for the fallacy of composition is: "a fallacy in which what is true of a part is, on that account alone, alleged to be also true of the whole."

assets. What is called the "market line" for one individual is the "market line" for every individual, and hence for all individuals aggregated. This market line, observable from market data, then provides the price of risk for individuals. Unfortunately, the logical error committed is the fallacy of composition, generalizing from one to the market.

If the theoreticians used demand and supply curves, the problem would be more obvious. The demand curve derived from one investor's behavior is multiplied by the number of investors involved (wealth-weighted), and this is presumed to be the marketwide demand curve. Of course, the actual mathematical methods used do not explicitly incorporate demand curves (failure to be explicit about how the individual demand curves combine to give a market demand curve is perhaps why the points made in this chapter have not been noticed before).[38] However, with heterogeneous expectations and without short selling, these shortcut methods do not work, as was shown above.

The basic problem is that the demand curves implied by each investor's optimization need not add up to an aggregate demand curve consistent with the security market relationship predicted by the capital-asset-pricing model. The reason is that the individual demand curves either stop at zero holdings (for most investors) or have a discontinuity at zero holdings (for those who go short if the profit potential is large enough). Basic economics textbooks show how aggregate demand curves can be constructed by adding up the demand curves of individuals. One adds up the amount an individual would hold at each price. Where the individual curves have a discontinuity at quantity zero, the aggregate curve may look quite different from the individual curves. This is why this model gives different conclusions than the CAPM. In going from theories of individual behavior to a theory of the market, there are unappreciated aggregation problems.

Growth Stocks and Divergence of Opinion

A natural question is what types of stocks are likely to have the greatest divergence of opinion. It seems that growth stocks are likely to have the highest divergence of opinion. In theory, a stock that will have growth in free cash flow and in dividends should be worth more. The next question is where this growth is going to come from.

The obvious sources are the existing investments of the company and future investments. If it is to come from the existing plant and

---

[38] The are of course some papers that discuss aggregation explicitly—such as John Lintner, "The Aggregation of Investors Diverse Judgments and Preferences in Purely Competitive Security Markets," *Journal of Financial and Quantitative Analysis* (December 1969), pp. 347–400—but often without incorporating the short selling constraint.

equipment, it must be because either the cash flows (and in practice earnings) are temporarily depressed for some reason (such as poor business conditions due to a recession) and are expected to recover. It seems plausible there will be more disagreement about the scope for a recovery than about the continuation of the profits currently being earned. For instance, the anticipated recovery in sales by the industry may not occur.

One may also expect higher earnings from existing plant and equipment because the management has a plan to solve an identified problem. Again, disagreements about the ability of the proposed solution to solve the problem are likely. It is possible to anticipate higher earnings because management will find a solution (even though they have not yet). Again investors can be anticipated to disagree about the ability of management to come up with a solution. Finally, even if current management cannot solve the problem, one may anticipate they will be replaced by management that can. Obviously, investors can disagree greatly about the probability of a management change (whether by board action or a takeover). Thus, the part of firm value that arises from future growth that takes the form of greater returns from existing plant and equipment appears subject to more divergence of opinion than the part of firm value from the continuation of current operations in their present mode. Due to restrictions on short selling, the price is set by the more optimistic investors for all of these conditions.

However, for more than short-term profit growth, it is usually necessary to have continued revenue growth. This normally means new plant and equipment, either for producing existing products or new products. Textbooks point out that much of the value in a correctly valued growth stock is the value of its opportunity to exploit opportunities to make high return investments.[39] If the investments that it can make merely provide a "market" rate of return, then the investors can make them on their own. They will not pay extra for a firm that will be making such investments, leaving out tax effects.[40]

Because these high return investments have not yet been made, the uncertainty about their return is relatively high. There is a great scope for disagreement about their existence and value. In contrast, the earnings from value stocks tend to come from products already in produc-

---

[39] Frank K. Reilly and Keith C. Brown, *Investment Analysis and Portfolio Management* (Hinsdale, IL: Dryden Press, 1994).

[40] The possible tax effect arises from the fact that long-term capital gains are taxed only when realized, and some investors may pay a premium for a company that invests profits in growing the business, rather than returning them to the owners to be invested at the same rate. Since the government will tax dividends when paid out (and until recently at a higher rate than long-term capital gains) an investor's wealth grows more rapidly if he picks the company that invests for him.

tion and investments that have already been made. The value of these assets (and the stream of income from them) is easier to determine. There will be less divergence of opinion about their value. Even in a business as prosaic as operating supermarkets or drugstores, there is likely to be less disagreement about the future profits of the already operating stores than about the future profits from the stores that are yet to be opened. Where the growth is to come from new products and innovations (some of which have not yet been made), the scope for disagreements about the value of the opportunity to make high return investments is likely to be great.

Since the new investments have not yet been made, there is scope for disagreement about how much they will cost to build and operate. Even more importantly there is scope for disagreement about whether the product or services from the new capacity can be sold. This happens even for existing products. It is often fairly safe to project that the product will continue to be used by the existing customers, and disagreement about this part of the business may not be great. However, continued growth in sales requires attracting new customers, customers who are likely to differ in important ways from the existing customers. People can legitimately disagree about the chances of attracting these new customers. Some may see market saturation as a problem, others may not. These optimists set the price (because they do not see market saturation as a problem).

Of course, if the current products are profitable enough so that it is worth investing in new capacity, it is likely that other firms will also see the market as attractive. New entry is a possibility. Again people will disagree about how likely that is. There are usually a large number of investors (and analysts serving them) who do not appear to consider this possibility (usually a mistake), or who after considering it do not expect it. History shows that entrance into expanding markets is extremely common. Again the optimists will set the price, and they are likely to be those who are not concerned about new entry.

Most nongrowing firms whose capacity is already adequate to supply its customers are in nonexpanding industries where profit margins are low enough so that new entrants are less likely. This makes these firms easier to project, and reduces the divergence of opinion below that which is typical for growing firms.

Many of the high-growth companies (probably most) are expected to get their growth not merely from selling more of their current models, but from new models that have not been introduced or even designed yet. Naturally there is considerable scope for disagreement about the prospects for such new products. Growth firms are frequently in high technology business, where new technologies are frequently being introduced, and new inventions are common. One should not expect analysts to know precisely what the new products will be. (Otherwise the analysts would have already patented them.) In these circumstances, there is considerable scope for disagreement about how the new products will do. Naturally, those that are the most optimistic will be those setting the price.

While it is very likely that average opinions are too optimistic, it should be noticed that even if every investor is on average correct in his estimates (i.e., if you collected estimates from him for all stocks, they would be unbiased on average, although of course there would be some errors), the above effect can still occur as long as investors' errors are not perfectly correlated with each other, and this divergence of opinion is greatest for the growth stocks. As explained earlier, when discussing the types of mistakes that investors may make and can be avoided by analysis, it does appear that the growth stocks have over long periods of time had lower returns than value stocks. The value stock anomalies (book-to-market value, price-to-earnings, cash-flow-to-earnings, dividend yield) to the efficient market model may be due to the uncertainty-induced bias effect discussed above.

This conclusion appears to differ from the empirical result of Diether et al. using analysts' estimates.[41] They found that the difference in returns between the lowest divergence-of-opinion growth stocks (identified by low book-to-market ratios) and the highest divergence of opinion growth stocks was less than the corresponding difference for the value stocks. However, as they noted, the analysts disagreed much more concerning the value stocks. For the growth stocks (low book-to-market), the lowest third had a dispersion of 0.04 and the highest third one of 0.49. For the value stocks (high book-to-market), the lowest third in dispersion average 0.10 and the highest third 1.04. The greater analyst disagreement for value stocks probably reflects the large number of stocks in this group, which are cyclical or exposed to short-term industry fluctuations (especially declines). Analysts probably disagree heavily as to how much weight to give to the recent earnings and as to the short-term outlook for the economy. Firms whose earnings have recently declined are likely to have had their stock prices knocked down low enough so they are classified as value stocks (high book-to-market ratio).

However, the difference in mean returns between the high and low dispersion thirds was 0.63% for the growth stocks and 0.80% for the value stocks. Per unit of analyst disagreement, the divergence of opinion effect seems to be more powerful for the growth stocks. They comment,

---

[41] Karl B. Diether, Christopher J. Malloy, and Anna Scherbina, "Differences of Opinion and the Cross Section of Stock Returns," *Journal of Finance* (October 2002), pp. 2,113–2,142.

"This is not surprising, given that the same amount of disagreement about earnings per share should translate into a higher level of disagreement about the intrinsic value of a growth stock." In the simplest application, the estimated value is the estimate of next year's earnings multiplied by a reasonable price-to-earnings ratio. Since growth stocks typically have higher price-to-earnings ratios, this would make their estimated values more sensitive to errors in the forecast earnings and to dispersion of opinion effects.

However, there is a more important factor. For growth stocks the principal uncertainties are not what earnings will be for the remainder of the fiscal year, but how long the firms will continue to grow. This is affected by issues such as when will new competition come in, and how quickly will the market for their product be saturated. The standard deviation of analysts' forecasts of near-term earnings is a relatively poor measure of these long-term uncertainties.

It is also very likely that analysts' opinions are a somewhat biased measure of the total divergence of opinion among investors. The reason is that growth stock analysts are likely to be believers in growth stock investing. Growth stock investors tend to believe that stocks that will show abnormal growth can be identified, often on the basis of historical data, or participation in high growth industries.

Those who apply a value-stock methodology to growth stocks will often arrive at values that are far below market prices. Such methods of analysis are likely to reach the conclusion that such stocks are not buy candidates. Analysts are usually expected to come up with buy recommendations, and their employers are frequently investment bankers. As a result, analysts whose preferred methods do not produce buy recommendations are less likely to be hired, are less likely to be true to their preferred methodologies if hired, and are more likely to be fired. Thus, we find that the sell-side analysts following growth stocks tend to use growth methodologies.

However, this does not mean that other methodologies are not being used by potential investors; they are. Those using other methodologies (including value-oriented methodologies) tend to arrive at lower valuations and tend not to be purchasers of growth stocks. Dispersals of (sell-side) analysts' opinions computed from published data will understate the total divergence of opinion among all potential investors. While this bias may affect value stocks also (few analysts using growth stock methodologies will be found to be following such value stock groups as tobacco, utilities, railroads, or food companies), the bias is likely to be much larger for growth stocks. Thus, it is argued that the winner's curse effect will be greater for growth stocks, and will be stronger the more the value of the stock depends on future growth in the company or industry.

As an extreme example, during the internet boom virtually all of the internet analysts were using growth-stock methodologies. They were frequently using methods that other growth stock analysts would not have used (price-to-sales ratios applied to sales projected several years into the future with little regard to profitability). Those who traded internet stocks would not have directed much business to a brokerage firm whose analyst of Internet-retailing stocks compared them to mail order catalogue houses, or who asked questions about the value of the warehouses and inventory, and then based valuations on what these were worth. As a result, the opinions of investors whose valuation methods were based on the above would not have been reflected in a dispersion of opinion calculated from published analysts' opinions.

Diether et al. citing McNichols and O'Brien argue that analysts are so reluctant to issue low earnings per share forecasts or to issue sell recommendations, that they simply stop covering the stocks about which they are pessimistic.[42] They do that because such negative reports would be bad for their careers. Diether et al. documents that there is a strong positive relationship between optimism in consensus forecasts (measured by error in quarterly earnings per share forecasts) and the standard deviation of analysts forecasts of the stock's earnings per share. The t-statistic for the regression is a very high −33.42. This relationship is probably a major reason for high dispersion of analysts' forecasts helping forecast returns, because an earnings disappointment is frequently followed by lower prices.

The analysis of this section shows that theories about individual investor behavior are very hard to test with aggregate data. Because of the way markets aggregate individual behavior, the slope of the market's return-versus-risk line will be different from (and in general flatter than) the average of the individual slopes. This makes it very hard to extrapolate from aggregate data to individual preferences, as well as difficult to reason from individual preferences (and introspection) to market relationships.

Future Exploitability

Will the various investment opportunities pointed out by divergence of opinion theory continue to exist? Anytime someone shows how better than average risk-adjusted returns could be earned by using a rule that has been shown to work in historical data, one naturally asks whether it will continue. Simple theory says that investors learn, and techniques that have proved profitable in the past are likely to be adopted by other

---

[42] Maureen F. McNichols and Patricia O'Brien, "Self-Selection and Analysts' Coverage," *Journal of Accounting Research* (1997), pp. 167–199.

investors in the future. The buying by these newly informed investors then eliminates the pricing error.

If the explanation for the flatness of the risk-return relationship is indeed uncertainty-induced bias, the odds would be good that the effect will continue to occur. The effect does not result from systematic errors in estimating investment returns. Indeed, as shown, it can occur when all investors make unbiased estimates. It results from a very subtle bias in which the returns conditional on being selected are lower than the unselected returns (and this bias varies with the risk). This effect has been called uncertainty-induced bias by Miller[43] when discussed in the context of capital budgeting.

However, there is another standard argument against effects persisting, even if the number of people trading against the effect does not increase. In cases where an investment rule earns more than average returns, the wealth of those using the rule increases. This will lead to more dollars being invested using the rule even if no other investors learn of the rule.

However, where the effect of an error is to cause investors to underestimate risk, or to underestimate the returns on the riskiest investments, the less-informed investors may choose to invest in riskier investments than is really optimal for them. Suppose these investors do overinvest in risky assets and the risky assets earn more than average (as theory suggests they should). Then the share of these investors in total wealth is likely to increase, even though these investors are earning less than they expected. They have made a mistake, but the faction of the wealth controlled by investors making this mistake may still increase.[44] This may slow down or even prevent correction of the error.

An example of this effect may be interesting. Consider the question of should you drop out of Harvard to start your own business. In wealth-maximization terms, the best move may be to drop out since you can get very wealthy. However, in terms of utility, a small shot at great wealth probably adds less to utility than the sacrifice of the opportunity for good earnings from a Harvard degree. However, the fraction of wealth controlled by those who took the risk is probably increased by making the utility-decreasing mistake of dropping out. One Bill Gates success with Microsoft can create such vast wealth that the faction of wealth controlled by such risk takers increases, even if the risk taking is a mistake in rational (utility-maximizing) terms. Aggregate wealth fre-

---

[43] Edward M. Miller, "Capital Budgeting Errors Seldom Cancel," *Financial Practice and Education* 10, 2 (Fall/Winter 2000), pp. 128–135.
[44] Edward M. Miller, "Equilibrium with Divergence of Opinion," *Review of Financial Economics* (Spring 2000), pp. 27–42.

quently flows to risk takers. Paradoxically, this may leave more and better investment opportunities for those who are not willing to take on as much risk. The aggregate growth in wealth of the risk takers gives them more resources to bid up the prices of the risky assets.

IMPLICATIONS FOR VALUE ADDITIVITY

Divergence of opinion in the presence of restrictions on short selling has implications for mergers and for value additivity.

A stock's equilibrium price will be just adequate to attract the marginal investor. Furthermore, marginal investors will generally be those who are most optimistic about a particular stock's outlook. Recognizing the marginal investor's role opens the possibility (indeed probability) that the marginal investors may be different for different securities.

It is well known that different investors use different methods for evaluating investment opportunities.[45] Also, different methods frequently lead to quite different portfolios. For instance, managers are often classified by "style" into "value" managers and "growth" managers. Investors with different styles buy different securities, with growth investors often being the marginal investors for growth stocks and value oriented investors for "value" stocks (those with low price-to-earnings ratios, or low price-to-book ratios). Stocks can be described as having clientele groups, that is, groups who view them as being worthy of inclusion in their portfolios.

Conglomerates
The implications for mergers of divergence of opinion theory can be understood with the aid of a simple example using the data shown in Exhibit 14.3. It is assumed that there are two types of investors, those

EXHIBIT 14.3   Conglomerate Price Determination

	Growth Drugs	Value Brands	Diversified Industries
Growth Investors	$100 ($240)	$50 ($120)	$150 ($360)
Value Investors	$50 ($120)	$100 ($240)	$150 ($360)
Market Price	$100	$100	$150

[45] As shown in Madelon DeVoe Talley, *The Passionate Investors* (New York: Crown Publishers, 1987); John Train, *Dance of the Money Bees, A Professional Speaks Frankly on Investing* (New York: Harper & Row, 1974); and John Train, *The Money Masters, Nine Great Investors: Their Winning Strategies and How You Can Apply Them* (New York: Harper & Row, 1980), for example.

who are willing to extrapolate a history of growth forward several years (growth investors), and those who base decisions on estimates of value with no allowance for growth (value investors). Imagine there are just two securities, Growth Drugs and Value Brands. Growth Drugs appeals to the value investors who forecast a future value of $240 for it versus a forecast of only $120 for Value Brands. After discounting, the growth investors are willing to pay $100 now for a share of Growth Drugs and $50 for a share of Value Brands. Likewise, the value investors estimate that Growth Drugs will be worth only $120 in the future, while Value Brands will be worth $240. After discounting, they are willing to pay only $100 for Value Brands and $50 for Growth Investors.

If the two companies are separate, Growth Drugs will sell for $100. All of the value-oriented investors will offer their stock for sale when the price rises above $50. Then competition among the growth investors will bid the price up to $100. In equilibrium all of the Growth Drugs stock is held by the growth investors. The value-oriented investors regard the stock as overvalued. Notice that although they view the stock as overvalued, they do not regard it as a good potential short sale since they believe that it will rise in price to $120. To sell short at $100 and to buy back at $120 (a higher price) is not a profitable trade for the investor who does not get prompt use of the proceeds.

Likewise, Value Brands would sell for $100. The growth-oriented investors view it as a stodgy company not expected to experience further growth, and will sell if offered more than the $50. The value-oriented investors will offer more (since from their view point it has a comparative advantage for inclusion in their portfolios) and competing among themselves will bid the price up to $100. Thus, both Growth Drugs and Value Brands would sell for $100 per share.

How much should a merged company sell for where each share represents a claim to the cash flow of one share each of Growth Drugs and Value Brands? Textbook theory suggests the merged company should sell for $200, the sum of the values of the parts.

However, inspection of Exhibit 14.3 above shows there are no investors who would be willing to pay $200 a share for the new company. The growth investors would view the merged company as a claim on Growth Drugs, worth $100 because of its growth prospects, and a claim on Value Brands, which their valuation methods estimates to be worth only $50 because of its poor growth prospects. Thus, they would view the merged company as worth $150 per share, with most of this attributable to Growth Drugs.

The value-oriented investors view the merged company as being worth $150 also; $100 for the well-established Value Brands unit plus $50 for Growth Drugs (their valuation methodology gives little weight to the growth history of the drug unit, perhaps because they have seen too many failures to maintain historical growth rates).

Thus, there are no investors who will pay more than $150 for the merged company. The supply/demand analysis shows that the merged company would be worth only $150, even though theories assuming perfect information among all investors predict that value additivity will hold and the total price will be $200. A simple implication is that it will not be in the interests of the two firms to merge.

Suppose the merged firm was already in existence. There would be an immediate profit from breaking it up. The stock would be trading at $150 while the component parts could each be sold for $100. The stockholders would be tempted to break the company up for an instant profit. If the management did not make the proposal, an outside entrepreneur would be tempted to buy control and then sell the parts separately. In some cases he might desire one unit, and realize he could acquire the desired unit by purchasing the whole and then selling the unit he did not desire to others (who presumably would pay more for it because their valuation methods indicated it to be worth more). For instance, someone who desired the Value Brands operation might realize he could purchase the combined units and then sell the Growth Drugs unit to someone optimistic about its prospects.

How do firms ever come to be in different industries? Many conglomerates exist because they make possible real cash flow improvements. There is a very large industrial organization literature on when combined firms may be more economical.[46] In some cases, there are economies from combining different operations. Sometimes these may disappear after the operations are large enough to be self-sustaining, creating a situation where a break up is value enhancing. For instance, much hard rock mineral exploration is conducted without being certain what if anything will be found. There are also economies to maintaining expertise in mine design. Thus, many mining companies find themselves mining a variety of minerals. However, since gold mining seems to appeal to a different group of investors than other forms of mining, it may later develop that splitting the firm up is optimal.

Successful research and development may give a company a strong position in an industry outside of its primary industry, or outside of the type of industry that appeals to its primary investors. Often in a new industry a firm will find that it must manufacture the machines it needs for producing its products. Exploiting a new invention may require both producing the machines and then using them to produce a product. Thus a firm may find itself in both the highly cyclical machinery busi-

---

[46] See for instance David J. Ravenscraft and F. M. Scherer, *Mergers, Sell-Offs, and Economic Efficiency* (Washington, D.C.: Brookings, 1987).

ness as well as in the more stable business of producing a product for consumers. After the business is established, there may be fewer economies from having both machinery and consumer products produced by the same firm and a split up may be feasible.

A common production process may cause a firm to produce several different products or a common marketing arrangement may cause it to produce its own products. These different lines of business may later become candidates for divestitures as conditions change and there are no longer major economies from having production done by one firm.

In other cases, there are clientele groups for mergers. For instance, in the 1960s there were many investors who believed that conglomerates improved the management of the firms they acquired. Other investors used analytic methods that used a price-earnings ratio based on historical growth rates in earnings per share. These investors did not distinguish between growth arising from mergers with firms with lower price-earnings ratios, and growth arising from being in a true high growth industry. The investors who applied the acquirer's high price-earnings ratio to the post-merger earnings (without realizing the new company probably was not as fast growing and should have a lower price-earnings ratio) constituted the price-setting optimistic investors. Thus, a strategy of continued mergers was wealth creating (for the original stockholders). Later, when the environment changed or the stream of mergers stopped, being a conglomerate turned into a disadvantage. Then there was money to be made from breaking the firms up.

In particular, many financial management textbooks describe how a takeover of a firm with a low price-earnings ratio by a high growth, high price-earnings ratio conglomerate will raise the earnings per share of the conglomerate (as well as assets per share). Several years of such mergers will leave a statistical series that looks as if the conglomerate is growing rapidly (which in turn can be used to prove the superiority of its management). The illusion of growing profits is increased by financing with convertible securities and warrants, which do not hurt current earnings. This appears to have happened in the 1960s with conglomerates.[47]

The above illustrates how divergence of opinion can cause a stream of cash flows to be worth more in parts than the whole is worth. This contrasts with the predictions of the mainstream value additivity theory that the whole equals the sum of the parts. Since the predictions of divergence of opinion theory differ from mainstream value additivity theory, it is interesting to look for empirical evidence on the theories.

---

[47] Uwe E. Reinhardt, *Mergers and Consolidations: A Corporate-Finance Approach* (Morristown, NJ: General Learning Press, 1972), pp. 22–25.

Closed-End Funds and Spin-Offs

To test value additivity, it is necessary to find cases where prices of assets are available as a package and for the components separately. One case is closed-end funds and another is where divisions of firms are spun-off.

A closed-end fund is an investment company that holds stock in other companies, but does not offer continuously to redeem its shares at net-asset prices (unlike a mutual fund). The prices of closed-end funds are set in the competitive markets in which they trade, as are the prices of the stocks of the companies they hold. Usually, closed-end funds sell at a substantial discount to their net asset values,[48] a fact Brickley and Schallheim call "an interesting anomaly."[49] A graph of the discounts from 1933 to 1982 shows only two periods with negative discounts.[50] Similar puzzling discounts were found for dual-purpose funds.[51] Richards et al. found closed-end bond fund discounts of 12.3% (December 1979).[52]

Malkiel proposed several possible explanations for these discounts but decides that none are adequate, and eventually concluded the market was inefficient here.[53] Thompson showed that profitable trading strategies existed.[54]

The closed-end fund discount is contrary to the value additivity theory but is predicted by the divergence of opinion theory. An investor

---

[48] See Thomas J. Herzfield, *The Investor's Guide to Closed-End Funds* (New York, NY: McGraw-Hill, 1980); and Rex Thompson, "The Information Content of Discounts and Premiums on Closed-End Fund Shares," *Journal of Financial Economics* (June 1978), pp. 151–187.

[49] James A. Brickley and James S. Schallheim, "Lifting the Lid on Closed-End Investment Companies: A Case of Abnormal Returns," *Journal of Financial and Quantitative Analysis* (March 1985), p. 107.

[50] William F. Sharpe, *Investments* (Englewood Cliffs, N. J.: Prentice Hall, 1981). p. 592.

[51] See Robert H. Litzenberger and Howard B. Sosin, "The Theory of Recapitalizations and the Evidence of Dual Purpose Funds," *Journal of Finance* (December 1977), pp. 1433–55, and Robert H. Litzenberger and Howard B. Sosin, "The Performance and Potential of Dual Purpose Funds," *Journal of Portfolio Management* (Spring 1978), pp. 49–56.

[52] R. Malcolm Richards, Donald R. Fraser, John C. Groth, "The Attractions of Closed-end Bond Funds," *Journal of Portfolio Management* (Winter 1982), pp. 56–61.

[53] Burton G. Malkiel, "The Valuation of Closed-End Investment-Company Shares," *Journal of Finance* (June 1977), pp. 847–859. For other attempts, see Kenneth J. Boudreaux, "Discounts and Premiums on Closed-End Mutual Funds: A Study in Valuation," *Journal of Finance* (May 1973), pp. 515–522; and Rodney L. Roenfeldt and Donald L. Tuttle, "An Examination of the Discounts and Premiums of Closed-End Investment Companies," *Journal of Business Research* (Fall 1973), pp. 129–140.

[54] Rex Thompson, "The Information Content of Discounts and Premiums on Closed-End Fund Shares," *Journal of Financial Economics* (June 1978), pp. 151–187.

will find that a portfolio of stocks selected by someone other than the investor himself will contain some stocks he would not have chosen himself, either because they did not meet his own unique needs, or because he was less optimistic about them than the portfolio managers for the closed-end fund were. The closed-end fund discount has long been recognized as an anomaly. No alternative explanation able to explain the magnitude of the discount has been offered, although some are plausible and could explain part of the discounts.

Another opportunity for testing the implications of value additivity is to observe what happens when a firm spins-off a subsidiary. Pure value additivity predicts that if the cash flows are not changed by the spin-off then the market value of the separate units will equal the prebreakup value. However, studies have shown that spin-offs create wealth, with the stockholders being wealthier after the spin-off than before.[55]

At first glance the wealth increases do not appear to be large since the total increase in wealth is small in percentage terms (7% according to Hite and Owers). However, as Hite and Owers put it (the size factor referred to is the percentage of the value of the firm spun-off):

> The reevaluations seem quite large in relation to the fraction spun-off. For the overall sample, the median size factor is 0.066 of the combined firm value, and the revaluation of 0.070 during the event period is of the same order of magnitude. Similarly, the point estimate for the small group is roughly the same as the size factor. Even for the large group, the revaluation is about a half the fraction spun-off. That spin-offs per se could generate gains roughly equal to the value of the divested unit is to suggest that the market

[55] Kenneth J. Boudreaux, "Divestiture and Share Price," *Journal of Financial and Quantitative Analysis* (November 1975), pp. 619–626; Gailen L. Hite and James E. Owers, "Security Price Reactions Around Corporate Spin-Off Announcements," *Journal of Financial Economics* (December 1983), pp. 409–436; Oppenheimer (quoted in Ronald J. Kudla and Thomas H. McInish, *Corporate Spin-offs: Strategy for the 1980's* (Westport, CT, 1984), pp. 46–50; Ronald J. Kudla and Thomas H. McInish, "Valuation Consequences of Corporate Spin-Offs," *Review of Business and Economic Research* (Winter 1983), pp. 71–77; Ronald J. Kudla and Thomas H. McInish, "Divergence of Opinion and Corporate Spin-Offs," *Quarterly Review of Economics and Business* (Summer 1988), pp. 20–29; Katherine Schipper and Abbie Smith, "Effects of Recontracting on Shareholder Wealth: The Case of Voluntary Spin-Offs," *Journal of Financial Economics* (December 1983), pp. 437–469; James A. Miles and James D. Rosenfeld, "The Effect of Voluntary Spin-offs Announcements on Shareholder Wealth," *Journal of Finance* (December 1983), pp. 1597–1606; and James D. Rosenfeld, "Additional Evidence on the Relation Between Divestiture Announcements and Shareholder Wealth," *Journal of Finance* (December 1984), pp. 1437–48, to name a few.

value of the parent's equity is hardly diminished even though assets are distributed to the subsidiary. The gains seem quite large, to be explained by the savings from using separate specialized contracts in which the parent and subsidiary have comparative advantages.[56]

Schipper and Smith report similar values for the overall gains.[57]

The literature discusses several possible explanations for the gains from spin-offs. Both Hite and Owers and Schipper and Smith consider the possibility that the spin-off reduces the assets backing the firms' bonds and transfers wealth from bondholders to equity holders, but find no evidence of bondholders being made worse off.[58] Some spin-offs are done to facilitate mergers but most are not, and those for other reasons report comparable gains. Regulatory factors explain some spin-offs, but Hite and Owers report that the legal/regulatory inspired spin-offs actually had negative excess returns over the whole preevent period, but positive returns around the announcement date that were similar to those for all spin-offs.[59] Schipper and Smith report higher returns for regulatory related spin-offs.

Separating operations in different industries might permit better and more specialized management or incentive compensation plans for managers related to stock prices. Ravenscraft and Scherer, drawing on both interviews and statistical studies, present evidence that profitability gains in the spun-off units frequently do occur with spin-offs.[60] Both Hite and Owers and Schipper and Smith discuss this possibility at length, with Schipper and Smith concluding that it explains the wealth gains with spin-offs. Hite and Owers (in the quote above) question whether it can explain the magnitude of the effect.

While there clearly can be disadvantages to a single management trying to manage several different businesses, most of these managerial specialization economies could be obtained by a separate management team for each unit. If anything, if the operation remained a subsidiary, the concentration of ownership in the parent would appear to permit more efficient monitoring than could be done by numerous uninformed stockholders. Evidence suggests that stock in small firms is valued at less than

---

[56] Hite and Owers, "Security Price Reactions Around Corporate Spin-Off Announcements," p. 430.

[57] Schipper and Smith, "Effects of Recontracting on Shareholder Wealth: The Case of Voluntary Spin-Offs."

[58] As discussed by Dan Galai and Ronald W. Masulis, "The Option Pricing Model and the Risk Factor of Stock," *Journal of Financial Economics* (January/March 1976), pp. 53–82.

[59] Hite and Owers, "Security Price Reactions Around Corporate Spin-Off Announcements," p. 432.

[60] Ravenscraft and Scherer, *Mergers, Sell-Offs, and Economic Efficiency.*

that of large firms.[61] A spin-off typically creates a much smaller firm, one that is usually traded over the counter where transactions costs and liquidity are less. Thus, the gains from improved contracting and management (as Hite and Owers noted) appear unable to fully explain how assets can be spun-off without perceptible effects on the parent's stock price (the result Hite and Owers report for small spin-offs).

Very closely related to complete spin-offs are equity carve-outs in which only part of a subsidiary's stock is sold to the public. Schipper and Smith have shown that announcement of carve-outs are accompanied by an average increase in the parent's stock price of just under 2%, a strong contrast with the typical price lowering effect of announcing a stock sale.[62] Although at first glance a 2% stock price gain appears small, it is large relative to the value of the subsidiary interest being sold, which was reported to have a median value of 8% of the parent's value. This wealth increase represents either a belief that the carve-out was actually going to raise the value of the parent's interest in the subsidiary by an appreciable amount or a belief that the equity interest sold would be sold for about 25% (2% gain divided by 8%) more than its value as part of the parent firm. The latter interpretation implies an appreciable violation of value additivity.

Predicting Firms for Which Spin-Offs and Divestitures Are Likely

Given there are often stock price increases (as shown above) when spin-offs or carve-outs are announced, it would be useful for investors to be able to predict the types of firms for which these are most likely. Spin-offs are presumably most likely when the parts will be worth more than the whole, as discussed above. One distinguishing characteristic of firms that do spin-offs is a firm with operations in widely differing industries. There are not likely to be any appreciable synergies from combining operations in different industries, and thus there are no lost economies of scale from breaking the firm up or diseconomies from dissolving integrated operations.

Schipper and Smith examine the industries of spun-off operations and document that in only 21 out of 93 spin-offs is the parent in the same broadly defined industry.[63] They interpret this as supporting their

---

[61] For instance, Donald B. Keim, "Size Related Anomalies and Stock Return Seasonality: Further Empirical Evidence," *Journal of Financial Economics* (June 1983), pp. 13–32.

[62] Katherine Schipper and Abbie Smith, "A Comparison of Equity Carve-Outs and Seasoned Equity Offerings," *Journal of Financial Economics* (January/February 1986), pp. 153–186.

[63] Schipper and Smith, "Effects of Recontracting on Shareholder Wealth: The Case of Voluntary Spin-Offs," p. 462.

hypothesis that spin-offs raise productivity by alleviating "diminishing returns to management, which arise with expansion in the number and diversity of transactions under one management."[64] Ravenscraft and Scherer report that operations sold are often in different industries, and frequently in ones with quite different characteristics than the parent.[65]

While the difference in industries between the parent and the operation sold or spun-off is certainly consistent with managerial specialization considerations, it is also consistent with the clientele group for the separated assets differing from the group owning the parent company. Earnings forecasts are frequently made by projecting sales for a particular industry and then applying these (with adjustments) to a particular firm. Ownership will come to be concentrated in those investors who are relatively optimistic about that industry (relative to other industries). It follows that the current stock owners are likely to have on average somewhat lower expectations for other industries. Thus, situations where spin-offs of operations in other industries would increase stockholder wealth should be common.

However, in identifying candidates for break up, another thing to look for is a case where the assets appeal to different types of investors. In some cases there may be a specific type of investor to whom assets of a particular type appeal. A particularly interesting example is the "gold bugs." There seems to be a distinct group of investors who highly value gold related assets. This arises from some combination of optimism about gold prices, and a belief that gold is very useful for diversification. Gold has historically done well in times of inflation and during periods of political instability. Thus, gold and gold-mining stocks are often bought by individuals who want a hedge against these risks.

In one short period, no less than six firms spun off all or part of their gold mines.[66] Such a concentration of spin-offs in this industry is hard to explain in models where spin-offs are motivated by a desire to motivate managers, or to otherwise increase cash flows. However, it can be explained with the clientele paradigm that emerges from the divergence of opinion model. At the time of the spin-offs, gold mining stocks appealed to a particular group of investors ("gold-bugs") who would pay high prices for them (the price-to-earnings ratios for the five profitable operations were reported as 31, 37, 113, 59, and 36, which were higher than other mining firms in 1986). These gold bugs appear to be different investors than those holding the parent companies (which were

---

[64] Schipper and Smith, "Effects of Recontracting on Shareholder Wealth: The Case of Voluntary Spin-Offs," p. 464.

[65] Ravenscraft and Scherer, *Mergers, Sell-Offs, and Economic Efficiency*.

[66] Sandra D. Atchison, "Gold Mines: Pay Dirt on Wall Street," *Business Week* (August 4, 1986).

conglomerates and general mining companies). When these mining assets were part of a much larger firm, the valuation was that of investors who lacked unusually optimistic expectations for gold prices, or who did not desire gold's diversification benefits. The contribution of earnings from gold mining to the parent firm's value was less than these assets value when sold to gold bugs.

In many cases a firm will have operations both in mature, stable industries (appealing to investors who seek high and stable dividends with a low level of risk), and in high-growth risky industries that are currently "sexy." One of the earliest financiers to exploit this technique was James Ling. In his Project Redeployment, he exchanged stock in three subsidiaries of Ling-Temco-Vought (LTV Aerospace Corporation, LTV Electrosystems and LTV Ling Altec) for stock in the parent corporation (which retained control of the subsidiaries). The subsidiaries' publicly traded stock sold for good prices, and this led other investors to conclude LTV must be worth at least the market value of the stock in the subsidiaries it owned. (Banks also proved willing to lend on these market values.) As one author asked, "Could it be that 1 + 1 + 1 could equal more than 3?"[67] Ling suggested that this was so that the shares in three companies, each of which was in a single industry, would be worth more than that of a single corporation involved in three different enterprises, and then went on to say, "Thus, in a way, 1 + 1 + 1 worked out to around 4."

The clientele theory explains what happened; stock in each company appealed to those most optimistic about the subsidiaries' industries. Those believing military aviation had a bright future would pay well for the aerospace company, those believing in military electronics would pay well for LTV Electrosystems, and those optimistic about civilian sound and testing equipment bought Ling Altec. The sum of the amounts certain investors would pay exceeded the original willingness to pay for the parent.

Another early example is provided by the LTV takeover of Wilson, followed by its division into three parts: Wilson & Company, Wilson Sporting Goods, and Wilson Pharmaceutical & Chemical. Sales of minority interests in the three companies brought in enough cash to pay much of the acquisition costs. What had happened? Wilson Sporting Goods was a "pure play" in the then fashionable leisure industry; Wilson Pharmaceutical & Chemical was in the growing drug business. Both appealed to investors convinced that these industries had bright futures, and hence deserved high price-to-earnings ratios. As Sobel put it, "Almost immediately Sporting Goods and Pharmaceutical & Chemical

---

[67] Robert Sobel, *The Rise and Fall of the Conglomerate Kings* (New York: Stein and Day, 1984), p. 91.

became semiglamour issues, and their stocks took off."[68] Wilson & Company, the heart of the original firm, remained an old line meatpacking firm which appealed to its traditional clientele, those who thought a major meatpacking firm was a desirable investment (presumably value investors since it was clearly not a growth firm).

Why had Wilson & Company not been valued at the sum of its parts? In pure financial theory, rational investors would compute the value of each part separately and offer this amount for the whole. If they use a dividend discount model, the sum of the potential dividends form the parts would equal the dividends from the whole (leaving out any possible tax related effects), and the discount rate would be a suitably weighted average of those applicable to the different parts. The dividend discount model of the textbooks implies value additivity. The observed valuation behavior supports a model where investors are using a variety of methods to evaluate potential investments, and hence disagree.

Another example of spinning off a subsidiary in a glamour industry is provided by the Imperial Industries spin-off of "Solar Systems by Sun Dance." Imperial Industries was a Florida building material company specializing in wallboard and gypsum products. As an extension of this, it had gotten into rooftop solar hot-water heaters. At the time, the press was filled with stories about the bright future expected for solar energy. Stock in any new solar energy company was in immediate demand. Thus, it could be predicted that those optimistic about solar energy would value highly stock in the solar subsidiary. However, solar energy was a small part of the operations of the parent company. Investors who hold stock in a building material company are not the type who will attach much value to a not yet profitable solar energy subsidiary. The solar operation was too small a part of the parent for those interested in solar energy to be attracted to the parent. The solution was to spin-off the subsidiary, keeping control with the parent, and hoping that this would cause the remaining interest to be valued at the price solar energy enthusiasts were willing to pay.

An example in the carve-out area is provided by the creation of Interferon Sciences from National Patent Development. Schipper and Smith use this as an example of a carve-out to try to explain why it was easier for the firm to raise capital by selling stock in the subsidiary rather than by any other technique.[69] The theory presented in this chapter provides an alternative explanation. By selling only 25% of the equity in the new subsidiary, the firm was able to raise all of the capital needed to finance the development of the interferon technology transferred from the parent to the new

---

[68] Sobel, *The Rise and Fall of the Conglomerate Kings*, p. 95.
[69] Schipper and Smith, "A Comparison of Equity Carve-Outs and Seasoned Equity Offerings."

subsidiary. At the time there was much discussion in the popular press about the wonders of interferon and its potential for curing cancer and other diseases. A very simple explanation for the decision to sell stock in Interferon Sciences exists. Most likely, the stock sold was valued at less by the stockholders in the parent company than by those members of the public who were enthusiastic about the future of the wonder drug, interferon.

The same explanation probably extends to other carve-outs. Schipper and Smith state that growth opportunities financed include Atlantic City casinos, Hawaiian condominiums, oil drilling, and bioengineering products, and note that, "There is a tendency for sample subsidiaries to belong to industries that, at the time of equity carve out, were expanding relatively rapidly (e.g., gambling, health care, sporting goods and games, home video and biotechnology.)"[70] This sounds like a typical list of fads. It seems very plausible that stock was carved out simply because the most optimistic members of the public would pay more for the stock than the management thought the stock was worth, a simple divergence of opinion explanation which Schipper and Smith ignore.

Another way to classify investors, not exclusive to classifying them by the type of industry they are optimistic about, is by the type of analytic methods they use in valuing stocks or in deciding whether or not to purchase them. In what Nobel laureate Herbert Simon calls "substantive rationality," all relevant facts are known and incorporated into valuation decisions.[71] However, in practice investors cannot realistically collect that much information, nor can the human brain process it. Observers of the investment scene believe that no one individual or firm can master all the available methods, and that investors or investment managers who try, end up doing worse than those who pick a consistent strategy and diligently employ it.[72] Thus, investors use what Simon calls "procedural rationality:" They find valuation methods that give reasonable results and help them to build what they regard as acceptable portfolios. (Notice that if a method undervalues a stock that could have been included in the portfolio; but this stock is comparable to those included in the portfolio, so there is no great loss.) Observers report that the two most popular approaches currently are growth stock investing and "value" oriented procedures.

---

[70] Schipper and Smith, "A Comparison of Equity Carve-Outs and Seasoned Equity Offerings," Note 17.

[71] Herbert Simon, *Models of Bounded Rationality: Behavioral Economics and Business Organization* (Cambridge, MA: MIT Press, 1982).

[72] Charles D. Ellis, *Investment Policy: How to Win at the Loser's Game* (Homewood, IL: Dow Jones Irwin, 1985), Chapter 3; Train, *Dance of the Money Bees, A Professional Speaks Frankly on Investing*, and Train, *The Money Masters, Nine Great Investors: Their Winning Strategies and How You Can Apply Them.*

Probably the most common of the procedurally rational methods is basing valuations on price-earnings ratios depending on industry or on historical or estimated growth rates. A perusal of the practitioner oriented publications (*Business Week, Wall Street Journal,* etc.) shows price-earnings ratios to be commonly used. Before such methods are summarily put down as too primitive, it should be noted that the simple procedure of ranking securities by price-earnings ratio and then choosing the stocks with the lowest ratio has been repeatedly shown to outperform the stock averages (which in turn usually outperform most actively managed portfolios).[73]

For instance, a Zacks study using the 3,300 companies (excluding companies forecast to lose money), which had forward price-earnings ratios, found that from October 1987 to September 2002 the portfolio with the top fifth of the stocks by forward price-to-earnings ratio had an average annualized return of 2.5%, versus 19.4% for the fifth of stocks with the lowest price-to-earning ratios with the other quintiles spread out in between.[74] Incidentally, forward price-earnings ratios are the analysts' projected earnings divided by the current price. When the absolute standard was used of stocks that had forward price-to-earnings ratios that exceed 65, the annualized rate of return was negative, −0.1%. Interpreted in terms of the theory of this chapter, optimistic investors can bid stocks up to values well above what they should be.

Obviously, selecting securities by current price-to-earnings ratios may fail to select some securities, which would be logical candidates for inclusion in a portfolio. For instance, some firms may have no earnings or earnings that are below those their assets should produce. However, it should not be assumed that these stocks, which are obviously undervalued by price-earnings ratio based rules, are true investment bargains. They are not, simply because investors using other procedures, perhaps asset-based, provide clientele groups for these securities. These groups often purchase stocks that are not currently profitable, but which have a potential for being profitable in the future, perhaps under new management.

Some growth-oriented investors specialize in identifying stocks with low earnings, or even with no earnings, but which have prospects for high growth and for being much larger in the future. Other investors

---

[73] By studies starting with S. Basu, "Investment Performance of Common Stocks in Relation to their Price-Earnings Ratios: A Test of the Efficient Markets Hypothesis," *Journal of Finance* (June 1977), pp. 663–682; and continuing through Jeffrey Jaffre, Donald B. Keim, and Randolph Westerfield, "Earnings Yields, Market Values, and Stock Returns," *Journal of Finance* (March 1989), pp.135–148; to Zacks, *Ahead of the Market.*

[74] Zacks, *Ahead of the Market,* p. 231.

specialize in selecting stocks on the basis of their assets or their breakup values.

These and many other investment procedures are in use, with the price of each security set by the investment procedure that attaches the highest valuation to it. If any of these procedures consistently gives much better investment results than another, money will flow to those managers using it, and other managers will adopt the technique. The final result could easily be that most securities (maybe even virtually all) are priced at close to efficient market levels, although other parts of this chapter and my other chapters in this book, argue this is not so. However, security prices for firms that are close to efficient market levels may still leave profitable opportunities for restructuring.

However, even if all securities are priced at approximately appropriate levels, it should not be assumed that a business unit makes an equal contribution to firm value regardless of the firm it is part of (even if cash flows remain the same). Some business units have a higher value when evaluated by one method than by another. They may add more to the value of a firm whose dominant investors use the valuation method which gives them the highest valuation than they add when part of a firm whose investors use another method. For instance, if a firm trades on the basis of the value of its assets, a unit with a high book value, but low earnings will probably add more to the total value than it would as part of a firm valued by applying a price-earnings ratio to the latest earnings.

In practice, investors do differ in their optimism about industries or about new technologies and very often the shareholders in the parent firm (only a small part of whose value is related to exposure to a particular technology) are not among those who are most optimistic about a subsidiary's industry or technology. When spun-off as a separate firm or sold to a new owner already in the subsidiary's business, the value may be based on a more optimistic evaluation of the prospects.

Those investors who have high growth projections for a particular industry or technology are likely to have bought stock in that industry and to have hired managers who make high growth projections. Thus, they will use a similar growth factor when evaluating a new project in their home industry, while there is no reason for the managers to choose unusually optimistic growth factors for other industries. When this is done, a firm in an acquiring industry (or a spin-off) will value the division at a higher multiple than it had as a small part of a larger firm in a slowly growing industry.

Big investment banking profits have been earned (and will continue to be earned) by identifying companies whose divisions and other assets appeal to different types of investors and selling the pieces off to them.

Selling Money-Losing Divisions

A particularly common case arises for money-losing divisions. A common procedure is to value a stock by multiplying its latest or projected earnings by a reasonable price-earnings ratio for a stock in that industry and with that growth history. If a unit is losing money, it reduces the firm's total earnings, and hence its market value. It is not hard to see how eliminating the losses would raise the stock price. In some cases the loss is simply eliminated by shutting the money losing operation down and selling the assets for their scrap value.

However, in many cases the operation can be sold as a going concern for more than its scrap value. In some cases, a currently unprofitable unit can be expected to return to profitability at the end of the current business cycle. In other cases, future profitability cannot be forecast with certainty, but a return to sustained profitability is possible. If there is no recovery, the new owner can close the unit. In this case, a purchase of the money-losing operation contains a valuable option; it can be shut down if the adverse conditions continue.

The sale of a money losing operation raises the earnings and, hence, the firm's market value in two ways: The losses are eliminated; and the sales proceeds can themselves be invested to bring in additional earnings.

In these cases, the selling firm can receive considerably less than the present value of future cash flows from the operation and yet find that the sale raises its stock price. This result contrasts with the predictions of value additivity. This may help to explain why so often firms choose to sell their money-losing operations even though, in theory, they should be worth no more to the purchaser than to the seller. Indeed, in general, it may add less to the purchaser's ability to pay dividends than it subtracts from the sellers ability to pay dividends because of the disruption attendant a sale and the costs of the sales process and the transfer.

An obvious question about the above is why purchase a money losing division if doing so lowers the purchasing firm's earnings. In some cases, the acquiring firm's management does not seek current stock price maximization. They might believe that their stockholders' long-run interests are best served by owning the unit, even if in the short run their reported profits and their stock price are lowered. Also, the acquiring firm may be privately owned without a publicly traded stock to be adversely affected.

However, just because the parent's stock price is lowered by ownership of a unit does not mean that ownership will hurt a purchaser's stock price. Such differences are possible even when investors in both the acquiring and selling firms are rational.

How the Relevant Details Depend on Firm Size

Here it is useful to return to Herbert Simon's distinction between "procedural" and "substantive" rationality.[75] When it is claimed investors are rational, the claim is that they are procedurally rational. They have discovered methods for making investment decisions that, considering the costs and time involved in decision making, give satisfactory results, and probably better results, than any other decision procedure they could use. Such decision procedures are rational, and to use them is to display "procedural rationality."

This concept of rationality is not the "substantive" rationality used in economics and mainstream financial theory. "Substantive rationality" assumes every investor has made the best possible estimate of all relevant numbers. In practice, having this level of information and doing the required analysis would be rational only if information and analysis were free. Of course, information and analysis do have costs. Thus, investors do not acquire all possibly relevant information about all securities that might be candidates for acquisition, but only information whose estimated value exceeds the costs of acquiring it.

In investing, a key number is the expected rate of return from ownership of a stock. Notice that how big an impact the operations of a particular unit has on the rate of return of a firm depends on the size of a firm. If a turnaround in a particular unit will add 1 million dollars per year in profits to the parent company, this is an additional 100% return for a company whose other operations are worth 1 million per year, an extra 10% for a company otherwise worth 10 million dollars, an extra 1% for a 100 million dollar company, and only 0.1% for a 1 billion dollar company. Someone trying to decide whether to invest in a small company will be very much interested in whether a particular unit is likely to have a 1 million dollar jump in profitability, while this will not be material for the larger companies.

While some people's intuition is that the gains from information about a large company (in which the market has a larger position) should be more valuable than the same information about a small company, the intuition is not supported by the formal optimization models. The list of variables in Markowitz optimization includes expected return, variances, and a list of covariances. Firm size is not a variable. The loss to the investor from making a mistake in the expected return (or for that matter any other parameter) for a small oil company is the same as for Exxon. If the return is grossly underestimated for either company, it is likely to be excluded from the portfolio. If it is overestimated, the stock will be included in the portfolio. As long as the

---

[75] Simon, *Models of Bounded Rationality: Behavioral Economics and Business Organization.*

assumption is maintained that the rate of return is independent of the amount purchased, and there are no constraints on the amount of a stock that can be purchased, the utility gain from a 1% improvement in the accuracy of the rate of return estimate for two otherwise similar oil companies (i.e., same variances and covariances) is the same. Notice the decision variable is the expected rate of return on the security, not the total profits of the firm. The contribution of an accurate forecast of the earnings of a unit to the accuracy of the forecast for the firm it is part of depends on the ratio of the units profits to that of the whole firm. Getting the details right about a unit that is small in relation to the whole firm contributes little to the accuracy of the forecasts for the whole firm.

Where there is a turnaround possibility for a unit that is part of a small company, it is procedurally rational to collect the information and do the analysis; when the same unit is part of a larger firm it is not procedurally rational to analyze the unit separately. When a large firm is contemplating selling a small unit to a smaller firm, the unit's turnaround possibilities will often be material to the investment merits of the small firm, but not material to those of the large firm. Instead, the valuation of the large firm is based on procedurally rational rules of thumb, such as mechanical projections of historical earnings, followed by use of a dividend discount model or application of a price-earnings ratio.

The above discussion has shown that while substantive rationality with its implicit assumption of free information implies that all investors use the same information (all relevant information) and do the same analysis (all analysis which could possibly be relevant), procedural rationality implies that the information gathered about a unit depends on the size of the parent company whose stock is being considered for purchase or sale. Given that different information is used by investors in the buying and the selling companies, the amount that a particular unit adds to the market values of the two companies need not be the same.

The above clientele theory makes a prediction about the size of firms that will be buying and selling money-losing units. The sellers will be large firms because owning a money losing unit lowers the current earnings and the stock price. The buyers will be smaller companies whose stockholders find it rational to explicitly analyze the unit's business prospects, recognizing any probability of a turnaround, any options that the unit may represent, and any liquidation values the unit may have if it is finally shut down.

Spinning the subsidiary off as a separate company, or selling it to its management merely represents extreme cases of selling to a small firm (one that has no assets beyond its option to buy the subsidiary). In this case the stockholders of the zero assets buying firm will quite rationally calculate the present value of the unit considering any expected turnarounds, any imbedded options, and any potential liquidation value.

The above argument was developed for a unit that is actually losing money, but its essence holds for units that are marginally profitable, or which are producing a profit below a normal return on the present value of expected future earnings.

The same argument would also apply to units in the developmental stage. A research intensive unit or one with a product with great prospects may make only a small contribution to the parent firm's value, because it is not procedurally rational for investors to estimate the value of the unit's growth opportunities. Even if the new product succeeds, it may make only a small percentage difference to the value of the parent firm (especially after allowing for the investment needed to make the product succeed and to produce it once it is established). However, evaluated separately, the unit may have a growth opportunity which has an appreciable value, and this would be recognized if the unit was spun-off (or sold to a small firm specializing in the industry).

Of course, if the academic theories about perfect markets with unlimited short selling were true, arbitrage would prevent all of the above effects. However, the inability to sell short the divisions of a large company make the textbook value additivity theory incorrect and create opportunities for investment bankers to exploit.

Value Additivity Theory

The above conclusions about spin-offs violate the widely held belief in value additivity. Value additivity holds that the market value of the whole is equal to the market value of the parts. Value additivity has been "proven" in several places. There appear to be two main types of proofs, and an answer to each has already been given.

One approach is to develop a model of rational valuation of a stream of cash flows and then to show that with this valuation model that the value of the whole is equal to the sum of the parts. Mossin deduced value additivity from homogeneous expectations, risk aversion, and no transactions costs.[76] That firm diversification serves no purpose under the assumptions of the capital asset pricing model was pointed out by Levy and Sarnat.[77] Alberts earlier made the same point.[78] Myers

---

[76] Jan C. Mossin, "Security Pricing and Investment Criteria in Competitive Markets," *American Economic Review* (December 1969), pp. 749–756.

[77] Haim Levy and M. Sarnat, "Diversification, Portfolio Analysis, and the Uneasy Case for Conglomerate Mergers," *Journal of Finance* (September 1970), pp. 795–802.

[78] William W. Alberts, "The Profitability of Growth by Merger," in William W. Alberts and J. Segall (eds.), *The Corporate Merger* (Chicago: University of Chicago Press, 1966), p. 271.

has shown that the state preference model implies no gains from diversification.[79] Galai and Masulis (working with no restrictions on obtaining prompt use of short sales and homogeneous expectations) argue that value additivity applies for total values when firms are merged or spin-offs occur, but they show how wealth can be shifted among stockholders and bondholders by mergers and spin-offs.[80]

These proofs for value additivity all involve substantive rationality and perfect short selling. All investors are assumed to make the substantively optimal choices, which is to say the choices they would make if they had all potentially relevant information. However, it would be rational for them to acquire all potentially relevant information only if information was free. Of course, information is not free. Where information and analysis have costs, investors acquire only that information whose benefits are worth the costs. As pointed out above, even where all investors pay the same price for information and analysis, the amount of information and analysis about a particular unit worth purchasing depends on who owns the unit or is considering purchasing it. Thus, buyers and sellers of businesses should rationally expect that some pieces of information will be acquired by the investors owning one firm, but not by those owning another. The result is that the divergence of opinion leads to violations of value additivity. The nonarbitrage proofs of value additivity are "substantive rationality" proofs that contain an assumption, implicit or explicit, that all investors are using the same information sets.

The other argument for value additivity is an arbitrage one.[81] It is argued that value additivity could be enforced by buying the parent and then selling short one of the parts, thus creating a stream of cash flows exactly equivalent to the remaining parts. It is then argued that the remaining part must sell at the same price as the difference between the parent and subsidiary. If otherwise, there would be profitable arbitrage opportunities. Unfortunately, this argument is weak.

Where none of the parts are separately traded, there are no shares to be shorted—and probably no accounting data to permit creation of securities with the same cash flows as an independent company would have. However, failure to earn a market return on proceeds of a short sale prevents this arbitrage from actually being carried out. As pointed out, individuals normally receive no interest on the proceeds, and insti-

---

[79] Stewart C. Myers, "Procedures for Capital Budgeting Under Uncertainty," *Industrial Management Review* (Spring 1968), pp. 1–20.
[80] Galai and Masulis, "The Option Pricing Model and the Risk Factor of Stock."
[81] Lawrence D. Schall, "Asset Valuation, Firm Investment, and Firm Diversification," *Journal of Business* (January 1972), pp. 11–28.

tutions experience a gap between market rates and the rates they receive. Notice the arbitrage argument requires holding the short position open indefinitely, or an infinite holding period. The present value of the difference between the competitive rate and the rate earned on the proceeds benefits from the power of compound interest. This difference increases steadily with the holding period. For the infinite holding period required for the arbitrage argument, the difference becomes infinite if there is even a small difference in the rates. Thus, arbitrage cannot be argued to assure value additivity.

Although value additivity has been discussed here mainly in the investment context of spin-offs, closed-end funds, mergers, and the like, it should be noticed that it plays a much wider role in finance. For instance, the usual theoretical arguments for the net-present-value rule in capital budgeting use value additivity to argue that the net present value of a project is the amount that it would add to the wealth of shareholders if the project is accepted.

With procedural rationality, most investors will not spend the resources needed to estimate all future earnings from a project, or even the nature of a firm's investment program. Once this is realized, it becomes clear that the effect of an investment on the current wealth of the shareholders is more likely to be determined by its immediate effect on earnings than by a net present value calculation. In turn, this means that managers have a real choice between strategies that maximize short- and long-term value.

In turn, portfolio managers trying to maximize return in the long run may be able to find firms that are maximizing long term, but which are priced on the basis of low current earnings.

CONCLUSIONS

Mainstream financial theory has been built on unrestricted short selling along with substantive rationality in which all investors are aware of all potentially relevant facts, and are able to do the optimal analysis. Among other things, this implies that investors will agree on measures of expected return and risk (homogeneous expectations). An alternative is that investors are merely procedurally rational, collecting data and using complex analytic methods only when the apparent benefit exceeds the costs. In this case, investors will exhibit divergence of opinion.

Interesting effects emerge when divergence of opinion is combined with real-world obstacles to short selling. Since divergence of opinion, uncertainty, and risk are correlated, this shortfall can be expected to increase with risk. It might even cause a reversal of the usual risk versus return relationship.

In particular, the systematic risk measured by beta is likely to be correlated with divergence of opinion. The uncertainty induced bias (winner's curse) effect will be greatest for high-beta stocks. The result is that when we aggregate across all securities, the market line showing the expected return versus beta should have an appreciably lower slope (and could easily be negative). A flat or negative security market line is consistent with every investor being willing to accept systematic risk only if promised a higher return. This explains the empirical observation that incurring beta risk is not rewarded by higher returns. The practical implication is that a low-beta portfolio can be designed that will hold up well in a market crash with little or no sacrifice of return. One of the reasons for the low-return to high-beta stocks is that growth stocks have tended to have lower returns than value stocks. This appears to be because the divergence of opinion about growth stocks is greater than about value stocks.

Recognitions of the obstacles to short selling has implications for the valuation of closed-end funds and for mergers and divestitures. The marginal investors who set stock prices will be different for different clientele groups. Closed-end funds and conglomerates will force investors to hold securities that they would not otherwise have held and will sell for less than the sum of their parts. This can explain the discounts on closed-end funds and the frequent gains from spinning off a subsidiary.

Index

395